THE SECOND ATTACK
on
PEARL HARBOR

OPERATION K
AND OTHER JAPANESE ATTEMPTS TO BOMB AMERICA IN
WORLD WAR II

STEVE HORN

Naval Institute Press
Annapolis, Maryland

Naval Institute Press
291 Wood Road
Annapolis, MD 21402

Library of Congress Cataloging-in-Publication Data
Horn, Steve, 1927–
The second attack on Pearl Harbor : Operation K and other Japanese
attempts to bomb America in World War II / Steve Horn.
    p. cm.
  Includes bibliographical references and index.
  ISBN 1-59114-388-8 (alk. paper)
  1. World War, 1939–1945—Campaigns—Pacific Area.
2. World War, 1939–1945—Campaigns—Hawaii. 3. World War,
1939–1945—Aerial operations, Japanese. 4. World War, 1939–1945—
Naval operations, Japanese. I. Title.
  D767.H594 2005
  940.54'26693—dc22

                                        2005016993

Printed in the United States of America on acid-free paper ∞

12 11 10 09 08 07 06 05   9 8 7 6 5 4 3 2
First printing

CONTENTS

Abbreviations and Acronyms

2nd Lt.	second lieutenant
Adm.	admiral
ASW	antisubmarine warfare
Brig. Gen.	brigadier general
CAP	Combat Air Patrol
Capt.	captain
Cdr.	commander
CinC	commander in chief
CinCPac	commander in chief, Pacific Fleet
Col.	colonel
Com 14	Fourteenth Naval District command post
CPO	chief petty officer
Ens.	ensign
FRUPac	Fleet Radio Unit, Pacific
Gen.	general
IFF	identification, friend or foe
IGHQ	imperial general headquarters
IJA	Imperial Japanese Army
IJAAF	Imperial Japanese Army Air Force
IJN	Imperial Japanese Navy
IJNAF	Imperial Japanese Naval Air Force

JMSDF	Japanese Maritime Self Defense Force
Lt.	lieutenant
Lt. (jg)	lieutenant (junior grade)
Lt. Cdr.	lieutenant commander
Lt. Col.	lieutenant colonel
Lt. Gen.	lieutenant general
Maj.	major
NATC	Naval Air Testing Center.
NGS	Naval General Staff
OKW	Armed Forces High Command
Op-20G	U.S. Navy's cryptanalytic office, Pacific
Pan Am	Pan American Airways
Pfc.	private, first class
PO	petty officer
Pvt.	private
RAAF	Royal Australian Air Force
RAF	Royal Air Force
Rear Adm.	rear admiral
S1c	seaman, first class
SeaBees	Naval Construction Battalions (CBs)
Seaman	noncommissioned
SIS	Signals Intelligence Section
SubRon	Submarine Squadron
TAIC	Technical Air Intelligence Center
USAAF	U.S. Army Air Force
Vice Adm.	vice admiral
VMF	U.S. Marine fighter squadrons.
WARDS	Women Air Raid Defense Service
WO	warrant officer
WPL-46	War Plan 46

The Second Attack on Pearl Harbor

INTRODUCTION

The battered remnants of Adm. Isoroku Yamamoto's once-mighty combined fleet straggled westward in retreat from the Battle of Midway. What had been the largest invasion fleet ever assembled up to that time was returning to Japan after a crushing defeat. Admiral Yamamoto had listened to his staff officers propose a dozen or more plans to recover from their loss of thousands of sailors and experienced combat airmen, four aircraft carriers, a cruiser, and 332 aircraft. The admiral disapproved of each of the proposed recovery plans as unworkable. He was painfully aware of the mistakes that had been made in the planning and execution of what the Japanese had thought would be an easy and perhaps final victory against the U.S. fleet.

The morose admiral overheard his officers wondering aloud, "How can we apologize to His Majesty for this defeat?" The admiral responded quickly, "Leave that to me! The fault is mine. I will apologize to the Emperor myself."

The Battle of Midway has been regarded as the turning point of the war in the Pacific for both the Japanese and the American forces. The Japanese had exceeded their own expectations in military and naval operations up to June 1942, and Admiral Yamamoto included himself in the ranks of those Japanese suffering from what came to be called *victory disease* (i.e., when a nation or armed force has military victories and becomes arrogant and complacent, developing established patterns of fighting, stereotyping opponents, or refusing to recognize alternatives). Their stunning successes in conquering larger Allied forces had made them cocky and arrogant. They believed that their fighting spirit was superior, and that it would allow them to defeat their enemies in every encounter. The Battle of Midway shook the Japanese out of their overconfidence.

This narrative will tell the story of some of Japan's failures. Some operations were planned and never carried out because of simple bad luck or unfortunate timing. Some operations were initiated and abandoned. Others were planned but never completed because the Japanese lacked the resources to carry them out.

Some operations were carried out, and, in the opinion of the Japanese, they were successful simply because they were completed, even if no real damage was done. Except for a handful of military history buffs and scholars who paid particular attention to the details of the Pacific War, few people know that the Japanese made a second bombing raid on Pearl Harbor just three months after the December 7 attack. In the early morning hours of March 4, 1942, two massive Japanese flying boats attempted to bomb Pearl Harbor. The bombs fell but did no damage because a thick cloud layer obscured the target area; each missed its intended target by miles. The bombs fell into the sea at the entrance to the harbor and in the trees on Mount Tantulus. Despite the technical sophistication of the mission—the bombers had taken off from the Marshall Islands and had been refueled by submarines—the Americans considered the attack a failure because no damage was done. The Japanese considered the attack a success because they had been able to attack Hawaii again, this time with impunity.

This was the first sortie of Japan's Operation K, a series of planned attacks on the United States and its possessions. Other missions were planned, but cryptanalysis by American naval intelligence officers thwarted those plans, ultimately making the Battle of Midway a disaster for the Japanese. Had Operation K been successful, the Battle of Midway and the remainder of the Pacific War might have turned out differently.

The Imperial Japanese Navy (IJN) had ambitious plans for attacking the United States, especially after Lt. Col. James H. Doolittle led sixteen bombers off an aircraft carrier to attack the home islands of

Japan. This bold raid demonstrated to the Japanese that such a mission was possible. Japanese planners, anxious to avenge that raid, allowed their imaginations free rein in brainstorming retribution against the Americans.

Plans were formed for using the large, long-range Emily (H8K) flying boats to be refueled by German submarines in open sea to conduct terror bombings on East Coast U.S. cities. The Germans liked the plans and even readied a few submarines for this operation, but priorities changed for the Japanese. A similar, but all-Japanese, plan would have had the submarine-refueled flying boats bombing West Coast cities, defense plants, and the oil fields of Texas. Another plan would have had giant submarines launching bombers to demolish the Gatun Locks of the Panama Canal. The subs and the bombers were built, but the war ended before they could be used.

The Japanese dreamed of building fleets of huge six-engined bombers similar in many ways to the postwar American Peacemaker (B-36). The Fugaku (Mount Fuji) bombers would have the extended range to make them capable of flying from Japan to bomb targets in the United States. The Japanese started constructing a plant where those bombers were to be built, but Japan's resources ran out before the bombers left the drawing board.

A combination of submarines and floatplanes was used in one of the first terrorist attacks on the United States: A Japanese submarine took a small, foldable floatplane to within fifty miles of the American coastline and launched the tiny bomber from a catapult. Small incendiary bombs were dropped on Oregon on two occasions in attempts to start raging forest fires. These were the only bombs from an enemy airplane to fall on the continental United States in World War II. As a feasibility test, the raids were a success. The Japanese were unaware of the effects of the rainy season in the American Northwest, however. Fortunately for the United States, heavy rains quenched any fires started by the bombings.

Probably the most controversial of all the failed Japanese attempts to attack American forces was the December 7 attack on Pearl Harbor.

Although it was regarded as a brilliant tactical victory for the Japanese, military historians and scholars of warfare generally agree that it was a monumental strategic blunder. Dr. H. P. Willmott, in his excellent book *Pearl Harbor,* states flatly that the attack was a failure. He argues that the Japanese attack was "directed against the tools, and not the basis, of sea power." He points out that the Japanese erred in knocking out just ships and airplanes but left the docks, repair facilities, and oil "tank farms" unharmed. This error allowed the American fleet to recover and continue to operate from Pearl Harbor.

Adm. Samuel E. Morrison, who wrote the official history of U.S. naval operations in World War II, agrees with Dr. Willmott. Admiral Morrison wrote that "the surprise attack on Pearl Harbor, far from being a 'strategic necessity,' as the Japanese claimed after the war, was a strategic imbecility." Dr. Gordon Prange explains these statements by pointing out that "the Japanese attack succeeded in unifying the American people so completely by arousing the ire and the full might of the United States that it was assured that the Japanese would lose the war."

Because he had spent a fair amount of time in the United States, Admiral Yamamoto should have known better than to insist that the war begin with an attack on Pearl Harbor. The Japanese generally had a poor regard for the fighting capabilities of Americans and believed that the United States would quickly opt for a short war, settling in negotiations for peace that would be favorable to the Japanese and allow them to enjoy their rich gains in Southeast Asia. In his *Pearl Harbor: The Verdict of History,* Dr. Prange devotes an entire chapter to the Japanese psychological blunder in underestimating the reaction of the Americans to the Pearl Harbor attack.

In 1941, the Americans were not yet ready for the war, but the Japanese had inventoried their dwindling resources and knew that their time was running out for a victorious war. Ironically, the Japanese concluded that if they could not have access to the resources for conducting their war against China, they were willing to go to war against a larger enemy to gain those resources. As a result, the Japanese painted themselves into a corner. They considered that war and possible defeat were more acceptable than status as a second-class power. The Japanese, especially Admiral Yamamoto, believed that unless they had a stunning victory to eliminate the U.S. Pacific Fleet at Pearl Harbor, the Japanese could not win the war.

Dr. Willmott suggests that if the Japanese had not moved against the U.S. Pacific Fleet at Pearl Harbor, "it is doubtful if the Pacific Fleet could have moved to contest the various Japanese moves in the central Pacific." In other words, the Japanese might have been able to carry out their invasion of Indochina, Thailand, Malaya, Sumatra, Burma, Borneo, and Java without American reaction or intervention. These were not U.S. territories, though, and the American government was more interested in the war in Europe at that time. The Philippines would have been threatened, but the United States was bolstering its military might in those islands for the Japanese threat that they expected in the spring of 1942.

In December 1941, the Japanese fleet was superior to the U.S. fleet in numbers and quality; many historians have expressed the belief that the U.S. Navy would not have succeeded in opposing the Japanese anywhere in the Pacific. Dr. Willmott believes that even if the Japanese had completely destroyed the Pearl Harbor base to force the American fleet to retreat to the U.S. West Coast, the American fleet would have eventually recovered. He states that there is "little doubt that the American national determination [would] see this war through to victory," and that victory would not depend on basing the fleet at Pearl Harbor. He cites this as a second reason why the attack on Pearl Harbor was a failure.

In effect, the Japanese attack on Pearl Harbor may not have been necessary. The attack made it imperative that the United States enter the war immediately. Without that attack, the United States would probably have delayed entering World War II for several more months, and even then would probably have entered only on the other side of the world from the Pacific.

The motion picture *Tora, Tora, Tora* was a 1970 joint effort of Japanese and American filmmakers. The film portrayed fairly accurately the events of the December 7, 1941, attack on Pearl Harbor. In the closing moments of the film, the actor Soh Yamamura, portraying Admiral Yamamoto, is portrayed pensively looking across the Pacific, saying, "I fear all we have done is to awaken a sleeping giant and fill him with terrible resolve." Admiral Yamamoto, in reality, probably never said that, but it was a correct statement. The admiral, who had been the architect of the Pearl Harbor attack, owed a profound apology to the emperor for insisting that the war with the United States begin in the manner in which it did.

1

"Another Strike Is Needed"

It was nearly 10:00 AM, December 7, 1941. Cdr. Mitsuo Fuchida focused his binoculars on the burning and sinking ships below him as his bomber banked in a wide circle ten thousand feet above Pearl Harbor. As the commanding officer of the Japanese air strike force that had devastated the American armed forces on Oahu, he wanted to be able to give an accurate assessment of the damage to Vice Adm. Chuichi Nagumo, the commander of the First Air Fleet. He had dropped his single bomb on the USS *California* and, with his bombing chore complete, Fuchida's primary duty as mission commander was to assess battle damage.

Thick, black smoke from burning oil obscured most of Fuchida's view. More smoke from exploding ammunition magazines and burning American airplanes on the ground made it difficult for him to get a clear view of the harbor and the surrounding airfields. Between the rolling columns of smoke he could see the blazing hulk of the *Arizona,* the dull red bottom of the capsized *Oklahoma,* and the low-in-the-water hulls of the settling *California* and *West Virginia.*

The *Oklahoma* had taken three torpedo hits and careened on her port side. Another torpedo struck her port side and the battleship capsized, with many members of her crew trapped inside the inverted hull. Some were rescued, but many men perished. The *West Virginia* took six torpedo hits and two bomb hits before she sank. The *Arizona* exploded when a bomb hit the magazine in the forecastle in the area of the second main turret. The *Tennessee,* berthed inboard of the *West Virginia,* was protected from torpedoes. She took only two bomb strikes, but was damaged by debris from the exploding *Arizona.* The *California* was badly damaged by two torpedoes and two bombs. All her watertight compartments had been opened in preparation for an inspection scheduled for December 8. With watertight integrity absent, she sank into the mud of the harbor, taking three days to settle to the bottom. The *Nevada* actually got under way and was attempting to reach the open sea when a torpedo and two bombs hit her. The *Pennsylvania* was in dry dock across the channel from Battleship Row and was only slightly damaged.

In all, eight battleships, three light cruisers, three destroyers, and four auxiliary craft were sunk or damaged. American loss of life at Pearl Harbor on December 7 was 2,403 killed and 1,178 wounded.[1]

There had been little or no resistance from the stunned American gunners for the first ten minutes of the attack, which allowed the Japanese to do most of their damage to the fleet anchored in the harbor. Fuchida observed that most of the antiaircraft fire was bursting behind the attackers. He did not know it at the time, but American gunners had been trained to fire at towed-target sleeves at speeds no greater than 127 miles per hour because the U.S. Navy's fire control directors could only track airborne targets moving at 150 miles per hour or less. None of the attacking Japanese airplanes involved in the attack that morning flew that slowly, and American gunners had not yet learned to aim ahead of such fast-moving targets. Now, at the end of the attack, black puffs of exploding antiaircraft shells dotted the sky. Fuchida's own bomber had been slightly damaged by antiaircraft fire, but he was confident that he would be able to return to his carrier, the *Akagi.* The almost complete absence of opposing American fighter planes in the air told him that the strikes on the army and navy airfields had been successful. Japanese control of the air over the island was almost complete.

An earlier message from imperial headquarters in Tokyo had informed the First Air Fleet that U.S. Navy ships were currently anchored in Pearl

Harbor. Information from the Japanese consulate in Honolulu was that there were eight battleships and seven cruisers present, but that as of December 7, 1941 (Tokyo time), there were no aircraft carriers in the port. Fuchida had been disappointed that the targets that the fliers of the First Air Fleet most wanted to hit—those American carriers—would not be present at Pearl Harbor.

Two Jake (E13A) reconnaissance floatplanes had been catapulted at 6:00 AM local time from the fast, new cruisers *Tone* and *Chikuma* that were racing ahead of the carriers. The floatplanes flew in to observe Oahu and Maui, primarily to determine that the U.S. fleet was really at Pearl Harbor and not at its Lahaina anchorage. The floatplanes were also able to provide a weather report while confirming the location of the American ships and state of alertness. Neither of them flew directly over their targets, but made their observations from a slight distance. The radar operators on Oahu were still in training, which may account for why the Japanese floatplanes were not reported.[2]

Lasting only one hour and fifty minutes, the two-wave attack had already accomplished more than the Imperial Japanese Navy (IJN) had planned, but Fuchida made note of the neat rows of destroyers tied up in their own area of the harbor. They had not been touched. He could see that many cruisers and all of the American submarines were unscathed. Some of the ships were beginning to get under way and were sending up an increasing barrage of anti-aircraft fire. The dry docks and ship repair facilities had not been targeted, nor had the storage tanks full of aviation gasoline and bunker oil.[3]

The air raid had been meant to cripple the American forces in the Pacific for at least six months. Fuchida realized that the complete surprise of the attack had created an unexpectedly favorable situation for the Japanese. A follow-up attack could finish off the damaged battleships, add the cruisers, destroyers, and submarines to the tally, complete the destruction of any remaining aircraft, destroy the U.S. Navy's repair facilities, and wipe out the fuel supply for the U.S. forces in Hawaii.[4]

Fuchida took one last look around the sky to reassure himself that all the Japanese aircraft still flying had completed their attack runs and were on the way back to their carriers. Closing his canopy, he requested his pilot, Lt. Mitsuo Matsuzaki, to proceed to the mission rendezvous point twenty nautical miles off the northwest coast of Oahu. His rearseat gunner, PO1c Norinobu Mizuki, kept his canopy open as he swiveled his 7.7-mm machine gun and watched anxiously for any pursuing American fighters.

So that no American aircraft would follow the attackers back to the Japanese task force, several return routes were designated in an elaborate deception plan. One group was to fly west from Oahu for no fewer than thirty miles before turning north toward the carriers. Another group was to take up a course due south for at least twenty miles from the island before swinging in a wide circle to the north. In the meantime, Admiral Nagumo's carriers had sailed forty miles closer to Oahu since the morning launch. He had intended to remain at least two hundred miles from Pearl Harbor, but he was aware that any planes short of fuel or damaged by enemy action might welcome the shorter distance.[5] At the rendezvous point, Fuchida's bomber descended to three thousand feet and met a couple of straggling Zero (A6M) fighters. They closed formation with Fuchida's aircraft to follow him back to their ships.

Military and naval historians agree on the facts of the first Pearl Harbor attack up to this point. For many years, these same historians have puzzled over why the Japanese did not launch a third wave strike to knock out the oil "tank farms" of aviation fuel and bunker oil, or why the Japanese did not at least attempt to destroy the dry docks, cranes, machine shops, power stations, and facilities that would be used to repair the damaged ships to return them to fighting condition. It was generally acknowledged after the attack that if the fuel supplies had been eliminated and the repair facilities wrecked, the U.S. forces might have been forced to withdraw from Hawaii to fight the Pacific War from the mainland West Coast. The course of the Pacific War might have gone quite differently had a third wave strike by the Japanese attackers been successful in destroying the repair facilities and the fuel storage areas. The United States would probably have achieved victory over the Japanese, but the process would have taken much longer. Adm. Samuel E. Morrison wrote that

celled by war requirements. These seven flattops were the entire carrier strength of the U.S. Navy.[10]

Fuchida believed that another attack might draw the American carriers into a rescue mission of their Hawaiian base. He recommended that, instead of retreating along the same route by which it had come, the Japanese strike force could sail south toward the Marshall Islands, with air searches as it went. With luck, there was a chance that the American carriers could be found and attacked.[11]

After Fuchida's bomber came to a stop on the flight deck of the *Akagi,* his excited friend, Commander Genda, now Admiral Nagumo's air officer, clambered up to Fuchida's cockpit to greet him. Fuchida asked him, "How many planes were lost?" "About thirty—some of *Akagi*'s planes are missing," Genda replied. "No more will return. Mine is the last," Fuchida said. Genda quickly calculated that twenty-nine had been lost in combat. Ten or fifteen of the returning planes were so badly damaged that they were pushed overboard, and another forty or forty-five planes were damaged but repairable.

Fuchida could hardly contain his eagerness to get the follow-up wave on its way. He could see that airplanes were being fueled and rearmed. Several engines were being run up and tested. Some airplanes were ready for immediate launch to defend the carriers if the Americans were able to find the attack force. Fuchida was ordered to report to Admiral Nagumo immediately for an account of the battle. Fuchida delayed his trip to the bridge just long enough to check his observations with those of his flight leaders in the operations center. He wanted to ensure that his findings were accurate, but before he could finish he received a second summons to report to the admiral on the double.

On the admiral's bridge, Nagumo waited with his chief of staff, Rear Adm. Ryunosuke Kusaka. They were already engaged in a heated discussion with staff officers concerning the launching of more aircraft against Pearl Harbor. Fuchida told the admiral that four battleships had been sunk and three more had been seriously damaged. Using a berthing chart, Fuchida pointed out the other ships that had been hit. Nagumo was pleased at this news and stated, "We may then conclude that anticipated results have been achieved." Fuchida nervously sensed that the admiral was not favoring follow-on attacks, but he admitted honestly that the main force would not be able to come out of the harbor for battle for at least six months. Fuchida hastily added that other targets—the oil storage tanks, the repair facilities and docks, the cruisers, destroyers, and submarines—would make it worthwhile to launch a third wave strike.

Admiral Nagumo had dozens of questions about whether or not all of the American fighters had been destroyed and the whereabouts of the U.S. aircraft carriers. One of the major weaknesses of the Hawaiian operation was that no provision had been made for aerial reconnaissance following the attack, so the Japanese were unable to locate those American carriers. Admiral Nagumo asked about the ability of the land-based bombers to counterattack, and—now that the element of surprise had been lost—the extent of the antiaircraft fire that could be expected. Fuchida answered all Nagumo's questions as well and as truthfully as he could, knowing that the admiral and his staff were concerned that the results of a follow-up attack would have to be worth any anticipated losses. Fuchida pointed out that the targets should be the damaged battleships, dockyards, and fuel tanks. He considered the job to be incomplete and told the admiral flatly, "Another strike is needed."[12]

When Commander Genda planned the Pearl Harbor attack he recommended the landing of Japanese troops to overrun and occupy the island following the attack on Oahu. The Japanese admirals of the naval general staff (NGS) had turned down this idea as unsupportable, but the approved plan did call for follow-on attacks. Carrier Striking Force Operations Order No. 3, issued on November 23, 1941, read as follows:

Immediately after the return of the first and second attack units, preparations for the next attack will be completed. At this time, carrier attack planes capable of carrying torpedoes will be armed with such as long as the supply lasts. [This was to enable the task force to counterattack any U.S. Navy ships that might show up in pursuit of the task force.] If the destruction of the enemy land-based air strength progresses favorably, repeated attacks will be made immediately and thus decisive results will be achieved. In the event that a powerful enemy surface fleet appears, it will be attacked.[13]

According to Fuchida, the Japanese fliers were eager to return to Pearl Harbor, even though they were aware that they no longer had the element of surprise. They knew that those alerted American antiaircraft gunners and fighter planes would be waiting for them, but the Japanese aircrew members were flushed with excitement by their successes thus far: They were feeling invincible.

Admiral Nagumo believed that the battleship was the primary offensive weapon of any navy, and that their thick armor and bristling antiaircraft protected the battleships adequately against any threat. In his opinion, aircraft carriers, with their thin hulls, large tanks of aviation gasoline, and the bombs and torpedoes they were loaded with made them vulnerable. He believed that aircraft carriers should be used to scout for the battleships, with offensive attacks by aircraft as their secondary responsibility. Because he had put the Pacific Fleet's battleships out of action with one blow he considered his assignment accomplished with far fewer than the expected losses.

Admiral Nagumo dismissed Commander Fuchida with congratulations on a job well done. Commander Genda took up the plea for continued attacks on Pearl Harbor. Genda knew that his aircrews had given the Japanese a marvelous opportunity that would never come again. Like Fuchida, he wanted to finish the job. Genda urged the admiral to "stay in the area for several days and run down the enemy carriers." Once the U.S. carriers had been located, they would attack them, also. If the carriers were eliminated, Pearl Harbor could be totally destroyed at the leisure of the Japanese task force. Genda glanced up at the dozens of Zero fighters droning overhead in a protective umbrella. "If the American heavy bombers do come after us," Genda added confidently, "our fighters will take care of them."[14]

The aggressive Commander Genda wanted to destroy the American carriers. He argued that the confusion that had been created by the Pearl

Harbor raid had provided the chance of a lifetime to totally destroy the U.S. Navy presence in the central Pacific. He was aware that nearly all of the Japanese fleet's flyable torpedo bombers were now loaded with torpedoes in preparation for attacks on any American ships that might be searching for the Japanese strike force. Repairing battle-damaged aircraft and refueling and loading bombs for strikes on ground targets might take too long to permit another attack on December 7. Even with the element of surprise gone, Genda believed that follow-on attacks the next day would be successful. His friend Commander Fuchida had even volunteered to lead another strike on Pearl Harbor. Genda enthusiastically agreed with Fuchida that the follow-on attacks would draw the U.S. carriers back to the islands from wherever they might be. Admiral Nagumo reminded Genda that their fuel tankers were already on their way to the prearranged rendezvous with the returning attack fleet. He did not want to break radio silence to change their orders. He added that they would never be able to catch up with the task force in time to furnish them with much-needed fuel, even if the tankers were redirected to the south.[15]

On board the carrier *Soryu,* Adm. Tamon Yamaguchi reported that his ship and the carrier *Hiryu* and their aircraft were ready to launch the third wave attack. Capt. Jisaku Okada of the carrier *Kaga,* the second carrier accompanying the *Akagi,* recommended that the fuel tanks and dock facilities be included in the list of targets, even if the attack sorties were flown the next day. The remaining two carriers—*Shokaku* and *Zuikaku*— reported that they were ready to return for another attack on Pearl Harbor.

Admiral Nagumo, however, believed that with the unexpected success of the raid the task force's job was complete, and that now his concern should be to keep his six carriers out of harm's way. In his mind, a Japanese proverb kept repeating itself: *Yudan kaiteki* (Carelessness is the greatest enemy). He did not know the whereabouts of the American carriers. He did not even know the exact number of U.S. Navy carriers currently in the Pacific. However, Nagumo did know that, wherever the American carriers were, they had been notified of the attack on their base at Pearl Harbor and they would be sending out scout planes to find his task force.

Actually, the *Enterprise* had been only two hundred miles from Oahu when Fuchida led the first wave attack. The American task force had been providentially delayed because the escorting destroyers had difficulty refueling in the heavy seas. Eighteen of the Dauntless (SBD) scout bombers from the *Enterprise* had arrived over Oahu during the attack. Five of them had been shot down—some by Japanese Zeroes and some by nervous American antiaircraft gunners—but thirteen of them had landed safely at Kaneohe. Those remaining had to run the gauntlet of U.S. Navy machine gunners there, but nine of them were undamaged. Those flyable Dauntlesses were quickly refueled and armed with 500-pound bombs. They then returned to the air to search for the Japanese fleet. They went in the right direction, but found only vacant ocean. Six army Flying Fortresses (B-17s) had taken off thirty minutes earlier to search the area to the south of Pearl Harbor. Naturally, they did not find the enemy fleet. Adm. Bill Halsey, on the *Enterprise,* did not know the location of the Japanese fleet and remained all day to the west of Oahu. He wanted to strike the attacking Japanese but could not determine if they were to the north or to the south. His ship's radar picked up blips 160 miles to the north. These indications were probably the Japanese fleet, but radar was new and unreliable. The inexperienced radar operators did not have confidence in their equipment.[16]

The Japanese carriers were certainly within the range of the American Flying Fortress bombers. Knowing this, Nagumo decided neither to attack Pearl Harbor again nor to hunt for the American flattops. He believed he had successfully accomplished his mission with only one-tenth the anticipated aircraft losses. He had expected to lose up to a third of his ships in the task force, but not one had been scratched.

Admiral Nagumo was not an aviator, but his seniority had positioned him to lead the Pearl Harbor attack. Nagumo placed a great deal of faith in his chief of staff, Admiral Kusaka, who had supported Nagumo's initial opposition to the Pearl Harbor attack. Admiral Nagumo had not been in favor of the Pearl Harbor attack, but once the IJN had given its approval of Admiral Yamamoto's daring plan for the raid, Nagumo had put aside his objections and earnestly prepared himself as leader of the operation.

On the bridge of the *Akagi,* Admiral Kusaka ended the discussion about launching a third wave attack. He announced, "There will be no attacks of any kind. Now we must prepare for other operations ahead. We will withdraw." Admiral Nagumo nodded his assent, saying curtly, "Please do."[17]

Admiral Nagumo had already made up his mind to withdraw his carrier force. His greatest concerns were with the American heavy bombers that might have survived the attack and any submarines that could be stalking his fleet. The signal flags were run up the yardarm of the *Akagi* at 1:30 PM to signal the other ships in the task force to retire at full speed to the northwest, away from Hawaii.[18]

Commander Fuchida was in the command post on the upper flight deck, gulping a lunch of rice cakes with bean paste—his first food since a predawn breakfast—when he learned that the carrier force was withdrawing. He rushed to the admiral's bridge to protest. He saluted Admiral Nagumo and demanded, "Why are we not attacking again?" Before Nagumo could answer, Kusaka interrupted by saying, "The objective of the Pearl Harbor operation has been achieved." He repeated that the First Air Fleet must now prepare for other upcoming operations. Fuchida was so enraged that he did not trust himself to speak. He saluted, turned on his heel, and left the bridge, a bitter, angry, and frustrated man. For the remainder of the voyage, Fuchida spoke to Nagumo only when duty and courtesy demanded it.[19]

Commander Genda shared Fuchida's disappointment, but even the scrappy Genda had to admit that Nagumo was right in not attacking Pearl Harbor again without first knowing the location of the American carriers. Genda, writing in 1967 about the Pearl Harbor operation, denied that any discussion ever took place about a third wave strike on December 7, and that he certainly did not participate in any urging that such a strike be made. He wrote, "According to Dr. Prange's book *Tora, Tora, Tora* and others, a fierce argument took place on the bridge of the *Akagi* [after the recovering of second-wave aircraft] as regards the proposal for a second strike [i.e., the third wave attack]. This is not true. The author [Genda] had been on the bridge for some eight hours before the start of operations and remained there over the following four days. Such a proposal was never made."[20]

One of the major shortcomings of the Pearl Harbor attack plan was that it made neither provision for poststrike reconnaissance nor a plan to send out scouts to locate the U.S. carriers if they happened to be absent from Pearl Harbor when the attack was made. These omissions were serious flaws in the plan and one of the first major errors made by the Japanese in their planning of the Pearl Harbor attack. Lack of extended range reconnaissance would plague the IJN for the remainder of the war.

Genda had worked on several alternative plans that would do the most damage to the Americans, even while the cruise was under way. He held out the hope that Nagumo would send out patrols to locate the carriers and attack them as soon as possible. Genda even advocated calling the fleet tankers down from their locations in the north so that the First Air Fleet could remain in the area to continue the search. Certain that the Japanese fleet had enough power to sink the American carriers, Genda proposed that they could return home by way of the Marshall Islands, attacking Oahu repeatedly as they passed that island to the west.[21]

Fuchida claimed that he reproved himself for not having hedged on his answers to Nagumo's questions, thinking that his answers might have justified the admiral's caution. In reality, Nagumo's mind had already been made up. Too many threats to the First Air Fleet existed to be ignored: the missing American carriers, the possibility of attack from the island-based Flying Fortresses, and the submarines that must be searching for the Japanese fleet. These were all factors that supported Nagumo's decision. Admiral Kusaka backed that decision, writing that the attack should be carried out "as swiftly as a demon flashing by and also it should be withdrawn as fast as the passing wind."[22]

On board the battleship *Yamato* in Japan, Adm. Isoroku Yamamoto, the commander in chief of the combined fleet, waited patiently to hear the reports of the attack on Oahu. Atmospheric conditions caused radio waves from Hawaii to be bounced so that radio operators on the *Yamato* had heard the famous broadcast message from Commander Fuchida—"*Tora,*

tora, tora" (Tiger, tiger, tiger)—indicating that the Pearl Harbor strike force had achieved complete surprise in its attack.

There was unabashed jubilation at combined fleet headquarters in Japan when the news came in of the success of the first two wave attacks. In Tokyo, imperial headquarters announced that Japanese forces had "entered into a state of war with American and British forces." Excitement ran high with the news announcement of the "huge victory at Pearl Harbor." Prime Minister Tojo broadcast that Japan had done its utmost to prevent war. He reminded his audience that Japan had never lost a war in twenty-six hundred years and finished his broadcast by saying "I promise you final victory."[23] Crowds gathered in the plaza near the imperial palace, singing the national anthem and other patriotic songs. Thousands pledged their loyalty to the emperor. Japanese newspapers announced "the day we have been awaiting impatiently has arrived," and "the Imperial forces are invincible."[24]

Admiral Nagumo held off sending his final full damage report until he was well clear of the Hawaiian waters and possible threats. On December 17, he sent "Battle Report No. 1." Considering the cloud cover and smoke over the target area, Fuchida and his observers had been fairly accurate in their damage assessment in that report. They took credit for sinking an oil tanker and damaging five cruisers that they did not hit. They overlooked the damage inflicted on the battleship USS *Pennsylvania,* the minelayer *Oglala,* the repair ship *Vestal,* and the seaplane tender *Curtiss.* The special attack unit of the advance force (of five midget submarines) that had participated in the opening moments of the war was highly praised for "much damage by its bravest attack," when actually the subs had probably caused little if any damage to American ships. The report erred significantly in its estimate that 450 U.S. aircraft had been set afire, destroyed by bombing or strafing, or shot down. American aircraft losses—army, navy, and marines—actually numbered 169.[25]

Although the initial assault on Pearl Harbor had involved two separate waves, forty-five minutes apart, the Japanese thought of the December 7, 1941, onslaught as one attack. Each of the aircraft—fighters and bombers—participating in the two waves flew only one sortie that day.

All the officers of the combined fleet staff expected Admiral Yamamoto to order Nagumo to launch follow-on attacks. The staff met to discuss more attacks and agreed that they should be accomplished if the American carriers could be located right away. Nagumo's orders had included a clause for repeated attacks, but did not provide the details of follow-on assaults. The staff concluded that Nagumo, as a battleship admiral who had knocked out the enemy's battleships, would probably consider his mission accomplished, and that to order him to attack again might be taken as a rebuke.[26]

Oddly enough, even before the message came from Nagumo, Yamamoto predicted that the Hawaiian *Kido Butai* (Strike Force) would withdraw from the area without additional sorties against Pearl Harbor. Admiral Yamamoto believed that Nagumo was not a cowardly leader, but a conservative, cautious man in battle. Admiral Yamamoto himself was a cautious warrior and he understood Admiral Nagumo's concerns.

Yamamoto had left the decision up to his tactical commander on the battle scene. He did not change Nagumo's orders. Rather, because Nagumo knew his own situation better than any other commander, Yamamoto believed that Nagumo should be allowed some latitude in making his decisions. Japanese intelligence and reconnaissance efforts had failed to locate any of the American carriers. Yamamoto shared Nagumo's caution because they both suspected that as many as five American carriers might be operating in the Pacific. They believed that the *Enterprise, Yorktown, Lexington,* and *Hornet* were based at Pearl Harbor. They had correct information that the *Saratoga* was at San Diego and would be joining the Pacific Fleet at any time, however.

Admiral Nagumo's decision to withdraw begs the question of what might have been achieved if he had allowed a third wave attack. He had fulfilled his part in directing the first attack, but Yamamoto's chief of staff, Rear Adm. Matome Ugaki, likened Nagumo to "a sneak thief . . . contented with a humble lot." Ugaki commented on the lost opportunity, saying, "since our loss is not more than thirty planes, it is most important for us to expand our results." Ugaki believed that Nagumo had departed early without finishing the job he had been sent to do.[27] Admiral Yamamoto was disappointed that Nagumo had not eliminated the American carriers, but he did not admonish Nagumo directly. A consummate bridge player, Yamamoto described Nagumo's withdrawal in bridge terms, as "a small slam, barely made . . . second class thinking."[28]

The world's attention was so riveted on Pearl Harbor on December 7, 1941, that little has been written or said about the Japanese attack on Midway Islands that night. The complex plans for the attack on Pearl Harbor included a provision for Midway Islands to be attacked on the same day by the Midway Neutralization Unit. Commanded by Capt. Kanamo Konishi, this auxiliary unit was made up of the destroyers *Ushio* and *Sazanami,* accompanied by the tanker *Shiriya.* The assignment of this small group was to "bombard and neutralize the air base at Midway" to ensure the safe passage of Nagumo's returning carriers and ships and to "divert American attention by decoying reconnaissance flights."[29] It is ironic that the Japanese planners concerned themselves with American reconnaissance flights, yet made no provisions for poststrike reconnaissance flights from their own fleet, other than the normal scouting flights and patrols for protection of the withdrawing strike force.

The report of the Midway Neutralization Unit was received at combined fleet headquarters and the operation was regarded as unsuccessful in carrying out its mission. Yamamoto's staff proposed another attack on Midway by either sending the two destroyers back to fulfill their task or by ordering Nagumo's First Air Fleet to hit Midway on the way home. Because the two destroyers had not done the job, the choice was awarded to the much more powerful First Air Fleet.

Admiral Nagumo read the orders to conduct a raid on the Midway Islands on his return voyage from the Pearl Harbor attack, but because he was feeling pleased with himself for the stunning success of that operation he chose to ignore the second orders. He claimed that bad weather and low fuel prevented the Midway operation. Actually, he was displeased with the orders for the raid on Midway, as was his chief of staff Admiral Kusaka, Commander Genda, and other members of his staff. They considered that the Midway operation was beneath their accomplishments and likened the request for an attack on Midway to "asking a junior sumo wrestler who's just beaten a grand champion if he'd mind buying some vegetables for dinner on the way home."[30]

The air raid on Pearl Harbor was a tactical masterpiece of air-to-surface warfare and resulted in a stunning tactical victory for the Japanese. Strategically, however, it was a colossal blunder because it had not damaged the ships that would become the primary battle force of the U.S. Navy—the aircraft carriers that were absent from the harbor on that December morning. The U.S. Navy's carrier air power was still almost completely intact. The majority of the 250 navy and marine aircraft present in Hawaii when the attack took place were newly arrived Catalina (PBY-3 and PBY-5) flying boat patrol bombers. Most of the fighting muscle—the fighters, torpedo bombers, and dive-bombers—were on the carriers.[31] Only two of the American battleships were permanently out of action, and most of the U.S. fleet at Pearl Harbor was back in operation within six months or less.

The fundamental error committed by the Japanese was that they failed to anticipate how the American people would rally in outrage at the attack. Any voices calling for the United States to isolate itself from the European and Asian wars were drowned out in the pledges of resolve for vengeance and the volunteer oaths of enlistees signing up to join the fight against the Axis powers. Americans were now willing to buckle down to fight a long war to achieve nothing less than unconditional surrender from their enemies. As Adm. Chester W. Nimitz put it, "The Japanese attack served to unify our country which was not at all sure that it wanted to get mixed up in World War II."[32] The Japanese had committed a monumental strategic blunder in failing to destroy the fuel tanks, docks, cranes, shops, and the repair facilities that would immediately begin the restoration of the damaged American ships.

During 1940 and 1941, the U.S. Navy had painstakingly built up its fuel reserve of 4.5 million barrels of aviation gasoline and oil in Hawaii. Nearly all of it was stored above ground and was therefore vulnerable to attack.[33] Admiral Nimitz, who arrived at Pearl Harbor on December 25, 1941, to take command of what was left of the Pacific Fleet, said that even these tanks could have been destroyed if the Japanese had machine-gunned them with incendiary bullets. The admiral commented that an underground bomb-proof storage for all petroleum products was being constructed at Red Hill, behind Pearl Harbor, at the time of the December 7 attack and that he had "sweated blood" until that underground storage facility was completed and the oil supply safely piped into it.[34] This enormous fuel cache on Oahu was far more than the Japanese possessed in all of their fuel reserves. Admiral Nimitz stated that had the American gasoline and oil storage tanks been bombed, the entire U.S. fleet would have had to retreat to the West Coast of the United States because it would not have had the fuel with which to operate from Pearl Harbor. He affirmed that it would have altered the course of the war significantly.[35]

By not carrying out the destruction of the U.S. Navy's shore installations and fuel storage tanks, Admiral Nagumo committed a mistake that helped to ensure that Japan would lose the Pacific War. The Japanese failed to exploit the advantages that their sudden strike had presented them. Their initial victory blinded them to the necessity of finding and attacking the American carriers: The weapons that would later defeat the Japanese had been spared.

American forces on Hawaii fully expected the attacks to continue throughout the remainder of the day and night on December 7. Adm. William L. Calhoun, commander of the base force, believed that there had indeed been a third wave, but claimed that it did little damage. He stated that he believed that the third wave's purpose was primarily photoreconnaissance. Lt. Gen. Walter C. Short, Hawaii's U.S. Army commander, reported to Gen. George Marshall, who subsequently reported it to President Roosevelt, that there was a "definite third wave attack at 11:00 AM." The belief that a third wave attack had occurred was so strong that Secretary of the Navy Frank Knox, after his inspection tour of Hawaii, was convinced of a third wave attack.[36] Ships' logs contained entries such as those of the destroyer-minelayer USS *Tracy*: "At 1040: Air attack continued by smaller group of planes." Battleship USS *Maryland,* the auxiliary *Sumner,* and the submarine *Pelias,* as well as the submarine *Dolphin* and the cruisers *St. Louis* and *Helena,* claimed to have fired on this third wave. Some ships' gunners even claimed to have shot down attackers during the supposed third wave attack.[37]

Wild rumors of invasion by the Japanese that Sunday were passed on to every military and naval installation on Oahu. Many anticipated an invasion. Adm. Husband E. Kimmel expected an invasion. So did his chief of staff, Capt. William Smith and the fleet aviation officer, Capt. Arthur C. Davis.[38] Fear and confusion set in at every base on Hawaii. Paratroopers wearing blue denim coveralls were reported to have landed on the North Shore. (This rumor might have been started by a U.S. Navy gunner, clad in dungarees, who bailed out of his crashing Dauntless dive-bomber after Japanese fighters had attacked it.) Four Japanese troop transport ships were supposedly seen off Barber's Point. An enemy sampan was said to be landing at the Naval Ammunition Depot. Col. William J. Flood and Col. William F. Farthing have said that, had the Japanese followed up the attack with landing troops, they could easily have gained control of the island in that one day: "Everybody thought that the Japanese would be back and could not understand why they didn't land."[39]

Admiral Nimitz hinted that by sinking several old or obsolescent battleships, the Japanese did the Americans a favor by forcing the U.S. Navy to abandon the battleship as its capital ship and form its striking forces around aircraft carriers.[40] Admiral Halsey echoed his beliefs.

The IJN's traditional strategy had been to entice the enemy fleet into home waters, wearing its strength down with tenacious attacks by submarines as the enemy made its way toward Japan, and to destroy remaining enemy ships in one great decisive battle. Instead, Yamamoto's planners convinced him that a direct attack on the U.S. Navy at Pearl Harbor would hold the greatest chance of success and do the most damage. It was a risky plan. Yamamoto convinced himself that the Pearl Harbor attack would be the most effective way to buy the six months needed to ensure the success of Japanese expansion in the Pacific, and he fought for this operation to be approved. He chose Genda to do the detailed planning of the raid, Fuchida to lead it in the air, and Nagumo's First Air Fleet to take the war to the Americans on Hawaii.

Commander Genda had been an assistant air attaché in London during 1939 and 1940. Some sources say that Genda got his inspiration for the Pearl Harbor attack from the brilliant British attack on Italian ships in the harbor at Taranto in southern Italy, but Genda's fertile mind had already conceived a torpedo attack against ships in a harbor, and the Taranto attack only reinforced his theories. In Taranto harbor, on the night of November 11, 1940, two waves of antiquated frame-and-fabric Fairey *Swordfish* biplane torpedo bombers were launched from the British aircraft carrier HMS *Illustrious*. The slow but agile old aircraft dropped special torpedoes, sinking half the Italian fleet at anchor, including three battleships. The British lost only two of their *Swordfish* and one crew. The harbor at Taranto was eighty-four- to ninety-feet deep.[41] Pearl Harbor was much shallower—thirty- to forty-feet deep. For this reason alone, the American admirals thought that Pearl Harbor was immune from torpedo attack. Not only was the harbor not deep enough for submarines to operate submerged, it was too shallow for bombers to drop their torpedoes against anchored ships. The U.S. Navy did not consider that torpedo nets were necessary to protect the ships berthed on Battleship Row. The nets were cumbersome and a great deal of trouble to place and operate; they were strung only at the entrance to Pearl Harbor.

Genda knew that conventional torpedoes would dive to about sixty-five feet and bury themselves in the mud in a shallow harbor when dropped from a normal launch. Working with torpedo experts, Genda applied information that he had gained from the British attack at Taranto to modify torpedoes by adding wooden stabilizing fins. Genda instructed his torpedo-bomber pilots to experiment with release altitudes and airspeeds. The pilots found that a release altitude of sixty-five feet and airspeed of one hundred knots (115 miles per hour) worked well. Practicing with the new torpedoes and using precise altitudes for release, the scores for successful hits rose to 82 percent.[42]

In August 1941, Fuchida initiated the training of the torpedo-bomber pilots at the air base at Kagoshima; Kagoshima Bay resembled Pearl Harbor in many respects. Cautious about revealing the Pearl Harbor attack plans, he informed the pilots that they had finished their preliminary fleet engagement training and that they would begin training in shallow-water torpedoing against anchored ships as part of their advanced training. His casual manner convinced the pilots that this was nothing out of the ordinary. He told them that the training torpedoes were not yet ready, so they would only be going through the motions. He went on with these detailed instructions: "You will climb to 2,000 meters [6,500 feet] under the flight commander's lead and charge over the eastern tip of Sakurajima [the extinct volcano jutting into Kagoshima Bay]. Then circle down the valley of the Kotsuki River at 500 meters [1,640 feet] intervals. Maintaining an altitude of 50 meters [160 feet], go down the valley from Iwasakidani toward Kagoshima, flying over the city at 40 meters [130 feet]."[43]

There was a collective gasp as the shocked pilots listened to these instructions. They were being ordered to fly over a city at dangerously low altitudes. Fuchida continued, "As you pass over the Yamagataya Department Store, to port you will see a large water tank on the shore. After you pass over it, come down to 20 meters [65 feet] and release a torpedo."[44]

He then added that a target buoy would be anchored about five hundred meters from the shore. As they released their torpedoes, they were to maintain their wings level at 160 knots (185 miles per hour), and climb to return to base. Although the pilots knew that these tactics allowed no room for error and that the maneuvers were dangerous, Fuchida cautioned them to be bold but careful. He ended his instructions by informing the group that their instructor, Lt. Shigeharu Murata, would demonstrate the procedures. As he walked Murata to his Kate (B5N2) bomber, Fuchida muttered under his breath, "I hope you can do it!" Murata had been highly amused by Fuchida's casual manner of briefing the fantastic instructions and remarked, "You could be a fine actor!" Murata took off and performed the entire series of maneuvers flawlessly.

The citizens of Kagoshima were dumbfounded as they watched plane after plane roar over the city, barely clearing the rooftops. Each bomber executed the intricate ballet as it zigzagged down the narrow valley, leveling out low over the water as if shot from a giant gun. This practice went on for days and the fliers loved it. Not one of the pilots made a mistake, but the townspeople of Kagoshima tired of the roar of engines and the near misses of airplanes over their homes. The women of the red-light district assumed that the navy pilots were buzzing the city for their benefit as practice flights screamed low over their area day after day. But even they eventually complained that the pilots were becoming "unusually fresh."[45]

After solving the torpedo problems, Commanders Genda and Fuchida continued tirelessly to plan the thousands of details that had to be addressed in the attack on Pearl Harbor. A large crate was brought to Admiral Kusaka's office on the carrier *Akagi,* which was anchored off Kyushu. The crate contained a highly detailed seven-foot-square model of Oahu, showing Pearl Harbor and its surrounding bases and airfields. Commanders Genda and Fuchida spent the next several days memorizing every terrain feature, every defense installation, and every detail that would affect their planning.

They decided on which aircraft would be armed with bombs, what size bombs, and which aircraft would be assigned to carry torpedoes. (The earlier model Kate torpedo bombers would be used as level horizontal bombers, and the newer models would be armed with torpedoes.) Genda and Fuchida assigned targets to be hit by each type of aircraft, the crew member who would lead the various flight elements, the times each target was to be hit, the directions of flight, and the different axes of attack. Genda even insisted that all the aircraft be winterized as a precaution, because the carrier fleet's route would be going fairly far north: All propellers received a thin coating of oil to prevent freezing. Genda and Fuchida went over their plans again and again to ensure that no detail was left unattended.

There were three main reasons for the stunning success of the tactics of the Pearl Harbor attack: The first was the complete surprise of the attack, the second was the meticulous planning done by Genda, and the third was the thorough training program conducted by Fuchida.[46]

On November 3, Admiral Yamamoto took his key staff officers to brief the IJN's chief of staff, Admiral Nagano, on the details of the attack on

Pearl Harbor. Nagano ended the lengthy discussions by sighing to Yamamoto, "As for the Pearl Harbor attack, my judgement is not always good, because I'm old. So I will have to trust yours."[47]

Admiral Yamamoto issued the bulky 151-page "Combined Fleet Top Secret Operations Order No. 1" on November 5. It detailed the strategy for the beginning of the Pacific War at Pearl Harbor with simultaneous attacks on the Philippines, Malaya, Guam, Wake, Hong Kong, and the South Seas area. Plans for the invasion of Thailand, the Dutch East Indies, and the Philippines were drawn up by the imperial staff to be carried out as the Southern Operation. The two primary purposes of the attack on Hawaii were to eliminate the U.S. Navy's presence in the Pacific, and to guarantee the unhampered success of the Southern Operation.[48]

In the spring of 1941, Cordell Hull, the U.S. secretary of state, had stated his four principles, which established acceptable (to the United States) foreign policy for the Japanese. These required the Japanese to moderate their plans for territorial expansion. The United States opposed Japanese aggression against China and the moves threatening the southwest Pacific areas. There was pressure from groups in the United States and in Japan to work out a compromise. Negotiations between Secretary Hull and Japanese Ambassador Nomura ground on during 1941, but the prospects of agreement grew dimmer with each passing day.

The Japanese had no idea that the Americans had broken their diplomatic ciphers as a result of the intensive codebreaking operations known as Magic. From the Magic messages, President Franklin D. Roosevelt learned that the Japanese planned to conduct parallel diplomatic and military offensives in Asia and he decided to intensify the economic warfare against Japan. From reading the Magic traffic, the U.S. State Department knew that November 25 was a key date in the negotiations and that after that date, if the differences were not resolved, Japan might commit to war. The diplomatic messages made no mention of military or naval actions or movements, however. Secretary Hull knew that the Japanese were making military and naval preparations while appearing earnest in their diplomatic efforts. On November 26, Hull stated United States' final position: Japan was to withdraw its troops from China, recognize the Chiang Kai Shek government, and withdraw from the Tripartite Pact with Germany and Italy.[49]

There have been many accounts of how the Japanese government's ultimatum message ending negotiations was presented to Secretary Hull. The message did not openly declare war, but informed the United States that negotiations had become futile. The Japanese government used the message to break off negotiations and diplomatic relations. The message was to have been delivered at least thirty minutes prior to the first bombs falling on Pearl Harbor, but the Japanese embassy in Washington was tardy in getting that important message to Secretary Hull. (An inexperienced typist had difficulty in completing a readable copy of the deciphered message.) The attack had begun seven minutes early and the Japanese message that was to have preceded it was delivered an hour and five minutes late. Hull already knew of the attack on Pearl Harbor when the Japanese finally delivered the message to him.

Admiral Yamamoto was extremely disappointed that negotiations had not been successful between his country's ambassadors and the United States—and that the attack had started before the message had been received by the U.S. government. When Yamamoto heard phrases like "sneak attack" and "day of infamy," he knew that one purpose of the Pearl Harbor attack had not been achieved. The Japanese intent had been to destroy the U.S. Navy's ability to fight and to wipe out the American will to fight, but in fact they had achieved the opposite: The attack on Pearl Harbor had served to infuriate the Americans and to unify their resolve to seek revenge on Japan.[50]

In spite of the fact that Admiral Nagumo believed that the Pearl Harbor attack had been a tremendous success, he fretted for days during the withdrawal phase. He was worried that his fleet was short of fuel, so he elected to return to Japanese waters by the northern route. He wanted to make his rendezvous with the tankers that were heading for the prearranged refueling point. This was probably a fortunate decision for the U.S. Navy's aircraft carriers, the *Lexington* and the *Enterprise*. Had Nagumo's carriers sailed south toward the Marshall Islands, his scout aircraft would certainly have located the U.S. carriers. The Japanese had the capability to launch 350 aircraft to attack the American ships, whereas the Americans had only 131 aircraft on board the two ships. The Japanese aircrews already had a high degree of combat experience. With a three-to-one advantage in carriers and aircraft in favor of the Japanese, there is little doubt that the Japanese would have sunk the American carriers. Had the Japanese made the follow-on attacks on Pearl Harbor and located the U.S. carriers, the final outcome of the war might not have been different, but years might have been added to the war. Admiral Nimitz stated that if the Japanese had destroyed the fuel tanks on Oahu, the war would have been prolonged by at least two years.[51]

Admiral Nagumo and his task force returned to Japan by the end of December, extremely pleased with what they had done at Pearl Harbor. Admiral Yamamoto was also pleased, but not satisfied. He had known all along that the Japanese must deal a crippling blow to the U.S. Navy from the beginning of the war so that his nation could then negotiate a peace with the Americans from a position of strength. He considered that Japan's position of strength could not last more than eighteen months. Nagumo had turned away from securing a complete victory, just when it was within his grasp.

When Nagumo and his staff arrived, they expected to receive smiles and praise from Yamamoto. Instead, Yamamoto gave them frowns and grumbling. Yamamoto did not scold them directly, but with cool deliberation informed them that they had not defeated the Americans. He told Nagumo to begin preparing for the next battles in the southern areas and the Indian Ocean. In his mind, Yamamoto already was forming new battle plans, because he knew that Hawaii and Midway would have to be revisited.[52]

The Japanese had opened the war in the Pacific with the longest-ranged attack ever conducted by one nation against another. Having chosen to do battle in such a vast arena, the Japanese would have to use many methods to extend the range of their aircraft, their ships, and all their fighting forces to fight such a war. They would be forced to experiment with schemes that were almost bizarre to challenge the Americans and the Allies to meet those long-range attacks.

The emperor was briefed on the Pearl Harbor attack, but he was given only the figures of the number of ships and aircraft destroyed. He was not given the details of what had not been destroyed. The briefing practically glowed with praise for the results that had been achieved by the imperial forces against the Americans in their first encounter.

2

Planning the Attack

The beginnings of the clash between the United States and Japan over China had roots in the early twentieth century. Both countries saw China as a vast market and treasure trove of raw materials, and were fiercely competitive for those treasures. Then, just before the beginning of World War I, the Japanese replaced the Russians as the main threat to American policy in the Far East. The Japanese had annexed Korea in 1910, marking the beginning of Japanese territorial expansion. The proud Japanese liked to point out that their country was the only Asian country that had not been colonized by the major Western powers. In fact, Japanese nationalistic pride was so great that they considered themselves to be justified in demanding that their country should be a colonial power equal to the Western powers. At the end of World War I, the rift between the United States and Japan was widening. The differences centered on America's insistence on its Open Door trade policies; the American possession of the Philippines versus the Japanese control of the Marianas Islands, the Caroline Islands, and the Marshall Islands; the open racial discrimination (from both sides); and the animosities of conflicting trade interests.[1]

As a member of the Allied coalition in World War I, the Japanese had seized the German foothold and concessions in the Shantung peninsula of China and taken the German-held islands in the Pacific. In the Versailles

Peace Conference in 1919, the Japanese offered to barter their interests in China for a seat in the League of Nations. The Japanese also asked for a declaration favoring the rights of nonwhite nations, citing the need for "just treatment in every respect, making no distinctions either in law or in fact, on account of their race or nationality."[2]

Although many nations supported the clause, the Japanese were keenly aware that President Woodrow Wilson's abstention helped to defeat the proposal. The failure of the proposal was not lost on the leaders of Japan. Adding to the perceived discrimination against the Japanese, the U.S. Congress had passed the Immigration Act of 1924, barring Asians from immigrating to the United States. This was regarded as insulting because, in the Gentlemen's Agreement made in 1907 with President Theodore Roosevelt, the Japanese had imposed the same ban on themselves.[3]

The Japanese believed that a semidivine emperor ruled them. Between the twelfth and nineteenth centuries, the country had evolved into a true feudal state. During this period, a strong sense of militarism blended well with the Japanese character at that time. The Japanese believed that they were descendants of lesser gods, and that they owed their lives to the emperor.[4] Whereas Westerners used racism to the denigration of others not like themselves, the Japanese held to their own unique form of racism, believing themselves superior because of the purity of their race. They concerned themselves with what it meant to be Japanese, and why the Yamato race was special among the races and cultures of the world. The Japanese did not claim to be mentally or physically superior to others; instead they claimed to be more virtuous and moralistic.[5]

Japanese nationalism had been based on the throne of the emperor from the beginnings of the Meiji period. Emperor Hirohito's grandfather, Emperor Mutsuhito, known posthumously as Meiji the Great, had been the guiding force behind Japan's modernization since 1868. At the beginning of the Meiji Period, Emperor Mutsuhito separated the imperial court from the government and reorganized his court to European standards, complete with a constitution that stated that the emperor was always to be the successor in a sacred blood lineage. The government was to be subordinated to the emperor who was "sacred and inviolable" as head of the empire and commander in chief of the armed forces.[6] Japan's focus on the emperor lasted until it was defeated in 1945. Since that time, the Japanese believe that the emperor's role concerns itself with culture rather than politics. Only the older Japanese still regard him as a political entity and semideity.[7]

More resentment was created by the Five Power Naval Agreements Treaty of 1922, which placed limits on the tonnage of capital ships of Great Britain, the United States, France, Italy, and Japan. The formula allowed Japan 40 percent less tonnage that the United States and Great Britain.[8] The "5:5:3 ratio" created a strong resentment among the young Japanese officers who would rise to become the naval leaders of World War II. They believed that the ratio imposed was adequate to protect Japan in its own waters, but that the Western powers remained superior on the open ocean. When the militant young leaders—including young Isoruku Yamamoto—came to power in Japan, they ended Japan's participation in the treaty.[9]

The Japanese wanted the advantage of cultural prestige as much as, or more than, the economic advantages of colonial possessions. The Japanese interests in expanding its territory in Manchuria and China through invasion had created strong opposition in the United States. Before 1931, Japan had no grand plan to go to war with China, but the government in Tokyo appeared to have become unable to control its increasingly obstinate, strong-willed army. In 1932, Prime Minister Inugai was killed by a group of hotheaded army cadets and naval officers. In the name of patriotism and Japan's "divine mission," other army officers and civilians were assassinated. The weak Japanese government would not censure the army for fear of loss of public support, but at the same time it would not admit to foreign governments that its armed forces were out of its control. In a relatively short time, the Imperial Japanese Army (IJA) was able to sweep aside most civilian opposition to its aggressive foreign policy in China. The increasing influence over the populace evolved into total military control. Unauthorized and artificially created incidents gave the Japanese an excuse to pour troops into China. Popular support for these victories led to the

Japanese people leaning toward a stronger military and weaker civilian government.[10]

Japan's opening moves on December 7, 1941, were based on planning that had really begun in July 1937, when serious fighting had spread in China. Japan rapidly took over large amounts of Chinese territory, until there was little of value left for the Japanese to conquer. The Japanese announced their establishment of the New Order of Eastern Asia, which they envisioned as a confederation of China, Korea, Manchukuo, and Japan under Japanese leadership. This grand dream came at a high price. Japan gradually began to realize that it was involved in a war that, under its present economic circumstances, it could not win. The IJA could not pacify the areas that it held, but neither could it force the final battle that would end the war. After March 1939, the nation was virtually ruled by decree from the military leaders, with the emperor's blessings. The Japanese government was forced to impose rationing on its citizens on certain items in 1938; nearly all production was geared for war. The IJA committed 1.5 million troops to China and the war was costing Japan $5 million a day.[11]

The United States, leading the nations that would become wartime allies, demanded that Japan withdraw its troops from China but took no real action. Japan wanted not only to remain in China, but also to have a free hand in its dealings with China. When the League of Nations condemned Japan for its invasion of China, the Japanese believed that the League and the Americans had shown their weakness when they failed to act on their initial moral indignation against Japan. Japan withdrew from the League in 1933; its withdrawal eventually led to the League's collapse in 1937.

More fuel was added to the fire when—"by mistake"—Japanese warplanes sank the American gunboat USS *Panay* in the Yangtze River on December 13, 1937. A quick apology and restitution from the Japanese defused what almost became a war-threatening incident. Within a few days, the infamous incident that came to be known as the Rape of Nanking began as Japanese soldiers were unleashed in an orgy of looting, burning, murder, and rape. Hundreds of thousands of Chinese men, women, and children were victims of one of the worst atrocities of the century. Following that horrific event, President Franklin D. Roosevelt called for a moral embargo of Japan by American arms manufacturers. Emperor Hirohito maintained his silence.[12]

After a major clash with the Soviets in 1938 where the borders of Korea, Manchukuo, and the Soviet Union converged, the Japanese emperor had to intervene to restrain his troops in that area. The conflict with the Russians erupted again in 1939 around Nomonhan in Mongolia. The Russians gave the Japanese a sound thrashing, and the IJA had another opponent to guard against at its newly established mainland borders. The threat of another clash with the Russians haunted the Japanese throughout World War II, and it was not mere paranoia. Premier Josef Stalin had hinted to China's Generalissimo Chiang Kai Shek that an alliance was brewing between Russia, Great Britain, and the United States against Japan.[13] The IJA considered that its war in China was its primary concern and resisted the Imperial Japanese Navy's (IJN's) preference to aim its attacks toward the east in the Pacific and south into Indochina, Malaya, and Australia.[14]

American aggravation with the Japanese was increased when Japan signed the Tripartite Pact (known in the United States as the Rome-Berlin-Tokyo Axis) in 1940 with Germany and Italy. The democracies' condemnation of Japan's actions against China steered Japan to align its policies with the totalitarian governments. Even though the Japanese were unhappy when Adolf Hitler and Stalin signed a nonaggression pact in 1939, they considered that it was to their advantage to be allied with Germany and Italy in case Russia threatened Manchuria again (or "Manchukuo," as it was redubbed during the Japanese occupation). In an effort to secure that northern flank, Japan's Foreign Minister Yosuki Matsuoka signed a nonaggression pact with the Russians during his visit to Moscow in March 1941. In reality, the Axis was never much of a true alliance. Although Japan was relieved when the Germans shattered their own nonaggression pact with the invasion of Russia in June 1941, the Japanese did not bother to notify Germany or Italy that the Japanese attack on Pearl Harbor would begin hostilities with the United States, nor did Hitler inform his Japanese allies that he was going to attack Russia before he did so. Germany and Italy did declare war on the United States on December 11, 1941, as a result of the Axis alliance. Hitler believed that the United States was weak, therefore unwilling to fight and that the Germans should support their Japanese "honorary Aryan brothers." This was to the delight of the British, who could now welcome the Americans openly as allies against all the Axis powers.[15]

Hitler had given the Japanese "honorary Aryan" status as allies and entertained the idea that the Japanese could rule Southeast Asia, Burma, and India and the Germans and Italians would rule Europe and Africa. Hitler was also aware that there was great discontent with British rule in India and the Axis powers fully expected that, if the British could be banished from Burma and India, these countries would support the Axis ambitions. Weak British and Dutch forces defended the Indian Ocean area. The Japanese learned just how weak the British were when the British steamer *Automedon* was captured and sunk by the German raider *Atlantis* in the Indian Ocean in November 1940. On board the *Automedon* were many highly secret documents that the Germans passed on to the Japanese. These were copies of the British War Cabinet discussions (intended for the commander in chief, Far East) stating that the British government was too weak to oppose any Japanese moves in Indochina or Thailand.[16]

If the Japanese had seized the island of Ceylon, the possibility existed that it might become unnecessary for the IJA to invade and hold India because, from Ceylon bases, the Japanese could have attacked the British oil fields of the Persian Gulf countries. The Axis leaders theorized that if the Japanese could meet with German forces to threaten southern Russia, Turkey would have to abandon its neutrality in favor of the Axis powers. One source claims that Hitler met Lt. Gen. Hiroshi Oshima, the Japanese ambassador to Germany, in the spring of 1941 to discuss plans for global war. Hitler was reputed to have called this joint plan Operation Orient. He proposed that the Japanese and Germans cooperate in their efforts to defeat the British and Americans by an exchange of German technology, machine tools, optical equipment, and military equipment for Japanese precious metals, rubber, silk, and vegetable oils. He further suggested that the IJA invade and occupy the island of Ceylon and use the Vichy French port of Diego Suarez on the northern coast of the large island of Madagascar for joint German-Japanese submarine operations in the Indian Ocean.

The Japanese did, for a short time, conduct joint submarine operations with the Germans from Diego Suarez. Nine surface-ship blockade runners managed to deliver sixty-five thousand tons of strategic materials from Japan to Germany, a dangerous run of twelve thousand miles.[17] A British invasion of Madagascar ended the threat to the British lifeline to Australia and New Zealand, at the same time cutting the Axis routes across the Indian Ocean. If the Japanese had deemed to launch a major offensive in the Indian Ocean, it is possible that Britain and the Russians could have been defeated and forced out of the war. Almost incredibly, the Japanese considered that they had their own higher priorities elsewhere.[18]

The freezing of all Japanese assets in July 1941 followed the American imposition of embargoes on strategic materials—primarily scrap metals and petroleum products. Historian Dr. H. P. Willmott claims that there was a probability that Japan may have become embroiled in a civil war if it had backed down before the United States' challenge in the summer of 1941. He points out that the IJN was calculating then that its strength would be only 30 percent that of the U.S. Navy by 1944, forcing a now-or-never challenge to Japan. Willmott also claims that, even before the embargo, Japan was trading at such a furious rate to finance the war in China that the country would have exhausted its gold and foreign currency reserves by early 1942. The country would have faced national bankruptcy by that time, which would have been a crisis of Japan's own making.[19]

The lengthy negotiations for a peaceful agreement between the United States and Japan degenerated into a situation where both nations were issuing ultimatums to each other which, to save face, both nations rejected. There were gross misunderstandings on both sides as to what the other nation really wanted. It became evident to both sides that no agreement would be reached.

Because Japan could not sustain itself from its own limited national resources, the island nation cast covetous eyes on the riches available in

Southeast Asia. To conduct its military operations against China, Japan required a ready storehouse of war materials. Japan believed that it had to fight the Americans, the British, and the Dutch to gain oil, rubber, metals, and strategic raw materials that were being cut off from Southeast Asia and Malaya.

The Japanese oil reserves were down to a two-year level—even less if they were to go to war with the United States and Britain. The Japanese military leaders claimed that they must go to war for their national survival and convinced the Japanese people that this was their only choice. In reality, the Japanese chose to go to war to gain the materials that they considered were necessary to continue to fight a war.[20]

As an island nation, Japan's economy required roughly 10 million tons of shipping to survive. In 1941, the Japanese tanker and cargo fleet could handle only 6 million tons; the remainder had been furnished by what would become enemy nations in the Pacific War. Japan had hoped to make up the deficit by its acquisition of oil and strategic materials, but actually the country would regain only a fraction of what it needed of these materials in its early territorial surges. As the war progressed, American submarines and aircraft brought Japanese shipping almost to a complete stop.[21]

A study by the Japanese military had shown that there were alarming contrasts between American and Japanese war potential in fundamental ways. In steel production alone, the United States led by a ratio of twenty to one; in oil production, more than two hundred to one; in coal ten to one; in aircraft five to one; and in shipping two to one. In addition, the American labor force outnumbered the Japanese by a ratio of five to one. Overall, the U.S. potential was more than ten to one over the Japanese.[22] Nevertheless, the prevailing militarists in the Japanese government considered that, with France defeated and England fighting for its own existence, Japan should not miss the bus and allow the opportunity to expand the empire slip by. The Japanese regarded Indochina with its rubber, tin, tungsten, coal, and rice as "a treasure lying in the street just waiting to be picked up." The weak Vichy French government quickly signed an agreement allowing Japan to establish air bases in northern Indochina and to use that area for attacks on China. Again, the United States strongly opposed this move. Hopes for a peaceful resolution of the differences between the two nations diminished almost daily during 1941.

With Gen. Hideki Tojo as prime minister of wartime Japan, the army was now in control of government plans and policies. The army's primary focus was still the resolution of the China Incident. This, as far as the IJA was concerned, was the principal reason for going to war with the British, the Dutch, and the Americans—to gain the strategic resources held by those powers. There were now over 2 million Japanese soldiers tied down in China and another 1 million stationed along the northern border in anticipation of a possible attack by the Russians. Adding an occupation force in Southeast Asia would stretch the IJA's abilities to its limits.[23] The IJN, though, knew that its time—and its oil supply—was running out for its opportunity to strike the Allied powers.

Today's U.S. Navy brass often say, whenever a military or naval world crisis arises, that the president's first question is invariably, "Where are the carriers?" Similarly, in World War II the planning strategists and intelligence specialists for the IJN always wanted to know the locations of the American aircraft carriers. In the weeks after the initial attack on Pearl Harbor, Japanese intelligence was not even certain of how many U.S. carriers were still left in the Pacific. Even though the submarine-launched floatplanes had provided some reconnaissance capability to provide limited information about the repair progress being made at the Hawaii bases, the Japanese were painfully aware that the submarine forces around the islands had not been successful in interrupting military operations and resupply.

Originally, all the Japanese submarines prowling the West Coast waters and around the Hawaiian Islands were to seek out and sink American warships. In the IJN's tactical doctrine at that time in the war, merchant and cargo ships were the secondary targets for their submarines' torpedoes and guns. Prior to returning to their Marshall Islands bases for refueling and resupply, the Japanese boats were supposed to surface and fire their deck guns at onshore targets if conditions were favorable for such action. American intelligence experts had already deduced that the submarines operating in Hawaiian waters were about to return to their bases whenever they surfaced to expend their deck gun ammunition on land installations.

The Japanese Mandate Islands, including the Caroline Islands and the Marshall Islands, were heavily fortified and secretly developed as bases primarily for submarine and air operations years before the opening of hostilities in World War II. The Marshall Islands, consisting of two dozen atolls and more than 867 reefs, had been claimed by Germany in 1885, but were mandated to Japan by the League of Nations in 1920 as war reparations. Under the League's specified conditions, these islands were not supposed to be fortified. By 1935, the Mandate Islands were held in absolute sovereignty by the Japanese. The total land area of the Marshall Islands was only seventy square miles, but they encompassed forty-five hundred square miles of lagoons that were ideal for submarine and seaplane bases.[24]

In great secrecy, the Japanese built a large submarine base and three long runways in the Kwajalein Atoll in the Marshalls, more than twenty-four hundred miles southwest of Pearl Harbor.[25] Jaluit Atoll, also in the Marshalls, was designated as an important base for seaplanes. Construction of the seaplane base was begun in early May 1941 and completed by the end of October 1941. A unit of Pete (F1M) biplane floatplanes began arriving on Jaluit in early 1942, with Mavis (H6K) flying boats permanently based there by May 1942. No land runways were ever constructed on Jaluit, probably because of the lack of shipping available for construction materials. There were two hangars to accommodate the large flying boats, and a smaller hangar for floatplanes. The service apron adjoined two seaplane ramps sloping into the lagoon, and there was a pier. Antiaircraft guns and searchlights completed the defenses for the base. Later, radar was added to the radio and direction-finding gear.

The town of Jabor on Jaluit was the prewar capital and administrative center for the Marshall Islands. The Jaluit-Emidj base was the most important center of military activity, so there was fuel storage for the other islands as well as for the base itself. The barracks, shops, hangars, and other buildings encompassed 320 thousand feet of floor space prior to U.S. bombing attacks, which began in early February 1942.[26]

Wotje Island is located on the eastern half of Wotje atoll, 189 statute miles east of Kwajalein. It is the largest piece of land in the atoll and had an airfield and a seaplane base. The airfield, with two runways, was situated on the northern half of Wotje Island. The main runway was oriented on a northwest-southeast direction, and was five thousand feet long. The secondary runway was thirty-five hundred feet long and ran perpendicular to the main runway. These were excellent poured concrete runways with large turning circles at each end. There were connecting taxiways and revetments for fourteen fighters. The field had a control tower, radio station, direction-finding equipment, barracks, and two hangars on two large service aprons.

Wotje's seaplane base was integrated with the airfield with its seaplane ramp running up to a service ramp and one of the hangars. Zero (A6M) fighters were stationed on the airfield. Antiaircraft guns and searchlights were placed all around the island. About three thousand Japanese soldiers, sailors, and airmen manned and defended the airfield and seaplane base.[27]

Maloelap in the Marshall Islands was developed as a bomber base, as were Eniwetok and Mili Atolls. Air bases were built in the Mariana Islands beginning in 1933 at Pagan and Saipan with three thousand–foot runways. A base with runways of suitable length for bombers was finished in 1940 on Tinian. An airfield and air base were constructed on the island of Rota, which was actually in sight of the Americans on Guam. In the West Caroline Islands, a bomber base with four thousand–foot runways was constructed on Palau and a fighter and seaplane base was completed in 1934 at Yap. In the East Carolines, three large bases were started in 1933 with improvements being made as late as 1943 at Truk. Ponape was furnished a runway for smaller planes by 1941, with bases also at Namuluk, Kusaie, and Mortlock Atolls.[28]

The IJN had given the construction and development of these island bases a high priority in the late 1930s and early war years. The deplorable working conditions on nearly all these desolate islands—unrelenting heat, high humidity, mosquitoes, tropical diseases, lack of potable water, and lack of facilities for housing or feeding construction crews—made the recruiting of normal work crews from Japan impossible. Local labor was not available because most of the islands were uninhabited. The distances from the Japanese home islands created more problems of getting work crews and building materials to these islands. The Japanese had used prisoners for construction of naval and air bases in Japan, so the IJN turned to prison authorities for the needed labor. There were two major advantages in using prisoners: the obvious saving of labor costs, and the easier control in maintaining the secrecy of the projects. Prisoners could not quit, nor could they escape from the islands to reveal the purpose of their labors. The prisoners, known as the *Sekisei Tai* (Loading Group) were used for the heavy labor, augmenting the engineers, guards, traders, and a few natives brought to the islands. At that time, prison conditions in Japan were so unpleasant that prisoners actually volunteered for the work. The islands of Tinian and Wotje were each assigned at least one thousand prisoner workers in 1939. By 1940, there were more than ten thousand prisoners involved in the work of building the bases in the Mandate Islands. Construction work in such heat and humidity was brutal. Accidents and disease took a heavy toll. On Tinian alone, twenty prisoners and two guards died. After two years of toil, the prisoners were returned to Japan in October 1941.[29]

By the beginning of the war, the IJN had dozens of bases with runways, seaplane ramps, maintenance facilities, weather stations, guns, searchlights, bunkers, and barracks on many of the islands scattered all across the central southern Pacific. After Amelia Earhart's plane was lost in June 1937 on Earhart's trans-Pacific flight, the rumors started, and persist today, that she had been on a secret mission to gain information about these secret bases. One story goes that several Marshall Islanders claimed that they had witnessed the ditching of an airplane near Barre Island in Mili Atoll (the location of one of the Japanese bomber bases). Other rumors claim that the Japanese shot down her plane, and that she and her navigator, Fred Noonan, were taken prisoner and held in a cell in a prison on Saipan. Although the truth may never be known about her mission, the Japanese were concerned about the search mission conducted by the U.S. Navy with aircraft from the carrier USS *Lexington*. The U.S. Navy had launched a massive search effort to locate Earhart's downed twin-engined Electra. Secret Japanese messages stated that the "U.S. Navy has set up such an exaggerated search plan (that it) raises a suspicion that they may be trying to collect materials for a strategic study under the pretense of such an air search." In other words, the Japanese considered that the search was an excuse for the U.S. Navy to gain intelligence information about their new bases in the Marshall Islands.[30]

The U.S. armed forces intelligence agencies had little information about the Japanese bases. In late November 1941, a top secret message from the war department notified General Short, the army commander on Oahu, that two Liberator (B-24) bombers would be sent to Hickam Field to conduct covert special photoreconnaissance missions of the Marshall and Caroline Islands. The new Liberator bombers had a longer range than the Flying Fortress (B-17) bombers already in use in the Pacific, so the Liberator was better suited for the extended-range requirements of the intelligence-gathering missions. The bombers were prepared for their photoreconnaissance mission at the Sacramento Air Depot, and moved to Hamilton Field near San Francisco for the flight to Hawaii. Both airplanes departed Hamilton Field on the night of December 4, but one had a serious nose wheel shimmy on takeoff and aborted its flight.

New technologies were coming into play to enhance the extended-range concept. Radar allowed longer-range reconnaissance by ships, which augmented the information received from scout planes. Approaching enemy aircraft could be detected and located by radar that provided precise range and bearing information. Combat Air Patrol (CAP) fighters, guarding the air space over a task force, could be directed more effectively and at greater ranges with radar.

With the opening of the Pacific War, the Mandate Islands were fortified even further with antiaircraft defenses, limited radar capabilities, and the stationing of IJA and IJN personnel units as defenders. The islands made that vast area of the Pacific a virtual Japanese lake, with ideal bases for aircraft and ship operations, especially seaplanes and submarines. Submarine tenders were based on Kwajalein and Eniwetok. From his flagship *Katori* anchored at Kwajalein, Vice Adm. Misumi Shimizu conducted the operations of his Sixth Fleet (Mandate Area Submarines). Shimizu was a brilliant officer who had participated in the planning and execution of the first Pearl Harbor strike.[31] Shimizu considered that these island bases were situated to give his submarines excellent access to the sea-lanes between Australia, Hawaii, and the West Coast of the United States.

Admiral Yamamoto was the commander in chief of the combined fleet. He was fifty-seven years old when the war with America was started, but he could easily have passed for a man of forty-five. Having placed second among three hundred applicants in his entrance exams for the Japanese Naval Academy at Eta Jima, he had graduated from that institution with honors. As a new ensign aboard the cruiser *Nisshin,* he served under Admiral Togo when the Japanese fleet annihilated the Russian fleet in 1904 at Port Arthur. He lost two fingers of his left hand in the battle that opened the war that made Japan a world power. His unusual first name, Isoruku, translates to fifty-six, commemorating his father's age when he was born, but giggling geishas later gave him the nickname "Eighty Sen." They allowed him a discount when they gave him a manicure: "Ten fingers, one yen; eight fingers, eighty sen." (One sen is 1/100th of a yen.)

Yamamoto was a passionate gambler and was fascinated with games of strategy. He gained fame as the navy champion at go and shogi, Japanese games similar to chess and checkers. He was sent to Harvard University in the United States after World War I to study economics, but he also avidly studied two other subjects: oil and American airplanes. He was an early visionary for military aviation, telling an American reporter that "the most important warship in the future will be a ship to carry airplanes."[32]

In 1923, he was named as the director of a new naval air training school at Kasumigaura (the IJN's equivalent of Pensacola), having established his reputation as a builder of the new Imperial Japanese Naval Air Force (IJNAF). Yamamoto was regarded as the father of Japanese naval aviation. Along with his students, he took the entire course of instruction—aeronautics, gunnery, communications, and even some flying lessons.

Japan's finest pilots usually came from the Yokaren flight training program (from the full name Hiko Yoka Renshu-sei—meaning Preparatory Course for the Aviators) or formally, the Flight Reserve Enlisted Trainee system. There were three levels of Yokaren: Ko (A) for junior high school graduates; Otsu (B) an added course for senior-elementary school graduates; and Hei (C) for nonaviator sailors who wanted to fly or were recommended by their supervisors. The different courses were based on each trainee's education level. Trainees from colleges and universities were dubbed Yobi Gakusai (reserve students). This training was popular among the college students who did not want to be drafted into the army. Not all of them wanted the navy, either, but the image of being a navy officer, especially a flyer, had more appeal. The Eta Jima graduates regarded these reserve flyers as dispensable and the Yobi Gakusai responded by referring to them as Annapolis officers. Many of the Yobi Gakusai did gain a degree of respect from their Eta Jima brothers because they usually possessed a more cultured education.

The Yokaren program had started on June 1, 1930, with seventy-nine students. They studied general high school subjects and took courses related to aviation for about three years. On graduation from ground school, they were usually promoted to the rank of leading flyer to begin a ten-month flight-training program for basic pilot training, then on to specialized aircraft training (fighters, bombers, and so on). Those who failed any course became observers, gunners, radiomen, or maintenance crew. On graduation from flight training, most were promoted to a petty officer rank. The navy program focused on young men aged fifteen through seventeen, with the training lasting two to three years, shortened to two years later in the war. Yokaren graduates could be promoted to officer rank, but they were restricted to holding rank no higher than commander. Eta Jima graduates discriminated against them by never allowing the Yokaren to be promoted to the rank of captain.[33]

Unlike most of the pilots of the world's navies of World War II, the majority of the IJNAF pilots were enlisted men, rather than officers. The famous Japanese ace, Saburo Sakai, was trained in a similar prewar course known as Sohren (Soju Renshu-sei). Sakai was a petty officer first class in the opening days of the Pacific War, but was eventually promoted to lieutenant (junior grade). This system resulted in bitter resentment by the enlisted pilots. They knew that they performed the same hazardous duties as the officers in their squadrons, but did not receive the pay and privileges afforded the officers. Sakai apparently never lost his antipathy for the officer-enlisted relationship, even though he was promoted to officer rank. One enlisted Zero pilot went so far as to say: "These green lieutenants didn't know how to fight and would get shot down right away. So he [the lieutenant] was assigned a veteran enlisted [pilot] to protect him. If he was unpopular, the wingman might become 'separated' during combat and the officer would surely die. *Do you understand?*"[34]

In 1925, Yamamoto was back in America as a naval attaché in Washington. He studied American defense industries and defenses, focusing on the aircraft carrier—the combination of sea and air power. The diminutive Yamamoto was a popular guest at Washington dinner parties and gained a reputation as a brilliant bridge and poker player. He had an opportunity to become familiar with Americans and the United States, and traveled throughout the country. He was impressed with the enormous potential of American industry, but held the U.S. armed forces in low esteem. He came to regard the U.S. Navy as "a social navy of bridge and golf players . . . a peacetime navy."[35]

As Japan's chief delegate to the London Naval Conference in 1934, Yamamoto was determined to break the 5:5:3 capital ship tonnage ratio that favored the United States and Great Britain over Japan. He called this ratio, which had been forced on Japan in 1921 at the Washington Disarmament Conference, a national degradation. Convinced that the warship tonnage limitations placed on his country by the treaties among the member nations were not acceptable, Yamamoto rejected the proposal. The talks ended without agreement and, considering that treaties were no longer binding, Japan made the decision to build the ships that the IJN wanted.[36] Yamamoto returned to Japan as a diplomatic hero, and was made vice minister of the navy.

In the early 1930s, Japan had begun a series of what it termed Replenishment Programs to expand the size of its own fleet. Shortly thereafter, the keel of the first of four superbattleships was laid and Japanese shipyards began work on two new aircraft carriers, the thirty thousand–ton *Shokaku* and the *Zuikaku*. The new Japanese warships would be designed strictly for combat; crew comfort was not a consideration. Design specifications called for an advantage over U.S. or British warships in speed, armament, and armor. Japanese light cruisers were capable of thirty-knot speeds with powerful 152 thousand horsepower engines propelling them. The new *Fubuki*-class destroyers were regarded as the best of their kind in the world.[37] Following President Franklin Roosevelt's first inauguration in 1933, the United States began to increase the size of its own navy.

The armed forces of Japan gained absolute veto power in national affairs in 1936. The powerful army was in complete control of the press with its censorship powers. The army was determined to broaden its adventures in China and wanted to join Germany and Italy in a world war. Yamamoto knew that the Americans were opposed to the direction that the IJA was taking and he worried about the army's ignorance of American industrial power. He became outspoken in his opposition to the IJA's stampede in the direction of war. The army's feelings toward Yamamoto became so heated that Adm. Mitsumasa Yonai, his superior as prime minister and also navy minister, assigned a police bodyguard to protect Yamamoto from assassination attempts. Yamamoto objected, so Yonai appointed him commander in chief of the fleet and sent him off to sea in 1940 for his own protection.[38] Yamamoto was no pacifist, but he resisted the army's ambitions and at the same time pressed his navy to prepare for war. When he realized that his homeland was determined to go to war with the Allied powers, he knew that the U.S. Navy would have to be eliminated or at least neutralized in the Pacific for Japan to establish its expanded empire. At the same time, he knew that the industrial capabilities of the United States would ultimately overwhelm Japan and that his country would not be able to win a lengthy war.

Admiral Yamamoto had opposed the war hawks in Japan's military government and had not wished to go to war with the United States. In spite of this, once the course of war had been chosen by Japan he devoted his energies to ensure that his navy would be prepared for that war. Although most of his naval combat experience had been aboard battleships, he favored the aircraft carrier over the battleship as the IJN's best weapon. He was the driving force behind the planning of the Pearl Harbor attack.

In presenting his war plans, Yamamoto had pointed out that the army did not need to be involved in the navy's Pearl Harbor mission. The army would need only a small occupying force in Southeast Asia and the newly conquered territories in Malaysia, Java, and the Philippines. The army generals finally agreed to Yamamoto's war plans, because they envisioned the Southern Operation as a means of encircling China's Chiang Kai Shek on the south and shutting off his war supplies. Earlier, Yamamoto's Pearl Harbor attack had been opposed by the IJA. They were more concerned with navy support for their Southern Operations—the taking of Southeast Asia, Malaya, Singapore, and the Philippines. Yamamoto had threatened to resign if the Pearl Harbor attack was not used to begin the war with the United States. He believed that the gamble on striking U.S. naval power at the opening day of the war was the only way that Japan could hope to gain an advantage over the Americans.

There were many highly placed officials of the IJN who were against the Pearl Harbor attack—Vice Adm. Chuichi Nagumo, who commanded the carrier fleet that ultimately made the attack, was among those who opposed the operation. Despite his personal misgivings, once Admiral Yamamoto had named him to lead the Pearl Harbor attack, Admiral Nagumo pledged every effort to make the attack successful. Nagumo and Rear Adm. Ryunosuke Kusaka, his chief of staff, considered that the true purpose of the attack on Hawaii was to protect the rear and flank of the Japanese amphibious forces that would be advancing against Malaya and the Philippines. The admirals later considered themselves to be justified in returning to Japan with their six carriers that came through the Pearl Harbor raid unharmed. They believed that they had ensured that the U.S. Navy's battleship fleet would be out of the Pacific War for many months to come.[39]

Admiral Yamamoto knew it would not be possible for Japan to win a war of attrition. In a conference in 1940 with Prince Fumimaro Konoye, then the premier of Japan, Yamamoto expressed his own disdain for the Tripartite Pact. Admiral Yamamoto is said to have told Prince Konoye, "If we are ordered to do it, then I can guarantee to put up a tough fight for the first six months, but I have absolutely no confidence as to what would happen if it went on for two or three years. It's too late to do anything about the Tripartite Pact now, but I hope that you'll at least make every effort to avoid war with America."[40]

As a true Japanese patriot, Yamamoto reluctantly accepted the responsibility for planning the IJN's war with the United States. As commander in chief of the combined fleet, he summoned Japan's best and brightest to come up with a workable plan for defeating the U.S. Navy in the Pacific. He personally chose Adm. Takijiro Onishi, an unconventional officer and a highly experienced aviator, to study the feasibility of the Pearl Harbor attack. Onishi had been on Yamamoto's staff at the training school, Kasumigaura. Admiral Onishi, in turn, chose Cdr. Minoru Genda, a brilliant tactician and flyer, to work out the details of such a complex attack.[41]

America's answer to the rising level of Japanese military and naval strength was the prewar Plan Orange that established the doctrine under which U.S. forces would fight a war with Japan in the Pacific. Plan Orange took its name from the color plans that had originated early in the twentieth century. The Joint Army and Navy Board had assigned color code names to the countries involved. The United States was Blue, and Japan was Orange. The Orange designation was later dropped and the formal title of War Plan 46 (WPL-46) became Rainbow 5. The latter term acknowledged the worldwide scope and involvement of the multicolored symbols of friends and foes of a world war. It was the basic policy guideline for the United States in World War II.[42] Plan Orange, the portion of the plan that applied to the war with Japan, stated that the U.S. Navy's primary mission was, basically, to move quickly to invade and capture positions in the Marshall Islands to establish forward fleet and air bases. The purpose of these bases would be to protect communication and supply lines between the Philippines, the South Pacific islands, Australia, and the U.S. mainland. The newly won U.S. bases in the Marshall Islands would deny the Japanese access to the area to threaten those lines. These strategies had been originally set forth during President Theodore Roosevelt's administration.[43]

The agreements between the United States and Great Britain placed these statements in the language of Rainbow 5: "If Japan does enter the war, the military strategy in the Far East will be defensive. The United States does not intend to add to its present military strength in the Far East but will employ the United States Pacific Fleet offensively in the manner best calculated to weaken Japanese economic power, and to support the defense of the Malay barrier by diverting Japanese strength away from Malaysia."[44] With the attack on Pearl Harbor, the Japanese forced the United States to postpone the provisions of Rainbow 5. The Americans lacked the surface ships, aircraft, and amphibious forces to take the tactical offensive in the Marshall Islands. An even more serious deficiency was the dearth of intelligence about Japanese strength and defenses in that area.[45]

The Japanese had no real interest in the Philippines, but wanted the oil and other raw materials available in the Indies. Japan lay to the north, the equator bisected the Indies, but Pearl Harbor was in the latitudes between the two. To protect the Japanese lines of communication and supply between Japan and the Indies, they had to have control of the entire Philippine archipelago. The weak forces maintained in the Philippines by the United States did not worry the Japanese, but they knew that, under Rainbow 5, those forces could and would be strengthened quickly by the American's industrial potential for building war machines. The Japanese worried about those American lines of communication that lay across their own lines to their mandate areas.

Admiral Yamamoto argued that an attack on the Indies had to be thrust through, not around, the Philippines. At the same time, the American fleet had to be at least neutralized from the beginning of the war to keep the U.S. forces at bay while Southeast Asia was being taken. If the U.S. Pacific Fleet was crushed from the start, they could not mount a campaign against Japan. If enough damage to American forces could be inflicted, it was possible that the worst threats could be turned away long enough for Japan to gain long-term security for its newly acquired wealth in Southeast Asia.

Once the decision to go to war with the United States had been made, Yamamoto was convinced that the attack on Pearl Harbor would be the only way to begin that war. His rationale was that the attack—with battleships, the symbols of naval power, as the primary targets—would damage American morale and buy time for the Japanese.[46] Contrary to the popular opinion that the American aircraft carriers were the primary targets of the Pearl Harbor attack (and the Japanese were indeed disappointed that the first attack failed to find even one of those carriers), the "Carrier Striking Force Operations Order No. 3," issued on November 23, 1941, clearly specified that "the targets for the first attack units were limited to about four battleships and four aircraft carriers; the order of targets will be battleships and then aircraft carriers.[47]

Admiral Yamamoto's operations officer, Captain Kuroshima, had argued during the planning of the Pearl Harbor attack that Japanese troops could invade Hawaii, taking advantage of the Americans' anticipated paralyzing confusion following the air strike. During that discussion in September 1941, Yamamoto had rejected Kuroshima's recommendations as risky. Yamamoto, the commander in chief, believed that there were two purposes for the attack on Hawaii. One was to create a diversion for the main thrust of the Southern Operation, which would secure the oil, rubber, and other resources of Southeast Asia. The other was to destroy as much of the U.S. Pacific Fleet as possible so that it could not interfere with Japan's taking of Southeast Asia's resources. With the unexpected stunning success of the raid on Hawaii, Yamamoto changed his mind about the invasion of Hawaii.[48]

Admiral Yamamoto knew that the Japanese could not win a long war, but just after the tactical victory at Pearl Harbor he considered that Japan had a short-term tactical edge and superior political willpower. He believed that the Japanese military and naval forces possessed a much higher level of fighting spirit than their enemies. He believed now, after receiving the battle reports from the returning First Air Fleet, that an invasion of Hawaii would not only have been possible, but relatively easy, if Nagumo's carrier force had been accompanied by invasion troops. In the confusion created by the surprise attack, the American defenses were seriously damaged and demoralized.

Adm. Chester W. Nimitz stated later in an interview, "In spite of the reverses we suffered on December 7, 1941, there were some spots on which we could congratulate ourselves on our luck." Admiral Nimitz pointed out that it was best that the American fleet had been inside Pearl Harbor during the attack. If the battleship fleet had been at sea, Adm. Husband E. Kimmel would have been forced to use the battleships with little or no air cover. The U.S. Navy's battleships would have been able to muster only eighteen knots, whereas the Japanese task force could operate at twenty-two knots. Their advantage in speed would allow the Japanese to choose to engage the U.S. Navy at their own time preference. Admiral Nimitz added that the men saved from the sunken ships in Pearl Harbor formed the cadre of experienced sailors for new ships being built. Had the old ships not been so completely destroyed, he said, "there might have been difficulty in securing the funds to build the ships needed to match the more modern Japanese ships."[49]

Almost ten hours after the initial attack on Pearl Harbor, IJA and IJN aircraft bombed American bases in the Philippines. Morning fog on their Formosa bases prevented the majority of the Japanese attackers from taking off at their earlier scheduled time. Even so, their late attack was even more effective than the attack on Pearl Harbor, because it established Japanese air superiority to ensure the success of the concurrent invasion. A commercial radio station in Manila had broadcast the news of the Pearl Harbor attack at 3:30 AM local time and all American armed forces had been placed on alert.

The first attack came at dawn in the Philippines when thirteen Kate (B5N2) and five Claude (A5M) fighters from the light carrier *Ryujo* bombed and strafed the naval base at Davao. Gen. Douglas MacArthur did not react to this raid, or to another attack three hours later when twenty-five Lily (Ki-48) twin-engined bombers bombed Tuguegarao Airfield.

MacArthur's inaction in the first hours of the Pacific War has been called "so irresponsible as to approach criminal negligence."[50] The largest concentration of American heavy bombers—thirty-five Flying Fortresses—had been assigned to MacArthur in the Philippines by the beginning of the Pacific War, but he waffled on his decision to use them. General MacArthur did not really understand airpower and how to make proper use of it. He thought that his force of Flying Fortresses would be his greatest asset and that the Japanese would be too intimidated to face such power. Instead, they quickly and effectively eliminated the Flying Fortresses as threats to their invasion plans. MacArthur's Far Eastern Air Force commander, Maj. Gen. Lewis Brereton, went to MacArthur's headquarters requesting permission to send his Flying Fortresses to counterattack the bases on Formosa. General Brereton claimed that General Sutherland, MacArthur's protective chief of staff, denied him access to see MacArthur for several hours. Sutherland would only authorize reconnaissance by the Flying Fortresses. In one of the first attacks on the Philippines, Japanese bombers destroyed twelve of them on the ground and crippled five more—half of the Flying Fortresses in MacArthur's command. Ninety-six aircraft at Clark air base were destroyed as they sat neatly lined up. A furious President Franklin Roosevelt, when told of the loss, lamented that they were wiped out "on the *ground,* by God, on the *ground!*"[51]

At the same time that the Philippines were being invaded, Japanese forces that would capture the Dutch East Indies began operations. Even before the Pearl Harbor task force had returned to Japan, Thailand was occupied and the Japanese were streaming through Malaya to overrun Singapore.

On December 10, land-based twin-engined Betty (G4M) bombers of the 22nd Air Flotilla, flying from bases at or near Saigon, sank the British battleships HMS *Prince of Wales* and *Repulse* in the waters off Malaya. This marked the first time that capital ships at sea had been sunk by aircraft alone.[52] Capt. Kameo Sonokawa, commander of the *Genzan Kokutai,* described the attack on the British ships by eighty-eight Betty aircraft armed with bombs and torpedoes. He claimed that the Japanese bombers scored, in addition to bomb hits, twelve torpedo hits on the *Repulse* and ten torpedo hits on the *Prince of Wales* by flying as low as seventy-five feet above the water to release their missiles. Four of the Betty bombers were shot down. One aircraft was left on the scene to watch the British ships sink. Ten Royal Air Force (RAF) Buffalo (F2A3) fighters arrived in the area too late to save the vessels and the remaining Japanese bombers managed to escape.[53]

Guam, defended only by a few Marines and a locally manned militia, was taken over and occupied when the war was only two days old, and the vital oil fields of Borneo were captured at Miri on December 16. Makin and Tarawa Islands in the Gilbert Islands and Wake Island were occupied before the end of December 1941.

Initially, tiny Wake Island would be the most difficult conquest for the Japanese to make. All their other conquests had gone down with surprising ease, but the resistance they encountered from the marine defenders of Wake Island came as a surprise. Three days prior to the Pearl Harbor attack, Adm. Bill Halsey's *Enterprise* carrier task force had delivered twelve Wildcat (F4F) fighters for the marine fighter squadron VMF-211's use to defend Wake. The island defenses included six five-inch former naval guns in three batteries, plus three batteries of four 3-inch antiaircraft guns. The marine garrison comprised 365 Marines and thirteen marine officers.

The invasion force sent by the Japanese to occupy Wake on December 11 consisted of three light cruisers and six destroyers, commanded by Rear Adm. Sadamichi Kajioka, with transports carrying 450 landing troops with their equipment and supplies. Twin-engined bombers from Kwajalein began three days of raids on December 8, destroying all but four of the marine Wildcat fighters, but those surviving four fighters damaged a cruiser and sank the destroyer *Kisaragi*. The marine shore batteries seriously damaged the cruiser *Yubari*, Kajioka's flagship, sank the destroyer *Hayate*, and scored damaging hits on three other ships. The Japanese withdrew after losing about five hundred sailors and airmen, for the loss of only one American at this stage of the siege.[54]

Admiral Nagumo had ignored the request to strike Midway Island on his return trip to Japan, but the setback in the invasion plans of Wake Island caused a stir. On December 15, Admiral Yamamoto ordered Nagumo to divert part of his returning force to assist in the elimination of the Wake Island defenses. Admiral Nagumo may have resented the suggestion that he send his triumphant fliers and sailors to batter Midway, but he was left no choice but to dispatch them to aid in the attack on Wake. In this instance, Nagumo could not ignore his orders and, without arguing, he sent the carriers *Soryu* and *Hiryu* with their escorts to assist the Wake Island invasion force.[55] The remainder of the IJN and its air force, along with 20 percent of the IJA, was striking at the British and Dutch empires and American holdings in the Southwest Pacific during this time. Admiral Yamamoto pondered the next moves of the combined fleet.[56]

The rest of Admiral Nagumo's First Air Fleet returned to Japan, sending their planes on December 22 and 23 to their respective bases in Japan from their carriers. Flying in groups of ten and twelve, they swept the sea ahead of *Akagi, Kaga, Zuikaku,* and *Shokaku,* looking for reported American submarines.[57] Meanwhile, Admiral Najioka, in his patched-up flagship, returned from the Marshall Islands with a large invasion fleet comprising two more cruisers, eight destroyers, four transports, and two troopships for another try at taking Wake Island. To assist him, four heavy cruisers and several destroyers were sent from Guam. Capping off this armada were the planes and carriers coming from Admiral Nagumo's returning Hawaii strike force. Additional bombing raids by the land-based bombers from Kwajalein added their punch to the attacks by carrier bombers and fighters. The incessant bombardment succeeded in eliminating the remaining four Wildcats. With all the marine fighters out of action, Wake Island finally fell to the Japanese on December 23.[58]

When the First Air Fleet's carriers and escorts sailed into Hashirajima on December 25, Admiral Yamamoto had already decided that, after some crew rest, reprovisioning, and repair, he would be sending Admiral Nagumo's fleet south to Truk in the Caroline Islands. From there, the First Air Fleet would support landings in the Australian mandated islands of New Guinea, New Britain, and New Ireland. They would assist the Second and Third Fleets in the taking of the Philippines, Borneo, Java, and the

Celebes. When the *Soryu* and *Hiryu* completed their tasks at Wake Island, they would be sent to the Celebes as a separate force. Occupying all these islands, along with Malaya and Burma, would complete the conquests that Japan hoped would supply the oil, rice, rubber, tin, and other strategic commodities needed to sustain its war.[59]

In the meantime, the Japanese continued the frenetic pace of the war, keeping the Allies off balance. Admiral Nagumo departed the Truk base with the carriers *Akagi, Kaga, Shokaku, Zuikaku* and their escorts on January 17. For three days their planes struck the British base at Rabaul on New Britain. Planes from *Shokaku* and *Zuikaku* hit Lae and Salamaua on the northeastern coast of New Guinea, meeting with no serious aerial opposition on any of these strikes. With no resistance on the ground, Japanese troops landed to occupy Rabaul and nearby Kavieng on New Ireland. Now the Coral Sea would be within the range of medium-range shore-based bombers. If bases in the Solomon Islands could be established, these would facilitate Japanese operations against Australia.[60]

The four carriers had returned to Truk when a U.S. carrier raid on the Marshall Islands was reported. Nagumo and his fleet dashed eastward, but the American carriers had escaped. *Shokaku* and *Zuikaku* were ordered back to Japan to guard against a possible American raid on the home islands. *Akagi* and *Kaga* sailed for Palau in the Carolines to meet with the carriers *Hiryu* and *Soryu* that were returning from their tasks at Wake Island. From Palau, the latter two carriers steamed to the East Indies with their planes striking the Dutch port Ambon on January 24 and 25, and attacking American and Dutch warships in the Java Sea. After joining up again at Palau, Nagumo's four carriers sailed to within 220 miles of the port of Darwin on the northern coast of Australia.[61]

A report of the Japanese air raid on February 19, 1942, on the port of Darwin states that it was the largest Japanese air attack since the first attack on Pearl Harbor, involving about 180 aircraft. The raid so terrified the town that it was briefly evacuated. The raid commenced at 10:00 AM with twenty-seven high-altitude bombers conducting pattern bombing, in which each aircraft dropped its bombs on a signal from a formation leader. This formation made two attacks in this manner. A number of dive-bombers, escorted by strafing fighters, attacked shipping in the harbor and the Royal Australian Air Force (RAAF) air base. The first attack lasted about forty minutes and was followed by a second attack of pattern bombing by heavy bombers from about fifteen thousand feet at 11:55 AM that lasted twenty to twenty-five minutes. The attack sank ten ships in the harbor, including the ammunition ship *Neptuna* that exploded. Other ships sunk were the *Zealandia, Meigs, Manualoa,* the *British Motorist,* and an American destroyer, the USS *Peary.* Damaged ships included the *Barossa,* the hospital ship *Manunda,* and the American SS *Port Mar.* A large section of the pier was destroyed. On land, the administrator's office, police barracks, police station, post office, telegraph office, and cable office were destroyed. The hospital was damaged and three private residences were destroyed.

At the RAAF air base, the Australians lost six Hudson (A-29) bombers. Another Hudson and a Wirraway (CA-1) trainer were damaged. American losses were eight Kittyhawk (P-40E) fighters shot down, two more destroyed on the ground, and a Liberator (B-24) bomber damaged on the ground. It was estimated that 250 people were killed in the attack. An inquiry centered on the fact that little or no warning of the raid was given before the bombs started to fall, with many people losing their lives as a result. No blame for the fiasco was ever established, but some believed that the RAAF station commander was guilty of being lax.[62] After the Darwin attack, Nagumo sailed to Staring Bay in the Celebes to support the Japanese invasion of Java.

After three months of war, the IJN had suffered the loss of five destroyers, seven submarines, seven minesweepers, three patrol boats, and one minelayer. None of its capital ships—battleships and aircraft carriers—had been scratched. Their Zero fighters had bested any opposing aircraft that the Allies had been able to put into the skies. Japanese victories and successes had come with such ease and in such a short time that the Japanese were forced abruptly to consider how to consolidate these victories and successes.

In a completely new venture, Nagumo's carriers entered the Indian Ocean to join Adm. Nobutake Kondo's Second Fleet in a huge operation to convince the people of India to increase their resistance to British rule. On April 5, Cdr. Mitsuo Fuchida led 180 aircraft to raid the British naval base at Colombo on the west coast of Ceylon. The RAF put up stiff opposition and both sides lost about 25 planes. Four days later, a similar force struck Trincomalee on the east coast of the island. Again, the RAF put up strong resistance, shooting down 15 Japanese raiders and losing 11 of their own. In this attack, the Japanese sank two cruisers, a destroyer, and six merchant vessels. On April 9, they sank the small British carrier *Hermes* and an escorting destroyer, and planes from the carrier *Ryujo* raided ports on the east coast of India, creating panic. Even as the Japanese forces withdrew, the British expected an invasion of India, but this was to be the only major Japanese sortie into the Indian Ocean. Such an invasion might have been successful in pushing all the way to the coast of Africa and the Persian Gulf with little trouble. If the Germans had been successful in taking the Suez Canal, India would have been completely isolated. Such a situation would have been a disaster for the Allies, but the Japanese did not press their advantage.[63] If the Japanese emperor recognized this situation, he made no mention of it. He was, in fact, stunned by what successes his forces had accomplished in so short a time. He was delighted at what he regarded as his nation's good fortune and the gains of his invincible warriors.

Admiral Nagumo could be proud of the achievements of his aircraft carriers. They had sailed over fifty thousand miles, destroyed hundreds of Allied aircraft, and sunk one British carrier, five American battleships, two British cruisers, and several Allied destroyers. He had also lost forty of his veteran pilots, which was the beginning of an attrition of one of Japan's most valuable wartime assets.[64] With eight aircraft carriers, the IJN's superiority would allow it to dominate the Pacific Ocean for the first six months of the war.[65] In the earliest days of the war, the Japanese armed forces were running far ahead of their own schedule of conquests in nearly all the areas that they had planned to take. They had surprised themselves with their own rapid progress and the ease of taking Guam, Makin Island, Hong Kong, Singapore, Borneo, and the Malay Peninsula. In less than three months of war, the Japanese were enjoying total success in Southeast Asia.

By bold action, meticulous planning, and the fighting spirit of their armed forces, the Japanese had achieved nearly all their goals.

In spite of their successes in battle, the Japanese were now involved in a different type of war than they had fought with China and Russia. The Japanese made the mistake of attempting to limit a naval war with the two greatest naval powers in the way that they had limited their earlier wars against continental powers. The IJN had not accomplished its primary objective in the war, which was to destroy or to neutralize the enemy's main forces as it had done in 1894 and 1904 against the Russians.

Japan's initial plan had been to wage a defensive war behind the defensive perimeter until their enemies' forces had been exhausted and the will to continue was broken. Now the island nation had to face the problem of how to consolidate its success and bring the war to a favorable close. It had become impossible to assume a defensive posture after such stunning victories. The Japanese had three major options—to push westward into the Indian Ocean, to push south toward Australia, or to push east into the central Pacific. Even the navy did not feel that it could go in all three directions, but the Japanese military and naval forces attempted exactly that combination, with necessary modifications. A direct attack on Australia was out of the question because the IJA did not have the strength or transportation for such an ambitious undertaking. They faced overwhelming logistical problems with operations against the British in the Indian Ocean. It was only natural, therefore, that they should elect to challenge the U.S. Navy for the decisive battle to eliminate that threat to all their other operations.[66]

The Japanese had never meant for the attack on Pearl Harbor on December 7 to be their only assault on the American forces based there. There were dozens of proposed attacks in various stages of planning that were to be achieved with aircraft, submarines, and other warships. Some of these attacks were eventually carried out as planned, but most of them were never more than the dreams of the planning staffs of the Japanese armed forces.

Less than forty-eight hours after the opening of the Pacific War, Admiral Yamamoto signed orders directing his staff to prepare plans for an invasion of Hawaii. He reasoned that the Hawaii base was the only direct threat to the Japanese homeland. It contained the headquarters of the U.S. Pacific Fleet and combined the crucial repair and storage facilities for all the American armed forces there. Until 1940, the Pacific Fleet had been head-quartered at San Diego. Hawaii was now the home of communications and intelligence operations for the entire Pacific area and would serve as the launching pad for any U.S. counteroffensive against Japan. The U.S. Pacific Fleet had temporarily lost its battleships, but those American aircraft carriers remained a dangerous fighting force. The loss of facilities on Oahu alone would have required the United States to consider its options in a long-distance war with Japan. The U.S. armed forces would have been compelled to operate from mainland bases on the West Coast. Australia and New Zealand, as well as Alaska and the Panama Canal, would be exposed and vulnerable. With Hawaii in Japanese hands, nearly five hundred thousand American citizens would be living as hostages. President Roosevelt might have been forced to negotiate a peace that would be favorable to the Japanese, ending the war and allowing them to enjoy their newly gained resources in Southeast Asia. Some of the officers on Yamamoto's staff even put forth the ideas of using Hawaii as the springboard for an invasion of the West Coast of the United States.[67]

The Japanese naval general staff (NGS) and the IJA engaged in another heated debate as to how to exploit their gains and how to conduct the second stage of the war. Despite their differences, the IJA and the IJN had agreed that the Philippines did not contain the materials that Japan wanted or needed. At the same time, both entities agreed that the American presence there could not be tolerated. The Philippines had to be in Japanese hands to secure free access to Borneo, Java, Malaysia, and the remainder of Southeast Asia. The Japanese anticipated that Australia would be the base from which the Allies would be forced to operate.

At first, the navy favored an invasion of Australia, claiming that only key points of that island continent would need to be occupied. The army rejected this option, saying that the entire landmass would have to be held and this would require too many troops. The army preferred what was named the FS Operation that would not require conquering Australia, but would isolate it by holding key islands near its shipping routes to the United States. Air bases on these islands would extend Japanese control. The army and navy reached tentative agreement on the FS Operation, with the army assuming responsibility for operations against India and the navy for those against Australia. The navy introduced a new plan for a limited invasion of Australia and new attacks on Hawaii. Admiral Yamamoto's sponsorship of the planning of the Pearl Harbor attack had placed him in a powerful position that could not be ignored in the mapping of future Japanese war plans. His chief of staff, Vice Adm. Matome Ugaki, went through the pendulum swing from expressing his doubts that Hawaii could be held even if captured, to a new position that would put him in charge of planning what would become known as the Eastern Operation—the taking of the entire Hawaiian archipelago.[68]

The arguments between the IJA generals and IJN admirals seemed at times to take on the elements of a kabuki drama. Positions were changed with each new briefing or war game. For at least two months, liaison conferences led to new maneuvering, new agreements, and new disagreements. At first, the IJN proposed taking Palmyra Island, a central Pacific post southwest of Hawaii. Another IJN proposal advocated the invasion of Australia. The IJA believed that it could not support an invasion of Hawaii. A new agreement reverted to the FS Operation, but left out the assault on Hawaii. They discussed an invasion of Ceylon (known today as Sri Lanka), but the army refused to back that option. Another navy scheme called for operations against Hawaii as early as the summer of 1942. Early in March 1942, the army and navy returned to a modified version of the FS Operation, with points in New Guinea to be occupied. Even this agreement was later altered.[69] The opposing factions of the IJA and IJN realized that they would have to reach a compromise. They did agree that pressure would have to be kept on the Allies to strengthen and protect the outer perimeter of the new Japanese empire, but not to the extent that it would draw on the already strained resources of the army.

The navy high command then told General Tojo that not until December 1943 would the U.S. Navy be able to mount any counterattacks, although they did admit that the Americans might use the Aleutian Islands to launch air strikes against the northernmost Japanese home islands. American aircraft carriers, the navy said, would have to come within two hundred miles of the home islands to launch any attacks. Japanese patrols, they were sure, would detect them before they got that close.

All the arguments came to an end when Lt. Col. James H. Doolittle led sixteen Mitchell (B-25B) bombers on a raid launched from the aircraft carrier *Hornet* (see Chapter 6). On April 18, 1942, Doolittle's bombers hit targets in Tokyo, Nagoya, Osaka, and Kobe. With protection of the emperor as their highest priority, the Japanese liaison conferees quickly agreed that the army and navy would cooperate to take the Aleutian Islands. They planned to seize Samoa, Fiji, New Caledonia, and parts of British New Guinea (Papua) to protect the home islands and to control the supply lines between the United States and Australia. Admiral Yamamoto, stunned by the Doolittle raid, quickly realized that their perimeter defense had holes in it. All the gaps must be sealed and the closest gap was the Midway Islands, 2,250 miles from Tokyo. The conferees agreed with Admiral Yamamoto's plan—the navy was to capture Midway. These moves, both services thought, would not be difficult for the various forces. Both services could operate from bases at Rabaul in the Bismarck Islands in the southern areas, with elements of the combined fleet stationed at Truk. Because the Allies had shown such a reluctance to fight in the southern areas, the army anticipated withdrawing five divisions from those areas once the perimeter was established, leaving only battalion strength units to hold the area.[70]

The Japanese armed forces planners—especially those of the navy—had a tendency to draw up complex battle plans in which every function of those operations had to be conducted exactly as planned for the entire operation to succeed. Even when contingency plans were included, the Japanese had a strong bias against using those alternative plans. Thus far, they had not been required to rely on any contingency plans. In many cases, for those operations to be successful the enemy had to do exactly what the Japanese planners expected them to do. This tendency seemed to stem from the symptoms of what some Japanese had recognized and named victory disease, enjoying one military or naval triumph after another and savoring the hubris that came from easy victories.

In his book *The Barrier and the Javelin,* a thorough analysis of the Japanese situation at this point in the war, H. P. Willmott states that "Paradoxically, their military and naval staffs had both overplanned and underprepared for the second phase of operations."[71]

Admiral Nagumo's carrier forces had returned to their homeports in Japan or were operating in the southern areas, while Admiral Yamamoto worked on plans for the occupation of Midway, which would become the base for the invasion of the rest of the Hawaiian Islands.[72] Those plans would include the largest battle fleet ever assembled up to that time for extended range operations.

The IJN probably had more highly qualified seaplane pilots than any other warring power of World War II. These skilled pilots also had more total experience in operating seaplanes, flying boats, and floatplanes than any other nation, either of Allied or the Axis powers. The cream of these seaplane experts was concentrated at the Yokosuka Naval Air Test Center. The IJN's 801st Kokutai (Air Group) was charged with the development, testing, and crew training for the new Emily flying boat. Assigned to the 801st Kokutai was Lt. Hisao Hashizume.

Hisao Hashizume was born on July 19, 1910. From his first days at school, he was recognized as a bright, exceptional child. Throughout his education, young Hashizume received excellent marks in all his studies and was regarded by his classmates and teachers as an outstanding student. On completion of his public schools, he applied for and was accepted by the Japanese Imperial Navy Academy at Eta Jima (the IJN's equivalent of Annapolis) in April 1929. He graduated from Eta Jima in November 1932, a member of the sixtieth class from that institution.[73] Hashizume had grown to be a handsome, muscular young man. He had excelled in athletics and was a top scholar. His ambition to become a naval aviator was fulfilled when he was assigned as Aviation Student (Hiko Gakusei), one of thirty-four members of the twenty-sixth class at the navy's flight training center at Kasumigaura. His flight training began there on November 21, 1934. As in his earlier preparations, Aviation Student Hashizume quickly gained a reputation as an enthusiastic flyer. His instructors were extremely impressed by the way he quickly grasped the knowledge of aerodynamics and how well he performed in flying an airplane. Hashizume's flying skills, coordination, and judgment developed rapidly and it was obvious that he was going to become an exceptional aviator. On graduation from flight training on July 31, 1935, he received an Imperial Award, the highest honor given to an aviation student.[74]

The IJN had begun a rapid expansion of its aviation arm in 1937. After his graduation as a naval aviator, Hashizume volunteered to fly at every opportunity to gain experience and to sharpen his pilot skills. His fellow pilots said that he flew an airplane as if it were an extension of his mind, his eyes, and his body. He was gifted as a natural flyer and he obviously loved every minute that he spent in the air.

Recognizing his talents as a pilot and leader, the IJN school directors retained him as a flight instructor at the Kasumigaura flight school. Hashizume especially liked seaplanes and quickly became proficient in flying this special type of airplane. All IJN pilots, of course, were at that time required to master seaplane flying, as were their American counterparts. His students claimed that in the Japanese naval flight-training program, there were, for a time, two methods of flying seaplanes. One method was based on the old standard IJN seaplane operations and the other was the new (preferred and quickly adopted) set of techniques that Hashizume had developed. The young instructor's procedures made seaplane takeoffs, landings, and water operations much more precise, more efficient, and safer. The IJNAF flight training school wisely discarded its old methods and integrated the Hashizume techniques into its seaplane training curriculum.[75]

Now regarded as an expert seaplane pilot, Hashizume requested an assignment as a combat pilot and was assigned early in 1938 to one of the IJN's unique vessels, the seaplane carrier *Kamikawa Maru.* Capt. Masafumi Arima, who would later skipper the aircraft carrier *Shokaku,* and who was shot down while leading an attack with kamikaze forces, was the commander of the *Kamikawa Maru*. Arima would have a great effect on Hashizume's career. Hashizume flew his first combat missions in the Sino-Japanese war.

Hashizume's early combat flights involved bombing Chinese transport ships in the South China Sea and reconnaissance patrols, searching for Chinese naval vessels and surface transports. His oversize biplane was rarely, if ever, threatened by Chinese opposition, except light antiaircraft fire from a few of the ships that carried such defense. Even in such mundane duties, Hashizume's talents were recognized as a superior pilot and leader.

Captain Arima was transferred from his command of the *Kamikawa Maru* and assigned to command a large shore-based flying boat air group at Yokohama. Captain Arima had been so impressed with Hashizume that he became his sponsor and mentor, arranging for the young ensign to be transferred along with him to his new unit. In November 1938, Hashizume was made a squadron leader at Yokohama Air Station and was soon qualified to fly the new four-engined Mavis flying boats that had recently entered the inventory of the IJNAF.

Now a lieutenant (junior grade), Hashizume applied himself with characteristic zeal to learn everything that he could absorb about the operation of large flying boats. He received special permission from Captain Arima to experiment with handling the airplane in simulated combat conditions. Hashizume and his crew practiced unannounced emergency landings and anchoring in the lee (downwind) side of small islands. They practiced dicey takeoffs and landings in the open ocean, learning to cope with various wind strengths, ocean conditions, waves, and swells. They practiced hazardous refueling from supply ships and submarines in the open ocean whenever calm conditions allowed it—practice that would soon prove useful. Hashizume's crew experimented in airborne antisubmarine warfare (ASW), an area of specialized techniques that, until that time, had been practically ignored by the IJN. They incorporated these experiments into their actual antisubmarine patrols over coastal home waters from their base at Yokohama. Hashizume's crew honed their skills and developed techniques that would be adapted later by the flying boat crews of the IJN in ASW. Hashizume studied submarine operations closely and made it a practice to get to know submarine skippers. He questioned them at length about their boats' capabilities and limitations. His commander authorized Hashizume and his crew to exercise extremely long-range and long-endurance flights of up to thirty hours—such training would also be useful later. Hashizume insisted that his crew record data on all their experiments (whether or not the experiments were successful), so that this information could be studied and used in additional research. Each crewmember maintained detailed records of his specialized duties, responsibilities and the results achieved in training. Hashizume reviewed these data and assimilated them into a training program for use by other flying boat crews to improve their overall efficiency.[76]

Hashizume became an extremely proficient over-water navigator, practicing navigation by celestial observation through the use of sextants, chronographs, and celestial tables. Most pilots left this work to a crew navigator, but Hashizume insisted on learning these skills himself. He realized that flying boats operated over vast distances of trackless ocean with no other navigation aids. Radio beams and bearings would not be available under most combat conditions because the enemy would deny the use of these aids for navigation. Hashizume taught celestial navigation skills to his copilot and observer, so that they formed a three-man navigation team. Any one of the team could take over these navigation duties under most circumstances.

Hashizume took the Mavis flying boat to the edges of its performance envelope to determine just what the airplane was capable of doing in combat conditions. His crew worked extremely hard, but always accepted the risks to which their leader exposed them. They knew his capabilities and trusted him completely. He had earned his crew's respect and he made it clear to each of his crewmembers that he, in turn, respected them and relied on them as well.

The lieutenant had read that Adm. Richard Byrd had had his appendix removed before he made his famous exploration of Antarctica, even though Byrd was perfectly healthy. Byrd had wanted to be able to remain in that hostile environment alone for an extended period without having to be concerned with a possible attack of appendicitis. In similar fashion, Hashizume insisted that his appendix be removed in the summer of 1940 so that he could devote himself to his flying duties and training, uninterrupted by possible illness. He counted himself among those Japanese naval officers who believed that conflict with America was inevitable and it was coming soon. He did not wish to have any unexpected illness interfere with his duties when that time came.[77]

When the first new Emily arrived at the Yokohama Air Station for evaluation and training, Lieutenant Hashizume was tremendously impressed. He immediately asked Captain Arima to assign him and his crew to fly the new Type 2 flying boat. Of course, Arima gave his approval. Hashizume and his crew were among the first to qualify to fly the new airplane. Hashizume was enraptured by the new flying boat; to him, this new assignment was a divine marriage. He quickly began a program to explore its capabilities. Recognizing that the new airplane had great potential, he began to test the limits to which the airplane could be taken—just as he and his crew had done with the earlier Mavis. He suggested many new missions using the expanded capabilities of the Emily flying boats to his friends in operations and mission planning. One of these suggested missions involved the refueling of the flying boat by a submarine tanker to extend the range of the already long-legged new patrol bomber. Hashizume was excited by what the new airplane was able to do and he was eager to take the Emily into combat. He would soon be able to put all of his training and preparation into that purpose.[78]

In the days following the December 7 attack on Pearl Harbor, the Japanese naval imperial staff was searching for more ways to cause problems for the American forces on Hawaii. Cdr. Tatsukichi Miyo, head of the planning staff, noticed that the new Emily flying boat was going to live up to all his expectations and that the IJN now had a weapon that would be capable, with some careful planning, of taking the war back to the Hawaiian Islands. Miyo began checking distances on his charts and talking to his planning staff counterparts who were submariners. A grand plan was being formulated in his fertile brain that would use the stealth of the submarines to extend the range of the new flying boat. He could hardly wait to present his plan to the admirals on the staff, whom he believed would, without doubt, be delighted with his ideas.

When Miyo presented his proposal to the general staff, they were favorably impressed with the proposal to attack Pearl Harbor again. A new raid on Pearl Harbor would cause the Americans to have to increase their defenses of Hawaii and tie up combat units that were needed for any Allied offenses against the new Japanese empire holdings. Repeated attacks could keep the U.S. Army and Navy off balance so badly that any new actions that they were planning would have to be cancelled or delayed. Japanese intelligence could certainly learn more from these armed reconnaissance missions about the locations of the elusive American aircraft carriers. Repeated attacks might even catch one or more of the carriers at anchor in Pearl Harbor and the carriers could suffer the fate of the American battleship fleet. The planning staff moved into high gear. As with most operations planned by the Japanese, a new attack on Pearl Harbor would be complex and it involved several forces having to converge and mesh to accomplish the task. The complicated plans had to be timed precisely to be successful.

The planned attacks were given the name Sakusen K (Operation K), K being the Japanese code designator for Hawaii. Operation K would be the baptism of fire for the new Emily flying boats, and would involve the second air attack on Pearl Harbor. This plan seemed brilliant, but needed more thought. The distances between the launching bases in the Marshall Islands and the Hawaiian Islands would be at the outer limits of the new patrol bombers' ability, so it was decided to extend their range comfortably by having them refueled by specially modified submarines at a sheltered atoll nearer the target. In their eagerness to test their new weapons, the Japanese planners failed to provide for many contingencies and they did not consider the inevitability of Murphy's Law ("Anything that can go wrong will go wrong") yielding negative results in the far-reaching consequences. The planners had hoped to send at least five bombers on the first sortie of Operation K, but only two would be available. They planned a series of raids by the Emily bombers, but they settled for a modest beginning—with the two preproduction prototype aircraft—for the first attack. The Japanese knew that only two bombers would be a pin-prick irritation, but they hoped to make up for the lack of damage inflicted by gaining desperately needed information about the Americans' principal base in the Pacific.

The reconnaissance portion of the mission was more important than the bombing damage that might be achieved. Even so, the sortie would arrive over Pearl Harbor in darkness. Although the flight was planned to take place during a full moon, a full moon's light does not allow the visibility needed for good military reconnaissance. A certain amount of arrogance might have affected the desire to show the Americans that the IJN had the capability to perform just such an attack less than three months after the first attack. The Japanese, by revealing that they possessed such a capability, may have cost themselves a great price that they had not anticipated. They had tipped their hand, and U.S. Navy intelligence got a good look at the cards that the Japanese held. The first sortie of Operation K would bring negative results for the Japanese and have dire consequences for their future operations.

3

The Second Attack on Pearl Harbor

From the opening weeks of the war, the high command planning staff began exploring ideas to take advantage of their new flying boat's capabilities. In some of their proposals, the planning staff allowed their imaginations to run wild.

Admiral Kinsei, impressed with the phenomenal range of the Emily (H8K), proposed that a flight of six Emilys would fly to a point near the California coast, land on the ocean, take on fuel from submarines, bomb the city of Los Angeles, and fly back to Japanese-held island bases. The Japanese were intrigued with the idea of extending the range of their airplanes by refueling them from submarines. The Japanese planners realized that if a few of the problems involved in the aircraft-submarine combination could be solved, the attacks over the extreme distances of the Pacific Ocean could give them a capability that they believed their American enemies would not possess. This plan was actually approved prior to the Battle of Midway, but was quietly dropped after that battle.

Another idea that the planners developed involved thirty Emily aircraft that would refuel from tanker submarines in the calmer waters of the Gulf of California east of Baja California, and fly across Mexico to bomb the Texas oil fields.

Still another scheme involved the cooperation of their German allies. The German Navy had a number of large tanker submarines that were known as milch cows. These large submarines supplied German unterseeboots (U-boats) with fuel, torpedoes, ammunition, food, and supplies while operating on the East Coast of the United States. The Japanese planned to have the flying boats refuel from those German submarines. The Emily bombers would operate up and down the East Coast, bombing major American coastal cities. These raids were to be conducted primarily for their terrorist and propaganda value. The Germans liked the idea and prepared their tanker subs for working with the Japanese flying boats, but the deteriorating war situation for the Japanese caused these plans to be abandoned.[1]

In his excellent U.S. Naval Institute *Proceedings* article, "Rendezvous in Reverse," Capt. Edwin T. Layton describes a fictional account of a bombing raid conducted by flying boats that had been refueled by submarines to extend their range. The original story, titled "Rendezvous," appeared in the August 2 and August 9, 1941, issues of *The Saturday Evening Post*, written by "Alec Hudson," which was the pen name of W. J. Holmes, then a reserve U.S. Navy lieutenant on active duty as an intelligence specialist.[2]

Published just four months before the first Pearl Harbor attack, the magazine story relates how a fictional attack by Catalinas (PBYs) was carried out against troops and transports in a port more than three thousand miles distant. The Catalinas lacked such round-trip range, but submarines at an uninhabited atoll refueled them in order to carry out their mission. Captain Layton suggested that this fictional yarn was the inspiration for the tactics used on the second attack on Pearl Harbor by the Imperial Japanese Navy (IJN). Captain Layton wrote that the Japanese attack "followed too closely, in reverse, the general outline of Alec Hudson's story 'Rendezvous,' to have been coincidental or pure chance."[3]

In response to Captain Layton's suggestion, Holmes commented that "The truth is that the Japanese did not have to depend upon Alec Hudson and *The Saturday Evening Post* for plans involving the fueling of seaplanes from submarines. Such possibilities were well known the world wide."[4]

Holmes states further that an associate editor of the *Post* had suggested the story to him, but he had replied that he had no access to information that such operations were being practiced. Holmes suspected that they were in fact being practiced, and because of possible secrecy, he was reluctant to write such a story. Even after he learned that an illustration of an airplane being refueled by a submarine was planned for another story in the same magazine and that the navy department had approved a motion picture to be titled *Attack* to be made from that story, he still did not use the plot. In 1940, a British naval officer wrote a book that hinted that the admiralty was familiar with the possibilities of seaplane-submarine operations. At about the same time, *Time* magazine reported that the Italian navy was using submarines to refuel seaplanes. Only at that time did Holmes write his story "Rendezvous" which he maintains was "pure fiction, without benefit of access to either our or the Japanese plans for the future."[5] Ironically, the Office of Naval Intelligence informed him that it was "inappropriate at the time" to release a story about airplanes being refueled from submarines. Later, a navy public relations officer asked Holmes to resubmit the story for publication. This time, the Office of Naval Intelligence approved the story, provided that a couple of deletions were made. The deletions did not alter the story line that much, so it finally appeared in *The Saturday Evening Post.*[6]

Actually, the U.S. Navy had been experimenting with refueling patrol planes by submarines. The submarine *Nautilus,* one of the largest subs in the navy at the time, participated in successful tests in early 1939. The commander in chief, U.S. fleet, directed that such exercises should continue on a regular basis between Submarine Division Four and the Catalinas of Patrol Wing Two. Both units were based at Pearl Harbor.[7] In October 1940, the secretary of the navy approved a recommendation that twenty-four submarines be equipped to carry aviation gasoline for refueling seaplanes on the water. These "authorized" submarines would be in addition to the *Nautilus* that had demonstrated refueling capability. The *Nautilus* had also made a successful dive to three hundred feet with a load of aviation gasoline aboard. The submarines *Narwhal* (and sister ship to *Nautilus*) and

Argonaut (the largest sub in the navy at the time and designated as a minelaying submarine) were to be altered to carry nineteen thousand gallons of aviation gasoline each.[8] There are no known incidents in which the U.S. Navy used this submarine-seaplane refueling capability operationally during World War II, even though it was available. Later, it was learned that the Japanese had practiced refueling a four-engined Mavis (H6K) flying boat from a submarine in 1939 in a feasibility test for just such a long-range bombing or reconnaissance operation.[9]

Even before the beginning of the war, the IJN had begun the design of a submarine that was intended specifically to service and support flying boats in forward areas and remote atolls that had no shore facilities and where seaplane tenders could not operate. This was the large SH-type support submarine, 364 feet long, weighing 3,512 tons surfaced, 4,290 tons submerged. Six were planned for the fleet, but only one, the *I-351*, was begun in mid-1943 and completed early in 1945. She could carry 365 tons of aviation gasoline, 11 tons of fresh water, and sixty 550-pound bombs or thirty bombs and fifteen aircraft torpedoes. She was built to service as many as three large flying boats simultaneously. The *I-351* was essentially a submarine aviation gasoline tanker, with the gasoline tanks built outside her pressure hull. This design feature was meant to preclude the possibility that explosive fumes could penetrate the pressure hull. She was designed to act also as an aircrew transport and to carry supplies to isolated bases. Originally, she was to be armed with a 5.5-inch deck gun and was supposed to have four 25-mm antiaircraft machine guns installed. The larger deck guns were in short supply, so four 3-inch trench mortars were mounted instead, along with seven of the antiaircraft machine guns. She had four torpedo tubes of her own, but no "reload" torpedoes. She was fitted with a snorkel breathing tube and its endurance was sixty days. The *I-351* lasted less than six months, being sunk by the submarine USS *Bluefish* in the South China Sea in July 1945.[10]

One of the schemes that the Japanese did bring about consisted of a planned series of armed reconnaissance sorties over the bases at Pearl Harbor and other American islands. The Mavis flying boats did not have the range capability or the self-defense protection needed for these missions. It had served well as long-range bombers in some earlier raids, but the Japanese planners considered that Pearl Harbor would be too well defended to send the slower, less formidably armed Mavis to attack there. The five examples of the Emily preproduction prototypes being tested at the Yokohama Naval Air Force base were showing themselves to be a vast improvement over the older flying boats currently in service, but no other Emily aircraft would be ready for operational use in time.

Cdr. Tatsukichi Miyo, the brilliant planner who had helped to write the demanding specifications for the Emily flying boats, led the IJN planning team. He had envisioned using long-range flying boats for just such missions as the Pearl Harbor attack. The new Emily was Japan's only long-range bomber capable of making those attacks from great distances, and they were the fulfillment of his dream. He persuaded the navy command staff to authorize putting the Emily to its first combat test, to take place in early March, 1942.[11]

The plans were carefully put together to use the superior qualities of the new bomber; a study of the maps of the vast Pacific area was the first step. Cdr. Suzuki Sugaru, the last IJN officer to visit Pearl Harbor, did the detailed planning.[12] A copy of a confidential registered publication, entitled "U.S. Naval Air Pilot, Pacific Islands," had been captured on Wake Island in December 1941 and was extremely useful to the Japanese. This document contained detailed information on specific island air facilities and sea-plane landing areas.[13] Using these data, the Japanese planners became interested in French Frigate Shoals, an atoll lying approximately halfway between Midway Island and Oahu.

French Frigate Shoals was a desolate atoll with only thirty or forty acres above water. This group of islands was discovered by the French explorer Jean-François de la Perouse in 1786. Before World War II, the U.S. Navy had developed East Island (the largest island of the French Frigate Shoals with an area of ten acres) as an emergency air base.[14] French Frigate Shoals' coral reefs encircle a large lagoon nearly fifteen miles long. La Perouse Pinnacle on its western edge rises 122 feet above sea level, making the atoll easy to spot from a submarine periscope or from an airplane. On the southern end of the atoll is Disappearing Island, which does indeed sometimes disappear at a particularly high tide. At the northern end is Tern Island, which became the location of a three thousand–foot emergency coral runway. French Frigate Shoals was a favorite location for many of Adm. Ernest King's operations when he was searching the Pacific for seaplane base locations for his Catalinas (PBYs). The atoll had several openings to its kidney-shaped lagoon that were deep enough for submarine or small craft to enter.[15]

Submarine *I-22* was sent from Wotje Island to reconnoiter this atoll to determine its suitability for use by submarines to refuel aircraft. On January 15, after careful observation of French Frigate Shoals and other islands in the Hawaiian chain, the submarine reported that French Frigate Shoals would indeed be the preferred and most practical location for the refueling part of the planned operation.[16]

Other preparatory actions included the modification of several of the I-class submarines to replace their Glen (E14Y) floatplanes with fuel and oil-tank storage and fuel-pumping equipment in their deck canister-hangars. This modification included four hose connections, hoses, reels, floats, tanks, and compressed air pumps for forcing fuel at high rates of transfer at fifty-three gallons per minute. Submarines *I-15, I-19,* and *I-26* were selected for the remodeling for refueling operations. All three ships would spend the first two weeks of February 1942 in port in Japan for these alterations.[17]

Commander Miyo and the planning staff came up with three plans for Operation K. They considered that each of the three plans was feasible. Plan Number One called for the aircraft to take off from the Wotje seaplane base in the Marshall Islands for French Frigate Shoals, 1,605 statute miles away. There, the planes would be refueled from the waiting submarines and take off for Pearl Harbor, 560 statute miles away. After dropping their bombs, the planes would fly directly back to Wotje (1,980 statute miles). If conditions required it, the route could be reversed so that the aircraft could refuel again at French Frigate Shoals on the return to Wotje. Necker Island, eighty miles east of French Frigate Shoals, could be used for the refueling in case

American security or patrols made the planned refueling point unusable. Necker Island lacked a lagoon, but its leeward side of the island's tall ridges could possibly offer calmer waters for a refueling operation. Plan Number Two involved a direct flight from Wotje to Pearl Harbor, refueling from submarines on the return flight via Washington Island (1,010 statute miles south of Oahu), and returning to Wotje. Plan Number Three changed the departure point to Makin Island in the Gilbert Islands. From Makin, the bombers would fly to Christmas Island, a distance of 1,336 statute miles. After refueling from submarines there, the aircraft would proceed to bomb Pearl Harbor and return for refueling again at Christmas Island and return to Makin.

Plan Number One was preferred over the others in spite of the longer distances. It seemed to be the least risky of the three plans, because Japanese intelligence was not sure of the status of American defenses on Christmas and Washington Islands. Christmas Island did have an airfield with a five thousand–foot runway currently under construction. Washington Island had no based defenses at this time of the war.[18]

The timing of the flight mandated a takeoff from Wotje at least two hours before sunrise and departure from French Frigate Shoals two hours after sunset. This timing was to place the bombers over Pearl Harbor in the early morning hours. All of the plans called for each bomber to be loaded with four 550-pound bombs. The planners knew that the Emily flying boats possessed almost exactly the range capability to make the four thousand–mile round trip, from Wotje to Pearl Harbor and back. However, the refueling by submarines would give the bombers an extra safety margin against unexpected headwinds, bad weather, or navigation errors on such a long flight. These new airplanes were too valuable to risk by taking them to the edge of their performance capabilities on their first mission.[19]

These would be the longest bombing sorties of World War II flown by any of the combatant nations, in distance and total flying time. Spare crewmembers for each crew position would be included to relieve fatigue for the arduous flight. Being fully loaded, the large seaplanes would require long takeoff runs. Another consideration was that the flight crews needed the light of a full moon to minimize the hazards of floating debris or rough water. The nautical almanac promised a full moon condition for the night of March 2, with good illumination for the hazardous takeoffs, for navigation for the first leg of the journey, for target identification, and bomb-aiming during the bomb run. The Japanese mission planners had chosen the U.S. Navy's Ten-Ten Docks (so named because they were given the designation number 1010 on charts of Pearl Harbor) as the target on this first flight of Operation K. The bombardiers and pilots had pointed out that the massive fuel storage tanks would not be easily identifiable in the darkness. The tanks were not concentrated in only one area. The Ten-Ten Docks were much more recognizable from high altitude at night. The mission planners considered that they could target the fuel storage tank areas in the later missions of Operation K.[20]

In the latter half of January 1942, Vice Adm. Matome Ugaki, the chief of staff of the combined fleet, sent secret radio dispatch #81 to the Fourth and Sixth Fleets directing them to plan and prepare for a night bombing attack on Pearl Harbor. The aircraft were to be refueled by submarine at an atoll west of Oahu, and this operation would take place in the latter part of February to "disrupt and nullify the Americans' salvage and repair work" going on at Pearl Harbor. In addition, the bomber crews were to gather as much information as possible on the number and types of ships currently anchored there. This would be one of the first armed reconnaissance missions of the war. The message specified that two of the new Type 13 (13-shi [Experimental Type]) long-range patrol planes would be assigned to the 24th Air Flotilla for this mission, arriving in the Marshall Islands in early February. The Emily airplanes were not yet in full production, so they were still being called the 13-shi long-range flying boats in this first message. It is believed that only five of the preproduction aircraft, including the first prototype, had been completed at this time. The staff planners initially wanted all five of the new Emily prototypes to be used in the attack, but more testing and the need for more crew training dictated that only two airplanes and crews could be spared.

The response to the secret radio dispatch #81 from the combined fleet came from Commander Miyo and his planning staff of the navy ministry on January 25. A plan was submitted for approval to the respective chiefs of staff of the units concerned. The first operation was authorized for March 2, 1942. Two Emily flying boats would be refueled by two submarines at French Frigate Shoals, with a third submarine present as a reserve refueling unit. Another submarine would be stationed near Johnston Island to serve as a radio beacon for the bombers on their return leg, with still another sub positioned southwest of Oahu for rescue, if necessary. In case both flying boats could not arrive at the Marshall Islands bases prior to the departure of the refueling submarines, the Yokohama Squadron was to send one flying boat to Wotje by February 12 to conduct training and practice with the radio beacon submarine. The second aircraft was to arrive no later than February 19. To provide maintenance assistance, two aircraft mechanics were to be assigned to each refueling submarine.[21]

The planners had a conference on Kwajalein in early February with the units that were charged with the execution of their plans. The studies and concepts of the mission were discussed and a draft of the Operation K orders was drawn up. The first phase of Operation K called for two armed reconnaissance missions to be flown, with bombing attacks to be made in accordance with Plan One on two dates. The first date (P Day) scheduled an early takeoff on March 1, 1942; the second date (Q Day) was set for the morning of March 6. The five days would allow for crew rest and any needed repairs to the aircraft after the first mission. Careful scrutiny of the almanacs caused the planners to realize that delays beyond March 6 would jeopardize the second attack, increasing the hazards of a night takeoff with the reduced visibility of a waning moon. The weather was always a factor in planning long-range missions, but the Japanese had an efficient weather reporting and forecasting system already operating in the Pacific. In addition, the Japanese intelligence counterparts of the American cryptanalysts had been successful in cracking the fairly simple puzzle of the U.S. Navy's coded weather reports from the U.S. Naval air stations at Midway, Johnston, and the Hawaiian

Islands. By adding American weather data to their own system, the Japanese possessed far more comprehensive weather information in the Pacific than did the U.S. forces.[22]

The submarine fleet was given detailed instructions for its part in Operation K. Submarines *I-15* and *I-19* were designated as the primary refueling tankers, each to be loaded with ten tons of aviation gasoline. The *I-26* would also be on station at French Frigate Shoals as the back-up refueling tanker, but would remain outside the reef to act as a picket boat when the other two submarines went inside the reef. Periscope reconnaissance was to be conducted prior to the refueling submarines entering the confining lagoon of the atoll. If any American forces were present, either in the form of patrol boats, lookout towers, or security personnel, the submarines were to surface and destroy the Americans and any of their existing facilities with their deck guns.

Submarine *I-9* was to be the flag boat of the flotilla. She was to be placed at Point M along the flight path in a position seven hundred miles southwest of French Frigate Shoals. The *I-9*'s duty was to act as a radio beacon to aid the bombers in navigation thirty minutes prior to the scheduled passage overhead, and to continue broadcasting the navigation signal for an additional thirty minutes after they had homed in on the signal. This placement of the radio beacon on the inbound route was a change in plans. Originally, the radio beacon submarine was to be in the vicinity of Johnson Island on the return leg of the mission, but the flight crews involved informed the planners that they preferred the beacon submarine on the inbound leg.

The *I-23* was to act as lifeguard at Point N, ten miles south of the entrance to Pearl Harbor, in case battle damage forced either or both of the bombers down or, if needed, to refuel the aircraft for the return journey. The Japanese had used submarines for this lifeguard duty for their carrier task force attacks on Pearl Harbor and the Philippines. The U.S. Navy did not use submarines in this role until later in the war.

All the submarines were to be on station one day prior to P Day and again on Q Day to make observations and broadcast twice-daily weather reports. All radio communication frequencies, call signs, special codes, and transmission procedures between aircraft, submarines, and bases were firmly established in the mission orders. Two of the smaller RO-type submarines were to station themselves three hundred miles northeast of Wotje along the flight path to act as radio beacons to assist the returning bombers.[23]

Back in Yokohama, the two aircrews chosen for the mission were gearing up to an extensive and concentrated training program that included day and night overwater navigation, night takeoffs and landings, reconnaissance techniques, and night bombing. The radio operators reviewed their short- and long-range communication procedures. It was decided to delay the practicing of refueling aircraft from submarines until after the Emily aircraft arrived in the Marshall Islands. This was scheduled for mid-February. The submarine crews were trained in refueling techniques in late January, using *I-23* to practice with one of the older Mavis flying boats acting as the receiver.[24]

On February 13, two Emily flying boats lifted off majestically from the waters of their home base at Yokohama for the Marshall Islands, via Saipan and Truk, arriving at Jaluit three days later. Numbered Y-71 and Y-72 on their tall vertical tail fins, they were actually the only two Emily aircraft available for the mission at that time.[25]

Lt. Hisao Hashizume had been chosen to be the mission commander of the first sortie of Operation K. He and his highly trained crew would lead the mission. Ens. Shosuke Sasao and his crew would fly the second aircraft. Sasao was also an experienced seaplane pilot who had been involved, like Hashizume, in the testing and training in operating the large new Emily flying boat. Little is known of Ensign Sasao's training, except that he probably had been a former enlisted pilot who had distinguished himself as a highly capable flyer and leader deserving of promotion to his commissioned rank. It was unusual for an ensign to be assigned to such a high-level job early in the war. It can be assumed that he was a pilot and leader of exceptional abilities.[26]

The crews for this important mission had been carefully selected. Each crewmember was regarded as the IJN's leading expert in his particular crew position specialty. Each crewmember chosen had been involved at Yokohama in the testing of the Emily and had been trained in the operation of the airplanes as soon as he had become available.

On February 19, Lieutenant Hashizume's crew flew Emily Y-71 from Jaluit to Kwajalein to participate in ten days of refueling training with the submarine crews. The crews of *I-15, I-19,* and *I-26* took turns with both the aircrews. Ensign Sasao's crew and Emily Y-72 had remained at Jaluit while a damaged wing flap was repaired.[27]

In the late afternoon of February 19, IJN aircraft crewmembers reported that they had sighted and attacked an American task force containing the carrier *Lexington* east of Rabaul. Fearing that his fleet base at Truk might be attacked, Adm. Isoruku Yamamoto demanded that all available submarines in the area, including some of the Operation K boats, were to concentrate on searching for the American task force. The search proved fruitless for the Japanese, but when the submarines were released to return for Operation K, *I-15* reported that the submarine group could not possibly reach French Frigate Shoals until 5:30 AM on March 2. This made it necessary to delay the planned bombing raid on Pearl Harbor until March 3. The flaws in the complex plans for Operation K were already apparent.

Another glitch for the Japanese developed when the navy ministry informed the submarine and aircraft units involved that the Americans had changed their weather code on March 1. Therefore, a complete weather map based on information from the American bases could not be drawn. The ministry added that it was attempting to break the new codes and provided its own weather predictions for the second and third of March. Their weather experts predicted that the winds at Pearl Harbor would be approximately twenty-three knots from the northeast and east-northeast. French Frigate Shoals winds were estimated from the east and southeast at approximately twenty-six knots.[28]

On February 14, the *I-9* and *I-23* submarines received their Operation K instructions by coded radio messages. Both submarines acknowledged the orders, but following the acknowledgement, Cdr. Genichi Shibata and his *I-23* were never heard from again. It is assumed that this submarine was sunk by an operational error; neither American nor Japanese records show a sinking of a submarine in that area of operations. On February 24, the *I-9* recovered her floatplane after the night reconnaissance of Pearl Harbor, and proceeded toward her position at Point M along the planned inbound flight route for the Emily bombers.[29]

On March 2, special weather reconnaissance planes were launched to the northeast of Wake Island and the Marshall Islands to augment the weather predictions from ships and other bases in that area of the Pacific. The reports from submarines at Point M and French Frigate Shoals indicated favorable weather.[30] Both flying boats were moved to the seaplane base at Wotje Atoll on March 2 to be loaded with fuel and bombs.[31] On the night of March 3 (March 2 in Hawaii), the submarines at French Frigate Shoals broadcast the following report: "Wind velocity twelve knots [13.6 miles per hour], height of waves less than one meter. Enemy nowhere in sight." The weather and conditions were favorable for the attack.[32]

The aircrews were gathered for the final mission briefing. To emphasize the importance of the mission, Vice Adm. Shigeyoshi Inoue, commander in chief of the Fourth Fleet (Mandate Area) personally briefed the crews about the magnitude and historic significance of their mission. He expressed his admiration of their courage and wished them success in their attack. The pep talk was unnecessary—the crews were confident and eager to get their flight under way.[33]

The two new Emily flying boats and their crews had been positioned at the seaplane base at Wotje Atoll because it was nearly 250 statute miles north of Jaluit Atoll. The overall round trip of the mission flying time to Oahu would be nearly three hours shorter than if flown from the base at Jaluit. The Wotje base was not as completely equipped and staffed as the base at Jaluit, but the facilities at the more forward base were adequate for the mission launch. Food on Wotje was in short supply, but the new flying boats had brought a few scarce items with them from Japan. This elevated morale as well as the excitement level among those stationed there. Rumors among the lower-ranking maintenance personnel on Wotje were that Pearl Harbor was about to be attacked again by these magnificent new seaplanes.

On the day before the planned launch for the attack, a Mavis flying boat was sent out for weather reconnaissance for seven hundred nautical miles from Wotje along the planned route of the flight. This aircraft reported favorable weather thus far for the mission, as did submarine *I-9* at Point M and the waiting submarines at French Frigate Shoals.[34]

The aircrew members and maintenance specialists involved in the launching were lined up at 11:00 PM on the night of March 3 (Wotje time) for a final briefing and equipment inspection before boarding. The aircrews boarded rubber boats and were rowed out past the sloping seaplane ramp to their airplanes that were moored on the west side of the island. Chatting excitedly among themselves, they boarded their aircraft and quickly began their preflight inspections and checklists. They checked fuel, oil, and hydraulic fluid levels. They tested electrical circuits and interphone systems and—without transmitting—they tested their radios. They inspected their parachutes and life vests, and stowed their inflatable life rafts near the exit doors. Each crewmember checked his oxygen mask and his individual oxygen supply panels. When those checks were complete, the crewmembers turned their attention to inspecting the aircraft oxygen system and oxygen bottles for full servicing. They adjusted their helmets, radio headphones, and microphones. The navigators laid out their charts on their plotting tables and checked their chronographs and sextants. Gunners checked their turrets for operation, swinging their turrets around to ensure that the guns could be flexed in aiming and were free in their travel. The gunners inspected their weapons and inventoried ammunition. With the aid of armorers, they carefully checked the four bombs suspended beneath the wings of each aircraft, along with the security of the bomb shackles, fuses, and arming wires. The pilots worked their control yokes and flap levers, peering out of their cockpit windows to ascertain that all controls were functioning properly. They set their compasses and attitude indicators, twisted the barometer knobs on their altimeters, gently tapping the glass faces of their instruments to free any sticking needles. Each crewmember stowed his personal gear near his crew position and secured it in place. As the time approached for takeoff, the crew quieted down and settled into their duties, their conversations more focused on the business of operating their airplanes. There were terse checklist challenges and quick responses as the crew commanders led their crews through the final equipment checklists.[35]

Low clouds were scudding across the sky, sometimes hiding the bright full moon, as the massive propeller blades began to turn. The engines came to life, coughing out clouds of blue smoke from the exhausts. The engines warmed up as the crewmen waited for the moon to illuminate the lagoon. The mission commander, Lieutenant Hashizume, was in the lead airplane, Emily Y-71. Ensign Sasao was in the second airplane, Emily Y-72. Y-71 took off at 4:55 AM, and Y-72 took off shortly thereafter. (As was true at all Japanese bases, their watches, clocks, and chronometers were set to Tokyo time. From this point on in this part of the narrative, though, all times will be indicated in Hawaii Time, which was two and a half hours later than Pacific Standard Time in 1942.) Both Emilys, heavy with fuel, bombs, ammunition, and extra crewmembers, required long, spraying takeoff runs to lift free off the water. The seaplane base at Wotje broadcast a brief, coded departure report to all the agencies concerned. The mission was finally on its way.

With their engines throttled back only slightly to climb power, both aircraft began a slow ascent on their northeast heading toward French Frigate Shoals. Hashizume slowed his immense bomber slightly to allow the second aircraft to catch up and join him in formation. Several heading changes were required to avoid rainsquall clouds. An hour and thirty-seven minutes after takeoff, the seaplanes were able to join up at twelve thousand five hundred feet and settle down to cruising in a loose formation.[36]

Some of the younger crewmembers were participating in their first combat mission, and the level of nervous anticipation was high. The combat veterans who had flown missions in the war with China attempted to convey an attitude of calm professionalism to the neophytes on the crew. Once the climb was established, the crewmembers were able to turn their attention to their normal duties and their thoughts were occupied less with what they might encounter over the enemy island of Oahu. A few of the spare

crewmembers gathered in the crew lounge on the lower level of the seaplanes to have a snack, smoke, and relax. A few closed their eyes and tried
to nap, but no real sleep would come. No enemy fighters would be threatening in the early phase of the mission, so the gunners and lookouts kept
their guns stowed, but peered out of their turrets and windows to maintain
visible contact with the other airplane.

The climb phase was challenging because it was conducted through scattered tropical rain showers, and visibility was poor. Several more heading
changes were needed to avoid the rain and thick clouds. Once above the
clouds, the crewmembers were seldom able to catch glimpses of the ocean's
surface. Radio silence was imperative and communication between the airplanes was by signal lamps. After sunrise, the weather gradually improved,
but an almost direct headwind had slowed their progress slightly. A celestial sun shot showed that their most probable position was slightly north
of the planned course. Both aircraft made a slight course change toward
Point M, where submarine I-9 was positioned.

At about 1:30 PM, the planes began picking up the low-frequency radio
beacon transmission from the I-9 on their radio direction-finder receivers
and homed in on the submarine. As the flying boats passed over the sub
at 2:40 PM, the submarine crewmembers on deck sighted the aircraft and
waved their caps wildly until the planes were out of sight. From their altitude, the bomber crewmembers could see the submarine, but not the men
waving to them. The flying boats continued to use the beacon to keep their
course for thirty more minutes. The submarine broadcast a coded mission
report to all concerned, and shut down her transmitters.[37]

At French Frigate Shoals, the submarines waiting there reported mostly
cloudy conditions. The bottoms of the clouds were at about 7,500 hundred
feet, and visibility was 5 miles. The wind was more than twenty miles per
hour, and was whipping up waves of five feet or more, making the refueling operation tricky and dangerous. The two flying boats arrived over
French Frigate Shoals at 6:30 PM, but cruised slowly around the atoll area
for nearly forty-five minutes to ensure that no American submarines or
patrol craft were in the vicinity. The pilots checked the windsocks that were

attached to the submarine periscope shafts to give them a wind direction indication. After estimating the wind strength, the pilots entered a pattern to line up for their landing into the wind. Both of the massive flying boats touched down several hundred yards from the waiting tanker-submarines, and began maneuvering into their position astern of the boats. The aircrews had already flown for over thirteen and a half hours, covering a distance of slightly more than 1,900 statute miles. Pearl Harbor was still 560 miles away.

Both aircraft carefully taxied astern of the slow-moving submarines but did not shut down their engines. To be able to maneuver and maintain their relative positions for refueling, the aircraft had to keep their two outboard engines running in order to maintain position with the submarines, which had to keep moving forward slowly to maintain their own steering. The airplane's speed and the submarine's speed had to be synchronized exactly to avoid collisions or loss of contact with the refueling hoses. The aircraft pilots gently worked their rudders and their engine throttles to make small directional changes and to stabilize their forward progress. The submarine commanders, standing on the bridge of their boats, kept a watchful eye on their boats' slow movement. At the same time, they carefully monitored the distance that had to be maintained between their positions in relation to each airplane. Submarine lookouts maintained their vigils searching the skies for any American patrol airplanes. The submarines and their nursing aircraft would have to be able to react quickly in case an American patrol plane or ship discovered them. Pumping thousands of gallons of aviation gasoline in ideal conditions was hazardous enough, even if the aircraft had not been loaded with bombs and ammunition. However, to perform this operation in windy, rough conditions while the engines were running was perilous. The brisk wind and rough wave action would have prohibited the refueling transfer in peacetime or in training practice, but this was a war mission and the risk was deemed justifiable.

Each submarine deck crew sent out a mooring pendant with a loop at its unattached end that was buoyed up by small floats. The aircraft crews snagged their pendant with a long boat hook and hauled up four specially made lightweight gasoline hoses to reach fuel tank receptacles along the top of the airplane's wings. Grounding wires to eliminate static electricity had to be carefully hooked up between the refueling hoses and the aircrafts' metal surfaces. The crewmembers involved in the refueling had to be careful to keep the hoses away from the spinning propeller arcs, at the same time ensuring that the hose nozzles did not come near the hot engine exhausts. When the hose nozzles were in place and the aircraft was ready to receive fuel, the submarine was signaled to release the compressed air, which began forcing aviation gasoline into the seaplanes' tanks at a rate of fifty gallons per minute. Engine oil tanks were topped off manually at the same time. The brisk winds and moderate swells caused fuel lines to part several times. A great deal of the time was consumed in the operation to recover the mooring pendants, maneuver the airplanes back into position, and reconnect the gasoline hoses. In about two hours, 3,170 gallons were pumped into each aircraft, adding approximately nineteen thousand pounds of weight to each.[38]

Having completed their dangerous refueling task just before sundown, the crews gathered atop the wings of the airplane and had their evening meal. They had draped American flags over the Rising Sun insignias on the tops of the wings, with the hope that this would deceive any American patrol plane that might surprise them. Because the Pan American Clipper flying boats exhibited large American flags painted on them for recognition, they hoped any patrol airplanes would mistake them for a Clipper. With submarines connected to the large flying boats that bore only a faint resemblance to the Clippers, no American patrol airplanes would have been fooled by this ruse.

The wind began to rise. Even inside the atoll's protective reefs, the waves were now six feet high. When one of the mooring cleats connecting a line to a sea anchor was snapped off the nose of his airplane, Lieutenant Hashizume decided that they should prepare for the tricky takeoff immediately. It was near enough to the scheduled departure time, in any case. The crews quickly resumed their positions in the airplanes and prepared for departure. After a bumpy takeoff run, Hashizume lifted his thirty-two-ton flying boat off the choppy waters at 9:38 PM. The second aircraft launched right behind him and they joined formation in the climb and set their course to follow the rocky pinnacles and islets of the central chain of the Hawaiian Islands.[39]

In the bright moonlight, the crew of Emily Y-71 sighted the steep-sided narrow ridge of volcanic rock that was Necker Island at 10:29 PM and altered course for Nihoa Island. The weather was still fairly clear as the bombers passed over the twin peaks of Nihoa at 11:55 PM. Emily Y-72 was in close formation and both airplanes were now cruising at fifteen thousand feet. The weather below them became less favorable for a bombing and reconnaissance mission. The clouds were becoming thicker and now obscured most of the ocean's surface. Their planned route was to thread the narrow passage (twelve nautical miles) between Niihau and Kaua'i Islands and turn toward Oahu. This maneuver was intended to prevent the flight from being seen by any aircraft spotters on either island. Because they had no radar detection gear, the flying boat crews were blissfully unaware of the American radar stations sitting atop the hills of the islands beneath them. On Oahu alone, five radar stations were now operational. Thirty minutes prior to reaching Oahu, the wind was now coming from the northeast at twenty-four knots (27.5 miles per hour), visibility had dropped to only two and a half miles, and the undercast five thousand feet beneath the bombers obscured 80 percent of the surface. Hashizume was only slightly reassured that he could see one recognizable object on the ground—the lighthouse at Kaena Point on the western tip of Oahu island.[40]

The crews of Emily Y-71 and Emily Y-72 did not know it, but the U.S. Army radar station on Kaua'i had detected their approach at 12:14 AM at a true bearing of 290 degrees and a distance of 204 miles. The radar station immediately reported these radar blips to the Air Warning Service on Oahu.[41]

Radar stations reported their bearings and distances information by field telephone to the Hawaiian Air Warning Service Center. "Lizard Control" was the heart of the Oahu Air Warning System, located at Fort Shafter. The WARDS (Women Air Raid Defense Service) moved markers on the large plotting board to indicate the positions of friendly or suspect targets. At the Center were liaison officers from the naval and army air force commands to identify each aircraft's plot. By comparing their knowledge of aircraft capabilities, flight plans, and areas of flight operations, the officers on duty could tell which targets were friendly or a potential threat. If none of them could identify or claim a radar target as one of their own, that target was termed a "bogey" and considered hostile until proven otherwise. If the Fighter Director decided that the bogey was unfriendly, he would launch, or scramble, defending fighters, which were already on alert status (fueled, armed, and pilots at hand—sometimes even sitting in the cockpits). This was before IFF (identification, friend or foe) radar identification transponder equipment was installed on planes in the Hawaii area.[42]

When first placed on the plotting board, the Emily formation plot was labeled unidentified. Neither the army nor the navy liaison officers could positively identify the blips as one of their own, nor could they rule out the possibility that the radar blips indicated a friendly stray returning off course or outside the stray's assigned flight sector. The suspect blips were monitored closely as their distance to Oahu shortened. At 1:08 AM, as the plot approached the island, the radar showed two aircraft, still labeled unidentified. It was beginning to appear that the genuine threat of an air raid was developing. The word spread through the Center that an air raid alarm was about to be sounded. The navy's Patrol Wing Two received an alerting phone call. The operations officer of Patrol Wing Two authorized Squadron VP-21 to launch three torpedo-loaded Catalina (PBY) patrol bombers to search for Japanese aircraft carriers. The authorized takeoff time was 1:15 AM. Two more torpedo-laden Catalinas followed shortly thereafter. The air defense commander—who controlled the interceptor aircraft, radar network, searchlights, and antiaircraft artillery—then ordered fighter-interceptors to take off.[43]

On November 12, just weeks before the December 7 attack, there had been a practice exercise of the Air Warning Service when the navy had launched a mock strike from a carrier eighty miles at sea. The primitive radar on the island had detected the mock attack and scrambled alert pursuit planes within six minutes. The system had worked perfectly then, but not on the morning of December 7. Perhaps it was because the practice attack was more or less expected, or perhaps it was because it was "just" a practice attack. For whatever reason, the system did not function well in the early morning hours of March 4, either. The army's pursuit planes could not locate the fast Emily bombers, even though a sighting was reported. In the early days of the war, most army pilots had little night flying time, minimal instrument flying experience, and had received no training at all in night-interception techniques.[44]

A few minutes later, the radar plots showed the incoming planes to be passing over Kaena Point on a course for Pearl Harbor. At 1:59 AM, the Hawaiian defense commander ordered an air raid alarm sounded and all armed forces bases on Oahu went to general quarters, or full alert battle stations.[45] By now, at least three Oahu radar stations were tracking several bogeys.[46]

The flying boats were still at fifteen thousand feet, but the thick cloud cover beneath him was disheartening to Lieutenant Hashizume. Even though he estimated the cloud layer to be two thousand to three thousand feet thick, some faint light filtered up from the bright work lights and the welding torches at work on the ships in Pearl Harbor, creating patches of light through the clouds. Accurate visual bombing would be impossible. Reconnaissance of the ships in the harbor would also be denied to the Japanese, under these conditions. The Japanese could see that the chances of achieving their mission objectives were dwindling rapidly.

Pushing the overhead-mounted throttles forward, Hashizume brought his engines up to nearly full power for the bomb run as he turned the flying boat toward where he guessed his target area would be. He could be sure of only one clearly visible object on the ground—the lighthouse at Kaena Point that was still flashing its brilliant signal far behind him. Ens. Tahei Sasaki, the navigator, quickly plotted a bearing from the lighthouse to the Ten-Ten Docks (so named because they were given the designation number 1010 on charts of Pearl Harbor) and called this reading to Lieutenant Hashizume. The crews of both bombers would use the lighthouse at Kaena Point to help them find the directions to the target area, but the distance from Kaena Point to Pearl Harbor was roughly twenty-six miles and they could only estimate their distance from the lighthouse. The pilots of both the airplanes lined up for their bomb runs as best they could and ordered their bombs armed in preparation for release.[47]

Suddenly, Lieutenant Hashizume saw through a break in the clouds what he believed to be a portion of Ford Island, which was located in the center of the harbor. He ordered a quick left turn to circle back over the target. Ensign Sasao in Emily Y-72 did not hear the order for the turn and the two airplanes became separated immediately. Lieutenant Hashizume in Emily Y-71 completed his turn, but by now the break in the clouds had disappeared. He released his four bombs at 2:10 AM (although he logged the release time as 2:15 AM). Risking collision with the second airplane, he turned again to try to see the impact of the bombs. The actual time of fall from bomb release to their striking the target below would be about thirty seconds, from their altitude. Hashizume could not see the impacts, but Emily Y-71's four bombs landed harmlessly on the slopes of Mount Tantalus above and behind Waikiki Beach, destroying only a few algaroba and monkey pod trees more than five miles from the intended target. Hashizume had misjudged both azimuth and range in his twists and turns just before bomb release. Ensign Sasao had not heard the lead aircraft call either of the turns. When he peered out of the cockpit at the start of his bomb run, he realized that his leader was no longer in sight. Aware that they had probably flown past their target, Sasao turned back to the north and by dead reckoning released his bombs at 2:30 AM. His bombs splashed harmlessly into the sea at the entrance to Pearl Harbor. (For this reason alone, it was believed and reported in some accounts of the attack that the raid had involved only one aircraft.) Sasao's range estimate from the lighthouse was more accurate than Hashizume's, but Sasao's azimuth was off, too. Neither crew could see where their bombs had landed, "all of Pearl Harbor being then completely obscured by clouds."[48]

The G-3 journal section of the "Summary of Seventh Air Force Operations" contains a copy of the radar logs of the morning of March 4,

1942. The terse log entry comments tell the story, beginning with the initial radar contact with the incoming Japanese bombers at 12:12 AM. The army radar had detected a "number of plots" west of Kaua'i. The air defense controllers at Lizard Control alerted the navy. At 12:33 AM, the radar reported that the number of targets had decreased to one, but this one was "very definite." This was probably Hashizume's Emily Y-71 in the lead with Sasao's Emily Y-72 in close formation. The primitive early radarscopes had a tendency to blend two closely spaced targets into one strong blip.

The navy wasted no time. They reported to the defense controllers that their VP-21 squadron had launched Catalina patrol bombers to search the area and that they would attempt to confirm the radar reports. The navy patrol bombers' markers were added to the plotting board. The army bided its time, allowing its fighter-interceptors to remain sheltered in revetments until the incoming Japanese airplanes were closer to the island. At 1:00 AM a second radar station reported that the plot (now code named Yehudi) had moved between the islands of Kaua'i and Niihau. The two planes apparently were still showing on the radarscopes as one target because they were in such close formation.

At the same time, three army fighter squadrons were alerted but not launched. Thirty minutes later and anxious for more information, the air defense controllers called the radar station to learn that the plot Yehudi still appeared to be one aircraft, now twenty miles southeast of Kaua'i Island. The defense controllers launched one flight of interceptors.

Just how many defending fighters were launched is not certain. Most sources say that only four Kittyhawk (P-40) fighters took off, but Airacobra (P-39D) fighters equipped the 46th Pursuit Squadron (Interceptor). An alert flight of the 46th had scrambled at 1:25 AM, led by 1st Lt. Othneil Norris.[49] More fighters took off at 1:36 AM.[50] The Kittyhawk could climb to fifteen thousand feet in about six and a half minutes. The climb performance of the Airacobra was similar. The Kittyhawk carried 281 rounds of .50-caliber ammunition for each of its six machine guns.[51] The Airacobra had four .30-caliber machine guns in its wings, but brandished a .37-mm cannon in its nose, firing its 15 rounds through the propeller hub.[52]

Both the Airacobra and Kittyhawk fighter airplanes were still rather new to Hawaii. These two airplanes were the most plentiful fighters in the army in early 1942. The Kittyhawk B- and C-model fighters that had been destroyed in the December 7 attack were being replaced with the later, heavier D- and E-models with better armament. The D-model had four and the E-model had six .50-caliber machine guns. The earlier model Kittyhawks were equipped with two .50-caliber and four .30-caliber machine guns.[53] The D-model Airacobra was armed with a 37-mm cannon firing through the propeller hub, and four .30-caliber wing guns.[54] In addition to their limited experience in instrument flying and complete lack of night-fighting training, nearly all of the fighter pilots were hampered by having to become acquainted with unfamiliar cockpits and newer types of aircraft.

Reporting to Maj. Gen. Clarence Tinker, commander of the newly designated 7th Air Force at that time, Brig. Gen. H. C. Davidson, commander of the 7th Interceptor Command, complained about his assigned airplanes. He said that "the P-40 [Kittyhawk] was an unsatisfactory interceptor airplane because of its lack of climbing ability and its inability to operate at high altitudes." The other fighter that the army sent to Hawaii to replace the losses suffered on December 7, the Airacobra, was also unable to operate efficiently at high altitudes.[55] Neither fighter was equipped with an engine supercharger, necessary for high-altitude flight. The Airacobra and Kittyhawk fighters were generally regarded as good fighters at low altitude, barely adequate at middle altitudes, but totally unsuitable as high-altitude interceptors.

U.S. Army Air Force (USAAF) and navy pilots from U.S. flying schools of the prewar era were given little night flying training. The aircraft at that time were not equipped with the instruments and radios for true instrument flight conditions. Formation flying was hazardous even in daylight, and night operations were not addressed in any of the current flight manuals. There was no tactical doctrine for aerial night fighting. The army and the navy had no dedicated night-fighter aircraft and no pilots from either service had been trained in night-fighting techniques. In the early days of the war, in a practice night scramble, sixteen Kittyhawks of the 47th Squadron had attempted to take off from their alert strip at Haleiwa on Oahu. Three of them cracked up on takeoff, and some of the following airplanes unknowingly took off through the wreckage on the runway.

Although the defending squadrons on Hawaii had fighters on alert for night interception duty, the airplanes and the skills of the pilots of the U.S. Army and navy were not yet up to the task. An army fighter squadron commander stated that, "night time panic that sent single-engine day fighters scurrying about in the Hawaiian darkness was a reaction, not a planned exercise." Army and navy fighter pilots knew that they had more to fear from night mid-air collisions and night spatial disorientation than from the Japanese.[56]

Ens. Wesley P. Craig later recalled that when he reported for duty at midnight of March 3, the sky was dark with a heavy, thick overcast. He had been assigned as a warning net and plotting officer with commander in chief, Pacific Fleet (CinCPac) operations, headquartered at the submarine base in Pearl Harbor. His ship, the destroyer USS *Cassin,* had been all but destroyed during the first attack on Pearl Harbor; she had shared a berth in the Ten-Ten docks with another destroyer, the *Downes,* and with the battleship *Pennsylvania.*

In his earphones, Ensign Craig heard different radar stations reporting the ranges and bearings of the incoming bombers. He said that it was quickly determined that they were enemy aircraft and he notified the operations duty officer, who called Admiral Nimitz, the commander in chief of Pacific Naval Forces. Ten minutes later, Admiral Nimitz sat down next to Ensign Craig at his plotting table. The admiral looked over the board carefully and asked a few questions about what forces were on alert. Condition Red went out to all ships and stations in Hawaii. The army was responsible for defending all shore installations and the navy was responsible for everything at sea, but these defenses were coordinated. Craig remembers that "everything was blacked out. It was extremely tense. . . . Around 0130, Admiral Nimitz turned to me and said, 'Let's send up six fighter planes.'" Fifteen minutes later, the admiral ordered that another six fighters be launched. These orders were passed quickly to the USAAF fighter bases, so as many as twelve fighters may have been in the dark skies over Oahu that night.[57]

Ens. Andrew Gennett was the gunnery officer on a converted fruit boat, the USS *Crescent City*. His ship, an attack transport, was anchored in Pearl Harbor on the night of March 3, having just arrived from the United States. Diaries would later be forbidden during the war, but Ensign Gennett kept one at this time. It contains this entry:

> 4 March 1942—Tonight around 0100, we were roused by sounds of General Quarters. General Alarm, Air Raid, was sounded. We dashed to our stations. The sky was dripping and clouds were cumulus at around 3,500 feet. Rain nimbus came down from the mountains eventually. Showers here are all localized. Liquid sunshine!
>
> I heard the far-off wail of a siren and watched the last of the lights in the whole area blink out. We stood dripping and sleepy, waiting. Engines were turned over. The Captain came up to the flying bridge to look around. Soon, we heard the roar of airplanes taking off and watched our searchlights pierce the sky. Every once in a while, the clouds broke and a brilliant moon shown down on us. I heard some dull explosions and few bursts of our anti-aircraft fire. Then, silence. We waited an hour more, then secured. A Nip plane had come over. One single plane dropped four bombs from considerable height, then left us. A mystery plane. My first air raid. I was not particularly impressed.[58]

Although his ship was equipped with a 5-inch gun on her stern and eight 3-inch guns at other positions on the ship, and numerous 20-mm antiaircraft cannons, Gennett said that they received no orders to fire, because there were no visible targets.[59]

At 2:10 AM, a teletype message was sent out to all stations on the island of Oahu to assume general quarters for an air raid. At the same time, a teletype message signed by Lt. Gen. Delos C. Emmons stated that the "Air Raid Not Sounded by this Hq." Ironically, Lieutenant Hashizume's bombs were released at that precise moment: 2:10 AM. A few minutes later, the signal office of the Hawaiian Air Force admitted that they had sounded the alarm at the direction of another officer in headquarters.

The ground controllers were still inexperienced in directing the airborne defenders, just as the fighter pilots themselves were inexperienced in following directions given to them by the operators at the ground radar stations. The fighters would take up an interception direction, only to find nothing to shoot at when they arrived where the radar showed a target to be. The complexities of radar interception had not been mastered by the pilots any more than they had by the radar controllers. The Japanese flying boats, in their dark blue-green camouflage paint, should have been fairly easy to see in contrast with the tops of the clouds, illuminated by a full moon. The engine exhaust flames from each of the four-engined bombers at high power should have made them even more visible, but apparently the fighters never got close enough to see any sign of the bombers. The patrolling Catalinas were directed to continue their search for Japanese ships or other aircraft.[60]

By 2:55 AM, the defending fighters, unable to locate the enemy bombers above the clouds, were recalled and began their descent for landing. Yehudi was now being shown on radar at forty-five miles south of Honolulu. At 3:05 AM, Yehudi was still being tracked, moving rapidly to the southwest. The bombers, turning and circling over what they presumed to be their targets, had maintained an average groundspeed of 150 to 160 miles per hour most of the time they were being tracked. In another thirty minutes, they had flown out of range of the Hawaiian radar stations.

The G-3 summary report includes the information that two pilots from Wheeler Air Base were positive that they had seen "four ships [aircraft] in a loose string" formation at nine thousand feet, with white lights showing, but the two Emilys were actually at about fifteen thousand feet in altitude and almost certainly showing no lights. Confusion and the "fog of war" are obvious in the G-3 report. The report is also fraught with errors. The Wheeler fighter pilots could not have seen four ships in loose string formation when only two widely separated bombers were involved, although they could have seen a formation of defending fighters. In addition, no attacking bombers would be showing white lights. Blue, red, or orange exhaust flames might be visible, but not white lights. The bombers were at a much higher altitude than the fighter pilots reported in their supposed sighting. The relatively primitive tracking radar saw only one aircraft when there were two aircraft—which were at times widely separated. Several comments were inserted that indicated that several agencies were "covering their behinds" in case this turned out to be another one of the many false alarms that were being sounded nearly every night during this period on Oahu.

John G. Eberhard was a staff sergeant and chief of the height-finder crew of an antiaircraft battery. He recalls that his crew was alerted to the incoming Japanese bombers by island defense command headquarters. He remembered that the gun crews were enthusiastically ready for action, but they were never ordered to fire. He said that "all the searchlight batteries on the island were in action" that night and that his unit remained on alert for three or four hours. Because of the broken overcast, they could see nothing to shoot at.[61]

In the field command post of Searchlight Battery E of the 64th Coast Artillery (Antiaircraft) was Pfc. Richard F. Ferguson, who confirmed many years later that their searchlights were piercing what was normally a nightly blackout. Searchlights brilliantly lit up the bottom of the low clouds. Because the Japanese flying boats were well above those clouds, though, the lights did not illuminate them.[62]

For most people on Oahu that night, the second attempted bombing of Pearl Harbor was almost a nonevent. A typical example is that of Pfc. Roy M. Foster, who was with the Fourth Defense Battalion on Oahu. He was alerted by his gunnery sergeant blowing a whistle. The sergeant formed his men (with their weapons) and dispersed them into a nearby sugar cane field. They whiled away the time by cutting, stripping, and chewing on the sugar cane stalks until the all clear was sounded. Foster says that they heard distant dull explosions, but could not determine what caused them.[63]

After they had dropped their bombs, neither crew of the flying boats was able to determine whether or not the bombs had hit their intended targets because of the extensive clouds below them. Both aircraft turned

southward to take up their withdrawal route from the target area. Each turret and gun position was manned and the anxious gunners peered over their
sights, searching for any pursuing American fighters. They knew that the
bright moonlight would have silhouetted the massive flying boats in their
dark camouflage for any fighters that might be above them, but no fighters threatened the Emilys. The two bombers had become widely separated
in their circling bomb run attempts, but they did not want to break radio
silence in the target area just to rejoin for their return flight to the Marshall
Islands. They were not now in visual contact with one another, so neither
crew knew how the other had fared during their brief and rather hectic run
over the enemy island.[64]

Twenty minutes after the second bomber had released its bombs and
when both aircraft were well clear of the target area, Lieutenant Hashizume
considered it was safe to break radio silence briefly to broadcast a coded
message that the attack had been successful. Both airplanes, even though
not within sight of the other, took up parallel courses for the return to
Wotje. Their flight altitude was reduced to twelve thousand feet so that the
crew could remove their oxygen masks and be more comfortable for the
long journey back to base. A thick layer of clouds kept them from going
lower for this portion of their flight.

Just after sunrise over the Pacific, S1c Kaichi Azume, the flight engineer,
began a careful interior inspection of Emily Y-71, Lieutenant Hashizume's
aircraft. Azume took his time, carefully peering into opened inspection panels throughout the voluminous interior of the flying boat. Opening up the
hull bilge access for inspection, Azume discovered that a hole about a foot
long and four inches wide had been gashed into the metal bottom skin of
the flying boat's hull. He concluded that, in the long, heavy takeoff run back
at French Frigate Shoals, the airplane had struck something in the water—
a floating log or even a submerged coral head. After receiving Azume's
report of the damage, Hashizume made a decision to alter his course in
order to return to Jaluit, instead of Wotje.

The base at Jaluit had more extensive repair facilities for the repair of
the hull damage. In his effort to keep radio transmissions to a minimum,

Hashizume elected not to inform Sasao in the second aircraft of his decision to fly to Jaluit instead of Wotje. Once they were out of range of the American fighter defense, the gunners relaxed somewhat, but maintained their vigil in case they encountered an American patrol plane. The remainder of the return trip to the Marshall Islands was uneventful. Sasao's aircraft landed at Wotje at 2:45 PM; he had expected the lead aircraft to be there already, but he and his crew were informed that no word had been received from Hashizume after his broadcast that the mission had been a success. Ensign Sasao's crew in Emily Y-72 was concerned about their comrades in Emily Y-71. It was not until 3:00 PM that Hashizume's flying boat arrived safely at Jaluit. Emily Y-71 had run into a severe rainsquall and had to reduce flying speed to ease the task of flying on instruments in acute turbulence. The mission had required over thirty-five and one-half hours, with thirty-two of those hours spent in the air. The flight had covered a total of over 4,750 statute miles. It was the longest bombing mission flown by any of the fighting powers during World War II.[65]

Hashizume's role in the mission was still not complete. His crew had stuffed a temporary patch over the hole in the hull, but they had no idea if or how long it would hold on landing in the water. To prevent his new airplane from sinking when he landed at Jaluit, he taxied rapidly to the seaplane ramp as seawater poured into the punctured hull. The beaching crew had been alerted to his problem and they made quick work of attaching the beaching wheels to the hull. As soon as he was given the signal that the beaching gear had been secured, Hashizume jammed his throttles forward to quickly bring the flying boat up on the sloping ramp from the sea. Hashizume personally supervised the repair of his airplane at the base at Jaluit. The seawater had to be drained and flushed from the hull before repairs could begin. With many of his crewmembers lending a hand to the maintenance specialists, the men worked to seal the gaping hole in the hull of the Emily. After satisfying himself that his airplane had been fully repaired, Hashizume was able to get some sleep. After loading more fuel the next morning, he and his crew flew back to the base at Wotje. The intelligence officers there scheduled a mission debriefing immediately after they landed.

The pilots and crews of both aircraft stated that, because of the dense clouds, the results of their bombing attempt were unknown. Through breaks in the undercast, they claimed to have observed one battleship in dry dock at Pearl Harbor, as well as an aircraft carrier and a cruiser at anchor there.[66]

The initial delay in the original P Day raid, which had just been completed, plus the delay caused by the damaged hull repairs of Hashizume's Emily Y-71, had now made the second Q Day impossible for its March 6 schedule. Hashizume agreed that the waning moon would not provide enough illumination for the required night takeoffs and refueling by submarine. He also knew that he and his exhausted crew needed rest.[67]

It is difficult to determine what the Japanese reaction to the second attack was, because sources disagree. On the one hand, throughout the war the Japanese were reluctant to release any detailed news about any of their military and naval operations except to make sweeping claims of victory without being specific about tactics or weapons used. When an operation was successful, only the general area of the operation was mentioned in the civilian press, which relied completely on the information supplied by the military and naval authorities. At this time of the war the Japanese government never admitted setbacks, much less defeats. Thus far, things were going well for the Japanese and there were no setbacks or defeats to discuss.

Like most Americans, many Japanese did not learn of the second attack on Pearl Harbor until long after the war had ended. The Japanese citizens were becoming somewhat jaded by the radio and newspaper accounts of one victory after another. Japanese naval authorities believed that the second attack—whether or not it had inflicted any major damage—had been an outstanding success. They had been able to drop bombs on Pearl Harbor a second time, less than three months after their first attack. This time, not a single bullet harmed the attackers, and the Americans seemed powerless to keep the Japanese from repeating their attacks.[68]

The Japanese press frequently gleaned its war stories from American sources. Reporting on the second attack on Pearl Harbor, Japanese radio broadcasts and newspapers claimed that a Los Angeles broadcast had told of "considerable damage done" to military installations at Pearl Harbor, with the death of "thirty sailors and civilians, and some seventy wounded."[69]

The U.S. Army's radar operators had done a creditable job of detecting and tracking the intruders, but the radar operators, ground controllers, and fighter pilots had failed miserably in attempting to intercept the Japanese bombers. Improvements in radar and radar techniques in controlling and directing fighter intercepts would create drastic changes in the tactics of aerial warfare for both sides as the war progressed. The need for airborne radar and dedicated night-fighters, along with the training needed to use these combat tools, was painfully obvious.

4

The Aftermath of the Attack

These were the blackest days of the war for the United States. The second attack on Pearl Harbor had taken place less than three months after December 7, 1941. Guam, Wake Island, Hong Kong, Singapore, and Thailand were in Japanese hands. All of Borneo had been taken. The Philippine Islands were being overrun and Port Darwin in Australia had been bombed. The Japanese seemed invincible, and their easy victories astonished even their own military planners. They were far ahead of their own schedule for conquests. Emperor Hirohito received almost daily briefings on the rapid progress of his armed forces. He became fascinated with German and Japanese newsreels showing one victory after another. The emperor conducted his first public celebration of the Pacific War victories by appearing briefly on his white horse, waving to the assembled crowds on the Nijubashi Bridge leading into the palace. But even then he was concerned, and commented to his cabinet member, Privy Seal Kido, "We are winning too quickly!"[1]

The armed forces on Hawaii certainly did not want to admit that the Japanese had attacked them a second time—this time, with impunity. At Pearl Harbor, the many members of the army and navy who were not informed that the bombs had been dropped by Japanese bombers were quick to try to place the blame for the incident. As soon as each service was absolutely certain that one of its own had not committed the error of jettisoning bombs in the wrong area, charges began to fly. The navy accused the army of carelessly dropping bombs by mistake and the army countered with similar charges against the navy. Navigational errors, procedural errors, or carelessness were cited as probable causes.

Although Allied intelligence experts knew of the earlier Mavis (H6K) flying boats, they were not yet aware of the existence of the new Emily (H8K) flying boats. The Emilys had been used in combat for the first time in this latest attack. These same intelligence experts were not aware of the outstanding performance of the new Emily bombers, especially their spectacular speed for such a large aircraft and their almost phenomenal range capabilities.

The local Honolulu newspapers were forced to rely on the armed services for information about the attack, but they were given scant or deliberately incorrect details about the bombing. The press's knowledge of what had actually happened was limited to whatever was obvious about smoking holes on the slopes of Mount Tantalus. As previously pointed out, the bombs from Ens. Shosuke Sasao's Emily Y-72 had fallen harmlessly into the ocean outside the entrance to Pearl Harbor, so for a long time the Americans believed that only one Japanese bomber had attacked. Army and navy intelligence specialists believed that the raid might have come from a cruiser's floatplane (or a single bomber from a carrier, which seemed unlikely). They knew that the lightweight Glen (E14Y) submarine-launched floatplane was incapable of carrying four medium-sized bombs.[2]

PO3c John C. Cash was in the radio room of the USS *Hopkins,* a World War I destroyer that had been converted to a minesweeper. He kept a war diary until April 1942, when he was told that personal diaries were against secrecy regulations. Regarding the attack, Cash wrote in that diary that the "average sailors on board a ship had little or no idea what was going on and [they] were not permitted to have radios on board ship for personal use. However, we in the radio gang could listen in on broadcasts in the Hawaiian area and short wave from the States." He learned of the second attack from one of these broadcasts. Most sailors had been made aware of the Glen floatplane, dubbed "washing machine Charlies" from their distinctive clattering engine sound, and of the submarines that were equipped to carry and launch the little observation aircraft. The rumors were that it was just another Glen over Pearl Harbor. (These sailors did not know that the Glen was incapable of such a bomb load.)[3]

The rumors were given more credence with an article that appeared on the front page just beneath the story of the second attack on the March 4, 1942, issue of the *Honolulu Star-Bulletin* with a London dateline:

JAPANESE MAY HAVE SUBS THAT CARRY PLANES

LONDON, March 4. (AP)—The Japanese are believed to be using at least one plane-carrying submarine and possibly more, informed sources here indicate.

They said that when the New Zealand armed merchant cruiser *Monowai* was engaged by an enemy submarine near New Zealand waters in January, the cruiser was attacked simultaneously by a plane believed to have come from the submarine. Neither attack caused any damage.

The submarine-carried aircraft probably would be a seaplane which could be stored in two sections in hangars on each side of the undersea ship and be assembled at sea, the informants explained.

The idea is not fundamentally new. Britain tried it in 1927. The ill-fated [British Royal Navy] *M2*, which had been built to carry a 12-inch gun, was adapted to take a seaplane with folding wings by removal of the gun and construction of a hangar in the space formerly occupied by the gun mounting. The seaplane was catapulted from the submarine.

Both the plane and the *M2* later were lost.

Jane's Fighting Ships, authoritative naval manual, lists the giant French submarine *Surcouf*, the largest [submarine] in the world, as carrying a small seaplane which is stored in a deck hangar.[4]

All servicemen in Hawaii had been warned not to include any information about military operations in their correspondence. Many of them were not even aware that the attack had taken place. Even today, many of the men who were stationed on Oahu that night declare that it did not happen because they had never heard anything about the raid. One correspondent proclaimed that his memory was "still perfect" and that, "if it had happened, he was in a position to know about it." (He is still convinced that it never occurred.)

Those who did know of the attack were cautioned not to mention it or write home about it. Pvt. Herbert G. Hunt, Jr., 27th Infantry Regimental Intelligence and Reconnaissance Platoon, was stationed in the command post located under the concrete stadium of Roosevelt High School near the spot where Lt. Hisao Hashizume's four bombs impacted. Hunt confirms that "the next day, nobody seemed to know anything about what had happened. The news media even reported that the air raid sirens were sounded by mistake that night. Then, the day after that, the newspapers came out with some of the story, but we were informed that we could not write home about it."[5]

Cpl. Donald Kennedy was on duty as a switchboard operator in the army's Diamond Head tunnel on the night of the attack. He recalls that all the army switchboard operators thought that it was great fun to listen in on their fellow soldiers making illicit phone calls on government phone circuits to their girl friends. He remembered receiving a message on the night of March 4 stating that the bombs came from a Japanese airplane. He recalled that he "pulled out all the phone plug drops and started calling various officers to advise them of the alert situation." He added that, "we were cautioned *never* to mention this incident, so that the Japanese would not know how close they came to actually bombing the place [successfully]."[6]

The two major Honolulu newspapers carried stories of the attack, but the military authorities gave them little information about what had actually happened. The March 4, 1942, headlines of the *Honolulu Star-Bulletin* read "Enemy Warplane Bombs Honolulu." The lead story read as follows:

3 [sic] MISSILES FALL IN AREA BEHIND ROOSEVELT HIGH

What was believed to be an enemy plane flew over Oahu early today and dropped three medium sized bombs on the lower slopes of Tantalus northeast of Roosevelt High School.

The incident occurred at 2:15 AM, army authorities announced this afternoon.

The plane was flying at high altitude.

Where the plane came from is not known.

It was the first enemy air attack since December 7 when Pearl Harbor and other military objectives were bombed.

There were no casualties and no damage with the exception of a few broken windows, the army said.

There were indications the plane might have come from a carrier or a submarine.

Presence of holes believed to be bomb craters were reported to the military authorities by three gangs of road workers.

Their location was given as about 1,000 yards northeast of Roosevelt high school and in an unpopulated forest area.

Army ordnance men were sent to investigate the holes and determine if possible what caused them.

Three sharp explosions which shook most sections of Honolulu, awoke thousands of persons, at about 2:10 this morning.

Although a siren was heard at the time of the detonations, army authorities said there was no air raid alarm.

Sounding of a siren just prior to the explosions was described as "inadvertent"—a mistake.

Residents reported having heard planes before and after the detonations, and searchlights were seen.

Hundreds of persons who heard the siren as well as detonations are reported to have rushed from their beds into bomb shelters.

Neither casualties nor major damage were reported, according to the police.

Police had reports that the detonations shattered windows in a house on Tantulus Drive. There were also scattered reports of other windows having been broken. A building at Kaahumanu school was shaken, but no damage was reported.

At the Tantulus Drive home of Lt. Harrison R. Cook, USN, the concussion from the detonations broke the glass in three large sliding windows and blew the windows off their tracks.

Occupants said they believed . . . that they smelled what seemed to be powder smoke.

Included with the article was a somewhat ironic two-column photograph showing two Japanese women (apparently servants in the home) examining the broken window mentioned in the story.[7]

The rival newspaper, the *Honolulu Advertiser*, printed only a short one-column mention of the attack headed "Night Alarm Wakens City" in its March 4 issue. This brief account read as follows: "Many Honolulans were awakened about 2:15 a. m. today by the sounding of a siren followed by three fairly heavy explosions. The nature of the detonations, which rattled windows downtown, was not immediately determined, and Army authorities stated that no air raid alarm had been sounded. Army authorities released the following statement: 'The inadvertent sounding of a siren, followed by three detonations, caused a belief that an air raid alarm was sounded. No air raid alarm was sounded, however. The cause of the detonations is now being investigated.'"[8]

Apparently, only brief mention appeared in two continental U.S. newspapers. Each of the rival San Francisco papers, the *San Francisco Chronicle* and the *San Francisco Examiner*, carried short speculative accounts of the raid the following day. The *Chronicle*'s story was an Associated Press release dated March 4 and titled "Army Hints at Raid by Single Plane." This narrative took its cue from the Honolulu papers:

The Army announced—today that "what was believed to be an enemy plane flew over Oahu island today and dropped three medium sized bombs on the outskirts of Honolulu. The plane was flying at a high altitude." The announcement said, "where it came from is not known. There were no casualties and no damage except a few broken windows."

Reports of some residents hearing many planes, and of others who reported even seeing several, went unconfirmed.

It is believed possible the plane was from a cruiser or other enemy ship at sea. It was the first reported bombing of the island since that of December 7 which precipitated the war with Japan.

Three heavy explosions shook Honolulu immediately after screaming air raid sirens wakened the city at 2:10 AM.

Army officials at the time however, said there was no air raid. They
said that the sirens were sounded inadvertently and did not disclose the
cause of the explosions.

Later, however, army authorities announced today that holes "resembling
bomb craters" had been found about two miles from the heart of the city.

The holes discovered by road workers are in forested terrain a thousand yards northeast of Roosevelt High School. The area is not populated.[9]

The other San Francisco paper, the *Examiner,* ran an even more speculative
article with a Washington dateline:

NEW HONOLULU RAID COULD HAVE COME FROM WAKE BASE
U.S. Points Out Japs Have Long Distance Bombers
Washington, March 4

(AP) Japan has several types of land based bombing planes which
could fly to Hawaii, drop bombs and return to their base.

Such an undertaking from the island of Wake, which Japan now controls, would be mere routine for long range bombers that could easily negotiate the 4,000 miles involved in a trip from Wake to Hawaii and return.

COULD FLY TO EUROPE
The United States possesses bombers which could fly to Europe with a full load
of fuel and bombs and, after unloading the bombs, return to the United States.

Another land base from which Japan could launch a nuisance raid
on Hawaii would be the Marshall Islands, also approximately 2,000 miles
away.

ATTACK FROM CARRIER
Carrier based planes have a much shorter range. The Pearl Harbor attack
December 7 was launched by carrier based planes that were comparatively
close to the Hawaiian Islands.

The fact that only three medium sized bombs were dropped on Hawaii today led to speculation that the raid probably was carried out by a land based bomber whose crew was eager to get back safely. Such raids are not considered profitable but may have a nuisance value.

(However, a single bomber plane might have been sent to "log" the route as the forerunner of mass attacks later.)[10]

The article had no basis in fact. The author of the article did not specify which aircraft—Japanese or American—had such capabilities, other than stating that the airplanes were land-based bombers. The Japanese did not have a land-based bomber at the time with such long range with any bomb load, and neither did the United States. For example, the first offensive mission flown by the Hawaiian Air Force on January 1, 1942, was a lone Flying Fortress (B-17). This airplane, with no bombs aboard, took off from Hickam Air Base on Oahu, flew to Midway Island to refuel, and flew to Wake Island, which had been taken over by the Japanese a week before. The Flying Fortress took photographs of Wake, returned via Midway to refuel, and flew on to land at Hickam with only fifteen minutes of fuel remaining in its tanks.[11] The Flying Fortress had a range of eleven hundred miles with a load of bombs; its longer-legged stable mate, the Liberator (B-24), could carry a normal bomb load for fifteen hundred miles. Even the new Emily had not made the round trip from the Marshall Islands to Hawaii without a refueling stop.[12]

On March 5, 1942, the *Honolulu Advertiser* carried much more coverage of the attack, but full details were still being withheld by the military. A three-column photograph of a bomb crater being inspected by helmeted soldiers indicating "Where Big Eggs Hit" topped the next-day story. The picture's caption read "NO DAMAGE DONE—Soldiers search crater on the lower slopes of Tantulus where four bombs burst in a shrub-covered area early yesterday morning. The craters were about 25 feet long, 20 wide and 10 deep, and apparently made by bombs weighing three hundred to six hundred pounds. Ordnance officers sought tell-tale splinters at the spot." The accompanying story follows:

MYSTERY PLANE DROPS FOUR BOMBS ON CITY
Deep Craters Blasted; Little Damage Caused.

A mystery plane, reportedly an enemy raider, dropped four heavy bombs in the . . . outskirts of Honolulu yesterday morning, blasting craters in the hillside brush approximately 10 feet deep but doing no other serious damage and causing no casualties. A few windows were broken in the vicinity and thousands of Honolulans were awakened at 2:15 AM by the detonations, causing wide-spread speculation on the cause until it was announced in the afternoon by Army authorities.

What the Army believed was an enemy plane flying "at extremely high altitude" dropped the missiles, the official Army communiqué said, emphasizing that they were medium-sized bombs and adding that "where the plane came from is not known."

Originally it had been reported that three bombs were dropped, but investigation during the morning disclosed a fourth crater in the woods on the lower slopes of Tantalus, not far northeast of Roosevelt High school. The craters, in a direct line, were about 25 feet long by 20 wide and bomb fragments were scattered over a wide area, some of them shearing off tree limbs 10 inches in diameter. Such fragments were picked up by ordnance officers, and examiners said the bombs had been from 300 to 600 pounds in weight.

"MEDIUM BOMBS"
Such bombs are described by the Army as "medium" bombs, as aerial missiles range from 50 to more than 1,000 pounds.

The explosions, which came in quick succession, were heard in most districts of the city, but particularly in the Manoa and Makiki sections, where houses shook and windows rattled. The police, radio stations and newspaper offices were immediately deluged with a flood of excited inquiries, and "several more cautious residents left their beds and took to their bomb shelters, despite the hour and the weather."

The phone calls indicated considerable confusion as to whether the explosions were caused by local defense batteries engaged in test firing, by enemy raiders or by enemy surface craft offshore.

No report was made that the nocturnal visitors were detected prior to the dropping of the bombs but shortly after the detonations, planes were reportedly heard overhead and searchlights pierced the black sky. Although it was later stated that there was no local activity, many Honolulans reported hearing anti-aircraft fire afterward, and one declared he had seen a plane caught in two cross-beams of the searchlights.

CITY ENTIRELY BLACKED OUT

Honolulu was completely blacked out at the time of the explosions. The craters were first discovered shortly after daylight by road workers en route to their jobs.

Residents awakened by the blasts said they heard an alarm siren sounded at the time, but authorities declared that the sounding of the siren was a mistake.

This was the first time Oahu has been reportedly attacked since Dec. 7, although other islands have since been shelled by submarines on two occasions, and many who heard the explosions thought another submarine attack was being made. Army authorities said no American planes were in the air before the detection of the attacker.

Where such planes might come from was a subject of much speculation in the city during the rest of the day. They might have come from aircraft carriers or enemy cruisers offshore, it was pointed out, or might have been long range bombers from the Japanese mid-Pacific bases, though this was considered unlikely, the distance being very great.

There have been recent reports from British observers in the south Pacific that the Japanese have been operating several large submarines capable of transporting aircraft aboard and assembling them at sea.

Meanwhile, the effect of the raid was to increase reports to the police last night of blackout violations, residents checking up more carefully on their neighborhoods in anticipation of further possible "nuisance" raids.[13]

On the second page of the same *Honolulu Advertiser* was a three-column photograph of a soldier climbing up to inspect a damaged tree. The headline read: "No B-B Did This," and went on to say, "When bombs dropped behind Honolulu yesterday morning digging four holes in an empty hillside, they threw jagged chunks of iron far and wide. One lopped off the top of this tree, some 25 feet from the nearest crater. The severed trunk is as big around as the soldier investigating it."[14]

Malcolm Aitken was assigned as an officer-agent in the army Counterintelligence Unit on Hawaii. He recalls that his office received a teletype message from the army intelligence section requesting that an investigation be conducted concerning several bomb or artillery shell strikes reported in the Tantalus-Roundtop area. With Special Agent George Scott he drove to the area where he found curious bystanders in and around a large crater. The two agents asked a police officer to clear the area for their investigation. Onlookers were asked to turn over any souvenirs that they may have taken from the crater. Scott and Aitken determined that the crater was the result of an aerial bomb or an artillery shell of medium weight. They were able to collect several fragments from the device and turned them in with their investigation report. Aitken later said that he had read the speculative reports in the newspapers, but was not convinced that the device had fallen from a Japanese bomber until he was contacted by the author many years later.[15]

The scarcity of forthcoming official details about the attack was prompted by the policies of the new Office of Censorship. President Franklin D. Roosevelt had created this agency on December 16 to monitor all media releases containing information or comments about military and naval operations.[16] Adm. Ernest J. King increased the reticence of the navy to issue information to the press. King cared nothing for publicity and disliked press conferences. He vowed that the Japanese would learn nothing of value from the navy's terse releases of information. The armed services began to garner the criticism of reporters and news gatherers who claimed that the military and naval authorities were overreacting to the original Pearl Harbor debacle. The services had clamped down on such information as ship losses, casualty lists, enlistments, and even figures for induction. When volunteers and draftees were loaded aboard buses and trains for boot camps or basic training, their numbers and destinations were regarded as classified information, because these were regarded as troop movements, right to the end of the war.[17]

On Hawaii, the frustrated defenders of the dozens of naval and military installations quickly realized the extent of their vulnerability to Japanese attack. With this attack, the Japanese had accomplished at least one of their objectives—to force the Americans to tie up more of their armed strength to defend the Hawaiian Islands. It was obvious that the increased defenses on the islands were still inadequate to fend off enemy attacks, especially night attacks. With this attack, the commanders of the fighter units charged with defending Hawaii realized that they were desperately in need of night-fighters along with pilots and crews trained in night-fighting techniques.

Following the second raid, fragments of the Japanese bomb body, fins, and fuses had been recovered (apparently the same bits and pieces gathered by Agents Aitken and Scott of the army's Counterintelligence Unit) and the bomb-disposal chief assured Adm. Chester W. Nimitz that they were of Japanese origin. The admiral asked Cdr. Edwin T. Layton how the bombing had been accomplished. Layton told him of the story that had been published in *The Saturday Evening Post* magazine, written by W. J. Holmes, a naval officer who was currently working in Station Hypo. Layton believed that the Japanese had gotten the idea of refueling aircraft from submarines from that story, titled "Rendezvous." Layton also told the admiral of the Japanese submarines that were known to be operating around French Frigate Shoals. Admiral Nimitz immediately ordered a converted destroyer–seaplane tender, the USS *Ballard*, to proceed to French Frigate Shoals to provide support for patrol planes and to deny the use of the area to enemy submarines for refueling aircraft. The atoll lagoon would later be mined to discourage Japanese subs.[18]

SSgt. Frank Rezeli was in the base engineering section at Wheeler Field at the time of the second attack. "We painted a P-26 [Peashooter] black so that it could fly night patrols."[19] Actually, the twelve remaining Peashooters that had escaped destruction on December 7 were pooled into the 73rd Pursuit Squadron. They were all painted matte black and relegated to the task of night patrol. The squadron commander of the 73rd and other veteran pilots were horrified by the prospect, but gamely followed their orders.[20] The old Army Air Corps had acquired the Peashooter in 1934 as its first monoplane fighter. It had fixed landing gear, an open cockpit, and a six hundred–horsepower engine. It was armed with one .50-caliber and one .30-caliber machine gun; its top speed was 35 miles per hour slower than that of the four-engined Emily. The Peashooter was certainly not a first-line fighter, but it was a familiar airplane to army fighter pilots and they were more at ease in the night skies over Oahu in it. During the daytime, the black Peashooters sat hunkered in revetments. They were not launched on the night of March 4. Even if they had taken off to pursue the Japanese flying boats, they were not speedy enough to have caught them.[21]

Ten days after the initial attack on Pearl Harbor, Lt. Gen. Delos C. Emmons had been named commander of the Hawaiian Department, replacing Lt. Gen. Walter C. Short. General Emmons had observed the night encounters in the Battle of Britain—both the British night defenses and the tactics used by the Luftwaffe's nocturnal air attackers. He realized that the U.S. Army Air Force (USAAF) would need a defensive night-fighter force when war came. When he had returned to the United States, General Emmons wrote a lengthy report that pointed out the urgent need for night-fighters and trained crews to fly them. The Emmons Board drew up the preliminary specifications for a dedicated night-fighter. Northrop Aviation was already working on a proposal to build a night-fighter aircraft for Britain, so the detailed specifications were turned over to that company. Northrop quickly adapted these USAAF requirements to their design and began work on prototype airplanes. Fast twin-engined army airplanes capable of carrying airborne radar and a radar operator were hastily modified to serve in the role of night-fighters. The first two of these were the Boston (A-20) light bomber and the Lightning (P-38). The Lightning was given a raised cramped seat for the radar operator behind the pilot, the AN/APS-6 radar set, a radar antenna installed in a streamline pod beneath the nose of the airplane, and antiflash gun muzzles. The manufacturer, Lockheed, received a contract to turn out seventy-five glossy black Lightning model-M aircraft that were just entering service as the war ended.[22]

The army had taken the idea of converting the Bostons into night fighters from the British. The Royal Air Force (RAF) had converted some of their lend-lease Boston bombers to night-fighters. The night-fighter version, called the Havoc, enjoyed only limited success as a night-fighter. The modified Bostons had a radar operator in the rear gunner's seat and the bombardier's glazed nose replaced with radar antenna and radar electronic equipment. One version of the Havoc was used to experiment with the dropping of small aerial mines in the path of German bombers. The experiment failed. Some of the RAF's Havoc aircraft were equipped with primitive radar and another version coupled the radar with a huge searchlight mounted in the nose to illuminate enemy aircraft for other more nimble accompanying night-fighters.[23]

Although few people on Oahu really knew what was taking place in the night sky over their island the night of the second attack, there were those who not only knew what was happening, but had suspected that it would take place. They had even put out the warning that some sort of air raid might take place. They were the men and women who worked in the U.S. Navy's Combat Intelligence Unit. The Combat Intelligence Unit was the radio intelligence organization that served the Pacific Fleet. It was a secret weapon of such potency that it would change the balance of power in the Pacific and alter the course of the war. Housed in the long, narrow, windowless basement of the Fourteenth Naval District's administration building near the Ten-Ten Dock in the navy yard at Pearl Harbor, the Combat Intelligence Unit and its secrets were protected by vault-like doors, steel-barred gates, and guards on watch twenty-four hours a day.[24]

Lt. Cdr. Joseph J. Rochefort had commanded the Combat Intelligence Unit since May 1941. The forty-three-year-old former enlisted man was the only man in the navy with expertise in three closely related and urgently needed skills: cryptanalysis, radio, and the Japanese language. Rochefort had a remarkable career. He had headed the navy's cryptographic unit from 1925 to 1927. Because of his outstanding abilities, he was then sent as a language student to Japan. This three-year tour was followed by a short six-month stint in naval intelligence. In the peaceful days of the early 1930s, Rochefort had entertained himself by breaking one of the State Department's codes, just to show that it could be done. (The State Department was not amused.) He spent the next few years in sea duty, with intelligence among his secondary duties. In 1939, the Imperial Japanese Navy (IJN) began using its fleet general-purpose code, known then as AN-1 by the U.S. Navy's code breakers.

In a rare instance of army-navy cooperation, because both services realized that the decoding project was a task too large for either agency on its own, the army's Signals Intelligence Section (SIS) joined with the navy's Communications Security Unit in an operation code-named Magic to attempt to break the Japanese diplomatic and military radio codes. The Magic project was initiated in 1939. Initially, each section had fewer than a dozen men assigned, but the navy unit had grown to about three hundred men by 1942.

The famous Japanese Purple code used a new cipher machine invented by Capt. Jinsaburo Ito, based on telephone switchboard stepping switches. The Japanese believed that it was impossible to break the codes transmitted through these cipher machines, and used this cryptographic system for Japanese diplomatic messages. After nineteen months of exhaustive work, the army's leading cryptanalyst, Col. William Friedman, broke the Purple code in September 1940, but suffered a nervous breakdown as a result of his work.[25]

Because the U.S. State Department was reading their mail, the Japanese plans to end negotiations were already known just before the first Pearl Harbor attack. Even though the Imperial Japanese Army (IJA) and IJN used the same type code machines that were used for the transmission of the diplomatic messages, the Purple code was completely different from JN-25, the IJN's operational message code system. For this reason, the Purple messages gave no hint of the Pearl Harbor attack, but did offer ominous information that something was about to happen somewhere in the Pacific.[26] The Magic project's solving of the riddle of the Purple code did not completely crack the IJN's JN-25 operational code, but it did enable Commander Rochefort and his unit to penetrate and understand vital portions of the messages sent by the Japanese.

Commander Rochefort had been the intelligence officer for the cruiser USS *Indianapolis* prior to being sent to organize and strengthen the radio intelligence unit at Pearl Harbor. To mask its true function, Rochefort renamed the organization the Combat Intelligence Unit, calling it FRUPac (Fleet Radio Unit, Pacific). Rochefort's mission was to learn, through communications intelligence, as much as possible about the dispositions, plans, and operations of the IJN. His unit ultimately analyzed all minor and one of two major Japanese naval cryptosystems. The one code never broken by the American intelligence experts was the IJN's Admirals' Code. Japanese intelligence, on the other hand, was able to break only the fairly simple weather reporting codes used by the U.S. armed forces. They were not able to break any of the other American military or naval operational codes throughout the war.[27]

Before the initial attack on Pearl Harbor, the Combat Intelligence Unit's primary task had been to monitor the IJN's radio messages, employing interception, direction-finding, and traffic analysis. The Hawaii-based unit was code-named Station Hypo and it listened to Japanese radio traffic with a similar station at Cavite on Corregidor named Station Cash, along with another station on Guam and the home base in Washington, D.C., known as Station Negat. The intercept station on Hawaii was receiving and copying the messages, but they could not decipher them. Breaking that code, up to the time of the December 7 attack, had been the task of the stations in Washington and the Philippines.[28]

Commander Rochefort stated in an interview that "an intelligence officer has one task, one job, one mission. This is to tell his commander, his superior, today, what the [enemies] are going to do tomorrow. This is his job. If he doesn't do it, then he's failed." Rochefort always considered that because he was not able to warn his superiors of the impending Japanese attack, he and the intelligence staff officers had failed to do their jobs. In fact, his organization, the Combat Intelligence Unit, had existed for only five months. They were critically lacking in the radio and communications equipment that they desperately needed because it was being sent to Europe. Instead of having several teletype machines to relay messages, the messages from the intercept stations were being delivered by jeep, motorcycle, or bicycle courier. The six or eight miles back to the Combat Intelligence Unit added hours to the tasks.[29]

Commander Rochefort said of the attempted raid on March 4 that, by that time in history, his cryptanalysts were partially reading intercepted Japanese radio traffic. He said that they had "received indications that the Japanese were going to conduct what I would prefer to call a reconnaissance of the Pearl Harbor area for the purposes of determining what progress we had made in repairing ships in the harbor and so on." He deduced that the Japanese would use land-based seaplanes, the distance required that the seaplanes would be refueled by submarines, and refueling would be done in the vicinity of French Frigate Shoals. He stated that he had told Admiral Nimitz that he believed this attempt (to at least reconnoiter Pearl Harbor) would take place and when. He furnished this detailed information to Admiral Nimitz's office and to Rear Adm. Claude C. Bloch, commandant of the Fourteenth Naval District. The first agency apparently did not share the information with the second. Rochefort said that "the next morning Com 14 [Fourteenth Naval District command post] sent for me and was quite irritated because these people appeared and had flown more or less unmolested over the island of Oahu. It was actually incredible. I told him that this information had been furnished (to) his office and had similarly been furnished to commander in chief Pacific [Admiral Nimitz] and in sufficient time for them to take any action they wished to take. Apparently they decided to take no action."[30] Rochefort was appalled, but said that he was later informed that both the army and the navy admitted that they had no planes capable of repelling the attack. He admitted that "it could have been the whole Japanese attack over again." He added, "I just threw up my hands and said it might be a good idea to remind everybody that this nation was at war."[31]

Just before the December 7 attack, the Japanese naval radio traffic had almost been silent. Japanese naval intelligence in Tokyo had changed the key to their JN-25 code and this threw the Americans off for a few days.

Rochefort and his colleagues had partially solved the new key by December 10 as traffic became heavy again.

Messages using the Purple code could be read in their entirety as soon as they were received and translated. The navy code breakers did not understand all messages in the JN-25 code clearly, however. That process rarely gave up more than 10 percent to 15 percent of a message. The content was usually solved by analysis: A ship's call sign suggested another with it (such as a submarine tender that would be in the company of certain submarines) or a previous operation might be associated with a current place name. Sometimes, a particular radio operator's touch on the transmitter key—known as his fist—was as recognizable as a signature and would reveal not only his ship, but also his location.

It took a combination of talents to make sense of all this. The combination of puzzle solver, linguist, and sailor was ideal. It should not be surprising that the men of the Combat Intelligence Unit were individualists. Rochefort himself was somewhat of a maverick—usually wearing an old red velvet smoking jacket and bedroom slippers—and he would work for days, catching a few hours sleep on a cot in his office, subsisting on strong coffee and sandwiches.[32]

Cryptanalysis was only a part of the task of the Combat Intelligence Unit. A majority of the radio work would involve direction finding and traffic analysis. Because radio signals are best heard when an antenna is pointed toward the transmitter, the direction from whence the signal is coming can be determined. If two or more direction finders can take bearings on a transmitter, the lines of those bearings will show the location of the transmitter where the lines cross on a map. By taking several successive bearings, not only the location, but also a ship's course and speed, can be plotted.

The U.S. Navy had established a network of direction-finding stations in the Pacific, beginning in 1937. By 1941, these stations made up a large arc from Dutch Harbor in the Aleutian Islands through Hawaii, Midway, Samoa, Guam, and Cavite in the Philippines. The dozens of men staffing these outposts reported their bearings to Hawaii, where Rochefort's unit translated them into fixes on a ship's position or course. This revealed not only the location of most Japanese ships, but also provided a rich source of messages for traffic analysis. By deducing which radios talk to which, the lines of command for a military or naval operation could be determined. When there was a significant increase in these communications, it usually meant that a military or naval operation was about to take place. Combined with direction finding, the intelligence analyst might be able to deduce where this operation would occur. Some of the gaps could be filled in by intuition, back-reference to other messages, and a general awareness of what was going on. Obviously, this method of gathering information has limitations. Codes and call signs could be changed. Radio silence or the clutter of the airways with false or misleading messages could confuse the listening analysts, but communications requirements could never completely prevent those analysts from gaining some of the information they sought.[33]

In an operation as complex as Operation K, a substantial amount of radio communication between the Imperial Japanese Naval Air Force (IJNAF) and the submarine units was involved. On March 2, Rochefort's Station Hypo intercepted and partially decrypted a message that indicated that an offensive operation would begin on March 5 (which was the fourth on Pearl Harbor). Station Cast in the Philippines copied and decoded a message that gave further indication of impending submarine and air attack for that date. The Combat Intelligence Unit was able to warn Admiral Nimitz on the afternoon of March 3 that something was in the wind.[34] Rochefort's radio intelligence report of March 3 noted specifically that Tokyo furnished the involved units with Hawaiian-area weather forecasts for March 4 and 5, even though the U.S. weather codes had been changed on March 1.

By March 2, Station Hypo had been able to decode the two-*kana* (phonetic letters of the Japanese alphabet) designators for all Japanese submarine tenders. This meant that the general operating areas and identities of some Japanese submarines could be determined. In early February, Rochefort's decoders had translated two messages from the commander in chief's Fourth Fleet (Mandate Area) addressed to "AA." The addressee AA was determined to be Wake Island by comparing Wake Island's response. The message requested information on the number of ships in AK. Again, Wake

Island's answer confirmed that AK referred to Pearl Harbor. Still another message referred to a pending offensive against AK.[35]

Commander Layton, Chief of the Pacific Fleet Intelligence office, considered that his group did not do well in predicting the second raid on Pearl Harbor. If there was an error that failed to forecast the attack, it was in analysis rather than interception. Station Hypo's direction-finders placed two Japanese submarines east of Midway in the vicinity of French Frigate Shoals and even identified them as the I-9 and the I-23. Rochefort had little doubt that some sort of operation would be directed at Pearl Harbor, but this time no aircraft carriers seemed to be involved. He suspected that the raid would be carried out using seaplanes to attack from the IJN's unique seaplane carriers, because he believed that the Japanese had no other aircraft capable of reaching Oahu from any of their land or island bases.[36]

The intelligence staff briefed Admiral Nimitz, and remarked that they had come up with where and when this pending operation would happen, but not what. Rochefort still believed that it might be floatplanes launched from Chitose-class seaplane carriers; the IJN was the only naval force in the world that used such vessels, but Rochefort knew also that Japanese floatplanes could carry only a small bomb load. Also, this ignored the submarines at French Frigate Shoals, so Rochefort really was not sure of what to expect. Nevertheless, the Catalina (PBY) patrol bomber squadrons were alerted to the possibility of a floatplane raid from the seaplane carriers.[37]

The citizens of a jittery Honolulu and the service personnel in and around Pearl Harbor were awash in rumors, just as they had been immediately following the December 7 attack. An already nervous and jumpy Oahu had been made even more nervous and jumpy by the night attack on March 4 by the flying boats.[38]

Three days after the second attempted attack, an indication of just how nervous Oahu was appears in the March 7, 1942, narrative report from the Pacific Fleet's chief of staff. The now-declassified secret log began by stating that at 10:23 AM that day army radar had detected aircraft twelve miles north of Kahuku Point (on the northern tip of Oahu). Army and navy plot officers denied having planes in that area, so the army sounded the air raid alarms one minute later for all the bases on Oahu.

Army fighter-interceptors took off immediately and all armed forces went into full air raid alert. Protective covers were torn from antiaircraft guns and ammunition lockers were unlocked and opened. Shells and bullets were loaded into the weapons. Gun tubs and turrets on nearly every ship in Pearl Harbor were manned and ready. At 10:35 AM, the Com 14 reported that submarines of Kahe Point (on the west coast of Oahu) were firing on the beach. Twelve minutes later, Com 14 reported that there were a total of five submarines, two of which were seriously damaged, and that the other three had retreated under return fire from the shore batteries. At 11:06 AM, Com 14 said that another submarine had been spotted off Nanakuli (on the southwest coast of Oahu). The sub was reported to be heading south. Com 14 followed up this report at 11:19 AM by stating that a friendly destroyer had reached a position five thousand yards off Kahe Point. The warship was investigating the submarine sighting and was "looking for possible survivors." With tongue in cheek, the navy report commented that all these sightings and reports were originated by the army and pointed out that the "reliability of these reports [was] decidedly questionable. Army is investigating." The report concluded with the entry at 11:26 AM confirming that the air raid had ended, the all clear had sounded, and the wartime condition readiness of Two was resumed.[39]

The army's report of this March 7 attack claimed that at 9:45 AM the navy reported to the army's control center that they were monitoring a Japanese radio conversation on a bearing due west of Oahu. The navy further stated that they believed the conversation was between aircraft. Twenty-five minutes later (but slightly earlier than Com 14's first reported contact), the army reported their radar had picked up the aircraft heading toward Oahu. As in the Com 14 memorandum, neither the navy nor the army could identify the aircraft. The air raid siren was sounded.

The army report indicates that only one pursuit (interceptor) unit had been launched because of poor weather conditions. The report is vague in that it does not declare how many aircraft were involved in a unit. That first interceptor unit was told to orbit over the western portion of Oahu. Compounding the vagueness, "three other units were scrambled and assumed battle stations around the island of Oahu." A unit of army Boston (A-20) light bombers was launched to aid in the intercept. All these aircraft were soon cluttering up the radar, their blips on the radarscopes intermingling. The fighters and the Bostons had intercepted each other. It was fortunate that none of the defenders shot down their friendly counterparts, because visibility was reported as poor. Once again, midair collisions were more of a threat than enemy aircraft.

Several reports came in from antiaircraft and coast artillery batteries on the exchange of gunfire with submarines and of aerial combats taking place overheard. The flying defenders aloft were shuttled from one location to another, but each time they reported no enemy aircraft to be found. Some marine aircraft armed with rockets were sent to search for the submarines, but found none. Four sub chasers raced to the locations of the reported submarines, but after an hour's search located no enemy boats.

After it became obvious that no enemy aircraft were threatening the island, one of the controllers informed his commander that he was sounding the all clear and notified the Aloha tower to sound that signal. Maj. Gen. Clarence Tinker, the commander of the army air forces in Hawaii, countermanded this order, and in fact, ordered all pursuit planes available to be made ready for immediate takeoff. At the time, four pursuit units were still in the air and all the other units had been on alert for over an hour. There were 139 fighters, including 26 marine and navy fighters, ready to take to the air in three minutes.

Finally, at 11:55 AM General Tinker called the control center to make it clear that, in the future, the all clear would not be sounded without his authorization. All the fighters were kept on alert until 12:30 PM, at which time they were allowed to relax to normal status.[40]

The afternoon *Honolulu Star-Advertiser* featured a one-column story on the front page of the March 7, 1942, edition:

Air Alert Sounds over Busy City at 11:28 [Actually, it was the All Clear that sounded at 11:28. Author.]

Army authorities announced that the air raid alarm was ordered sounded after defense units detected the approach of unidentified elements at sea.

At 10:22 this morning air raid alarms sounded over a busy city and Honolulu people by the tens of thousands took to shelters, trenches, basements and heavy-built buildings.

The all-clear signal was given at 11:28.

The alarm was officially announced, immediately as "precautionary," and it was also officially announced that this was not a drill.

Radio stations KGMB and KGU went off the air at 9:45 a.m. by order of Army authorities and it was announced at that time that the stations were ordered silenced as a precaution.

Invading airplanes might get bearings from radio station broadcasts, it is explained.

At about 10:15 a.m., all guards in Iolani palace, which houses the offices of the military and civilian governors, were ordered alerted with steel helmets and gas masks handy.

The police radio, which did not go off the air, notified all motor patrolmen and other officers to take their special posts immediately at the sounding of the air raid alarm.

Many schools were in session today and children were taken into air raid shelters.

Crowds which were downtown when the alarm was sounded took shelter in nearby buildings and the streets were cleared of all persons and motor vehicles except those having special authority to be abroad.

The streets were quickly cleared, with no disorder, confusion or apparent panic and equal order and celerity in getting to shelter were reported at schools and public buildings where numerous persons were congregated.[41]

Even though the air raid on March 7 had proven to be a false alarm, the armed forces on Hawaii had not calmed their fears of more attacks. A week later, at 9:43 AM on March 14, the army air defense center reported two unidentified planes about sixty miles southwest of Oahu and sounded the air raid alarm again. Two minutes later, the navy followed suit with its general quarters air raid alarm to the ships and installations in and around Pearl Harbor. The common lament went up with a sigh, "Here we go again!"

At 9:49 AM, the army information center said that an unidentified aircraft carrier was reported by one of her patrolling bombers southeast of Oahu at a distance of one hundred miles. It required another twenty minutes to unravel the error caused by a misunderstanding between the patrol bomber and the army controller who interpreted the word "carrier" for "bearing" in a ship position report.

Army bombers and fighters took off during the alert and many radar plots were reported of planes to the southwest of Oahu at distances ranging from thirty to seventy-five miles, but all these turned out to be false alarms. The same navy intelligence summary noted in passing that the USS *O'Brien* had arrived at French Frigate Shoals to relieve *Ballard*, the seaplane tender that had been on patrol there. The U.S. Navy was forcing the Japanese refueling submarines to keep their heads down and away from French Frigate Shoals.[42]

In fact, the Operation K follow-on attack originally scheduled for Q Day on March 6 had been cancelled by the initial delay in P Day (which had been delayed until March 4), plus the additional day required to repair the damaged hull of Hashizume's airplane on Jaluit. The planning of the follow-on attack had been unrealistic in the first place coming so close on the heels of the first attack. The crews were exhausted from the long flight and the schedule had not allowed for aircraft damage or any other needed maintenance. The planners back in Tokyo had recognized that the waning moon of March 6 would not be favorable for more night operations. The high command in Tokyo now had reconnaissance of Midway and Johnston Islands as its much more urgent priority.[43]

Rochefort and his Combat Intelligence Unit were able to score another success by partially decoding the messages ordering the 24th Kokutai (Air Group) in the Marshall Islands to conduct reconnaissance flights to Midway and Johnston Islands. This Kokutai was known to be operating four-engined flying boats (which the Americans assumed to be of the Mavis type, because the Type 2 Emily had just made its debut and they were not yet aware of its existence).[44]

An order for the Midway and Johnston Island reconnaissance missions came as a surprise to the 24th Kokutai on March 5, even before Hashizume had returned with Emily Y-71 to the seaplane base at Wotje. The order had requested that the missions be carried out on March 6, the next day. Both the crews were exhausted from their long mission, and both airplanes needed inspections, repairs, and maintenance before going out on another mission. The base at Wotje was in poor condition: There was a shortage of food and an epidemic of dengue fever among the maintenance personnel. Hashizume realized that it would not be possible to fly the reconnaissance missions until March 9. Higher headquarters reluctantly approved the necessary delay.[45]

The Combat Intelligence Unit on Oahu had intercepted all these messages. They could not decrypt all of the message contents, but their analysis was good enough to know that Midway and possibly some of the other bases in the Hawaiian area could expect the presence of Japanese airplanes around March 10. It also tipped off American intelligence that the Japanese were interested now in Midway Island.[46]

5

Photoreconnaissance Missions to Midway and Johnston Islands

When Lt. Hisao Hashizume and his crew, with the Emily (H8K) flying boat (Emily Y-71), finally made their return to the seaplane base on Wotje, there was great jubilation over the success of the long mission that they had completed. Hashizume taxied slowly to the anchoring buoys on the western side of the island, and shut down the engines. The anchoring party from the island base met the airplane in rubber boats and quickly secured the large plane, and greeted the weary flight crew with shouts of congratulations. The aviators climbed from the open hatches on the flying boat's hull, stepped carefully into the bobbing rubber boats, and were soon on the wide, sloping seaplane ramp. After three months of arduous preparation and training, the new flying boats and their crews had attacked Pearl Harbor again without even being threatened by the defense forces there. Even though the results of the bombing could not be known, they had been able to position their bombers over Oahu again, and the Americans had been unable to stop them.

The squadron commanding officer, Cdr. Toshio Yokoi, led the entire squadron in offering a sake toast to thank Hashizume, Ens. Shosuke Sasao, and their flight crewmembers for a job well done. Even with the miserable conditions on the island base, the morale of the flying boat squadron and the maintenance technicians based on Wotje had been given a tremendous boost from the second Hawaii mission.[1]

Back in Tokyo, decisions had already been made that would soon affect all these men. Adm. Isoroku Yamamoto had ordered his chief of staff Rear Adm. Matome Ugaki to "plan the second term strategy at once."[2] Ugaki was asked to submit his ideas for the Imperial Japanese Navy's (IJN's) next moves. His plans were consolidated and completed after a preliminary investigation that he and his staff conducted from January 11 through 14. They made a comprehensive study of the recent Japanese military and naval successes. At the same time, they attempted to anticipate what problems might arise in the upcoming actions. In his diary, Ugaki recorded his thoughts: "After June of this year, we should occupy Midway, Johnston and Palmyra, send our air force forward to these islands and dispatch the combined fleet with an occupying force to occupy Hawaii and at the same time bring the enemy fleet into decisive battle." This line of reasoning was exactly in tune with that of Admiral Yamamoto.[3]

The new interest in Midway created a problem for the IJN intelligence. They had few data on Midway except for outdated maps. Actually, the Japanese had hardly any data on what was going on in the defense build-up of any of the islands in American hands. The only information about what the Americans had done to improve island defenses was what had been observable from submarine periscopes from several miles offshore. Japanese naval intelligence desperately needed up-to-date photography that could be studied and analyzed to determine what the Americans had done to fortify the atoll islands. Surely, Midway's defenses had been bolstered since the island had been attacked on the first night of the Pacific War, but how many defending fighters were stationed there now? Did the atoll have radar? How many and what kind of antiaircraft guns had been added? Where were the guns placed on the atoll's islands? Were there heavier guns now on the island? How many troops were garrisoned there now? What strength would the Japanese need to overcome the Midway defenders? A high-priority request for photoreconnaissance went out to the flying boat squadrons in the Marshall Island bases, the only units in position and with enough range to accomplish the task.

Midway's defenses had indeed been increased significantly since the war had begun. Eastern Island now boasted three asphalt-topped coral-based runways ranging in length from fifty-three hundred feet to thirty-two hundred feet; each was three hundred feet wide. These facilities had been built by the 10th, 123rd, and 301st Naval Construction Battalions (SeaBees). Their work on Midway was just being completed as the war began.[4] Pan American Airways (Pan Am) had operated its famous Clipper flying boats with a stop at Midway until the first days of the war. Pan Am's facilities and seaplane ramp were on Sand Island facing the atoll's interior lagoon. This was now a base for the U.S. Navy's Catalina (PBY) flying boats. The marine garrison was the 6th Marine Defense Battalion that had replaced the 3rd Marine Defense Battalion on September 11, 1941. The 6th Marine Defense Battalion included a headquarters and headquarters battery, the 23rd Provisional Marine (Rifle) Companies, one 5-inch Artillery Group, two 7-inch Artillery Batteries, two 3-inch .50-caliber batteries, two 3-inch Antiaircraft Groups, four batteries of 37- and 20-mm guns, and two .30- and .50-caliber machine-gun batteries. Two companies of the 2nd Raider Battalion completed the marine complement of 34 officers and 750 enlisted men. A radar antenna and radar shack were located on the western edge of Sand Island and searchlights were placed at the most advantageous locations on both islands.[5]

Early in December, the maintenance technicians of Marine Air Group 21's three squadrons arrived on Midway to prepare for the delivery of eighteen Vindicator (SB2U-3) dive-bombers. A navy Catalina flying boat led these obsolescent machines to Midway from Pearl Harbor on a nine-hour and forty-five–minute flight—the longest overwater mass flight by single-engined aircraft at that time.[6] On December 25, 1941, the carrier *Saratoga* delivered the fighter airplanes originally intended for Wake Island to Midway—fourteen Buffalo (F2A-3) fighters of VMF-221. These elderly dive-bombers and fighters were all that were available on such short notice.

The Buffalo (F2A-3) fighter had been the U.S. Navy's first monoplane fighter when it entered the navy's inventory in 1938. The navy had quickly discovered that the Buffalo was cursed with a weak landing gear, engine cooling problems, and, in the later models, a heavy wing loading, making it unsuitable for aircraft carrier operation. When the superior

Wildcat (F4F) fighters became available to the navy, they were assigned to carrier fighter squadrons. The Marines inherited the portly Buffalo for land-based operation.

The export version of the Buffalo had been purchased from the United States by Finland and used with great success against Russian fighters and bombers in Finland's war with Russia in 1939. Several Finnish pilots became aces flying the Buffalo against the best Russian pilots and airplanes in that conflict. The newer Buffalo-3 models used by the Marines at Midway had been made heavier with added armor plating, fuel tank protection, and the installation of two synchronized .50-caliber machine guns in the nose cowling and two wing .50-caliber guns in place of one .30- and one .50-caliber synchronized machine guns. These modifications were believed to be improvements, but this added weight had an adverse affect on the later Buffalo's flight performance.[7]

The RAF had ordered the Buffalo to equip squadrons in the Far East and Burma. The IJNAF's fast, nimble Zero fighters had annihilated most of these. The Buffalo also equipped some Dutch fighter units in the East Indies and these were also quickly destroyed when they tangled with the Zeroes. At least nine ships were on their way to deliver twenty-one Dutch Buffalo fighters, but these were diverted to Australia. The Dutch fighters were quickly unloaded, assembled, and commandeered by the desperate USAAF. Somewhat mysteriously, these airplanes were called SB1A aircraft in official USAAF records, instead of being given a P designation (for Pursuit) like other army fighter airplanes. Some, if not all, were painted in standard U.S. Army olive drab and light gray camouflage and markings, with "U.S. Army" clearly showing on the underside of the wings. It is doubtful that these airplanes saw any combat in the hands of American pilots. By the middle of 1942, the Buffalo had been turned over to the Royal Australian Air Force (RAAF).[8]

On December 26 and 27, 1941, 864 civilian construction workers were evacuated from what was presumed to be an inevitable war zone. On January 25, 1942, the Japanese tested the Midway defenses when the submarine *I-173* surfaced and lobbed ten to fifteen shells into the lagoon, but it was driven under by return salvos from one of the atoll's three-inch batteries. On February 8, submarine *I-69* attempted to shell the atoll, then tried again two days later. Each time the sub was driven off by return fire from the Midway marine batteries or the Buffalo fighters armed with 100-pound bombs.[9] By March 10, 1942, the Marine Defense Battalion, the marine fighter and bomber squadrons, and the navy's Catalina units and their administrative and maintenance personnel boosted Midway's population to about 3,000 men.[10]

Johnston Island was of interest to the Japanese because it was even closer to Pearl Harbor than Midway, just 717 nautical miles (945 statute miles) southwest of Oahu. Johnston Island, at that time, actually consisted of two natural coral islands (Johnston Island and Sand Island). At just over five hundred acres, Johnston Island was the larger of the two and had been established as a seaplane base in August 1941. Dredging, reef blasting, land filling, and grading by the U.S. Navy had begun to clear coral heads out of the seaplane runway area and to enlarge the land area of the main island as early as 1936. This actually created two more small islands in the atoll, North Island and East Island. No land runway would be completed until December 1942, so no fighters were based at Johnston yet. Japanese submarines had shelled Johnston Island shortly after December 7. While the sub crews were surfaced, they could observe that construction work was going on at Johnston and gave limited reports of this activity, but only aerial photography would yield the type of information about Johnston's defenses that the Japanese needed.[11]

Palmyra Island was mentioned by Admiral Ugaki as the third island that should be taken by the Japanese to facilitate further attacks on Hawaii. Palmyra Island, one of the Line Islands, was made up of about fifty islets covered with dense vegetation, coconut trees, and balsa trees that stood up to 90 feet tall. It was located about halfway between Hawaii and American Samoa. The atoll's climate was equatorial: hot and rainy. An airstrip existed on the main island, measuring about 3,000 feet long and 200 feet wide, with a secondary strip only 150 feet wide. Two seaplane-landing areas were in the lagoon, 10,000 feet long by 650 feet wide.

Palmyra was important to the Japanese and the Americans, primarily because of its location about 850 nautical miles (1,150 statute miles) south of Pearl Harbor.[12]

The timing of the orders that came from the naval general staff (NGS) in Tokyo to the 24th Kokutai on Wotje requesting the immediate photoreconnaissance flights to Midway and Johnston Islands was considered unfeeling. The disregard for the weary crews created a rage of protest, even from the head of the unit, Commander Yokoi. The only aircraft available for such missions (and the authorities in Tokyo were aware of this) were Emily (H8K) Y-71 and Emily Y-72, just returned from their thirty-five and one-half hour mission, with thirty-two of those hours spent in the air. The only crews trained to fly the airplanes were those of Lieutenant Hashizume and Ensign Sasao. Every member of the 24th Kokutai wondered how the higher headquarters could be so inconsiderate as to order these exhausted crews back into the air on such a dangerous mission. What was the urgency behind such orders? The second mission against Hawaii had been cancelled because the conditions could not be met for Q Day and because the crews would be too tired to be effective in such a demanding mission.

One squadron member said later, "it was like a dash of cold water in the face." With the Americans now on full alert all over the Hawaiian Island chain, the missions would be extremely dangerous. They would place both flying boats over enemy islands, alone without fighter escort and in full daylight.[13]

Hashizume read the orders over carefully. He looked at each member of his weary crew, and sighed as he realized that his men would rely on him to make a decision. Hashizume believed that he really had no choice. He exchanged a knowing look with Ensign Sasao, and accepted the orders with a characteristic smile, saying, "Since the order is given, I will go."

Ensign Sasao's reaction was not recorded, but Hashizume quickly added that he would take the longer mission to Midway, leaving the shorter mission to Johnston Island for Sasao and his Emily Y-72 crew. Hashizume went to work immediately with the navigators to plan the mission and dispatched the remainder of his crew to ready the airplane. Hashizume submitted his proposed flight plans to Midway and Johnston Islands for approval by headquarters, Fourth Fleet.

The distance from Wotje to Midway is 1,400 nautical miles (1,620 statute miles). At a cruising speed of 160 knots (184 miles per hour), the flight to Midway would require nine or ten hours with a similar time for the return leg, depending on the winds encountered. The distance to Johnston Island was only a little shorter—1,160 nautical miles (1,340 statute miles), requiring a flight time of slightly over seven hours each way. Because the purpose of the missions was photoreconnaissance, each flying boat would be over the targets at a planned altitude of twenty-one thousand feet—close to the airplane's service ceiling of twenty-five thousand feet. Headquarters, Fourth Fleet, approved the flight plans. As a result of the unit commander's appeal, however, there was one additional day of rest for the crews indicated. The missions were to be flown on March 10 (Tokyo time). This would place the airplanes over Midway and Johnston Islands on March 9, local time. No refueling by submarines would be required, because the missions were shorter. No bombs would be carried this time— just cameras—which allowed more fuel on board. A full amount of ammunition for the airplane's cannons and machine guns would be loaded, however. They would concern themselves about flying a photoreconnaissance mission to Palmyra Atoll later, because this was not yet mentioned in the orders from Tokyo. Besides, no other aircraft or crews were available for a mission to Palmyra. The distances to each island were comfortably within the range capabilities of the long-legged Emily.[14]

The crew composition was changed on both aircraft, to increase overall combat flying experience, but Lieutenant Hashizume was still the mission commander and lead pilot on Emily Y-71, and Ensign Sasao again flew Emily Y-72.

Just as they had done a few days earlier, the crews boarded their aircraft from rubber boats, completed their preflight checks, and started the engines. At nearly midnight on March 9, Hashizume raised his hand to the top of the cockpit and pushed his four overhead throttles forward to begin his takeoff run. Once airborne, the flying boat banked gently and took up its heading for Midway as it climbed. On most Japanese multiengined aircraft, the pilot occupied the right seat and the copilot sat in the left seat. On some Japanese bombers, the mission commander would not occupy the pilot's seat but had his own position in the airplane, usually just behind the pilot and usually slightly elevated. In some cases, the mission commander might not even be a rated pilot, but he was the overall commander of a formation of aircraft, usually because of his rank.[15] On the earlier March 3 flight, after the two airplanes had joined in formation, Lieutenant Hashizume relinquished the pilot's seat to CPO Shiichi Ogawa and took the mission commander's seat behind the pilot. Hashizume and the two other pilots on board traded duties throughout the long flight to relieve the monotony, with Hashizume handling the landings, takeoffs, the dangerous refueling with the submarine, and the bomb run itself. On the flight to Midway, Hashizume had briefed his commander that, because only two pilots would be on board for this mission, he would remain in the pilot's seat for the entire flight. In the meantime, Ensign Sasao launched his mission shortly after Hashizume's Emily Y-71 lifted off the lagoon at Wotje. Sasao in Emily Y-72 followed a more easterly course toward Johnston Island.[16]

Earlier in the day on March 9, Lt. Cdr. Joseph J. Rochefort at the Combat Intelligence Unit had made another startlingly accurate analysis of decrypted messages. His intelligence specialists could read enough of the messages between Tokyo and the seaplane units based in the Marshall Islands to know that something was up and that it would happen in the next day or two. The radio traffic indicated that Japanese attention was focused on Midway and another island (that he suspected was Johnston Island, but could not be sure). Rochefort had the message center at headquarters, Fourteenth Naval District, send a warning message to Midway: "Possibility exists attack by enemy flying boats tonight or tomorrow night."[17]

Rochefort believed that, because the attempted March 3 attack had taken place at night, the attack on Midway would also be at night. The messages that he and his staff had intercepted and partially decrypted did not reveal that the mission purpose was only photoreconnaissance, nor that it would be different in any way from the bombing attack on Oahu. Thus warned, the island defenders' radar antenna at Midway Island was keeping its vigil in all directions and all units went on full alert. The marine fighter pilots based there had been training in radar intercepts at a feverish pace. They had also practiced launching as many aircraft as soon as possible in the shortest time possible, to reduce the chance of any airplanes, fighters, or bombers being destroyed on the ground. The attack on Oahu the previous week provided a strong incentive to master the intercept techniques required for working successfully with radar control. The Marines knew that these techniques would be useful in fending off the attacks that they believed were sure to come.

At 10:37 AM Midway time on March 10, the radar's electronic eye picked up a target forty-three miles from Midway on a bearing almost due west. Within one minute, air raid sirens on the island sounded. Within two minutes, Lt. Col. W. J. Wallace, commanding officer of Marine Aircraft Group 22, was in the command post. Seven minutes after the radar target had been sighted, twenty-seven marine fighters and scout bombers had cleared the Midway runway. Not only were the defending fighters airborne, the Marines were making sure that none of their flyable airplanes would be caught on the ground. At 10:46 AM the marine fighters were ordered by the task group commander to split into high and low patrols and to stand by for further orders.

Hashizume's navigation team had apparently missed Midway slightly, because the radar showed him to the west of the island, proceeding in a northerly direction with the distance increasing. It is possible, of course, that this was a ploy to approach the island from an unexpected direction. Like the attack on Oahu the week before, the Japanese had no way of knowing that they were being tracked by radar. In any case, the Emily crew either caught their error or deliberately changed direction because the flying boat made a wide turn directly toward the island. Its distance began decreasing rapidly on a bearing of 280 degrees. The photographic run over Midway was originally planned for twenty-one thousand feet, but cloud cover required a descent to a much lower altitude. This suited Lieutenant Hashizume and his crew, because they felt safer nearer the surface.

The marine fighters were ordered by Colonel Wallace to orbit on that bearing of 280 degrees twenty miles offshore and await attack orders.[18] The marine fighter aircraft awaiting Hashizume's flying boat were the venerable Buffalo. Of the Buffalo's fighting capabilities, Capt. Philip R. White, a marine Buffalo pilot who survived the Battle of Midway, said without hesitation that, "Any commander who orders pilots out in an F2A [Buffalo] should consider the pilots lost before leaving the ground."[19] On the morning of March 10, though, the Marines in Buffalo of VMF-221 Squadron, waiting west of Midway, were about to experience one of their rare victories.

At 11:01 AM, the height-finding radar on Midway acquired the Emily, now fifty miles away at nine thousand feet. The marine group commander ordered a flight of four fighters, led by Capt. James L. Neefus, to intercept and investigate the target. Four minutes later, Captain Neefus shouted "Tallyho!" after he sighted the flying boat five miles away at nine thousand feet. He could make out the Rising Sun insignia and could tell that it was a large four-engined flying boat. Colonel Wallace ordered him to intercept and attack.[20]

Ten pairs of eyes had been anxiously scanning the sky on board the Japanese flying boat. The oncoming flight of four stubby-winged Buffalo fighters was apparently spotted just as the marine pilots saw the Emily.

Captain Neefus led his three other fighters, flown by 1st Lt. Charles W. Somers, Jr., 2nd Lt. Francis P. McCarthy, and marine Gunner Robert L. Dickey, as they maneuvered for the first firing pass toward the Emily. The flying boat's alert gunners warned their pilot of the marine fighters' relative positions because the Emily turned away to the southwest and pushed over into a steep thirty degrees nose-down dive. Because of their hull configuration, flying boats lacked gun positions (like the ball turret on the bottom of the land-based army Flying Fortress) to protect their vulnerable undersides. Therefore, the normal tactic for flying boats was to dive to an extremely low altitude so that the attacking fighters could not get underneath the airplane. The disadvantage to this tactic was that, in many cases, a panicked pilot who put a flying boat into too steep a dive caused actual structural damage to the aircraft because of the extreme speeds and stresses of the dive. In addition, the attacking fighter pilots could correct their aim by watching splash patterns from their bullets striking the ocean below the target aircraft. The Emily did have a gun hatch in the lower aft part of the hull, but it was equipped with only a 7.7-mm machine gun. Hashizume was diving for the ocean surface to protect his airplane and crew as best he could.

Captain Neefus was having some difficulty gaining on the fast flying boat, even in a dive. He made one firing pass from a high side attack while in the dive. His right wingman, Lieutenant McCarthy, followed two hundred yards behind with his own firing pass. McCarthy saw trails of smoke coming from each of the flying boat's two outboard engines. He noted that his own diving airspeed was 240 knots (276 miles per hour) and that he was barely gaining on the diving seaplane. The Emily was trying to reach a cloud layer at three thousand feet. Lieutenant McCarthy crossed behind the Emily as he noticed another Buffalo making a firing pass. He saw the other fighter peel away.[21]

Lieutenant Somers aimed his fighter toward the left side of the diving Emily in an attempt to bracket it between the attacking fighters and to prevent the seaplane's escape. As he began his firing run, a fighter ahead of him finished its firing attack and broke away sharply. He delayed his pass until the target seaplane broke out of a small cloud, and followed it down to four hundred feet where he encountered another small cloud. The fleeing bomber was still in a rather steep dive and started a left turn when both the target and the attacking fighter entered clouds again. He saw no telltale flashes or tracers of return fire from the gun turrets of the Japanese bomber.[22]

Gunner Dickey, the only enlisted pilot in the flight, had turned and tried to get into position for a high side or overhead firing pass. He switched his engine supercharger to high blower and pushed his throttle forward for maximum power, but still had difficulty in closing the range to the fleeing bomber. In the heat of the chase, he lost sight of the other airplanes in his formation. Just as the Emily was about to reenter the low clouds, Dickey made a right-side approach and delivered a burst of fire. During the attack, he came in close astern of his quarry, and drifted down and to the left of the bomber. He tried to stay with his target as the Emily entered the undercast, turning sharply to the right to stay on its tail. Suddenly, he felt a sharp pain in his left arm. Seeing a hole in his windshield, realized that he had been hit by one of the flying boats' turret gunners. Dickey made a diving turn to escape the return fire and came out under the clouds at five hundred feet above the ocean. He used his right hand to place his useless left arm in his lap and tried to determine the most probable course for a return to Midway. His engine was now running rough and his windshield was covered with oil, but he radioed his flight leader that he thought that he could make it back to the island.[23]

Captain Neefus was maneuvering to set himself up for his second firing pass when he saw the flying boat enter the cloud layer followed by a firing Buffalo fighter. He saw no return fire coming from the Emily's turret guns. Pulling up above the cloud layer, Neefus flew on for about three minutes on the seaplane's last observed heading, waiting for the enemy airplane to emerge from the clouds. He could not see any other airplanes, friendly or enemy. The sky was empty above the clouds. He reversed course and dove under the cloud layer, hoping to sight his wingman and the other two airplanes of the second element. As Neefus emerged from the cloud layer, he saw a large fire on the water five miles ahead. He circled the black smoke and flame for a few minutes, but could not determine what was burning. He was worried that it might be one of the fighters of his own flight that had been shot down or had crashed. Neefus radioed a report of the fire to the command post at Midway. Climbing for a return to the island, he spotted two Buffalo off his right wing. Joining up with them, he recognized his wingman, Lieutenant McCarthy and Lieutenant Somers.[24]

The command post ordered the three fighters to continue their patrols south and west of Midway, after hearing Gunner Dickey reporting his safe landing at Midway. Dickey had considerable trouble maneuvering his control stick, throttle, landing gear, flap, and trim controls with one hand, but he managed to land his shot-up Buffalo at Midway safely. An ambulance met him at the runway and the medics helped him out of the cockpit of his fighter. The flight surgeon removed an armor-piercing 7.7-mm machine-gun bullet from Dickey's broken left arm and evacuated him to the naval hospital on Sand Island of the Midway Islands. Seven bullets had hit his airplane: one through the tail wheel bearing, three through the fuselage skin, one through an engine cylinder, one through the engine firewall, and the one through the windshield that had hit his left arm.[25]

Lieutenant Hashizume and his crew had perished in the crash and fire of Emily Y-71 in the ocean forty-five miles west of Midway Island. Hashizume was thirty-one years old when he died. On Wotje, the vigil by the radio went on well past the time that Hashizume and the crew of Emily Y-71 were expected to return. Finally, it was obvious that Hashizume would not be coming back. His friends in the 24th Kokutai on Wotje believed that he had a premonition of his death. When they went to his quarters to prepare his belongings for return to his wife in Japan, his squadron mates found his room in the officers' quarters spotlessly cleaned and all his clothing and personal belongings neatly arranged for shipment. As was the custom of Japanese fighting men during World War II, he had prepared fingernail clippings and short locks of hair, with a poignant farewell letter to his wife, to be included in a package of his personal effects. Fellow members of his squadron wept openly when they were forced to acknowledge that he would never return from the mission to Midway Island.[26]

With Lieutenant Hashizume's death, Japan had lost its top flying boat expert. The men who lost their lives with Hashizume that day were the most experienced flying boat crewmembers in the Imperial Japanese Naval Air Force (IJNAF). They had trained together for years. Just as it is impossible to know which of the Japanese gunners hit Gunner Dickey's fighter, it was impossible to determine which or how many of the marine pilots participated in shooting down Emily Y-71.

Captain Neefus, Lieutenants Somers and McCarthy, and Gunner Dickey each received a bottle of bourbon whiskey and congratulations from Colonel Wallace.[27] Admiral Bloch, the commander of the Fourteenth Naval District, recommended all four pilots and Commander Rochefort for medal awards. Captain Neefus was awarded the Navy Cross, with Lieutenants Somers and McCarthy each receiving the Distinguished Flying Cross. Gunner Dickey also received the Distinguished Flying Cross and a Purple Heart for his wound.[28]

Commander Rochefort was recommended for a Distinguished Service Medal, but a cryptic memo turned up regarding this recommendation. It was handwritten from "Pfeiffer" to "Murphy" and was apparently included with other correspondence concerning the medal award. It read, "These two communications should be handled together. I can't see Rochefort's part on the evidence presented. The actual attack took place just about as far from the time he predicted it was possible to do. Suggest asking Midway whether the message affected their readiness. If the answer is 'Yes'—more power to Rochefort and he should be recognized. [Inititaled "P."]"[29] It is not clear just who the writer and the recipient of the memo were, but their correspondence apparently had some effect. (Rochefort later hinted that Murphy might have been Capt. Vincent R. Murphy on the planning staff. Captain Murphy apparently resented Rochefort taking over some of the functions of planning.)[30]

Professional jealousies had existed in the competitive armed forces for hundreds of years in all armies and navies. The new war that had been thrust on these service members only caused more desperate scrambling to receive credit (or deny credit) for any outstanding achievements. Promotions were based on these achievements, along with the number of medals for recognition of achievement or heroic deeds. For whatever reason, Rochefort did not receive the medal, even though it is obvious that his warning did let the Marines on Midway know to increase their alertness. Through their increased awareness of a threat, the fighter defenders of Midway, with radar guidance, were able to shoot down the intruder.

Ensign Sasao and his crew in Emily Y-72 flew to Johnston Island with no problems. Sasao's Emily was over the American-held island at 10:30 AM on a clear day, but Johnston had not yet been equipped with a radar station for protection. There were no waiting fighters based there and Sasao's flying boat was not molested by antiaircraft fire at twenty-one thousand feet. His crew returned safely to Wotje with many excellent photographs of the island and its facilities. Ensign Sasao was told that Lieutenant Hashizume had sent only one brief message: "Enemy in sight." This broadcast probably went out when the crew of Emily Y-71 sighted the approach of the defending marine Buffalo fighters. No other word had been received from the flight to Midway and it was assumed that Emily Y-71 and its crew had met with enemy fighter opposition. The Japanese did not learn the true fate of Hashizume's crew until after the war.[31]

The American forces were still not aware of the new Emily's existence even though marine pilots had shot one down. Each of the pilots had described the flying boat as having twin rudders, which was the configuration of the earlier Mavis (H6K), an airplane that they knew existed because they had studied its shape and size in photographs and models in their aircraft recognition classes. It may be said that the Mavis was the airplane that they expected to see, because they recognized that they had shot down a large four-engined flying boat. In the swift movement and blurred confusion of aerial combat, it is not possible to observe every detail. American forces did know that Japanese flying boats were quite active then and they were appearing all over the islands of the Hawaiian chain and the central Pacific. They knew also that large four-engined seaplanes were based in the Marshall Islands. U.S. Navy intelligence officers now had deduced how the Japanese were able to bring off such long range raids successfully—by refueling them with submarines at sea, or at least in the calmer waters of atoll lagoons. The intelligence "Summary of the Situation" for March 11, 1942, carried the comment: "Indications are that renewed attempts at long range bombing of Hawaiian Islands by flying boats may be attempted."[32]

American forces remained on high alert now that the Japanese flying boats were appearing so often in so many places. Because the intelligence officers knew how the Japanese were able to carry out these overflights, they became expected almost on a daily basis. The accounts of false alarms of air raids on March 7 and March 14 were related earlier (see Chapter 4). Later, two U.S. Navy seaplane tenders were stationed continuously at French Frigate Shoals and patrols by Catalina flying boats were launched from that area. The navy ordered the atoll's lagoon to be mined to deny the area to Japanese submarines. Visits by patrolling surface craft were also increased.

Because minefields cannot distinguish between friend and enemy, the U.S. patrol boat YP-277 ran into this minefield by mistake and was blown up. The Japanese could understand this casualty, because their own anti-submarine defensive minefields had accounted for six Japanese ships thus far, totaling thirty thousand tons of shipping.[33]

After returning from his successful reconnaissance flight to Johnston Island, Ensign Sasao's crew of Emily Y-72 was the only operational Emily unit in the area. Production of the next new Emily flying boats would not be completed for months and crews would need training to fly them. The 24th Kokutai ambitiously issued orders for reconnaissance flights to be conducted over Palmyra, Fiji, Samoa, New Caledonia, Brisbane, and Midway (again), but with only one Emily and one trained flight crew, all these missions were impossible to carry out. The older shorter-ranging Mavis aircraft had to maintain their own patrols from the Marshall Islands and the many other seaplane bases scattered over the vast Pacific.

Ensign Sasao was ordered to return immediately with Emily Y-72 to the Yokosuka Air Group in Japan. He departed Jaluit on March 18, arriving back in Japan on March 25.[34] This was one of the earliest indications that the IJN was finally beginning to realize that combat crew expertise and experience were valuable assets that should not be squandered. Ensign Sasao was assigned as an instructor at Yokosuka, teaching other pilots and crews how to fly the new Emily flying boats just beginning to come off the production line. He was also instrumental in the development of the transport version of the Emily. Sasao remained at Yokosuka until March 1944.[35]

Even with the loss of Lieutenant Hashizume, his crew, and Emily Y-71, the Japanese were not discouraged from making plans for more Operation K–type attacks on Hawaii. The IJN was quite pleased with their new weapon and its capabilities. As more of the flying boats became available, and more new crews were trained to fly them, there were plans to revisit Midway and Hawaii many times in the near future.

6

The Doolittle-Halsey Raid and the Battle of the Coral Sea

On the first day of the New Year 1942, Vice Adm. Matome Ugaki, Adm. Isoroku Yamamoto's chief of staff, made this entry in his diary to record his thoughts on the surprising Japanese achievements: "It has been only twenty-five days since the war started, yet operations have been progressing smoothly and we have enough reason to hope for completion of the first stage of the war before the end of March. Then what will come next?"[1]

Admiral Ugaki was acknowledged as one of the Imperial Japanese Navy's (IJN's) top experts in strategy. The fact that he even asked the question points out that the Japanese had plunged into the war with no real long-range strategic vision of how it would ultimately be carried out, and that the Japanese really had many plans for the second phase of the war that had been thrust on them before they had an opportunity to prepare for their next moves. They were perplexed by their own stunning successes thus far in the war. Japan's urgent desire to secure a supply of oil had become foremost in the initial war strategy with little regard to the inherent risks. Sparse consideration had been devoted to what would follow, when and if success was achieved. The Japanese planners knew that the timing was not right for them to begin the war with the Allied powers, but they also knew that time was running out for them. Time was on the side of the Allies, not the Japanese. They believed that they had been forced to initiate the conflict.[2] The military planners had been able to convince the emperor that launching the war was necessary, but they failed to adequately plan for how the war would come to a conclusion favorable for the Japanese. The IJN had initially seen its war objectives in somewhat simplistic terms, with its Pacific War evolving in three stages. The first stage would be the attack on the Pacific Fleet in Pearl Harbor, with other naval and military forces destroying enemy ships and units as they conquered the territories in what they termed the Southern Area—the Philippines, Malaya, and the Dutch East Indies.

Two weeks after Ugaki wrote in his diary, Admiral Yamamoto directed him to come up with the navy's next tasks during the second stage of operations.

The second stage would be the completion of building bases in a sizeable perimeter extending from the Kurile Islands through Wake Island, the Marshall Islands, the Caroline Islands, the Mariana Islands, the Gilbert Islands, the Bismarck Islands, northern New Guinea, the Dutch East Indies, and Malaya. Of course, Wake Island had been an American possession; the Gilberts and Malaya were British. The Bismarcks and New Guinea were Australian property. The Japanese believed that the taking of these posts would be relatively easy.

The third stage would be the consolidation of these gains, with the interception and destruction of any Allied forces that threatened the perimeter.

These acts of attrition, the Japanese believed, would wear down the American will to continue the war. The Japanese could then dominate Burma and the Indian Ocean, perhaps even India itself, as Adolf Hitler's Operation Orient had envisioned. The success of the Pearl Harbor attack was of prime importance to this strategy. The Japanese believed that if the American fleet was not destroyed, the second and third stages would be impossible.[3]

The Japanese armed forces could not agree on their next objectives. As stated earlier, the Imperial Japanese Army (IJA) and IJN hated each other almost more than they hated their American, British, Dutch, and Chinese opponents. Their goals, ambitions, and plans for conducting the war were completely at odds. The organization of the Japanese armed forces was somewhat responsible for this situation. Before the war, the emperor had been the supreme commander of the Japanese armed forces under the Meiji Constitution, declared on February 11, 1889. For wartime only, an imperial general headquarters (IGHQ) was set up to conduct operational and strategic matters. The IGHQ consisted of two departments: a navy department and an army department, each independent of the other, with no chief of staff. The two departments rarely met.

In 1937, an IGHQ-cabinet liaison conference was established to conduct meetings in the presence of the emperor to receive imperial blessings for policy decisions prepared by his advisors. The emperor himself usually did not speak at these conferences. His silence was always taken as consent, even though he could have changed the course of all Japanese military and naval operations with a single sentence. All during the war, the Japanese government operated under a cabinet system, based on the emperor's decrees. The cabinet system had no power over command and operation of the armed forces because the heads of the army and navy—the powerful direct advisors to the emperor—handled these functions. The Diet (Japanese Parliament) could only vote on the annual defense budget, with no other voice in military or naval affairs.[4]

The Germans urged the Japanese to either attack the Russians in Manchuria or to invade India—or both. Either action by the Japanese would have been of great assistance to the Germans, but the navy considered that its primary enemy was the U.S. Navy; the army was preoccupied with China but was maintaining an uneasy front with the Russians in Manchuria. The IJA was willing to attack the Russians if the Siberian Army moved to the eastern front in Europe. The army could not gain approval for such a campaign and those plans were dropped.[5] The baffled Germans were not aware of the animosity that existed between the IJA and IJN. The Germans did not understand that there was no superior coordinating command similar to their own armed forces high command (OKW) that served to coordinate national war objectives.[6]

The Japanese had accomplished the first stage of the Pacific War almost too easily. They were as surprised as the rest of the world that by early

February 1942 the Stage 1 goals had been accomplished. The army and navy disagreed violently about their next objectives. One group of IJA generals wanted to push west by taking Ceylon (now Sri Lanka) and eventually swarm through India and the Middle East to link up with Germany's General Rommel in the Near East. The IJA had been worried about Russia, but since Hitler's assault against Russia those concerns had decreased. Surely the Russians would not attack the Japanese on a second front while engaged on another front with an advancing German Army. The IJN's general staff wanted to move south to isolate Australia by taking the Solomon Islands, Samoa, and Fiji. Only Yamamoto's combined fleet headquarters planning mentions the Midway Islands.

In keeping with the rivalry between the deck and desk sailors, even the naval general staff (NGS) (the desk sailors) balked at the idea of taking Midway. The islands were distant and shore-based air support would not be available for an attack on Midway, yet Midway was well within the range of American Flying Fortress (B-17) and Liberator bombers based on Hawaii. It would require a great deal of shipping to keep it supplied. Yamamoto's proposed June deadline made it an unpopular option. The main reason that it was even on the table was that Yamamoto wanted it. The admiral was absolutely unshakable in his belief that unless victory could be obtained quickly by the destruction of the American fleet, Japan would become involved in a long war that the country could not hope to win. He realized that Japanese sea power was at its zenith and was convinced that he had an opportunity to defeat the U.S. fleet. He was idolized in Japan since his successful initial attack on Pearl Harbor. This almost guaranteed that the NGS could not and would not stand up against him. Yamamoto believed that his nation should expand its perimeters toward the east by eliminating Midway as the closest American base. He yearned for a strategic triumph over the Americans. He also recognized the threat from the Aleutian Islands and added an attack on those islands to the Midway plan. He would use the Aleutians attack as a decoy to draw American defenders away from Midway while his main force attacked that atoll. To underscore his refusal to compromise on his Midway plan, he threatened to resign, as he had threatened when promoting his initial Pearl Harbor attack plan.[7]

The interservice and intraservice rivalry died hard. The squabbling was still going on because the NGS wanted to delay the Midway attack for another month. To make his plan more acceptable, Admiral Yamamoto promised that the Fiji-Samoan operation would be the next step following the assault on Midway. Reluctantly, the NGS finally gave the plan its blessing on April 5.[8]

Any objections to the Midway operation evaporated on April 18, 1942, when Lt. Col. James H. Doolittle's Mitchell bombers swept in from the sea to bomb targets in Tokyo and other major Japanese cities. The sixteen American twin-engined medium army bombers had been launched from the aircraft carrier USS *Hornet* six hundred miles from Japan.[9]

The idea for such a daring raid had stemmed from President Franklin D. Roosevelt's urging his military and naval chiefs of staff to conduct a bombing raid of any sort on the home islands of Japan as soon as possible to boost the sagging morale of the American people and the Allies. Questions about launching larger twin-engined airplanes from aircraft carriers were already being asked by army and navy planning staffs for other operations: Could the larger army aircraft be operated from the navy's carriers?

Several months earlier, on January 10, Capt. Francis S. Low, a submariner on Adm. Ernest J. King's staff, approached King with an idea for bombing Japan. Admiral King listened to Low's proposal and told him to confer with Capt. Donald B. Duncan, King's air operations officer, after cautioning both to maintain the utmost secrecy on their findings. Captain Duncan quickly informed Low that the twin-engined bombers then available could not land on the carriers, but perhaps could take off from the carriers. The army's bombers under consideration were the old Bolo (B-18), the Dragon (B-23), the Boston (A-20), the Mitchell (B-25), and the Marauder (B-26).

After five days, Duncan came up with a thirty-page hand-written analysis that chose the Mitchell as the only bomber for the job. With extra gas tanks, it could make a two thousand–mile flight with a 1-ton bomb load. Admiral King gave his approval, if Gen. Hap Arnold of the U.S. Army Air Force (USAAF) went along with the plan. General Arnold liked the plan and immediately chose Colonel Doolittle to lead the project. Doolittle was a famous racing and test pilot who was used to doing almost impossible things with airplanes. Doolittle was not only an experienced pilot, but also a pilot with masters and doctoral degrees from the Massachusetts Institute of Technology in aeronautical engineering. He had conducted extensive research on aircraft performance and instrument flight. Doolittle agreed that the Mitchell was the only airplane that met all the mission's requirements and began choosing pilots and crews for the raid. The navy selected the new aircraft carrier, the USS *Hornet,* skippered by Capt. Marc A. Mitscher, for the job.[10]

On February 3, two Mitchells were loaded aboard the *Hornet* at Norfolk, Virginia, but even Mitscher and the army flight crews were not told the real purpose of the successful experimental launches of the bombers from the carrier deck. The army pilots participating in the experiment were surprised that the bombers could get off the carrier deck with room to spare.[11]

Modifications to twenty-four Mitchell model-B bombers were begun immediately, using the top priorities authorized by General Arnold. The plans originally called for eighteen airplanes to be used, with six spares available for the mission. Aircraft modifications, crew selection, and training had to be completed by April 1.

Colonel Doolittle, working with his navy counterparts, drew up the plans for the mission. They hoped to take the bombers within four hundred to five hundred miles of the coast of Japan, and launch from the south-southwest to proceed directly to targets selected in the Tokyo-Yokohama, Nagoya, and Osaka-Kobe areas. The Mitchells would be launched from the carrier at night to arrive over their targets just after dawn. The bombers would approach Japan at a low level to avoid being picked up by radar. Doolittle believed that a daylight attack would guarantee easier target identification and better bombing accuracy. After hitting their targets, the bombers would return toward a southeasterly direction. Once well clear of the Japanese coast, the airplanes would turn to proceed westerly to specified airports equipped with radio homing beacons in China. After refueling, they would reform at the base at Chunking.

Each airplane would carry about eleven hundred gallons of fuel, enabling a range of twenty-four hundred miles. The bomb load would consist of two 500-pound demolition bombs and as near as possible to 1,000 pounds of incendiary bombs. The demolition bombs would be dropped before the incendiaries were let go. It was decided later that the bomb load would be three demolition bombs and 500 pounds of incendiaries.[12]

After all the necessary alterations had been made to the bombers, they were flown to the Alameda Naval Air Station, California, where sixteen of them were loaded aboard the *Hornet*. Task Force 16.2 (the *Hornet*, the cruisers *Nashville* and *Vincennes*, four destroyers, and an oiler) departed San Francisco Bay on April 2. Adm. William Halsey, heading Task Force 16.1 in the carrier USS *Enterprise*, with the cruisers *Salt Lake City* and *Northampton*, also escorted by four destroyers and an oiler, left Pearl Harbor on April 7. The task forces came together under the command of Admiral Halsey on April 12 at the international dateline well to the north of the Midway Islands. The two tankers were supposed to refuel the fleet when they had reached a point eight hundred miles east of Japan, and head back with the destroyers to Pearl Harbor while the carriers and their cruiser escorts proceeded to the launch point.[13]

The arrangements for the radio navigation beacons, airfields, and refueling in China were not going well. Because of secrecy, the authorities in China did not understand the urgency of their part in the mission. Generalissimo Chiang Kai Shek was not enthusiastic because he knew the Japanese would wreak massive retaliation on any Chinese who helped the American aviators.

While the American armada was plowing through bad weather, American forces on Bataan in the Philippines surrendered to the Japanese on April 9. The holdouts on the island of Corregidor in Manila harbor were battered incessantly by Japanese artillery. The situation in the Philippines was hopeless. Burma, followed by Sumatra, had fallen the month before, and the Japanese had taken over ninety-eight thousand Allied troops as prisoners in the Netherlands East Indies. America was in its darkest period in history.

Guarding the sea approaches to Japan were about fifty radio-equipped fishing boats that doubled as an early warning surveillance network, unknown to American intelligence. At 7:38 AM on April 18, a *Hornet* look-out spotted one of the fishing boat patrol vessels fewer than ten miles away by. A *Hornet* radio operator intercepted a message in Japanese that had originated nearby. The Japanese ship, now only six miles from the task force, was sunk by gunfire from the cruiser *Nashville,* but not before the word had been flashed to Japan that American aircraft carriers were 650 miles off the coast, headed for Japan.[14]

Admiral Halsey was forced to make an unpleasant decision. He could not risk losing the two precious aircraft carriers, so he decided that the army bombers would have to be jettisoned over the side of the carriers or launched early so that the carriers could withdraw from Japanese waters. Colonel Doolittle concurred with the decision that his bombers would be launched immediately. He led the force off the carrier deck with 620 miles to go to Tokyo. Each bomber left the deck successfully, although none of the pilots, including Doolittle, had ever made a carrier takeoff. By launching early, they would use up precious fuel, but each crew believed that they could still make the increased distance to China.[15]

Admiral Halsey was aware that Mavis (H6K) flying boats had been launched to find his fleet, but they failed to locate the American ships. Halsey said later that they had tracked the Japanese flying boats on radar and he was tempted to unleash fighters to go after them; he decided that it would be better not to risk revealing his position, however.

Halsey was also supposed to have signaled Washington when Doolittle and his bombers had launched. This was to be relayed to Chunking to let them know that the bombers were on their way, to alert the air defense net in China, and to have them turn on their homing radio beacons at the proper time. For unexplained reasons, the message was never sent. Doolittle said later that perhaps Halsey was still concerned about revealing his position by broadcasting. Halsey had reason to be concerned because Rochefort's Fleet Radio Unit, Pacific (FRUPac) at Pearl Harbor learned that

Admiral Nagumo's *Kido Butai* was now out of the Indian Ocean and could be searching for the Halsey task force.[16]

The Japanese, unaware that the carriers had launched twin-engined bombers, expected an attack by single-engined carrier aircraft with much shorter range. The Japanese believed that the carriers would have to approach to within two hundred miles to launch aircraft, so they felt no sense of urgency. They planned to send out several Mavis flying boats to patrol the area from which the Americans would come. They believed that the attack would not come until the next day, at the earliest, so considered that there was plenty of time to get ready for defense of the home islands.[17]

By coincidence, Tokyo had announced that it would conduct its first air raid drill on Saturday, April 18. A group of Japanese fighters engaged in mock dogfights over the city and barrage balloons were raised and lowered for practice. As an example of the animosity between Japan's armed services, the IJN knew that a threat was slowly approaching their shores, but did not inform the army's air defense commander. At noon, the exercise was nearly over and the barrage balloons were lowered for the last time. At 12:20 PM Tokyo time, the Mitchells swept over the city, dropping the first American bombs on Japan. Eleven Mitchells hit their primary targets; four diverted to secondary targets; and one was forced to jettison its bombs when it was attacked by Japanese fighters.[18]

None of the Mitchells made it to their planned destination airfields in China. One bomber, low on fuel, diverted to Vladivostok in Siberia and the Russians interned the crew and their airplane. The other fifteen crews were forced to bail out or to crash-land their bombers when they ran low on fuel. Doolittle believed that he would be court-martialed because all sixteen airplanes were lost in the raid. Instead, he was later promoted two ranks to brigadier general and awarded the Medal of Honor by President Roosevelt.

The Japanese captured eight American flyers from two crews and executed three crewmembers for crimes against Japanese civilians. The Japanese also killed several hundred thousand Chinese civilians as retribution for the raid.[19] The Doolittle raiders caused little actual damage to Japanese territory, but the damage to Japanese face was unbearable to the military. The Japanese government made no public acknowledgement of the raid to its citizens, but the daring attack had destroyed the myth of the impregnability of the homeland. The Japanese military was forced to increase the strength of their home defense forces.

The Doolittle-Halsey raid on Japan can arguably be called the most important strategic bombing mission of World War II. The psychological effect of the raid worked miracles for the morale of the American people who had received nothing but bad war news for five months. The effect on the Japanese, naturally, was just the opposite. They now realized that their homeland was not immune from the war and that their home defenses needed bolstering. The Japanese armed forces considered it a grave dereliction of duty that the emperor's life had been in jeopardy. Admiral Yamamoto took the attack by American bombers as a personal affront, blaming himself for allowing the Americans to attack Japan from the sea.[20]

The American attack convinced the Japanese that they should extend their defensive perimeter farther east. By seizing bases in the Aleutian Islands and the Midway Islands, it would be much more unlikely that American carriers could approach the empire's home islands again. Before those islands could be taken, Japanese forces were already in place to attack bases in southern New Guinea and the southern Solomon Islands. If bases in these islands could be taken, they could be used to attack the lines of communication between the United States and Australia. The preparations for these attacks set the stage for the Battle of the Coral Sea (see below).[21]

With Nagumo's aircraft carriers busy elsewhere in the southwest Pacific and Indian Oceans, the only available weapons to maintain pressure on Hawaii in the first months of the war were submarines. The main operating base for the mid-Pacific Sixth Fleet (Submarine) was Kwajalein atoll in the Marshall Islands. Just before the Pearl Harbor attack on December 7, the Sixth Fleet consisted of forty submarines.[22] The submarine fleet's part in the Pearl Harbor attack had been a complete failure. Twenty-eight submarines and five midget submarines had been assigned to augment the air attack. Admiral Yamamoto had been reluctant to allow the subs to participate because he considered that they might ruin the element of surprise—

and they almost did. It is believed that all of the midget subs were sunk or captured without inflicting any damage to the American fleet. One of the full-size submarines was sunk outside Pearl Harbor. After the initial attack on December 7, the IJN was operating a unique class of submarines with only limited success in the Hawaii area.

On December 7, 1941, the submarine *I-26* sank the American merchantman SS *Cynthia Olson* about 750 miles northwest of Seattle.[23] The *I-9* sank the SS *Lahaina* between Oahu and San Francisco. On December 9, the *I-10* sank the SS *Donnyvale* on her way north to the U.S. West Coast.[24]

The *I-1, I-2,* and *I-3* submarines, armed with 5.5-inch deck guns, shelled island ports during December. On December 15, a submarine fired ten deck gunshots into the Kahului, Maui, harbor area, hitting a pineapple cannery and causing about $700 worth of damage. On the night of December 30, Nawiliwili on Kaua'i and Hilo and Kahului on Maui were shelled, also with negligible damage.[25]

On December 10, Admiral Halsey's *Enterprise* was spotted off Kaua'i by the *I-6*. Nine of the twelve submarines stationed in the Hawaii area were ordered to pursue and sink the carrier.[26] The Japanese chased the carrier for two days and one submarine fired a long lance torpedo that missed the carrier by only sixty feet.[27] Finally, the *Enterprise* patrol planes found three of the Japanese pursuers. One submarine escaped unharmed, but another was believed to have been hit. A third, the *I-70*, captained by Cdr. Sano Takashi, was damaged and could not submerge and it was caught on the surface trying to make repairs. A dive-bomber piloted by Lt. Clarence E. Dickenson attacked and the *I-70* went down. The *Enterprise* had managed to elude her pursuers.[28]

Nine of the submarines were then ordered to proceed to the American mainland to begin attacking U.S. ships and to shell shore targets of opportunity with their deck guns. The *I-19* went to a strategic location off Los Angeles harbor, *I-15* proceeded to a point off San Francisco, *I-25* sailed to the mouth of the Columbia River, and *I-26* took up a position off the Strait of Juan de Fuca, the waterway approach to the port of Seattle. The other five submarines established their locations near Cape Blanco, Oregon;

and near San Diego, Monterey Bay, Cape Mendocino, and Estero Bay, California.

In the week ending with December 24, 1941, the Japanese submarines attacked eight American merchant ships. Two were sunk and two were damaged, with six seamen killed. On December 24, it was planned that eight of the subs would surface to expend all their 5.5-inch deck gun ammunition against shore targets before returning to the Marshall Islands. Admiral Nagano countermanded this order in Tokyo just hours before the bombardment of Los Angeles, San Francisco, and other West Coast targets was to begin. The admiral feared retaliation in kind against target cities in Japan from American submarines known to be just off the coast of Japan.[29] The admiral also did not want to have to apologize to the emperor for provoking such retaliation from the U.S. Navy.

At dawn on December 17, the submarine I-7 surfaced off the coast of Oahu to launch her Slim (E9W) biplane reconnaissance floatplane. It was the first Japanese aircraft to fly over Pearl Harbor since the December 7 attack. The pilot and observer confirmed that four U.S. Navy battleships had been sunk and three others seriously damaged and that many other ships in the harbor were sunk or damaged. The aircraft crew reported seeing an aircraft carrier in the harbor, five cruisers, and thirty smaller vessels, while dozens of destroyed airplanes could be seen still littering the army and navy airfields on Oahu.

When the floatplane returned to the I-7, the submarine commander was nervous about his surface exposure. The small floatplane landed alongside the submarine, but the captain did not want to take the time that would be required to swing the airplane aboard with the derrick, disassemble it, and stow it in the canister-hangar. The two aircrew men hastily dived into the ocean from the airplane and swam to the submarine. After the crew machine-gunned holes in the aircraft's floats, wings, and fuselage, the sub submerged, abandoning the Slim floatplane's sinking wreckage.[30]

Back in Japan, the IJN's strategic planners were becoming disenchanted with the lack of success in their submarine operations. The aviators on the planning staff recognized an opportunity to show what warplanes could do. They were keenly aware that their new Emily (H8K) flying boat, with its 125-foot wingspan and length of over 92 feet, was a world-beater aircraft; they were anxious to try its capabilities in combat.

Probably the most important result of the Doolittle raid was that it forced the Japanese to reconsider their war plans for the Pacific. Admiral Yamamoto was obsessively devoted to the emperor; the safety of the ruler, considered by the Japanese to be semidivine, had to be assured. Yamamoto took the Doolittle-Halsey attack as a personal affront and believed that he had failed in his duty to protect the emperor. The Japanese had quickly learned that the Mitchells had not come from a land base, but had been launched from an aircraft carrier. Nevertheless, the IJN and IJA agreed that the defensive perimeter had to be expanded to the east—toward Hawaii. Because the Midway Islands were the closest American real estate to Japan, they simply had to be held by the Japanese to eliminate any future threat. Admiral Yamamoto considered that the Midway operation would serve a twofold purpose. The first would be to invade Midway and convert it into a Japanese air base and the launch point for the invasion of Hawaii. The second goal would be to lure what remained of the U.S. fleet—especially the aircraft carriers—into the Midway area for the ultimate decisive battle that would spell the end for American naval power in the Pacific. The Japanese would then have free rein to conduct their operations, unhampered and at will, all over the Pacific.[31]

Plans were already being carried out to expand the Japanese perimeter into the New Guinea area and the Solomon Islands. Admiral Yamamoto's plans for this area were code-named MO. In early May 1942, the IJA wanted to put troops on the southern coast of New Guinea at Port Moresby and Tulagi in the Solomon Islands. Japanese air bases could then be used to threaten Australia and the lifelines from the United States. A task force under Vice Adm. Shigeyoshi Inouye of the Fourth Fleet would include the carriers *Zuikaku* and *Shokaku,* two cruisers, six destroyers, and 150 land-based aircraft. These units would cover separate invasion forces for Port Moresby and Tulagi. The Port Moresby force would sally from Rabaul. The smaller force for Tulagi would come from Truk in the Caroline Islands.

The typically complex Japanese battle plans gave the invasion group their own escorting forces, including the light carrier *Shoho*. Like so many of the IJN's operations plans, it relied on bringing together several groups of ships, with precise timing, and with the enemy behaving exactly as the Japanese expected them to behave. The plans were to withdraw the carriers used for this invasion as soon as it was completed, so that they could participate in the forthcoming attack on Midway.[32]

In March 1942, naval intelligence in Washington had asked Lt. Cdr. Joseph J. Rochefort to estimate Japanese intentions. With the information he had gathered and his remarkable intuition, he predicted that because the Indian Ocean had been swept clean of threats and the East Indies secured, the Japanese would move next against New Guinea. There were indications, he added, that a major offensive in the central Pacific would begin in the summer. In early April, radio traffic analysis linked the Japanese carriers *Zuikaku* and *Shokaku* with the commander of the Fourth Fleet. Other traffic yielded enough information to let Rochefort know that a cruiser division was being sent to Truk. Piecing all this together pointed to the probability that two large carriers and two more heavy cruisers would be participating in the Port Moresby operation.[33]

U.S. Navy cryptanalysts and traffic decoders of Rochefort's Combat Intelligence Unit learned of the impending Japanese foray into the Coral Sea area and quickly passed this information to Adm. Chester W. Nimitz. Commander Rochefort said later that he thought that the Combat Intelligence Unit had done a better job of predicting the Japanese moves in the Coral Sea than was later done in forecasting Japanese plans at Midway. He added that most of the credit should go to the unit in Australia headed by Lt. Rudolph J. Fabian. This group, with its code name "Cast" later altered to "Bellconner," had been evacuated from Corregidor and moved to Australia by submarines.[34]

The Battle of the Coral Sea was opened on April 30, 1942, as a Japanese occupation force with a strong defensive escort sailed southward from Truk toward New Guinea. On May 3, the Japanese landed unopposed at Tulagi, the base having been abandoned by the Australians. The Japanese immediately began to establish a seaplane base there.[35] Admiral Nimitz, having been informed by his intelligence officers that this would happen, sent two carriers, the *Lexington* and the *Yorktown,* carrying a total of 141 aircraft, to head off the Japanese invasion fleet that was moving south for an assault on Port Moresby.[36]

When Adm. Frank Jack Fletcher learned of the landing, he rushed toward Tulagi on his flagship, the carrier *Yorktown,* and left the *Lexington* to complete her refueling. At dawn the next day, Admiral Fletcher launched three waves of Dauntless (SBD) dive-bombers and Devastator (TBD) torpedo planes to attack the island and the Japanese ships there. The results were disappointing because there were few suitable targets at Tulagi. One Japanese destroyer and several small craft were sunk and five seaplanes were destroyed. The surprised Japanese put up little resistance.

For the next two days, both the opposing carrier groups tried to locate each other, but they failed, in part due to poor visibility. Gen. Douglas MacArthur's command was responsible for long-range reconnaissance in this area, but he did not have enough airplanes to cover this mission. Even so, he had forbidden Admiral Nimitz to send extended-range patrol planes into this zone of operations to provide assistance.[37]

Sighting reports and more intelligence information allowed Admiral Fletcher to deduce that the invasion force aiming at Port Moresby would come through the Jomard Passage. Fletcher positioned Task Group 17 (consisting of the American cruiser *Chicago* and two Australian cruisers, *Australia* and *Hobart*), commanded by Rear Adm. John G. Crace of the Royal Navy, to block the exit to the south.

Admiral Fletcher further ordered the fleet oiler USS *Neosho* and her escorting destroyer *Sims* to an assumed safe rendezvous to the south. At 8:15 AM on May 7, a Japanese patrol plane sighted the two ships and reported them to be a carrier and a cruiser. Rear Adm. Chuichi Hara immediately launched seventy-eight planes from the *Zuikaku* and *Shokaku*. Minutes later, another Japanese patrol plane found the American carriers. The frustrated Admiral Hara, unable to direct his airplanes to the correct location because they now had insufficient fuel,

ordered the two hapless American ships sunk. The *Sims* was sunk immediately and the *Neosho* was hit seven times but remained a floating
derelict for four days until a U.S. destroyer sank the oiler with gunfire.

The Americans made similar mistakes. That same morning, a U.S. scout
plane reported locating two Japanese carriers and four heavy cruisers.
Fletcher believed that this was the main enemy force and sent off ninety-
three aircraft from his two carriers. When they had almost arrived at the
reported scene, it was discovered that the scout plane's report was garbled—
only two cruisers and two destroyers had been sighted. Canceling that error
with another error, the leading Dauntless scout bomber from *Lexington*
wandered off course and found Adm. Aritomo Goto's invasion force that
included the light carrier *Shoho*, in beautifully clear weather. Most of the
Shoho's protecting fighters were away from their home ship, instead protecting the southbound Port Moresby invasion force. The attacking
American bombers blasted *Shoho* with thirteen bomb hits and seven torpedoes, sinking the Japanese carrier in fifteen minutes with about eight hundred crewmen aboard. As the carrier went down, Lt. Cdr. Robert E. Dixon
broadcast the famous "Scratch one flat-top" message to the *Lexington*.[38]

Both the American and Japanese carrier forces were now about equal
in number; both forces continued to grope for each other in the murky
weather. Early on May 8, each spotted the other and, at one point, attacking American and Japanese airplanes passed each other unseen on the way
to their targets. The forces were almost identical—122 American planes and
121 Japanese planes. The American carriers were exposed in clear weather
but the Japanese were conveniently sheltered by bad weather. The American
force finally located the Japanese, and in the first American strike against
Japanese heavy carriers the *Shokaku* received six hits by dive-bombers from
Lexington and *Yorktown*. The Japanese carrier could launch aircraft, but
was now unable to recover them. Zero (A6M) fighters or antiaircraft fire
shot down 43 American aircraft. The *Shokaku* put out her fires, but had to
return to Japan for repairs, having lost 108 men.[39]

The *Yorktown* was hit by only one bomb, but the 800-pound weapon
passed through three decks, caused sixty-six fatal and serious casualties,
and started a fire. The fire was quickly extinguished and the *Yorktown*'s

flight operations were not interrupted. Even though the *Yorktown* was severely damaged, she was still able to maintain a speed of thirty knots.

The *Lexington* came under heavy torpedo attack. After damage control parties fought valiantly to save the converted battle cruiser, leaking fuel fumes were ignited to set off a chain of explosions that rendered the ship past salvage. Capt. Frederick C. Sherman finally ordered the *Lexington* abandoned and her escorting destroyers finished the ship off with a spread of torpedoes, as several of her crewmembers wept openly. Ninety-two percent of her crew was saved.[40]

The Battle of the Coral Sea was the first naval battle in history in which the surface vessels never came close enough to actually fire directly at each other. Only the aircraft from Japanese carriers and American carriers inflicted damage on their enemies. The ships themselves never actually came close.

The Japanese regarded the Battle of the Coral Sea as a great victory. Radio Tokyo claimed that the American carrier *Saratoga* and a *Yorktown*-class carrier, a *California*-class battleship, a British warship of the *Warspite* class, another cruiser, a twenty thousand–ton oil tanker, and a destroyer had been sunk; and that a cruiser of the *Canberra*-class had been severely damaged. In addition, they reported that sixty-six American planes had been destroyed, and Japanese losses had been limited to one small aircraft carrier and eighty planes.[41]

Japanese losses in the Battle of the Coral Sea, and the sighting by a Japanese patrol plane of Halsey's carriers rushing west to the Coral Sea from Pearl Harbor, had another effect on Japanese plans. They abandoned their schedule to take Nauru and Ocean Islands, even though Admiral Nimitz quickly ordered the carriers *Enterprise* and *Hornet* to return to Pearl Harbor, because they were too late to participate in the Battle of the Coral Sea. Like a great chess player, Admiral Nimitz was already thinking ahead to the next moves. He recalled all his carriers—including the damaged *Yorktown*—back to Pearl Harbor on the double.

The final score for the Battle of the Coral Sea showed a tactical victory for the Japanese. In addition to the lost carrier mentioned above— the USS *Lexington*—a second carrier, *Yorktown*, was damaged. One oiler and a destroyer had also been sunk. The Japanese lost one small carrier, one destroyer, and several small craft, with one out of six fleet carriers in the Pacific damaged.

In spite of the score, Coral Sea was a strategic victory for the Americans. The Japanese left the scene of conflict assuming from their pilots' overstated battle reports that the American Task Force 17 (both carriers) had been destroyed. Even so, Admiral Inouye cautiously put off the invasion of Port Moresby because, although he was convinced that the American carrier strength had been smashed, the carrier air strength he had remaining was not sufficient to protect the invasion from the American land-based bombers. The planned Japanese invasion of Port Moresby was postponed. It was the first time in the war that the Japanese had been stopped in their plans for conquest.[42]

Admiral Inouye may have overreacted to the loss of the light carrier *Shoho*, in the first carrier battle with the Americans, but Yamamoto apparently believed that the setback could be remedied later. It was true that the superb new *Shokaku* had suffered severe damage with her flight deck shattered and her bow burnt out by American bombs. The more serious loss was that 30 percent of the ship's flying crews had been killed. The *Shokaku* had to limp back to Japan for repairs and would not be in action for several months. The *Zuikaku*, although not seriously damaged, had suffered the loss of 40 percent of her flying crewmen, some of the IJN's most experienced combat aviators. Even if the aircraft and crew replacements were completed immediately, these replacements would not be combat-trained and ready for battle for several weeks.[43]

Before the war, Japanese flight training was limited to a small and elite group. In 1937, only seventy trainees were selected out of more than fifteen hundred applicants. Of those seventy, only twenty-five actually completed flight training. Only Eta Jima graduates who requested it were sent to flight training, because there was no added incentive for naval officers to be pilots. The IJN considered that it could use enlisted pilots, reserving the leadership roles for its officer pilots.

Before the war, Japanese flight training programs for officer and enlisted pilots were much longer than those of pilot training programs of other countries. Including general education courses, ground courses, and flight training, some trainees took as long as four years to gain their wings as full-fledged pilots.

At the beginning of the Pacific War, the IJN had about fifteen hundred of the best and most experienced combat pilots in the world. Of these, probably no more than 10 percent were officers. The officers were regular academy graduates, a few reserve officers (college graduates), and special service officers (promoted up from enlisted ranks). Officer pilots and enlisted pilots were segregated into different flight training classes. The enlisted pilots were from the *Yokaren* flight training program, detailed in Chapter 2. This created a high degree of resentment between the officer pilots and the enlisted pilots. The enlisted pilots knew that they were doing the same job as the officer pilots, and in many cases doing it more effectively, but without the officers' higher pay and privileges of rank. The IJN chose to ignore these ill feelings. The war with China had provided excellent combat experience for Japanese pilots, but there were far too few of them for an all-out war.[44]

The U.S. Navy and the USAAF had enlisted pilots at the beginning of the war, but both services usually (and quickly) integrated their enlisted pilots into the officer ranks because of the desperate need for their experience. Enlisted pilots in the army, navy, and marines were used throughout the war in special duties, usually as liaison, glider, or service pilots. Flight officers were aviation cadets who "had not qualified (as commissioned officers) . . . appointed as flight officers with a rank equivalent of warrant officer, junior grade." Warrant officers in the American forces were granted most of the officer privileges, but not the higher pay or responsibilities of the higher ranks.[45]

As the Pacific War began, the Imperial Japanese Naval Air Force (IJNAF) had a fairly small force of about five thousand pilots. Of these, only about thirty-five hundred were front-line pilots. To maintain their qualitative advantage in combat, the Japanese policy of keeping their best aviators constantly in the fight was deeply flawed. Against the Americans, losses began to mount, and the IJN shortened the training curriculum but expanded its pilot training facilities in a desperate attempt to turn out pilots on a production-line basis.[46] This move came too late in the war. The accelerated inferior training resulted in disastrous losses for the Japanese. They did not rotate their more experienced pilots back from the fronts to instruct and train new pilots in the skills that were needed in combat. In 1943, the Japanese built twenty thousand eight hundred aircraft, then twenty-six thousand in 1944. The losses in training, ferrying, accidents, and combat were so high that the total front-line strength in pilots and aircraft was barely maintained. As the war progressed, the Japanese were flying inferior aircraft against better-trained and better-equipped American pilots. A Japanese pilot was likely to be shot down on his first combat mission without doing any damage to an American airplane or ship. The shortage of trained combat pilots resulted in a marked decline for the IJNAF and would be an increasing major factor in the upcoming battles.[47]

In toting up the score for the Battle of the Coral Sea, Admiral Yamamoto believed that two American carriers had been sunk and that the U.S. Navy had only two battle-worthy carriers (if that many) remaining in the Pacific, and no prospect of reinforcement. He would still be able to send four carriers in the force that would be attacking Midway. The carrier *Junyo* and a light carrier, the *Ryujo,* would be the centerpieces of the subsidiary northern force that would be invading the Aleutian Islands.[48] All the Japanese successes in battle thus far had served to reinforce the belief in *nihon seishin*—the inborn Japanese fighting spirit. This became evident when the war games were being played out on board the flagship *Yamato.* When it became evident in the games that no contingency plan existed if the American carriers were, in fact, waiting to strike the Japanese carrier force that was to bear down on Midway, the possibility was given little chance. As an example, during the games Admiral Ugaki overruled an umpire who had ruled that two of the Japanese carriers had been sunk, bringing the *Kaga* miraculously back to life.[49] Ignoring this cavalier attitude, Admiral Yamamoto remained optimistic about the forthcoming invasion of Midway. He suffered from victory disease just as severely as any seaman in the IJN, and victory disease was about to have a fatal effect on the IJN's plans for attacking Midway.

7

The Battle of Midway

The Midway Islands comprise two tiny coral atolls, Sand and Eastern Islands, enclosed in a forbidding reef some thirteen hundred miles west-northwest of Pearl Harbor. Except for smaller Kure Island sixty miles beyond, Midway is the final westerly point of the Hawaiian island chain. Prior to World War II, the atoll had served at various times as a coaling station, commercial cable relay point, and Pan American Airways (Pan Am) Clipper rest and refueling stop.[1]

Adm. Isoroku Yamamoto had called Midway the "Sentry of Hawaii," and regarded it as a direct threat to his emperor and homeland, especially since the Lt. Col. James H. Doolittle raid. Although he knew that the Doolittle Mitchells (B-25s) had not taken off from Midway, he believed that the Americans might use the island for future attacks. Yamamoto knew that the U.S. Navy would base patrol and reconnaissance airplanes as well as submarines there, posing another threat to the Japanese homeland.

Admiral Yamamoto set into motion an extremely intricate and grandiose plan using the largest and most powerful battle fleet ever amassed by any other navy in history, manned by more than one hundred thousand officers and men. He would deploy some two hundred ships that would take part in two separate but closely linked operations. Yamamoto, as combined fleet commander, would be in overall command of both campaigns: Operation AL, the planned invasion of the Aleutian Islands, and Operation MI, the planned invasion and occupation of the Midway Islands. The overall purpose of both operations was, in addition to protecting the emperor, to lure the American fleet into the final decisive battle that would destroy the American naval presence in the Pacific.

Initially, the Japanese had intended the Aleutians operation to be a reconnaissance in force. Adak Island was to be occupied, any American military facilities there destroyed, and its harbor mined. The occupying forces were to leave to augment the forces invading Attu. The Japanese, believing at first that the Aleutian weather was too severe to allow sustained air operations, changed their minds when they realized that it would be advantageous to have a base for long-range flying boats to conduct reconnaissance of the northern half of the fourteen hundred miles between Adak and Midway in the northern Pacific. This area of the Pacific was exactly the area through which the Pearl Harbor attack force had passed. By denying the Americans this area of the ocean, the likelihood of another Doolittle-type raid would be greatly reduced. They later abandoned plans for the occupation of Adak when the Battle of Midway went badly. Ultimately, they would only occupy Attu and Kiska.[2]

Operation AL, led by Rear Adm. Moshiro Hosogaya, included the Northern Force, consisting of a heavy cruiser, two destroyers, and five support ships. The Second Carrier Striking Force of Operation AL consisted of one heavy aircraft carrier and one light aircraft carrier, screened by two heavy cruisers, three destroyers, and an oiler. Sources disagree on the number and types of aircraft on the flagship light carrier, the *Ryujo*. Three sources state that the ship's fighter complement was sixteen Zero (A6M) fighters and twenty Kate (B5N2) torpedo bombers. Another source claims that the *Ryujo* carried only twelve Zeroes and eighteen Kates.[3] A fifth source states that the *Ryujo* could accommodate forty-eight aircraft, so the thirty-seven fighters and torpedo bombers figure is probably correct.[4] The Aleutian Support Force included four battleships escorted by two light cruisers and twelve destroyers, and supplied by two oilers; there were two invasion forces. The one for Attu Island consisted of four destroyers, a minelayer, and a transport. A larger invasion force for Kiska boasted three light cruisers, an auxiliary cruiser, three destroyers, two troop transports, three minesweepers, and a six-boat submarine detachment.[5]

The Midway fleet, of course, was much larger. This group included the First Fleet (Main Body), with Admiral Yamamoto riding in his favorite ship, which was the mightiest battleship in the world at the time, the *Yamato*. The admiral was accompanied by two other battleships, a light cruiser, nine destroyers, two oilers, and a special force of two seaplane carriers loaded with midget submarines for this operation. Oddly enough, the light carrier *Hosho*, the old pioneer, accompanied this group, bearing eight Kate torpedo bombers and a disputed number of Zero fighters. (One source maintained that this ship was operating with nine obsolescent Claude [A5M] fighters and six even older Jean [B4Y] biplane torpedo bombers on board.)[6] The Main Force (First Fleet) had as its main punch the First Carrier Striking Force, under the command of Vice Adm. Chuichi Nagumo. Four heavy carriers were loaded with a total of eighty-four Zero fighters, eighty-four Val (D3A) dive-bombers, and ninety-three Kate torpedo bombers. Screening these carriers were two more battleships, two heavy cruisers, a light cruiser, sixteen destroyers with a trailing supply contingent of five oilers, and three transports.

The Midway Occupation Force was made up of sixteen transports and three patrol boats carrying about five thousand troops of the Second Special Naval Landing Force and an army detachment. This part of the fleet was protected by the light carrier *Zuiho* with twelve Zero fighters and twelve Kate torpedo bombers on board, two battleships, eight cruisers, and twenty-two destroyers, all of them nourished by six oilers.

The seaplane tender group consisted of two seaplane tenders loaded with a total of twenty-four fighter seaplanes and eight scout seaplanes. Six submarines formed the underwater detachment accompanying the Midway invasion fleet; the advance submarine force would place ten submarines in the waters near French Frigate Shoals to scout for the American fleet's expected approach.

This armada was rounded out by a repair ship, and several smaller vessels—patrol boats (some carrying invasion troops), mine sweepers, sub chasers, and auxiliary craft.[7]

Long-range aerial search and patrol would be conducted by Mavis (H6K) flying boats of the 24th Air Flotilla based at Jaluit and Wotje in the Marshall Islands, aided by a few more Mavis aircraft of the 26th Air Flotilla stationed at Marcus Island. The Toko Air Group was alerted in May 1942 to send a detachment of six Mavis flying boats via Paramushir in the Kurile Islands to participate in the Aleutian operation. They were to be based at a seaplane facility to be established on Kiska in the Aleutian Islands. The distance from Paramushir to Kiska is approximately fifteen hundred statute miles, so the Mavis was quite capable of flying reconnaissance missions between the two bases. One source hints that a detachment of new Emily (H8K) flying boats may have been sent from the Yokosuka Kokutai to Marcus Island, some fifteen hundred miles west of Midway. These airplanes could have provided reconnaissance and patrol protection for the Japanese fleet headed to Midway.[8]

The first action in the Japanese battle plan involved the Northern Force. The carriers launched an attack on Dutch Harbor in the Aleutian Islands on June 3 in an attempt to draw the U.S. fleet from their base in Pearl Harbor to the north to oppose the invasion threat. It was hoped that this feint would keep the American forces' attention focused to the north, drawing their attention away from Midway.

On June 4, Admiral Nagumo approached Midway with the Kido Butai (Strike Force) to eliminate the island's defenses with air attacks. An ambush force of fifteen Japanese submarines was awaiting the American fleet along an arc imposed between Hawaii and Midway. On June 5, the Japanese invasion force approached from the southwest to land troops and take over the islands. Admiral Yamamoto himself in the mighty battleship *Yamato* arrived June 6 with the Main Force that included two more battleships (the *Nagato* and *Mutsu*) and heavy cruisers. He believed that the American fleet would recover from the Aleutians deception quickly and attempt to oppose the Midway invasion. When the U.S. Navy rushed south to interfere with the assault on Midway, the Japanese fleet would be waiting for them. This would be the final decisive battle that the Japanese had been dreaming of for decades that would eliminate the U.S. Navy's battle force in the Pacific.[9]

The IJN had considered the U.S. Navy to be its sole hypothetical enemy since 1909. For thirty years, the IJN had trained and studied for the great decisive battle against the U.S. fleet, in which an American onslaught would be countered and destroyed in the grandest battle in naval history. This was to have taken place in the waters near the Japanese homeland but, with the extended reach of carrier aviation, Yamamoto now saw the perfect opportunity to accomplish this victory at Midway.[10]

The first indication to U.S. naval intelligence officers that the Japanese were thinking about more operations against Midway, Hawaii, and the island chain was the March 4 raid by the two Emily flying boats. The fact that an enemy flying boat had been shot down near Midway on March 10 and that Johnston Island had received a visit from the Japanese on the same day added to the increasing evidence that more activity could be expected. On May 6, a message was decoded from the Japanese Fourth Air Attack Force based at Kwajalein: "Request we be supplied ten crystals for frequencies 4990 and 8990 kilocycles for use in aircraft in the second K campaign. Above to reach this headquarters [Kwajalein] prior to the 17th."

The answer came on May 10 to advise that the radio crystals required "for use in K operations" would be shipped by air from Japan on May 12. U.S. naval intelligence knew now that Operation K involved the use of submarine-refueled flying boats operating against Hawaii. So far, the flying boats had been operating only in the Midway and Oahu areas. The Japanese were obviously up to something, and were planning another bombing raid or reconnaissance sorties, or a combination.[11] The Combat Intelligence Unit had not known that the March 10 sortie that resulted in Lt. Hisao Hashizume's shoot-down was purely a reconnaissance mission, but it was already clear that the Japanese were showing increasing interest in Midway.

Admiral Yamamoto's typically complex plans for the Midway invasion needed complete tactical and strategic surprise to succeed. Lt. Cdr.

Joseph J. Rochefort's Combat Intelligence Unit would deny the admiral that most important element of his attack. Many of the intelligence triumphs were accomplished by traffic analysis, combined with cryptology. Traffic analysis was a highly technical skill used by self-taught enlisted analysts to piece together the identification and locations of ship and unit call signs. Their skill allowed them to gain knowledge of how the Japanese communicated. The Japanese used a completely different telegraphic code in their radio communications, based on the Japanese alphabet. It contained nearly twice the number of dot-dash combinations as the Morse code used by the rest of the world. Overcoming this obstacle and correlating ship identification, location, and the types of messages were monumental tasks. Their successes enabled the U.S. Navy's hard-working traffic analyst experts to assemble tables of organization and orders of battle for the entire Japanese fleet. Traffic analysis was the glue that patched together the readable with the unreadable decrypts, allowing the purpose of the messages to be decoded.

The code known as JN-25 was the primary operating code of the IJN. The Japanese were convinced that this code was completely unbreakable. It was based on a system using two codebooks that were actually dictionaries of forty-five thousand five-digit numbers in each codebook: one arranged alphabetically for encoding, the other organized numerically for decoding. The five-digit numbers were added to similar numbers (additives) in another codebook to read out the Japanese phonetic alphabet. Each message indicated by key numbers which page, line, and column of the second book was to be used for decoding. To check for garbled messages, all sums were divisible by five.[12]

By April, the U.S. Navy cryptanalysts had figured out about 30 percent of the IJN code system. They were compiling their own dictionaries of coded groups and tables of cipher numbers. The Japanese message encoders became complacent and usually used only the same first page of the additive book too often. If U.S. Navy cryptanalysts could gain a toehold on the differing additives, many messages could be at least partially read. An enlisted cryptanalyst, R. V. Anderson, who was formerly based on Corregidor, discovered that the numerical difference between any two enciphered code groups stayed the same if those code groups were encrypted by the same additive or cipher key. Anderson began compiling an index of those numerical differences that he believed would facilitate key word recovery. His colleagues ridiculed his efforts, but as he began to recover more key additives than all of them combined, everyone began using his index (which they dubbed the Handy Andy) as a standard tool in the decrypting of additives. Anderson was offered an officer's commission and a Bronze Star to reward his breakthrough.[13] Before they were shut down and evacuated to Australia, the Corregidor intelligence unit (Cast) furnished Hawaii with 950 new values for the JN-25 codebook, 650 additional code indicators, and 1,700 additives for new cipher keys.[14]

The 30 percent of the Japanese code vocabulary that the Americans could understand represented most of the terms used in the IJN's operations. At the same time, the airwaves all over the western Pacific were loaded with directives, questions, and responses coursing through the command channels to refit, equip, man, refuel, assemble, and dispatch the ships, men, and aircraft involved in the complex Midway plans. Even with such a traffic load, Rochefort had unraveled an amazing 90 percent of Yamamoto's plans. Rochefort knew almost everything about the upcoming operation except the main target and the date when the operation would be launched, yet the Japanese considered their code so complex that it could not be broken, and believed all their communications to be completely secure.[15]

A difference of opinion about the upcoming operation was developing between the cryptanalysts of Op-20G (the U.S. Navy's cryptanalytic office, Pacific) at headquarters in Washington and those of Rochefort's listening post in Hawaii. Rochefort's Hypo was technically an outstation of Op-20G not accountable to Adm. Chester W. Nimitz. The two agencies agreed that something big and complicated was about to take place, but they disagreed on Japanese objectives. The commander in chief, U.S. fleet—the strong-willed Adm. Ernest J. King—backed his Washington team. Their estimate was that the Japanese would begin their operation in mid-June, but reserved their decision on just where it would take place. The Washington team believed that the Japanese would be striking south toward Fiji, Samoa, and New Caledonia. One Washington-based intelligence officer believed that their next objective might be the invasion of Johnston Island south of Oahu. The entire Washington intelligence staff urged Admiral King to restrain Admiral Nimitz's orders withdrawing carriers from the Solomon Islands and the south Pacific. The Washington group considered that those areas would be unprotected while the navy's carrier strength was concentrated in the Hawaiian island chain.[16]

The acerbic Admiral King could not give his complete trust to Admiral Nimitz, saying that Nimitz "could lose the war in one afternoon." In addition, Admiral King held a personal dislike for Rochefort, considering him to be the antithesis of a naval officer in appearance and demeanor. King considered Rochefort to be a maverick, unorthodox and irrepressible, a nonconformist who disregarded most of the navy's rigid social protocol. Admiral Nimitz was willing to listen to his own Pearl Harbor–based intelligence staff, but was not yet convinced of their analysis of Japanese plans.[17]

The story of Rochefort's classic ruse to learn where Yamamoto's fleet would strike has been told in most of the stories about the Battle of Midway. Having intercepted a message referring to "AF" from the radio traffic from a Japanese scout plane flying near Midway, Rochefort was certain that AF was the code designation for Midway, but he couldn't prove it. The combined efforts of his Hypo crew and those of Cast on Corregidor had decrypted a message in which the Japanese assigned the geographical designator of AF to the Midway Islands.[18] Rochefort checked the letters AF on a recently captured Japanese grid map and discovered that A and F designated coordinates for an area that included the Midway Islands. Rochefort asked Admiral Nimitz for permission to have Midway send a spurious message "in the clear" that the island's water purification system had broken down. In a few hours, the Japanese dutifully reported to the imperial fleet that AF was having water problems and that water purification equipment would be needed for their occupying forces. Rochefort now had an absolute confirmation of the Japanese objectives and Admiral Nimitz now knew where Yamamoto's fleet would be going.[19]

The date of the assault still remained open to question. The deduced evidence placed it as early as June 1 or as late as June 10. The time was critical, because Op-20G's radio intelligence specialists had decoded messages detailing the procedures for the distribution of new codebooks. The Combat Intelligence Unit knew that the Japanese planned to place a new set of codes into operation on June 1. At that point, the Americans would have to start all over again to unravel the new system to decode enemy radio messages.

Two of Rochefort's cryptanalysts, both lieutenant commanders, Wesley A. Wright and Joseph Finnegan, puzzled over the date ciphers from four messages: One was a new message relating to Midway; the other three had come in earlier. Wright and Finnegan knew that the Japanese phonetic alphabet—the kana—was composed actually of two alphabets, the hiragana and the katakana. Each set has forty-six letters that are pronounced alike. Generally, the hiragana is used to form grammatical endings and the katakana is used to write in Japanese the words borrowed from other languages.[20] Up to now, one alphabet had been used for some messages, and the other alphabet in other messages. Deciphering each alphabet separately had produced nothing but gibberish. The idea dawned: Perhaps the elusive ciphers might come from the two combined alphabets. The two experts worked out a grid system, arranging the characters of one alphabet horizontally, and those of the other alphabet vertically. It took an all-night session, using an early IBM punch-card computer, to make the grid match the ciphers against the 2,209 possible combinations the system allowed. The theory worked! The squares on the final grid revealed real words and readable information. With triumphant confidence, they roused Rochefort from his cot to inform him that the Japanese would attack Midway on June 4.[21] For the remainder of the day, the intelligence staff reviewed the details of the information now at hand. Cdr. Edwin T. Layton, head of Admiral Nimitz's intelligence staff, was able to predict confidently that, "They'll come in from the northwest on a bearing of 325 degrees and they will be sighted at about 175 miles from Midway, and the time will be about 0600 Midway time."[22]

Admiral Nimitz had not been too impressed with the Combat Intelligence Unit in his early days at Pearl Harbor, but he was convinced now that Rochefort had been correct in all of his analyses of Japanese intentions. The admiral now backed his own Combat Intelligence Unit completely and would base his strategies on its predictions.

Admiral Nimitz flew to Midway to personally inspect the island's defenses and to provide what he could to bolster those defenses. He acted at once to concentrate his forces around Midway. He secretly recalled the carriers *Enterprise* and *Hornet* to Pearl Harbor, leaving a cruiser behind to imitate the radio messages and identifiers of the carriers so that the Japanese would not detect the carriers' withdrawal movement. The *Yorktown* was already returning from the Coral Sea battle. Of course, the *Yorktown* had not been sunk in the Coral Sea, but the Japanese believed that she had been sunk. The damaged carrier had rushed back to Pearl Harbor for repair and replenishment. The original estimates for the *Yorktown*'s repair of her battle damage were for three weeks of around-the-clock work. A direct bomb hit had done serious damage to the inner workings of the ship and two near misses had opened seams in her hull. Herculean efforts by the repair crews at Pearl Harbor made the ship seaworthy again in three days. The *Yorktown*'s repairs were not complete, but were sufficient to allow the ship to join American forces defending Midway.[23]

To meet the massive Japanese fleet at Midway, the U.S. Navy gathered its fleet of three carriers, one light and seven heavy cruisers, fifteen destroyers, and two more destroyers screening two oilers. Rounding out the seagoing forces were nineteen submarines. The three aircraft carriers had on board a total of 79 Wildcat (F4F) fighters, 112 Dauntless (SBD) dive-bombers, and 42 Devastator (TBD) torpedo bombers.

Admiral Nimitz dispatched additional men, planes, and armament to Midway. Many of the airplanes were obsolete, but they were the only ones available. The Marines were still burdened with their stubby Buffalo (F2A) fighters, now being called the Flying Coffins. The Marine Air

Group 22 on Midway had twenty Buffalo fighters, seven Wildcat fighters, and sixteen Dauntless dive-bombers. Eleven more marine dive-
bombers were the obsolescent prewar Vindicators (SB2Us). The
Vindicators, with a fabric-covered fuselage, was dubbed the Vibrator and
Wind Indicator. Augmenting these relics was a detachment of Torpedo
Squadron Eight of 6 new Avenger (TBF) torpedo bombers (that would
make their combat debut in the upcoming fray). The navy had 32
Catalina (PBY) patrol bombers conducting patrols from the island. The
army's 7th Air Force contributed 4 Marauder (B-26) twin-engine bombers
modified to carry torpedoes, and 19 Flying Fortress (B-17) heavy
bombers. In all, 141 aircraft lined the runways on Midway's Eastern
Island air base.[24]

On the American side, Admiral Nimitz had a complete picture of what
the Japanese were intending to do. Knowing that the threat to the Aleutian
Islands was only diversionary bait, he assigned minimal forces to deal with
it and kept his main strength ready to deal with the assault on Midway.
Yamamoto, on the other hand, was handicapped by his lack of knowledge
about American strength and location. He had even been denied the photographic reconnaissance that he had hoped would come from Lieutenant
Hashizume's fatal flight to Midway.

Admiral Yamamoto had been surprised that a second American carrier task force had appeared for the Battle of the Coral Sea. He wanted no
such surprises in the upcoming Battle of Midway. He desperately needed to
know how many carriers the U.S. Navy had remaining in the Pacific, and
where they were.

The new (Type 2) Emily flying boats had been so successful in their
March 4 attack on Pearl Harbor that the Japanese decided that the operation should be repeated just before the invasion of Midway. By now, the
eighth new Emilys had been completed at the Kawanishi factory. New crews
were completing their training in the operation of the potent new patrol
bomber. Two of the new flying boats were ordered transferred with their
crews from the Yokohama Kokutai to the 14th Kokutai at Wotje for a second K armed reconnaissance attack on Pearl Harbor. The operation would

be conducted almost exactly like the March 4 attack, with submarines refueling the two aircraft at French Frigate Shoals.[25]

The two flying boats, Emily W-45 and Emily W-46, were scheduled to take off at midnight on May 30 (Tokyo time May 29; 3:00 AM Wotje time) to reach French Frigate Shoals just before sunset, by 5:30 PM local time. After being refueled from the submarines there, they would depart for Oahu by 7:00 PM if all went as planned. Their primary mission on this flight was reconnaissance to determine the location of the American carriers but, as before, they would each carry four 550-pound bombs. They would arrive over Pearl Harbor at 1:15 AM local time with the light of a full moon on May 3, and fly nonstop back to Wotje, arriving at about 12:20 PM local time on May 31.

The submarine force commander, Vice Adm. Teruhisa Komatsu, had assigned six submarines to participate in the operation. Three submarines would act as refueling tankers to replenish the Emilys at French Frigate Shoals; another would act as a radio beacon between Wotje and French Frigate Shoals on the homeward-bound leg. This was the major change from the earlier mission. A fifth boat would be stationed off Keahole Point to act as a rescue boat in case of trouble, and a sixth would be positioned eighty miles southwest of Oahu for patrol, weather reporting, and rescue.[26]

The first submarine to arrive at French Frigate Shoals on May 26 was the *I-121*. The submarine commander was dismayed to see a U.S. Navy seaplane tender riding at anchor in the atoll's lagoon. The *I-121* was joined by the other two tanker-submarines, the *I-122* and *I-123*, that night. For the next three days, the Japanese submarines waited for the American ship to depart. Instead, a second American seaplane tender arrived. Apparently, the Americans planned to conduct flying boat operations themselves from French Frigate Shoals. On orders from Admiral Nimitz, these ships were the USS *Ballard* and *Thornton,* both destroyers that had been converted to seaplane tenders, placed at French Frigate Shoals for the specific purpose of denying the atolls' shelter to the Japanese for their Operation K. On the night of May 29, Lt. Cdr. Toshitake Ueno, commander of the *I-123*, took one last look through his periscope to see the two American ships still present. The three Japanese submarines were configured as tankers and therefore were not really able to launch an attack on two well-armed American ships to get rid of them. The U.S. seaplane tenders were possibly expecting Catalina patrol bombers to arrive at any time. Commander Ueno radioed the situation to his commanding officer on Kwajalein. Vice Adm. Eiji Goto understood the situation and radioed instructions back: the operation would be postponed for one day and to expect the Japanese flying boats on May 31. On the following night, the situation had not improved for the Japanese. In the fact, now the presence of American Catalina patrol bombers confirmed the Japanese suspicions that the Americans were already using the Shoals as a seaplane base themselves. Ueno again radioed the bad news to headquarters. This time, the answer came from Vice Adm. Nishizo Tsukahara, commander of the 11th Air Fleet. Operation K was to be suspended. The Japanese seaplanes would not be coming.[27]

The Japanese did have a contingency plan to use Necker Island (located ninty-four statute miles east-southeast of French Frigate Shoals) as an alternative site for the refueling rendezvous, but for an unknown reason they chose not to use this location. Necker Island did not have the sheltered atoll lagoon that was the best feature of French Frigate Shoals. Perhaps they believed that the Catalina flying boats operating from such a nearby base would surely detect the submarines, the Emily flying boats, or both during their exposed refueling operation. Ironically, had they used Necker Island, there was an excellent chance that the Japanese submarines would have sighted the U.S. carrier task forces on their way to Midway.[28]

Just at this point, another hitch in the Japanese plans developed. The submarines of Squadron Five, assigned to the B cordon line to be established northwest of Hawaii on June 2, were detained by repair delays in Japan. The A cordon line west of Hawaii was to be established by the boats of Squadron Three, but three of the four subs assigned were unable to reach their stations because of the delayed, then aborted, Operation K. Fifteen submarines had been scheduled for screening duty to spot and attack any ships from Pearl Harbor on their way to Midway. Only one reached her assigned post by June 2. The others arrived on June 4, far too late to see the American task forces that already had steamed through that area earlier on their way to their battle stations rendezvous area northeast of Midway. Admiral Yamamoto still did not know exactly how many aircraft carriers the Americans had to meet his assault on Midway.[29] Admiral Yamamoto deemed that radio silence was absolutely necessary, so he chose not to inform Admiral Nagumo that Operation K, the reconnaissance of Pearl Harbor, had been cancelled. Yamamoto incorrectly assumed that Nagumo's radios had picked up this information as Yamamoto's radios had; in the event, though, Nagumo's ships lacked the more sophisticated communications equipment available on Yamamoto's flagship. Nagumo's carriers maintained their course for Midway, believing that if the American carriers constituted a threat coming from Pearl Harbor, this knowledge would be furnished by combined fleet intelligence.[30]

The Japanese were overly self-confident and even arrogant at this point, which led to their downfall at Midway. In spite of the lack of intelligence information, the Japanese confidence in their success and underestimation of their enemy seems almost uncanny. Just as he was about to launch his attack on Midway, Admiral Nagumo issued the following information on the American situation:

1. The enemy fleet will probably come out to engage when the Midway landing operations are begun.
2. Enemy air patrols from Midway will be heavier to westward and southward, less heavy to the north and northwest.
3. The radius of enemy air patrols is estimated to be approximately 500 miles. [He was apparently not notified that his own patrol planes had encountered American patrol planes 700 miles from Midway on 30 May (1 June Tokyo Time).]
4. The enemy is not yet aware of our plan, and he has not yet detected our task force.

5. There is no evidence of an enemy task force in our vicinity.

6. It is therefore possible for us to attack Midway, destroy land-based planes there, and support the landing operation. We can then turn around, meet an approaching enemy task force, and destroy it.

7. Possible counterattacks by enemy land-based air can surely be repulsed by our interceptors and anti-aircraft fire.[31]

The admiral was wrong on all counts.

The details of the saga of the Battle of Midway will not be repeated here. The story has been told in great detail in books, motion pictures, television documentaries, museum dioramas, and even computer games. Among the best of the books about this battle are John B. Lundstrom's *The First Team*; Cdr. Mitsuo Fuchida and Masatake Okumiya's *Midway: The Battle That Doomed Japan*; Walter Lord's *Incredible Victory*; Gordon W. Prange, Donald Goldstein, and Katherine V. Dillon's *Miracle at Midway*; and the Naval Analysis Division of the U.S. Strategic Bombing Survey's highly detailed *Campaigns of the Pacific War*. World War II historians agree that the Battle of Midway was the crucial battle of the Pacific War. It was the turn of the tide with a great helping of pure luck on the side of the Americans. It marked the end of Japanese conquests and broke the back of the IJN. They abandoned plans for the invasion of Midway.

American losses were the carrier *Yorktown* and the destroyer *Hamman*, and 147 aircraft, including those destroyed on the ground at Midway and on board the *Yorktown*. The United States suffered 307 casualties. Japanese losses were four aircraft carriers—*Akagi, Kaga, Hiryu,* and *Soryu*—and the heavy cruiser *Mikuma*. The Japanese lost 332 dive-bombers, torpedo planes, and fighters with their precious pilots and crews. Japanese casualties numbered 2,500 men.[32]

For several days, Admiral Nimitz had monitored the battle through patrol plane reports, radio messages from ships in the battle fleet, and from units based on Midway itself. He took a great deal of satisfaction in learning that Nagumo's carriers had been located off Midway on the predicted day and area. Admiral Nimitz, noting the positions of the enemy carriers that were plotted on the board in his Operations Room, remarked with a smile to Commander Layton, his chief of intelligence: "Well, you were only five minutes, five degrees and five miles off."[33]

After the terse cable message, "Air raid Midway," the radios in the Nimitz command post went silent for two hours. Rochefort began telephoning the admiral with news that was gleaned from the decoded and translated Japanese radio reports to Nagumo of how the battle was going. Rochefort's radio traffic analysis listeners smiled to themselves as they recognized the heavy "fist" of *Akagi's* chief radio operator.[34]

Naval historians agree that the Americans were blessed with almost incredible luck during the battle, whereas the Japanese suffered from terrible timing and "unlucky breaks." Both sides made tragic errors, and both sides performed some brilliant tasks. Adm. Samuel E. Morrison and Commander Fuchida agree that the American victory at Midway was, overall, a victory of intelligence.

There have been many accolades from historians for Admiral Yamamoto's remarkable planning abilities. As the architect of the Pearl Harbor attack, he was given credit for the brilliant success of that raid when in fact, even though it was a tactical triumph, that attack has been called unnecessary and a complete strategic blunder on the part of the Japanese. Dr. Paul S. Dull, in his *A Battle History of the Imperial Japanese Navy (1941–1945)*, voiced the opinion that it was difficult to see how Yamamoto could be called a great admiral. Dr. Dull points out that Yamamoto's most significant contribution to the IJN was the admiral's planning of the original Pearl Harbor attack. When Yamamoto did "bring his Combined Fleet out, and carrier battles ensued, his tactics led to disaster."[35]

Yamamoto and Nagumo made many gross mistakes in the execution of the Battle of Midway. These were compounded by the many misfortunes suffered by the Japanese. Yamamoto had given Nagumo two distinct, but incompatible, responsibilities. Nagumo's carriers were to attack Midway in preparation for the landing assault. This severely restricted the movements of the carriers, because they had to maintain their formations for air operations. The other mission was to locate and destroy the American forces.

This demanded complete freedom of movement as required and at the same time made it necessary to keep their own location secret during the search for the enemy. Yamamoto failed to assign priority of one mission over the other. Once these complex plans were set in motion, there was no provision to change them.

To make the situation even more difficult, there was absolutely no up-to-date intelligence available to Yamamoto or Nagumo about the defenses of Midway or the location of the American ships. Operation K, the flying boat reconnaissance mission, would have confirmed for Admiral Yamamoto that the American carriers were not at Pearl Harbor. This knowledge might have convinced him that Admiral Nimitz had sent the American carriers out to meet him. He could and should have alerted Nagumo to this, and altered his reconnaissance and patrol plans in a new and highly concentrated attempt to locate the U.S. task forces. By altering his attack plans, Nagumo might have been able to carry out the anticipated ambush of the American fleet. But Operation K had been scrubbed and the submarines had not been at their assigned screening locations to report the movements of the U.S. carriers. Their fleet scouting planes were sent out in a single-phase search plan that was in several cases late and poorly executed. The search yielded insufficient, misleading, and inaccurate reports. The Japanese, nevertheless, still were confident of their victory and made the decision to keep to their complex schedule.[36]

The single remaining source of intelligence information for the Japanese forces was radio traffic. Yamamoto's flagship *Yamato* bristled with radio antennae and gleaned American traffic indicating a high level of American activity—especially patrol planes—in the Hawaii area. Such activity, even though the messages could not be decoded by the Japanese, was usually associated with a strong sortie by U.S. ships from Hawaii. Not wishing to break radio silence, even with such vital information, Admiral Yamamoto sent no warning to Nagumo. Yamamoto's combined fleet intelligence specialists blithely assumed that because Nagumo was closer to the source, he had probably received the same information. However, Nagumo had not, because his carriers did not have the same ability to pick up enemy radio traffic.

Yamamoto's failure to notify Nagumo of what little intelligence was available was one of the major Japanese blunders of their Midway fiasco.

The naval general staff (NGS) back in Tokyo told Yamamoto that it appeared that enemy radio traffic in the Solomon Islands placed the American carrier (or carriers) still in that area, presenting no threat to the Midway operation. Fuchida comments that the Emily flying boats of Operation K would have been too late to arrive over Pearl Harbor to see any of the American carriers. He postulates that the NGS's misinformation would have been confirmed if the Operation K flying boats had reported that no American carriers were in the Hawaiian anchorage.[37]

Another "What If . . . ?" scenario has been offered by Prof. Theodore F. Cook, Jr,. titled "Our Midway Disaster."[38] He wonders why some Japanese intelligence officer did not question the spurious message from Midway reporting problems with their water purification plant. Why was it sent unencoded and in the clear? Professor Cook believes that, if the Japanese had not insisted that their codes were unbreakable and if they had considered the possibility that the American intelligence specialists were deciphering their messages, they may have suspected that this unencoded message was a ploy to yield the code word for Midway. If Admiral Yamamoto had known, or even had strong suspicions that the U.S. Navy was aware of his plans for Midway, he certainly had the advantage of numerical superiority to devise an ambush of his own for the American carriers that he knew would challenge the assault on Midway. It would undoubtedly have brought about the great decisive battle that Yamamoto had been seeking. It was a perfect opportunity for him to choose the time and place for the battle that he had dreamed of as Japan's primary hope of gaining the upper hand in the Pacific War.

Fuchida admits that they did not guard their secrets closely enough. Throughout the war, the Japanese considered that their code that the Americans called JN-25 was unbreakable. At the same time, Admiral Yamamoto failed to pass along important warnings, intelligence, and precautionary instructions because of his preoccupation with radio silence. Yamamoto's insistence on the gallant but antiquated concept of being present at the battle scene (in his flagship, the battleship *Yamato*) hampered his own communications. The entire IJN from Yamamoto down to the lowest-ranking sailor suffered from overconfidence and hubris as a result of the long string of Japanese triumphs of the opening days of the Pacific War. Imperial headquarters had already renamed Midway Island and had chosen the officer who would be the new station commander. Admiral Nimitz was outraged by the undue overconfidence and impertinence of the Japanese.[39]

Yamamoto violated one of the basic principles of war by dispersing his fleets over wide areas instead of concentrating his forces. Each of the groups of ships was too distant to assist any of the other forces if they encountered unexpected contact with the American opposition. If Yamamoto's main body had operated with Nagumo's carrier force, the battleships could have provided a strong antiaircraft and antiship screen for the carriers. Yamamoto could have maintained direct control over the conduct of the battles had he been physically closer. The Japanese lost their focus on the primary goal of the entire operation—the annihilation of the American fleet. The primary purpose of the invasion of Midway was to lure the American fleet into battle. The ability to attack Hawaii and Pearl Harbor after the Japanese had established a base at Midway would have been a bonus.

The reconnaissance-bombing missions of Operation K were too complex and depended on all units involved functioning without interference or alteration in plans. The submarines in the screening cordons, even if they had arrived on station in time, were assigned somewhat static patrol stations and probably would not have been able to report sighting the American fleet from those positions.

Admiral Nagumo failed to insist on adequate search sorties preceding the Midway attack. His reluctance was prompted by the past tendencies of some search planes to lose their way and to request radio homing signals. (These signals could also reveal the presence of the carriers to the enemy.) With an earlier, two-phase extensive search, the American task force probably would have been sighted and Nagumo would have been able to launch the first strike, rather than having to receive it. The sloppy reporting by his scout planes gave him inadequate and misleading information.

Nagumo used airplanes from all four of his carriers on the first strike instead of sending the assault from two carriers and holding the aircraft from the other two carriers in reserve for the second strike. His vulnerability was increased by recovery operations taking place on all his carriers at the same time, leaving no capability to launch defending aircraft in case of enemy attack. Lt. Joichi Tomonaga, the leader of the first air attack on Midway, had radioed back to the carriers: "There is need for a second attack." Admiral Nagumo was in the process of loading his bombers and torpedo planes for an attack on ships. Because of Tomonaga's message, Nagumo made the decision to download the armor-piercing bombs and torpedoes to exchange them for high-explosive bombs for a second attack on the land targets. It was a fatal decision that had loose bombs and torpedoes strewn about the decks of his carriers just as American Dauntless dive-bombers screamed down in their attack.

Nagumo's gravest error was in not launching every available aircraft he had, whether or not properly armed with torpedoes or bombs, when he learned that the American task force included at least one carrier. When American dive-bombers did strike, three of the Japanese carriers were out of action in five minutes, and the fourth was sunk the next day. The Japanese Midway force was, for all practical purposes, wiped out before Admiral Yamamoto could do anything about it. For a time, Admiral Yamamoto even considered a desperate plan to move his battleship force into place to attempt a night surface battle with the American fleet. He still had three carriers in his fleet but they were scattered too far apart to coalesce into an effective battle force. As night fell, the American fleet wisely withdrew to the east to avoid just such an encounter and to stay out of range from Wake Island–based Japanese bombers.[40]

Yamamoto's staff officers began to make desperate proposals for saving the campaign, even though most of them acknowledged that they had, in fact, suffered a tragic defeat. Another attack using the few aircraft available from the light carriers and even floatplanes against the American fleet was suggested. The combined fleet gunnery officer proposed a night bombardment of Midway by the battleships and heavy cruisers to neutralize American air power on the island. An even more fantastic plan would have sent in all the battleships, led by the *Yamato,* to shell the island in broad daylight. With the odds against the success of any of these schemes, Yamamoto gave up the battle as lost as soon as he realized that none of these plans had any chance of success. The fear of the remaining American airplanes and shore batteries on Midway caused the cancellation of all these proposals.

At Midway, the Japanese had suffered their first crushing reverse. They were forced into a defensive posture for the remainder of the war. In the intelligence war, Yamamoto had lost. The thought of just ceasing the offensive was unbearable to the Japanese. Those staff officers were gambling their existence rather than admitting that the Japanese fleet had been defeated.

As the remaining Japanese fleet withdrew and turned back to Japan, hubris was replaced by low morale at all levels. There was much talk of suicides to atone for failures. Admiral Yamamoto remained in his cabin for two days. Then, after receiving reports of the defeat from several of his ship commanders, he attempted to restore morale to the survivors. His orders went out to provide the men with pocket money and sweet cakes.

Yamamoto radioed the bad news to Admiral Nagano, chief of the NGS. Nagano informed the emperor accurately of the carrier and aircrew losses, but the emperor elected not to inform the army immediately. The navy gave the emperor's liaison conference little information about the real results of the Midway battle because the navy considered that the real extent of the damage should remain a military secret. The emperor seemed not to absorb the grave importance of the serious losses suffered at the battles of the Coral Sea and Midway.[41] Nagano finally informed Prime Minister Tojo of the defeat. Tojo issued the comment that the navy was not to be criticized; that materials would be made available immediately to replace the losses, and that the news was not to be made public. The emperor approved this handling of the matter.[42]

In Tokyo, radio listeners were told of a great naval victory. They were informed that two U.S. aircraft carriers had been sunk and 120 U.S. planes had been shot down, that the Aleutian Islands were in Japanese hands and heavy damage had been done to the installations on Midway. The *Japan*

Times and Advertiser newspaper proclaimed "Navy Scores Another Epochal Victory." A later report added an American heavy cruiser and a submarine to the score. Japanese losses were reported as one carrier sunk, a carrier and a cruiser damaged, and only thirty-five planes lost.[43]

In reality, news reporters who had been on Japanese ships were barred from returning to Tokyo to keep the press from learning of the debacle. The returning ship crews were denied shore leave or kept on base. Over five hundred wounded officers and men were secreted from hospital ships at night and ushered into the back doors of hospitals guarded by the IJN's sea police. The wounded men were not allowed visitors, letters, or telephone calls. Most Japanese did not learn of the real outcome of the Battle of Midway until after the end of the war.[44]

If Yamamoto had destroyed the American carriers, he probably would have been successful in the taking of Midway at his leisure. With Japanese carrier strength undiminished in the absence of American carrier opposition, the Hawaiian Islands would have been under constant attack. This softening up of the Hawaiian bases would have facilitated the taking of Hawaii. This, in turn, would have forced the withdrawal of American forces all to the way to the mainland West Coast. Had the Midway campaign been successful and Hawaii under Japanese control, Yamamoto's next program would have been to concentrate on a campaign against the Solomon Islands, Fiji, and Samoa. With the air power of the U.S. Pacific Fleet eliminated, little would have stood in his way. Bases on these islands could threaten any supply lines between Australia and the United States. With those vital lifelines cut, Gen. Douglas MacArthur's forces would have been completely isolated. The Japanese would have had free rein in the South Pacific and Indian Oceans to exploit their gains in Southeast Asia. By conquering India itself, they might have pushed westward to link with the Germans in the Middle East. Certainly the possession of Midway would have provided the Japanese a means to harass Hawaii and its lifelines to the West Coast. The United States' strategy of "going after Hitler First" would have been drastically altered, and dealing with the Japanese would have become America's first wartime priority.[45]

8

Bombing the United States and the Panama Canal

During the production of the initial series of the Type 1 Emily (H8K) models, the Imperial Japanese Navy (IJN) had decided to improve subsequent models of this magnificent new flying boat by including protected fuel tanks and by adding armor plating of 20- or 30-mm hardened steel to the seat backs of all crewmembers. The recommendations for these improvements had been urged by the pilots and crews of the Mavis (H6K) flying boats who had encountered Allied fighters and patrol bombers in combat. One of these proponents was Lt. Cdr. Tsuneo Hitsuji, a Mavis crew commander of the 851st Kokutai. Hitsuji's crew had fought a harrowing, running battle with a patrolling American Flying Fortress (B-17) approximately 150 miles south of Guadalcanal. The two four-engined giants fought to a draw at low level with the Flying Fortress making at least seven firing passes at the Mavis. Hitsuji's gunners scored hits on the Flying Fortress, but several of the seaplane's gunners were wounded and the fuselage interior sloshed with leaking gasoline. The Japanese seaplane's hull was so full of holes that Hitsuji reported that they nearly sank on landing before they reached the seaplane ramp at their base on Shortland Island. Because of Hitsuji's encounter, he urged that self-sealing fuel tanks be installed on all flying boats, that defensive armament be increased, that armor plate be provided at each crewmember's seat, and that training in air-to-air gunnery be expanded. Hitsuji realized that these modifications would increase the Emily's weight by about three thousand pounds, but speed and range would not suffer by much.[1]

In the new, improved Emily Type 2 flying boats, this extra weight was accommodated by the installation of the more powerful engines that developed 1,850 horsepower for takeoff. The increased power shortened the takeoff run, boosted the rate of climb, raised the service ceiling, and increased top speed. The 20-mm cannon had been restored to the nose turret with a revision to the turret that increased weapon elevation and depression to increase the field of fire. The vertical tail surfaces were enlarged and a fin was added aft of the hull step to enhance water stability. With these improvements now standardized, the new craft were being supplied hastily to combat units. After the first twelve Emily Type 1s were produced, the added features of the newer airplanes coming off the Kawanishi assembly lines caused the IJN to designate them as Emily Type 2 flying boats.[2]

The first unit to receive the Emily for combat had been the 24th Koku Sentai (24th Air Flotilla) of the Fourth Fleet. This would be the detachment of the two airplanes of the Yokohama Kokutai sent to Jaluit in the Marshall Islands for the second attempt to bomb Pearl Harbor. As more of the Emily Type 1 aircraft were completed and their crews trained, they joined the Mavis crews in the Marshall Islands to form a new unit, the No. 14 Kokutai, which was tasked for surveillance duties. After the second Operation K armed reconnaissance by Emily flying boats had been cancelled in late May 1942, just before the Battle of Midway, the Emilys were kept busy, still operating from the Marshall Islands bases. Earlier, following the Battle of the Coral Sea, they had flown unsuccessful search and patrol missions north of the Solomon Islands, looking for the withdrawing U.S. fleet.[3]

Six Mavis aircraft from the Toko Kokutai were sent in May 1942 from Yokohama via Paramushir in the Kurile Islands to Kiska to participate in the diversionary operations against the Aleutian Islands by early June. Being serviced by the seaplane tender *Kamitsu Maru* there, the half-dozen Mavis bombers operated from a camp on Kiska Island's harbor for the next two months. The commanding officer of the detachment, Capt. Sukemitsu Ito, stated that their reconnaissance and bombing efforts were limited by unfavorable weather in the Aleutians. After losing five of their number to ground fire and bad weather, two replacement Mavis airplanes were sent to Kiska. The remaining three airplanes were returned to Japan on August 17.[4]

In August 1942, U.S. Marines, led by Lt. Col. Evans F. Carlson, conducted a commando-type raid on Makin Island. The Japanese garrison there consisted of only forty-three combat troops. Carlson's Raiders were transported to Makin in two submarines, the *Nautilus* and the *Argonaut*, to create a diversion from the Guadalcanal-Tulagi landings.

The Marines made their landings on inflated rubber boats with outboard motors. The Japanese were not completely surprised and quickly organized their defenses, but the defenders were being eliminated and efforts to bring in reinforcements were not successful. The Japanese responded with several air attacks against the Marines; one of these attacks involved two Emilys. The battle report stated that several groups of aircraft participated. At first, two biplanes (probably Pete [F1M] floatplanes) flew over Makin, forcing the submarines to submerge. The biplanes "reconnoitered" for fifteen minutes, dropped bombs, and then departed. The next group of twelve aircraft, which included two "large" flying boats (Emilys) and two "medium" seaplanes (type not identified), was sighted in the early afternoon. One of the Emilys landed in the lagoon and was quickly destroyed by machine gun and antitank rifle fire. The other ten aircraft of the group bombed and strafed the island for over an hour, then departed. Native islanders reported that the wrecked Emily had brought thirty-five Japanese reinforcements, but these had all been killed.

Carlson's Raiders were not meant to occupy the island, but their withdrawal from the island did not go well. Outboard motors balked, and some of the rafts overturned in the heavy surf. As the submarines departed, the Marines believed that all their living members were aboard. Unfortunately, nine Marines had been left on the island. They were captured and executed by the returning Japanese. The hulk of the Emily still lay on the beach when the island was occupied by American forces in November 1943.[5]

The Emily flying boats were also responsible for what has been called the largest loss of American supplies—after the December 7 attack on Pearl Harbor—of World War II. By early 1944, the island of Roi-Namur (one of the islets of the Kwajalein Atoll) had become a large supply base serving what were then American bases in the Marshall Islands. Roi-Namur was crowded with stored food, ammunition, trucks, bulldozers, cranes, landing craft of all sizes, and heavy construction equipment. In the invasion of Tarawa, the Marines had run short of ammunition, so those in charge of logistics had loaded the island of Roi-Namur with invasion supplies sufficient for at least two weeks. At least six enemy seaplanes (one source says as many as fourteen) conducted a raid on the island at 2:30 AM on February 12, 1944. These airplanes were Emilys of the Kaigun Kokutais based on Saipan; they had staged through Ponape for refueling.[6] The distance from Saipan to Ponape is 1,025 miles and from Ponape to Roi-Namur, 675 miles.[7] At least one of the Emily bombardiers scored a direct hit on the ammunition dump. The explosion wiped out 85 percent of the supplies on the island and one-third of the construction equipment. Combat correspondent Bernard Redmond described "solid sheets of flame" from the explosions. The raid lasted only five minutes, but the ammunition dump continued to explode for four hours. Thirty Americans were killed and four hundred were wounded. Two large landing craft were destroyed, and so was almost all the food on the island.[8]

As the war ground down the Japanese, the magnificent Emily flying boats that had been the stars of Operation K were reduced to flying passengers and supplies to and from the by-passed island outposts. Late in the war, one of the final combat missions flown by the Emily was to provide navigation for and to lead a large formation of Frances (P1Y1). Frances was a beautiful, clean-lined twin-engined bomber that was fast and maneuverable enough to be built in a fighter version. It had sufficient range and bomb capacity to be used on "special attack" missions, which was the Japanese euphemism for suicide missions (also called kamikaze attacks).

After their support of the Iwo Jima invasion had been completed, the American task forces withdrew to reform at Ulithi Atoll. This presented a target too lucrative for the Japanese to ignore. A Myrt (C6N) reconnaissance plane confirmed that dozens of U.S. ships, including many aircraft carriers, were anchored at Ulithi. The Japanese were eager to launch their long-planned Tan Operation to destroy the enemy warships at their base.

After confusing messages caused an aborted mission on March 10, 1945, the Special Attack Squadron Azusa was launched in earnest the following day. The force, consisting of twenty-four Frances bombers, was led by three Emily Type 2 flying boats flying from Kanoya Air Base in southern Kyushu to Ulithi Atoll, a one-way distance of fifteen hundred statute miles. The two dozen Frances bombers made their rendezvous with their guiding Emilys at 9:20 AM over Cape Sata to proceed directly to Ulithi. There the Frances bombers began their suicide dives into the nineteen American aircraft carriers based there at the time. The Emily flying boats were considered too precious to act as suicide attackers, even though their crews volunteered for such attacks. The Emily crews were ordered to observe the results of the attack and return to base.

The lead pilot in the first Emily was Commander Hitsuji, who described the mission. As they neared the island of Okino-tori Shima—the halfway point—the formation was forced to climb to avoid clouds and rain squalls. Thirteen of the Frances bombers developed engine trouble and had to leave the formation. Most of the bombers were able to land on Japanese-held islands, but two had to ditch in the ocean. When the formation descended through the clouds again they were at first unable to locate Ulithi, but they sighted Yap Island twenty miles to the east. Taking a bearing from Yap, the formation was able to make its run-in to the Ulithi lagoon. Commander Hitsuji remembers that the weather at Ulithi was bad and the formation battled strong headwinds all the way to the target area. This not only delayed the attack, but also caused many of the Frances bombers to run out of fuel before reaching their intended targets. At sundown (6:52 PM local time) eleven of the attackers finally reached the target area to make their final dives; by this time darkness was falling. Up to this point, the American fleet had not detected attackers and that fleet was not blacked out until the first Japanese attacker began its bomb run.

The first Frances began its dive at 7:05 PM, and the last made its attack twenty-five minutes later. The crews of the flying boats observed only two small fires as a result of the attack. The carrier *Randolph* was the only ship that was damaged. Of the three Emily flying boats, one had to make a forced landing on the open ocean and a Japanese submarine picked up the crew. One other Emily disappeared on the return flight and was never heard from again. Commander Hitsuji piloted the third Emily back to Kanoya; that was the only aircraft to return from the mission. Although he had volunteered to do so, he had been specifically ordered not to dive his precious Emily into enemy ships.[9]

Only a few months remained of the Pacific War and all the flying boat units of the IJN were severely hampered by constant attacks from Allied aircraft, fuel shortages, and lack of parts. When the surrender came on September 2, 1945, only three Type 2 Emily flying boats remained to be turned over to the Allies. One was made flyable for delivery to the U.S. Navy for evaluation by cannibalizing parts from the other two airplanes. The Americans had recognized that the Emily was an exceptional airplane and wanted to examine it closely to glean any useful secrets from it. It was shipped to the United States for testing at the navy test center at Patuxent River, Maryland. Years later, it was returned to Japan. That one remaining airplane still exists on display in the Maritime Museum in Tokyo.[10]

Throughout the war, Japanese seaplanes carried a significant load of combat duties. These specialized airplanes made some of the most daring strikes of the Pacific conflict. Beginning in early 1942, there were other attacks that came from Japanese submarine-aircraft combinations. The IJN already had elaborate plans to use submarines to extend the range of attack aircraft. The submarine-carried reconnaissance floatplane Glen (E14Y) was the only aircraft ever to bomb the continental United States during World War II. On two occasions, a Glen from the submarine *I-25* dropped incendiary bombs on Oregon forests, yet few Americans were ever aware that an enemy bomber had dropped bombs on U.S. soil.

A proposal to use the tiny floatplane for such attacks came from WO Nobuo Fujita, flying officer for the submarine *I-25*. Fujita conceived an idea that the little plane, armed with bombs, could search far ahead of the submarine to attack shipping, or at least create a diversion while the mother submarine attacked jointly with his airplane. He also believed that the Glen could bomb shore targets—such as the Panama Canal, West Coast aircraft factories, and the naval base at San Diego. He discussed his ideas with his boat's executive officer, who wrote a letter outlining a proposal to naval headquarters. The IJN planners favored testing those ideas. When Fujita was next in port, he was summoned to headquarters to be told that he would be the one to carry out his plan. Fujita was informed that his target would be the forests of Oregon, where it was believed that small incendiary bombs could start raging forest fires, possibly engulfing whole towns in flames. At first, Fujita was extremely disappointed that his targets would not be the Panama Canal, aircraft factories, or military bases. The Japanese planners explained to him that because his small Glen floatplane could carry only a small bomb load, they believed that a more effective tactic would be incendiary attacks on the forests, starting massive forest fires that could create terror and panic among the population. They considered that such attacks, the first aerial terrorist attacks on the United States, would not only boost the moral of the Japanese people as retaliation for the Lt. Col. James H. Doolittle attack on Japan, but that they would also be a great source for the Japanese propaganda mill. Fujita requested up-to-date maps of the Oregon area and he was furnished maps that had been captured on Wake Island.

Just before dawn on September 9, 1942, the submarine *I-25,* with Cdr. Meiji Tagami as her captain, surfaced off the Oregon coast near Cape Blanco lighthouse. After the crew prepared their aircraft for flight (it was jokingly referred to by the submarine crews as the Erector Set because they assembled it by unfolding the wings and tail surfaces before launch), Warrant Officer Fujita and his navigator-gunner PO2c Shoji Okuda were catapulted into the darkness. After climbing to cruise altitude, they flew at 150 miles per hour toward the lighthouse. Their tiny airplane was capable of carrying only two 170-pound bombs. After crossing the coast-line, they turned on a southeasterly course and climbed to eight thousand feet. At a point about 50 miles inland, the morning sun revealed that they were over dense forestland. Fujita signaled Okuda to release one of the bombs. They were elated to see a scattering of flickering flames in the trees of Wheeler Ridge, eight miles south of Brookings. Each of the small bombs could spread 520 matchlike firing elements over a circle three hundred feet in diameter, burning at 1,500° Centigrade. They flew on for a few more miles, and released their second bomb. They turned the tiny Glen toward the sea, diving to treetop level and racing back to the waiting mother submarine.[11]

At least five people on the ground spotted Fujita's Glen. Marvin Johnson, a truck driver, reported the sighting of a "single engine [aircraft] with a sputtering motor. My son Dave was with me." When Johnson called the Coast Guard to report the sighting, the answering serviceman said, "You wouldn't know what a plane looked like," then hung up. Johnson said that he never forgave the Coast Guard for being so rude. Three other people claimed that they had seen the small floatplane. Allen Ettinger, another local resident, said that he had heard the Glen, but did not see it. He remarked that "it sounded like a Model A Ford hitting on three cylinders."[12]

Fujita had sighted two merchant ships on his return trip and told Commander Tagami where the vessels could be found and attacked. The little Glen aircraft was quickly disassembled and stowed, then sealed in its hangar on the submarine. As Tagami maneuvered the sub for her attack on the ships, a Hudson (A-29) bomber dove out of the sun in an attempt to drop bombs near the diving submarine. They appeared to miss their target.[13]

Capt. Jean H. Daugherty of the 390th Bomb Squadron had piloted the bomber from McChord Field, Tacoma, Washington, with his crew. Captain Daugherty recalled that west of the California-Oregon border they spotted something dark in the water. He soon realized that what they saw was a large submarine, most likely Japanese. He dropped two 300-pound demolition bombs on the crash-diving submarine, but could not tell if he had hit or damaged her. He ended the mission without knowing the status of the submarine, and in fact did not learn that he had damaged the submarine until thirty years later. The *I-25* was able to repair her damage and escape. A Coast Guard cutter and three additional airplanes searched the area, but could find no evidence of the submarine.[14]

The American reaction to the bombing was swift. The Federal Bureau of Investigation began its examination of the first bombing no fewer than four hours after it had happened. Lt. General John L. DeWitt, commander of the Western Defense Command, dispatched staff officers to Washington to obtain authorization to increase his defenses. He ordered a flight of four Lightning (P-38) fighters from the 55th Fighter Group at McChord Field near Tacoma to be temporarily based for patrols out of a fighter strip near Hoquiam, Washington.[15]

The FBI continued its investigation by sending ground teams into the bombed areas, but could find nothing to support earlier beliefs that aircraft parts had secretly been landed on U.S. soil and then assembled for the bombing raid. One supposition was that, because it was a floatplane, it could have been operated from one of the many lakes in the region. At that time, American intelligence specialists suspected that the Japanese had submarines capable of carrying aircraft. At night, drivers were cautioned not to drive near the ocean with their lights on. Nine motorists were ticketed in the Crescent City, California, area in one night for failure to abide by these restrictions. Another motorist was charged with "driving with a flashlight in a 'dimout' zone."[16]

A few days later, Radio Tokyo quoted a San Francisco radio broadcast about a Japanese plane, believed to have been launched from a submarine that had dropped firebombs in Oregon's forests. The broadcast did not mention damage. In fact, there was little actual damage done—the fires did not spread. The Japanese submariners had not been aware of the heavy rains that had dampened the forests just prior to their flight.

On September 29, the crew decided to attempt a second bombing of the Oregon forests. This time, the launch was made at midnight. Commander Tagami told Fujita that he believed that the initial bombing had alerted the enemy and that this would result in increased patrols by the Americans.

The close call with the attacking Hudson was still fresh on his mind. The little Glen carried only one light 7.7-mm machine gun in the rear cockpit for self-protection. It was maneuverable, but slow—certainly no match for any American patrol bombers. Pilot Fujita was also worried about being able to find his mother ship in the darkness on his return. Fortunately, his skipper waited for a moonlit night.

The I-25 surfaced fifty miles west of Cape Blanco to reassemble and rearm the floatplane. Fujita and his gunner Okuda flew an estimated fifty miles inland and dropped their bombs in the Grassy Knob area east of Port Orford, Oregon. They could see the red flames in the forest easily in the darkness. To reduce noise, Fujita throttled his engine down as he crossed the coast and glided well out to sea before restoring full power to the engine. He located the mother submarine in the darkness by sighting, in the moonlight, a trailing oil slick that the ship was leaving. (The oil leak may have been caused by the earlier attack by the Hudson.) The crew quickly stopped the tell-tale leaking oil after recovering her floatplane. When the Glen had been disassembled and stowed, the hangar was sealed and the I-25 resumed her patrol. As before, there was little or no damage in Oregon because the forests were still soaked by rain.

Fujita knew that the ship had two more remaining bombs on board for the airplane, but the foul weather and rough seas precluded a third wave attack. He was satisfied to be the first Japanese flyer to bomb the American mainland. He told himself that this was partial retaliation for the Doolittle raid on his own country. As it turned out, his would be the only airplane that conducted aerial bombing attacks on the mainland United States in World War II.[17]

The crew of the I-25 believed that they had accomplished their primary mission of bombing the United States. In addition, in early October, the submarine had sunk two oil tankers, the sixty-six hundred–ton SS Camden and the SS Larry Doheny. The I-25 tallied one other rather strange score. With one torpedo remaining, the submarine was about to return to Japan when two southbound submarines were spotted on the surface. The torpedo launched by I-26 struck one of the subs, which sank in twenty seconds with all hands. After the war, it was learned that the submarine hit was the *L-16*, one of two Russian submarines bound for the Panama Canal. Japan and Russia were not at war at that time. Had all the facts about the sinking of the *L-16* been known then, it could have developed into a serious international incident.[18]

The *I-17* was the first Japanese submarine ever to fire on U.S. mainland shore targets. On the clear night of February 23, 1942, Cdr. Kozo Nishino ordered his crew to battle surface at 6:40 PM, just as darkness was falling on the southern coast of California. The black-painted submarine was only one mile off the beach in the Santa Barbara channel. The nine-man deck gun crew scrambled to their weapon and began firing at about the same time that President Roosevelt was beginning a radio address—one of his famous fireside chats. It was the first time that foreign artillery shells had landed on the U.S. mainland since the War of 1812.

The intended target was the group of oil storage tanks and the refining facilities of Richfield Oil Company's refinery near Ellwood City. Commander Nishino, formerly the captain of an oil tanker, had taken on a load of oil from this facility before the war. Nishino expected a quick response from any shore batteries that the U.S. Army may have placed to protect those facilities, so he did not take the time to fire any ranging shots. Explosions interrupted the dinner service at nearby Wheeler's Inn as the *I-17*'s gun crew blew five-foot craters in the foothills of the Santa Ynez Mountains for forty-five minutes. Nishino's gun crew scored no hits and caused no real damage because he lacked an adequate range finder in the gathering darkness and the submarine had to keep moving to maintain steerage.

The gun crew was now working in the increasing darkness and it was difficult for them to see their targets in spite of the short distance. At 8:20 PM, after expending her gun ammunition, the submarine slipped below the surface and headed back to the Marshall Islands. The only American reaction was to silence local radio stations. Automobile traffic along the coastal highway had immediately turned around and escaped out of harm's way.

To keep the Japanese from learning of any reaction to the shelling, the American government immediately warned newspapers and radio stations not to publicize the event. Oil refinery workers were ordered not to talk about the incident and were threatened with loss of exemption from the draft if they broke their silence about what had happened. *Life* magazine ignored the government orders and published three pages of pictures covering the story in its March 9, 1942, issue.[19]

Rumors of the bold submarine attack spread rapidly throughout southern California. Western defense commanders were nervous and placed all antiaircraft and searchlight batteries on alert on February 24. Naval intelligence had predicted that an attack on Los Angeles was imminent. False alarms brought an alert to the city at 7:30 PM that night, but the all clear was sounded by 10:30 PM.

Early the next morning, in the darkness at 2:15 AM on February 25, there were reports of unidentified aircraft approaching Los Angeles from the ocean. Radar had picked up a target 120 miles to the west, approaching the city. The regional defense authority ordered an immediate blackout. A flight of planes was reported over Long Beach. A colonel commanding a coastal artillery battery reported twenty-five more planes at twelve thousand feet. The Los Angeles Defense Information Center was deluged with enemy plane sightings. Nervous, trigger-happy antiaircraft gunners began firing at any suspected targets, expending some fourteen hundred rounds of 3-inch antiaircraft artillery alone, not including the shooting of larger and smaller caliber ammunition. At 3:06 AM the sky above Los Angeles was as bright as day. The shaken-awake citizens of Los Angeles opened their windows to see tracer bullets and the bright flashes of exploding antiaircraft fire in the darkness. Shrapnel rained over much of the city. Searchlights lit up the skies of Los Angeles and air raid sirens caused residents to panic. Bill Weller, Jr., ten years old at the time, recalls seeing (and hearing) an antiaircraft battery at Manchester and Western firing at what he thought to be "planes in V-formation heading north toward Burbank."[20] An air raid warden claimed seeing no fewer than ten flights of enemy planes. Another witness remembered that "Huge spotlights were on one plane and—oh my!—the artillery guns were really shooting."[21] The *Los Angeles Times* reported that two planes crashed and burned—one in Hollywood and another near 185th

Street and Vermont Avenue. The report did not identify either aircraft as friendly or enemy. Fourth Air Force headquarters in San Francisco said that at least one plane had been shot down in the attack.[22]

Ever since December 7, 1941, Americans had expected an attack by the Japanese against the city that was home to some of the nation's largest aircraft production plants and defense industries. One resident eyewitness interviewed recalled that "P-38s [Lightnings] and fighters were screaming back and forth all over the city at low altitude" and "flak was going off all over the place" in what became known as the Battle of Los Angeles. Other sources claimed that no defending American fighters were ever involved because of the heavy flak. Later, embarrassed army officers conceded that a few unidentified aircraft may have touched off the incident and that "our forces overreacted unnecessarily." Other high-ranking army officials never admitted that there had been an overreaction but resolutely maintained that the threat had been real and that the enemy had been successfully repelled. Even Secretary of War Henry L. Stimson said that Japanese planes had indeed been overhead during the so-called battle, but Secretary of the Navy Frank Knox stated flatly that there had been no such planes. The official U.S. Army Air Force (USAAF) history admits that accounts of that night are "hopelessly at variance."[23] The rest of the U.S. Navy scoffed at the whole affair, saying that there was never any reason for the so-called battle. The comedy 1941, featuring John Belushi as a cigar-chewing gung-ho Kittyhawk (P-40) fighter pilot, was based on the Battle of Los Angeles, and some of the incidents portrayed in the film had some basis in fact.[24]

The submarines I-25 and I-26 accomplished the only other shelling attacks by Japanese submarines on shore installations. The I-26, captained by Cdr. Minoru Yokota, lobbed about twenty 5.5-in. shells at the Estevan Point lighthouse on Vancouver Island on the night of June 20, 1942. Nothing of consequence was hit by the shells, but it was the only place in Canada to come under enemy fire in World War II.[25]

The only military installation to be attacked by the Japanese submarines was Fort Stevens, Oregon, a U.S. Army Coast Artillery station. The commander of the submarine I-25, Commander Tagami, using maps captured on

Wake Island, thought that he was shelling an American submarine base at the mouth of the Columbia River. The coast artillery batteries at Fort Stevens were alerted, loaded, and ready to return fire on the brazen attacker, but the commanding officer of Fort Stevens would not give the order to fire because he thought that the sub was out of range. Actually, the Japanese submarine was well within the range of the larger shore guns. He also admitted that he worried that the location of his gun emplacements would be revealed if he returned fire. Fortunately, once again no damage was done to the shore installation. The Japanese submarine commander later admitted that he would not have come near the fort if he had known it was a coast artillery base.[26]

It would be almost a year later after the bombing of the Oregon forests, on October 5–6, 1943, that the first American carrier forces equal to the Japanese strength of their Pearl Harbor attack struck Wake Island. The island had been attacked by smaller forces before, but the U.S. Navy was now definitely back on the offensive. New Hellcat (F6F) fighters with bombers from the carriers *Essex, Lexington, Yorktown, Belleau Woods, Cowpens,* and *Independence* bombed and strafed the island unmercifully. They destroyed twenty-two of thirty-four Japanese planes on the island.[27]

The heavy attack on Wake alarmed the Japanese high command with its concentration of force. They interpreted it to mean that an offensive against Wake Island or the Marshall Islands was about to begin. Because the Emily flying boats could no longer refuel at French Frigate Shoals, there was to be at least one more flight by the little Glen floatplane over Pearl Harbor to learn the level of American strength there.

The Japanese submarine *I-36* had been loitering in the Hawaii area for nearly a month waiting for an opportunity to get a look at the activity in Pearl Harbor. Each time the boat came close, the radar defenses, air patrols, and an alert inshore patrol at Oahu kept her at bay. Finally, in desperation, the *I-36* moved out three hundred miles to launch her Glen on a one-way special mission on October 19. The little floatplane could not carry enough fuel to make the round trip, but the doomed aviator successfully reached Pearl Harbor to radio his report back to the sub that he had sighted four carriers, four battleships, five cruisers, and seventeen destroyers in port.

After he ended his transmission, he signed off with a patriotic "Banzai!" and disappeared somewhere in the Pacific Ocean.[28]

Except for the earlier attack launched from the *I-25* by Warrant Officer Fujita to attempt to start forest fires in Oregon, the little Glen floatplanes were never used offensively for the remainder of the war. Fujita's attack had served as a feasibility test for a much more ambitious plan that had been brewing earlier with the IJN's long-range planners. Fujita's concept to use submarine-based bombers had originated elsewhere before and had already been given a great deal of importance. In 1942, in the Fifth Fleet replenishment program (corresponding to an annual defense budget), the IJN authorized a request for eighteen submarines of the *I-400* class (see Appendix).

In December 1944, the plan was for the submarines to take their aircraft near the mainland United States and use them in terror bombing or kamikaze strikes against New York City or Washington, D.C., or both. When these plans were cancelled, Capt. Tatsunoke Ariizumi formed Submarine Squadron One (SubRon1) consisting of *I-400, I-401, I-13*, and *I-14* for another special mission. With three airplanes on the first two and two each on the latter, SubRon1 could launch a ten-bomber strike force.

SubRon1's first mission, as selected by Vice Adm. Jisaburo Ozawa, was to be Operation PX. This was a top-secret plan to use the ten Seiran (M6A) bombers to conduct bacteriological warfare on the cities of the U.S. West Coast and Allied-occupied Pacific Islands. Infected fleas and insects were to be dropped in plague bombs to spread typhus, dengue fever, cholera, bubonic plague, and other plagues. These germ warfare agents had been developed by the Imperial Japanese Army's (IJA's) General Ishii's infamous Detachment 731 near Harbin, Manchuria, using Chinese, Korean, Russian, and American prisoners as test subjects. Fortunately, this diabolical mission was cancelled by Gen. Yoshijiro Umezu, chief of the army general staff, who decided that "Germ warfare against the United States would escalate to war against all humanity."[29]

It was apparent by early 1945 that Germany would be defeated and that the Pacific Fleet would be augmented by many warships from the Atlantic.

They would be coming through the Panama Canal to participate in attacks against Japan in the Pacific. Captain Ariizumi suggested that a more urgent, more realistic, and more useful plan would be to bomb the Gatun Locks of the Panama Canal. American air raids on the Aichi aircraft workshops, fuel shortages, and air-dropped mines interfered with submarine training exercises in Japanese home waters, but by mid-June 1945, pilots who had already joined SubRon1's specially formed 901st Air Group were practicing against full-size mock-ups of the Gatun Locks in Toyama Bay, Honshu.[30]

It was planned that the four boats of SubRon1 would sail to near Oahu on the same route taken for the December 1941 attack. They would then move south to the coast of Colombia, working their way northward to the waters off the Panama Canal to launch all ten of their Seiran. Each bomber would be loaded with a 1,764-pound bomb or torpedo. More than one source indicates that the airplanes would be painted silver and given American insignia to deceive and confuse the defending American fighter pilots into thinking that the Seirans were American Mustangs (P-51s). If intercepted by American fighters, the pilots would jettison their floats to increase the speed of their terminal suicide dives into their targets. (Without its floats, the Seiran's liquid-cooled engine and streamlined canopy made it resemble the American Mustang fighter at a distance.) The Japanese did not know that Mustangs had not yet been based in the Canal Zone area, but encountering Mustang fighters and especially float-equipped Mustangs might have caused some confusion among defending American fighter pilots. The Japanese believed that even a few seconds of delay in recognizing the Seirans as Japanese might give them the advantage that they needed for success in their attack.[31]

Before their training was complete, target plans were altered again. The IJN was running out of fuel in the final weeks of the war. The round trip of seventeen thousand miles to the Panama Canal would require at least sixteen hundred tons of fuel for each submarine. Only two thousand tons of fuel were available at the home base at Kure, so *I-401* departed in mid-May for Dairen, Manchuria, where a supply of oil was available. Barely out of port, *I-401* struck a magnetic mine laid by a Superfortress (B-29) and had to return to Kure for repairs. *I-400* was successful in getting a full load of oil from Dairen, but the threat of mines forced a change in plans to train the submarines to operate with their seaplanes in the Inland Sea. The operation was moved for training in the Sea of Japan. When the U.S. submarine *Skate* torpedoed the IJN submarine *I-122* on June 10 in the Sea of Japan, it became obvious that there was no place to hide. After two of the Seiran crashed during joint training exercises and Superfortress raids disrupted production schedules for the Seiran bombers and spare parts, the plan to bomb the Panama Canal was abandoned. In place of this plan, the Japanese hoped to bombard San Francisco, but ultimately they cancelled this plan, also.[32]

The Japanese learned that more than three thousand Allied warships and transports were already gathering at Pacific anchorages for Operation Olympic, the forthcoming invasion of the Japanese home islands. Against the fulminations and vehement objections of SubRon1's skipper, Captain Ariizumi, the naval high command decided that a higher priority would be a coordinated attack on the U.S. fleet anchorage at Ulithi Atoll where the Americans were beginning to gather many of the invasion ships. The Japanese wanted to destroy as much of this U.S. fleet as possible with an attack by the aircraft of SubRon1 and other submarines carrying the *kaiten* (midget suicide submarines) atop their hulls. In this plan, only the *I-400* and *I-401* would launch Seiran attack bombers. The *I-13* and *I-14* would instead carry, disassembled, the fast Myrt long-range reconnaissance planes to Truk. There, the Myrt would be reassembled to use as scouts over Ulithi in preparation for the attack scheduled for August 25.

The *I-13* and *I-14* sailed for Truk on July 15. The next day, planes of a hunter-killer group from the USS *Anzio* discovered the *I-13* about 630 miles east of Honshu. The submarine was damaged by aircraft rockets, and then sunk by the destroyer escort USS *Lawrence C. Taylor*. *I-400* and *I-401* sailed separately for a rendezvous off Ponape Island in the eastern Caroline Islands where they were to meet on August 16 to await orders for their attack. Those orders never came. The fighting ended on August 15 and the submarines were ordered to return to Japan to surrender. Captain Ariizumi directed his squadron to hoist black flags, jettison all documents, fire their torpedoes, and catapult all aircraft into the ocean.[33]

As skipper of the IJN submarine *I-8*, Captain Ariizumi had picked up ninety-eight unarmed survivors of a Dutch merchant ship *Tjsalak* south of Colombo on March 26, 1944, and massacred all of them. He performed a similar atrocity with ninety-six prisoners from the American transport ship *Jean Nicolet* in the Maldives on July 2, 1944. He and his crew tortured and murdered sixty members of the freighter's crew. When he was suddenly forced to dive by the appearance of an approaching aircraft, he left thirty-five bound prisoners on deck. The next day, a Royal Indian Navy escort ship rescued twenty-three survivors of this group who had managed to untie themselves and tread water all night.

Captain Ariizumi was unable to accept the fact that he had failed to carry out his missions to bomb the United States, the Panama Canal, or the American fleet at Ulithi. He believed that he would be tried as a war criminal for his atrocities. He believed that he owed an apology to the emperor. Ariizumi is reported to have committed seppuku by shooting himself as *I-401* entered Tokyo Bay to surrender at Yokosuka.[34] When the *I-400* surrendered to U.S. Navy ships, the boat was carrying no airplanes, nor did she have torpedoes or ammunition, having obeyed surrender orders to jettison all ordnance. The Seiran airplanes had been fired from the catapults with their wings and tail surfaces folded, then riddled with gunfire so that they would sink. The boat did carry a heavy load of provisions, making it obvious that nearly all Japanese submarines were being used to supply the starving garrisons of bypassed islands.

There was evidence that the submarines of SubRon1 made at least one pass at the Panama Canal. Charts found on the *I-400* and *I-14* indicated that the *I-400, I-401, I-13,* and *I-14* had completed a reconnaissance cruise of the Eastern Pacific in 1945. The charts show that on June 7 they were ten miles off the coast of Colombia, well within striking distance of the Canal. Apparently the Japanese were waiting for exactly the right time to strike but their reasons for withholding the strike against the Canal in early June were not revealed. Why the attack was not carried out in June was never determined.[35]

The realization of the lack of resources and the inability to overcome technical problems was a bitter disappointment for the Japanese. Their dreams of superbomber raids against the American mainland slipped away.

Not until the end of the war did the Japanese abandon plans for retaliation. The Japanese had been stopped in New Guinea, Midway, and Guadalcanal. The course of the war was definitely against the Japanese by the beginning of that year but they still yearned to bomb the United States. The Doolittle raid demanded retaliation and several Japanese admirals and generals believed that they had failed in their duty to protect the emperor and the Japanese homeland. Many of those Japanese generals and admirals with deeply rooted Shinto beliefs considered that they owed their lives to the emperor. His safety and well-being were the reason for their existence.

The Japanese bomb-balloons, called *fugo* or the *fugo*-weapon by their originators, were another desperate part of the retaliation offensive to regain face lost by the humiliation of the Doolittle bombing raid. The Japanese balloon-bomb idea originated in 1933 as part of a proposed airborne weapons program. Spurred by the Doolittle raid, the Japanese spent the next two years in testing and preparing bomb-carrying balloons.

The balloons were about thirty-three feet in diameter, made of six hundred separate pieces of tissue-paper glued with a paste sealant made from a type of Japanese potato to make a leak-proof sphere. Inflated with nineteen thousand cubic feet of hydrogen, the balloons had a lifting capacity of one thousand pounds at sea level and three hundred pounds at thirty thousand feet. The payload of the balloons was a thirty-three-pound high-explosive antipersonnel bomb and several of two types of incendiary bombs.[36]

Japanese high-school girls were the major labor force involved with the manufacture of the balloons. The girls labored to stitch and paste the balloon envelopes and the balloons were tested in large theatres and sumo wrestling halls. One girl told of how a factory was started at her school in 1944, with the girls being told that they would be making a secret weapon that would be going all the way to America, but they were not told what the weapon was. The school was closed as the war intensified and the girls were sent to a factory where the balloons were assembled and tested. They worked twelve-hour shifts with no lunch in an unheated building. Not until forty years later did they learn that their balloons had been used to attempt to bomb the American homeland.[37]

The world's first intercontinental weapon, these balloons would ride the fast east-flowing winds (later known as the jet stream) from Japan to the mainland of the United States and Canada. Through extensive tests by radio tracking, the Japanese learned that fifty to seventy hours were required for the sixty-two hundred–mile trip. Once the balloon had reached the mainland United States, small incendiary and antipersonnel bombs would be released by timers or barometers to "create death and destruction [which could] panic the nation."

These indiscriminate balloon-bombs were primarily a weapon developed by the IJA, but the IJN developed a type of balloon that consisted of components that could be loaded on board submarines through their small hatches. The balloons, equipped with an automatic altitude-control device and timing mechanisms for releasing the bombs, were to be inflated on the deck of the submarine. The balloons would be launched at night approximately 620 miles off the North American coast for a flight time of about ten hours. Two submarines, the *I-34* and *I-35*, were refitted for this mission and two hundred balloons were fabricated for this operation. The submarines were urgently needed for other higher priority missions and the balloon-submarine combination project was discontinued.[38]

The balloon-bomb attacks were not successful, even though thousands of the balloons were launched. Several small forest fires were ignited, but these fires never caused the damage that the Japanese had hoped for. There were 285 reported balloon incidents out of an estimated 9,000 balloons launched from Japan. One balloon was found in Alaska in late 1954 with its explosive potential still active. Fighters shot many of the balloons down, but there has been no accounting for thousands of them.

The U.S. government wanted to keep any news of America being indiscriminately bombed out of the news to keep the Japanese from launching more of the balloon-bombs. The strategy worked. The Japanese became discouraged because of the silence of the American press about any balloon incidents. This policy of silence denied the Japanese any knowledge of the effectiveness of the balloon attacks. The

Japanese believed that their balloon-bomb plan was a failure and shut down the launches in March 1945.

In reality, the threat was regarded as serious in the United States. To guard against forest fire damage, the army sent the first all-volunteer African-American 555th Parachute Infantry Battalion on a top-secret mission to Pendleton Air Base, Oregon, with a contingent to be stationed at Chico, California. On their way to the west, the troopers thought that they would be assigned to join Gen. Douglas MacArthur's Pacific forces to fight the Japanese. Instead, they were to participate in Operation Fire Fly. This assignment involved the paratroopers of the 555th battalion to train with the earliest smoke jumpers to fight forest fires. The soldiers of the 555th were not aware of the balloon-bomb threat—they just thought that they were to fight forest fires. The unit was ready after only two weeks of training as smoke-jumpers and they did quench at least thirty-six fires (most from natural causes), but they had hoped to prove themselves in combat. The troopers of the 555th made twelve hundred individual jumps from their bases in Oregon and California in the summer of 1945.[39]

Ironically, the only deaths caused by the balloons were six people—Mrs. Archie Mitchell, a Sunday school teacher, and five children—on May 5, 1945, a month after the Japanese ended the balloon launches. Mrs. Mitchell and the children were on a picnic outing with her husband and several other children. They were curious about the strange object that they had found in the woods near Bly, Oregon, and caused it to detonate.[40]

Detailed accounts of the entire balloon-bomb operation and the U.S. reactions to it are given in the thoroughly-researched *Japan's World War II Balloon Bomb Attacks on North America* by Robert C. Mikesh, former curator of the National Air and Space Museum, published by the Smithsonian Institute Press, and Bert Webber's well-done *Silent Seige—III*, published by the Webb Research Group.

EPILOGUE

In June 1944, the once mighty Imperial Japanese Navy (IJN) lost its prize carriers *Shokaku* and *Taiho*, along with nearly three hundred aircraft in the Battle of the Philippine Sea. By early July, it had become evident to even the most loyal of the emperor's subjects that the war was lost for the Japanese. With the taking of Saipan, the Americans now had island bases from which their Superfortresses (B-29s) could attack the Japanese home islands. Vice Adm. Chuichi Nagumo, who had commanded the powerful carrier forces that had attacked Oahu and Midway, had been reduced to commanding the naval units on Saipan. Nagumo, after leaving a letter of profound apology to the emperor, committed seppuku (ritualized suicide) to atone for his failures.[1]

Gen. Douglas MacArthur fulfilled his "I shall return" promise as he waded ashore on Leyte on October 20, 1944. With the ensuing Battle of Leyte Gulf, the U.S. Navy eliminated any serious opposition in the Pacific. In late November, Superfortresses began bombing Tokyo from bases in the Marianas Islands.[2]

The growing threats to Japan caused the imperial general headquarters (IGHQ) to form a new homeland defense operations plan optimistically called *Sho-Go*—Victory Operation. The plan's purpose was to inflict such delays and heavy losses on the Allies that they would be forced to accept a negotiated peace favorable to the Japanese. Even if that failed, it would give the Japanese more time to organize their home defenses. The *Sho-Go* plan covered operations in the Philippines, Formosa, the Ryukyu Islands, and homeland defense plans for the inevitable invasion of Japan. The plan emphasized beach defense and powerful counterattacks to take place before landing forces could establish beachheads. Extensive construction of coastal defenses in Kyushu began in the fall of 1944.[3]

After the war, it was discovered that the Japanese, even without breaking any codes, had made accurate estimates of American invasion plans. In April 1945, IGHQ finalized its *Ketsu-Go* plan—the blueprint for the entire structure of the homeland defense. The *Ketsu-Go* plan depended heavily on the *Tokko* or *To-Go* forces (a contraction of the Japanese Tokubetsu Kogeki Tai, or Special Attack Units). The desperate kamikaze attacks of these forces had proven their effectiveness in the Philippines and at Okinawa. In defense of the Japanese home islands, the Japanese plan was for the kamikazes to swarm by the thousands to destroy the Allied invasion fleet while it was still at sea. The optimistic Japanese planners estimated that there would be ten thousand Japanese aircraft of different types available for kamikaze strikes at the time of the invasion. They believed that at least half the invasion fleet would be destroyed before a single American soldier reached the beach.[4]

The estimate of the Japanese planners of the number of aircraft, including bomb-laden trainers and specially designed kamikaze airplanes, to be involved in kamikaze attacks to defend the home islands was right on the mark. The U.S. Strategic Bombing Survey placed the figure at nearly seventeen hundred Japanese aircraft that would have been used to participate in the *Tokko* tactics in the invasion defense of the Japanese home islands. Other estimates ran as high as 12,725 aircraft available for kamikaze attacks.[5]

Of all the crewmembers that had been on board the two Emily flying boats when they attempted to bomb Pearl Harbor in March 1942, only one man survived the war. This was PO2c Toshiaki Yamada, the radioman who had been on Lt. Hisao Hashizume's Emily Y-71 for the March attack, but who flew with Ensign Sasao's Emily Y-72 crew that went to photograph Johnston Island on March 10.

Ens. Shosuke Sasao, after returning to Yokosuka in March 1942, flew as an instructor for the Emily flying boats there. Sasao was listed as killed in action in the Saipan area in July 1944.[6]

Cdr. Mitsuo Fuchida, who had led the initial attack on Pearl Harbor, survived the Battle of Midway, the Battle of Leyte Gulf, a jungle crash, the atomic bombing of Hiroshima, and stood as a captain on the deck of the USS *Missouri* as the surrender documents were signed. His naval career was over. He worked briefly with the U.S. Strategic Bombing Survey, and testified in the war crimes trials, but these duties came to an end. He really feared that he would be tried as a war criminal himself. Unemployed, he tried to eke out a survival for his family and himself as a farmer. He hated the American occupation of his homeland bitterly and blamed his former enemies for all his troubles and those of his defeated country.

By a strange coincidence, a stranger handed Fuchida a religious pamphlet on the street one day. It had been written by an American sergeant, Jacob DeShazer, one of the crewmembers of Doolittle's Raiders. DeShazer had been captured by the Japanese when he bailed out of his crippled Mitchell (B-25), but survived the war in a Japanese prison camp. DeShazer had converted to Christianity after reading the Bible in prison. Fuchida's interest in that religion was sparked by the pamphlet and he became a devout Christian himself. After several successful speaking engagements that drew large crowds of Japanese, Fuchida realized that he had found his new calling and he became a minister. He worked for the remainder of his life in efforts to promote world peace through Christianity. He lived for several years in the United States and came to genuinely love the country that had been his former enemy. He returned to visit Japan later and died at the age of seventy-three on May 30, 1976.[7]

Cdr. Minoru Genda, Fuchida's close friend and chief planner of the Pearl Harbor attack, became a lieutenant general in the Japanese Maritime Air Self-Defense Force (JMSDF) after the war. Genda created quite a stir when he commented that if the Japanese had possessed the atomic bomb during the Pacific War, they would certainly have used it against the American forces. Genda died on August 15, 1989.

Fuchida's and Genda's mentor, Adm. Isoroku Yamamoto, did not survive the war. Late in March 1943, Yamamoto had initiated Operation I, a counteroffensive that was to strike Allied harbors and airbases in the Solomon Islands, focusing on destroying American airpower in the area. The admiral had flown to the Japanese base at Rabaul to oversee the operation. Operation I began on April 7, 1943, and even raided General MacArthur's New Guinea headquarters at Port Moresby in New Guinea. Yamamoto was given reports that the enemy was suffering heavy losses in ships, aircraft, and on their bases. The Japanese had never learned, nor did they suspect during the war, that the Americans had broken their radio codes. The code breakers of three of the Fleet Radio Units simultaneously intercepted and decoded a series of messages that went out on April 14 telling the units involved that Admiral Yamamoto would conduct an inspection tour of the bases at Ballale, Buin, and Shortland Islands. Included in that message was an itinerary of the admiral's tour, giving exact departure and arrival times, reminding all concerned that the admiral was a stickler for promptness.[8]

Cdr. Edwin T. Layton, Adm. Chester W. Nimitz's intelligence chief, had received a copy of the itinerary message that read as follows:

The inspection tour of the Commander-in-Chief Combined Fleet to Ballale, Shortland and Buin on April 18 is scheduled as follows:

0600 depart Rabaul by medium attack plane (Mitsubishi Betty bomber) escorted by six fighters).

0800 arrive Ballale. Depart immediately for Shortland by subchaser (1s Base Force will prepare one boat), arriving Shortland 0840.

0945 depart Shortland by subchaser, arriving Ballale 1030. (For transportation, prepare assault boat at Shortland and motor launch at Ballale.)

1100 depart Ballale by medium attack plane arriving Buin 1110. Lunch at Headquarters, 1st Base Force. (Senior Staff Officer, Air Flotilla 26, to be present.)

1400 depart Buin by medium attack plane, arriving Rabaul 1530.

At each base, the Commander in Chief will make a short tour of inspection and at one base he will visit the sick and wounded, but current operations should continue.

In the event of inclement weather, there will be a postponement of one day.[9]

Commander Layton knew that this inspection tour placed Admiral Yamamoto closer than ever before to American forces in the combat zone. He quickly took the decoded message to Admiral Nimitz. The admiral went to his immense wall chart of the Pacific Ocean. He checked Yamamoto's destinations on Bougainville, and measured the distances between those bases and Guadalcanal. He knew that Adm. William F. Halsey had army and navy fighters under his command that had recently attacked bases on Bougainville.

Nimitz then asked Layton, "Do we try to get him?" Layton replied, "You know, Admiral, it would be just as if they shot you down. There's nobody to replace you." Layton later wrote that Nimitz and Halsey had received the president's approval for the operation, but did not document the claim.

Admirals Nimitz and Halsey gave the job to Adm. Marc A. Mitscher who commanded all the navy and army air units on Guadalcanal. Mitscher responded with his assurance that the Lightnings (P-38s), with large drop tanks installed, had the range to accomplish the task. The navy's Wildcats (F4Fs) and Corsairs (F4U) did not have the range for this mission.

Led by Maj. John W. Mitchell, the squadron commander of the 339th Fighter Squadron, sixteen Lightnings took off from Guadalcanal's Henderson Field early on the morning of April 18, 1943. Mitchell's Lightning had been fitted with a carefully calibrated ship's compass. The mission planning had been meticulous, with headings, timing, and altitudes for each of the navigation legs that would avoid the Japanese-held islands east of the course. The Lightnings would remain low to avoid radar detection and they would observe strict radio silence until they reached the area where they expected to intercept Yamamoto's bomber.[10]

Yamamoto was known for his punctuality, but the Americans knew that the odds of intercepting the admiral's bomber after such a 410-mile rambling route were slim. The inbound flight would take nearly two hours for the Lightning. At one minute ahead of schedule, they were exactly on course when one member of the flight broke radio silence. "Bogeys, eleven o'clock high!" There, just ahead to the left and higher, were two Betty (G3M) bombers and six escorting Zero (A6M) fighters.[11]

Twelve of the Lightnings went into a rapid climb to cover the Zero escort so the four other fighters would go after the two Japanese bombers. (They had expected only one bomber.) Capt. Tom Lanphier and Lt. Rex T. Barber went after the bombers. Yamamoto's Betty crashed into the jungle from low altitude and the second Betty crashed into the ocean. In the confusion of battle, both Lanphier and Barber claimed to have shot down Yamamoto's bomber, and the controversy has still not been resolved as to which pilot should receive credit. One Lightning pilot, Lt. Raymond K. Hine, was seen being attacked by the escorting Zeroes and did not return from the mission. For a time, the Lightning pilots believed that a third Betty was shot down, as well as three of the escorting Zero fighters. The Japanese confirmed that two bombers had been shot down and that Admiral Yamamoto had died in one of them. Vice Adm. Matome Ugaki, Yamamoto's chief of staff, was in the second bomber and suffered severe injuries. None of the Zeroes was shot down, as the Americans had claimed, but the Japanese also erroneously claimed the downing of six of the Lightnings.[12]

The emperor ordered a rare state funeral for Yamamoto on June 5, 1943. The emperor promoted Yamamoto posthumously to fleet admiral and awarded him the Grand Order of the Chrysanthemum, equivalent to the American Medal of Honor.[13]

The American cryptanalysts and code breakers had scored another victory in the war of intelligence. Lt. Cdr. Joseph J. Rochefort, head of the navy's Combat Intelligence Unit, Pacific, whose group had done such brilliant work, did not receive his just rewards for his victories in the intelligence war. In October 1942, he was reassigned to duty in San Francisco, and in June 1943 he was assigned to the dead-end job as commander of a floating dry dock at Mare Island, California. Later, his Combat Intelligence Unit received the Navy Unit Commendation and he was awarded the Legion of Merit medal. He retired from the navy as a captain on January 1, 1947. Rochefort died at Torrance, California, on July 20, 1976.[14]

WO Nobuo Fujita, the pilot who bombed the Oregon forests in 1942, was invited in 1962 to visit Brookings, Oregon, by the local Junior Chamber of Commerce. Fujita and his family were to be the city's guests at the town's Azalea Festival. There was some opposition to this visit, but the Jaycees countered this by citing their creed that "the brotherhood of man transcends the sovereignty of nations." Fujita was overwhelmed by the friendliness of his welcome to America. One of the Jaycees was a pilot and took Fujita for a flight in a Piper Tri-pacer. Fujita took the controls to fly over Wheeler Ridge, where he had released his bombs twenty years earlier. At a banquet, Fujita presented the town of Brookings with the priceless *kai-gunto* samurai sword that he had carried on his bombing missions. He returned to the area again in 1992 and planted a small redwood tree at the site of his earlier bombing. He said that he was glad to act as a "bridge between Japan and America." Fujita died of lung cancer in 1997 and his ashes were scattered over the area of his first bombing.[15]

Even before the official surrender documents were signed on board the USS *Missouri* on September 2, 1945, the disarming of Japanese military and naval forces had been ordered and initiated with vigor. Aircraft were disabled by removing their propellers and puncturing gasoline tanks. Most were incinerated after being bulldozed into piles of smashed aluminum. Allied intelligence units wanted to examine and test some of the Imperial Japanese Army (IJA) and IJN's airplanes. Examples of certain airplanes were named and held for flight tests and evaluations by Allied intelligence teams.

The last official mission flown by a Japanese pilot in a Japanese warplane was the delivery of the one remaining flyable Emily flying boat, with Lt. Cdr. Tsuneo Hitsuji as its pilot. The U.S. Navy had been so impressed with the performance of its former enemy flying boat that it wanted to evaluate its features and abilities for possible use in the design of future American flying boats.

The final flight took place on November 13, 1945, from the Japanese Naval Base at Takuma to Yokohama. Commander Hitsuji was the commanding officer of the 801st Sentai (flying boat squadron) based at Yokohama. As such, he was responsible for the repair of the last Emily. Seven mechanics from the Kure Naval Air Arsenal nearby had needed approximately two months to bring this last remaining example of the Emily to flying condition. The squadron had only three Emily aircraft that had not been totally destroyed by Allied forces. All three of the remaining airplanes had been damaged to some extent. Two of them were used for spare parts to repair the last surviving airplane. Even in that aircraft, several bullet holes inflicted by American strafing attacks had to be patched. All radar equipment, cannon, and machine guns were removed prior to the ferry delivery flight.[16]

Commander Hitsuji was at the controls of the last Emily, accompanied by Lt. (jg) E. J. Silver, who was responsible for the safe delivery of the Emily to Yokohama. Lieutenant Silver, assigned to the U.S. Strategic Bombing Survey Mission, had arrived at Takuma the day before with a Catalina (PBY-5) that would be used to escort the Japanese flying boat.[17]

Takeoff was at 11:00 AM that November morning with the Catalina leading the Emily. According to the restrictions, at no time was the Japanese airplane to precede its escort and this posed a problem. The notoriously slow Catalina's cruise speed was only 105 knots (122 miles per hour), but the Emily could not cruise economically at that speed. The maximum speed for the Catalina was 154 knots (179 miles per hour). Wing flap deflection would have been required to slow the Japanese airplane, so a compromise speed of 130 knots (150 miles per hour) was agreed on for the Emily and it would fly a zigzag course behind the Catalina to maintain its trailing position. The Emily could normally have made the flight in an hour and forty-five minutes, but it had to stay with its American escort. The trip took two and a half hours.[18]

The Japanese flying boat was promptly loaded aboard a U.S. Navy seaplane tender for its trip to the United States. When the plane arrived at

Whidbey Island in Washington, inspection revealed that the aircraft was really not up to the three thousand miles overland ferry flight to the Naval Air Test Center (NATC) at Patuxent River, Maryland. The airplane was reloaded aboard ship and hauled to Norfolk, Virginia. After more preparation, it was flown the one hundred miles to the NATC at Patuxent River, finally arriving on May 23, 1946. There, the navy assigned two of its top Aviation Machinist Mates to bring the Emily up to flight test standards. To meet navy safety requirements for flight testing, a great deal of work still needed to be accomplished. Extensive hull repairs still had to be made. All controls, electrical systems, fuel, and lubrication systems had to be checked. Parts for repairing the engines' water-injection system were not available, so full power from the engines would not be possible.[19]

The Emily was finally judged safe for flight and made its first and only flight in the United States on May 23, 1946. The quick, short takeoff run impressed the American pilots and the Emily quickly climbed to twelve thousand feet. The flying boat was accompanied by a Privateer (PB4Y) (the navy version of the army's Liberator [B-24] bomber) that was acting as safety escort and chase plane while taking photographs of the flight. The Emily was being flown by test pilot Cdr. Thomas F. Connolly, former commander of a squadron of Coronado (PB2Y) four-engined patrol bombers in the Pacific. Connolly gingerly advanced the throttles of the Emily to maximum cruise power and the flight was going well until the flight engineer announced that the oil pressure on one engine had dropped to zero because of a broken oil line. The engine was quickly shut down. Power was reduced to normal cruise settings until a second engine quit. The remaining two engines were slowed; because the flight was near home base, the flying boat glided down to a safe landing on the Patuxent River. As the aircraft touched down, a third engine quit. A crash boat towed the big bird ignominiously into the seaplane basin.[20]

With doubts about the reliability of the engines, further flight tests were cancelled and the tests were redirected toward examining the airplane's water-handling stability, spray characteristics, and hull design. American aviation contractors were given an opportunity to inspect the Emily's design features. They were especially interested in the slender hull design and the use of chines to control the splash patterns. Navy test crews were impressed that bow spray in nearly all conditions was never any closer than two feet to the massive propellers. After eight of these water tests were completed in January 1947, the Emily was retired and then transferred back to storage at Norfolk.[21] For a while, the National Air and Space Museum considered putting the airplane on display, but its large size worked against these plans. East coast hurricanes and summer suns took their toll on the derelict airplane and the navy decided to cut the airplane up for scrap after several years of neglect. A group of Japanese businessmen persuaded the navy to allow them to return the Emily to its home country to restore it for display there. With financing arranged by the Maritime Museum in Tokyo and All-Nippon Airways, the Emily was brought by ship back to the grounds of the Shin Meiwa plant, at no expense to the U.S. Navy. Hitsuji, the pilot who had flown the delivery mission to the U.S. Navy in 1945, had risen to the rank of rear admiral in the postwar JMSDF. He assisted the company in arranging for the Emily to be returned to Japan.

The three massive *I-400*-class *Sen-Toku* submarines that were completed fared slightly better, having never been used operationally. All three were turned over to the U.S. Navy after surrender. Navy crews sailed *I-400* and *I-401* to Pearl Harbor for evaluation. Both submarines were torpedoed and scuttled off the coast of Oahu later in 1946. The *I-402* was scuttled near Japan in 1946.[22] Of the two other monster submarines, the *I-13* and *I-14*, only the latter survived the war. The *I-14* was surrendered to the U.S. Navy at sea on August 27, 1945. It was later scrapped.[23]

One of the Aichi M6A1 Seiran aircraft was brought back to the U.S. for evaluation, along with several dozen other Japanese aircraft. The Seiran rested in the Garber Restoration Facility at Silver Hill, Maryland, for many years. It was unique and significant enough to be fully restored to pristine condition at the Garber Facility in 1999 and displayed at the Udvar-Hazy Center at Dulles Airport near Washington.

Time magazine called Emperor Hirohito "the 20th century's greatest survivor." The magazine explained this distinction by stating that "history has not given too many the chance to lead a nation into appalling disaster, only to emerge with at least partial credit for its reform and rebirth."[24] Impressions of the emperor ranged from those images of the uniformed and plumed military monarch on his white horse, to the humble little man in a rumpled suit, waving his crushed hat to the bowing crowds of his people. He preferred to be regarded as mild mannered, but he could and did assert his authority harshly in dealing with an attempted military coup in 1936. At that time, a group of young officers killed several civilian officials, claiming that they were acting to protect the emperor. He ordered his generals to put down the revolt and had nineteen of the rebels executed. The emperor feared his own assassination by the growing power of the militarists. Later, he attempted to convey the impression that he was a pacifist and that his military government conducted the war without his consent. In reality, he followed his country's military adventures closely with daily briefings by his ministers. He was perfectly aware of what his generals, admirals, soldiers, sailors, and airmen were doing. From his war room, he issued instructions to his generals and admirals, reveling in their victories and commiserating in their defeats.[25]

When Japanese forces attacked China, the emperor claimed that any attempt on his part to stop the invasion might have created another coup. He was extremely anxious to preserve his dynasty and his seat on the throne. He wanted peace, but lacked the courage of his convictions, so he allowed his country to go to war. Hirohito made weak pleas for restraint and urged that the conferences with the United States go on to try to resolve the differences between the two countries. The ultimate result was the December 7 attack on Pearl Harbor.[26]

When Japan was facing inevitable defeat three years later, his ministers begged Hirohito to end the war. Now even more obsessed with maintaining his dynastic sovereignty, he refused to discuss surrender. He was afraid that he would be tried and possibly executed as a war criminal. For another year, he insisted on continuing the war, urging his military leaders to fight harder, to gain one last victory to inflict more casualties on the enemy, so that Japan could negotiate favorable peace terms from a position of strength. During that year an additional 1.5 million Japanese were killed.[27]

The two atomic bombs, the Soviet entry into the Asian war, the devastating fire bombings by Superfortresses, and the strangling submarine blockade finally forced the emperor to bear the unbearable, and agree to end the war by surrendering.

The emperor made a recording of his imperial rescript to announce to his subjects that Japan had lost the war and that he was ordering his military forces to cease fighting and accept the terms of unconditional surrender. The Japanese people heard his voice for the first time, broadcast on loudspeakers set up throughout the land, operating on a special ration of electricity for the purpose.[28]

A wave of suicides followed the broadcast. Minister of the Army Korechika Anami challenged the people of Japan to continue the fight, even if they had to "eat grass, wallow in the dirt, and sleep in the fields." Anami suffered the mixed emotions of loyalty to the emperor and shame that his army had been defeated. He wrote a poem of apology to the emperor, and on another sheet of paper he wrote, "Believing firmly that our sacred land will never perish, I, with my death, humbly apologize to the Emperor for the great crime." Anami's "great crime" was the defeat and surrender of his army. He faced the imperial palace and committed seppuku—ritualized suicide—in his home.[29]

Even before the surrender, Japanese military and naval officers by the hundreds followed suit. Admiral Ugaki, Yamamoto's chief of staff, climbed into the seat of a Judy (D4Y) dive-bomber beside the navigator. A flight of eleven of these bombers was about to depart Oita Air Base on a kamikaze mission on August 15. A final radio transmission reported that they were diving on the enemy. Like many others, Admiral Ugaki had written his apology to the emperor. Not wishing to disobey an order from the emperor, Ugaki nevertheless wanted to die honorably. There are no Allied records of a kamikaze attack on that date, so it is assumed that Admiral Ugaki and his flight deliberately crashed into the empty ocean.[30]

The Pacific War was finally over.

In his first meeting with General MacArthur, the emperor convinced the general that he would cooperate in every way, even by abdicating if necessary. The emperor explained to MacArthur that he had not dared to disagree with those military advisors who insisted on going to war with the United States. Hirohito said that, "I would have been put in an insane asylum or even assassinated." MacArthur's reply: "A monarch must be brave enough to run such risks." Hirohito changed the subject and hinted that Japan's entry into war may have been justified, but that he would accept responsibility for the decision to go to war.[31] This is probably as close as the emperor ever came to making an apology to anyone.

MacArthur was convinced that the Japanese needed the emperor to remain as their sovereign and that the emperor on the throne was necessary to keep the occupation of Japan peaceful. MacArthur insisted that the emperor was not to be tried as a war criminal. Instead, he believed that the emperor would be useful in putting down a rise of communism in Japan and keeping the now unemployed Japanese armed forces subdued.[32]

Three decades later Hirohito expressed "profound sadness" over World War II to President Gerald Ford during a visit to the United States in 1975. Asked by a Japanese reporter during that visit if he accepted responsibility for the war, Hirohito stiffened and replied, "I can't answer that question because I haven't thoroughly studied the literature in this field, and so don't really appreciate the nuances of your words."[33]

Even Japanese historians and scholars were angered when Hirohito claimed that the bombing of Hiroshima "couldn't be helped because it happened in wartime." At least two of them published documented accounts of Hirohito's involvement in all phases of the China and Pacific Wars. There was vigorous international reaction to the Japanese ministry of education's minimizing and toning down the harsher statements in textbooks about Japan's military expansion in the war years. The South Korean press complained that Japanese textbooks referred to Japan's invasion of China only as an "advance." The same books downplayed Japan's draconian colonial rule of Korea in calling the Korean Independence movement "a riot." In 1982, the Chinese press focused on blaming Japan for the Asia-Pacific War.

A survey of the Japanese public revealed that the majority of the emperor's subjects believed that the emperor was responsible for the war.[34]

Hirohito was eighty-six years old in 1987, when it was reported that he was suffering from an intestinal disease. His surgery was successful, but he was still very ill the next year. In 1988, his son Prince Akihito learned that the emperor had cancer. The Japanese media reported in great detail of the emperor's vital signs for one hundred and eleven days. During this time, the same Japanese media deliberately avoided any mention of the emperor's wartime military involvement, but the rest of the world press focused almost exclusively on the emperor's responsibility for the Pacific War and how Japanese officials and politicians were deliberately avoiding this subject. In effect, the Japanese were refusing to apologize for the emperor's wartime actions.

The emperor died in January 1989. Many elderly Japanese went into intense mourning. There was a great deal of difference between the emotions of the elderly Japanese toward their emperor and the feelings of the rest of the world.[35]

On January 1, 1946, Hirohito had issued an edict that volunteered the fact that he was not a deity. Under the new Japanese Constitution of 1947, the emperor became only "the symbol of the State and of the unity of the people, deriving his position from the will of the people with whom resides sovereign power." The Constitution went on to outlaw war forever for the Japanese and denied the emperor any power to choose war as an option.[36]

No more apologies were due the emperor.

Appendix

Extending the Range

The Pacific Ocean makes up about 35 percent of the earth's surface. Half of the earth's ocean surface is found in the Pacific—about 70 million square miles. When the Japanese moved into the southwest Pacific, they added about three hundred thousand square miles of territory to their empire. With the islands of Wake, Marcus, and Guam included in their conquests, the lines of communication and supply covered approximately 1 million square miles. This expanse ran from the Solomon Islands across the Philippines, Indochina, the Dutch East Indies, British Malaya, all the way to India's Bay of Bengal. The eastern edge of these holdings began with the Marshall Islands and included the Caroline Islands, the Gilbert Islands, and the Marianas Islands. By July of 1942, the Japanese occupied Attu and Kiska in the Aleutian Islands in the north and Tulagi and Guadalcanal in the south. A cursory inspection of a map of this vast area shows that the territory is more than 90 percent water. These waters were the approaches by which American forces could threaten Japan's entire empire. The Japanese were acutely aware of this threat.[1]

The Imperial Japanese Navy (IJN) was spread thin in its efforts to guard those approaches. In addition, they had to maintain communications, and transport munitions, food, supplies, and personnel to these remote bases and outposts. Japan had a shortage of cargo and transport ships well before it plunged into hostilities. Japanese shipyards were overtaxed just to provide sources for the warships needed by the navy, and cargo vessels were a lower priority. The American submarines in Japanese home waters had their periscope sights set on cargo vessels and transport ships, unlike the Japanese submarines that sought Allied men-of-war as their first priority targets.

From the beginning of the war, the IJN had a pressing need for long- and short-range types of reconnaissance aircraft. The ideal long-range patrol aircraft did not have to be particularly fast, but long range and great endurance were its most useful capabilities. A patrol aircraft had to be able to loiter in one area to track an enemy ship or task force.[2]

Extended range was the most desirable characteristic of any patrol, scout, or reconnaissance airplane. Long-range scouting was essential for warfare on the open seas, because opposing forces might close the distance between them by as much as five hundred miles overnight. The extended range capabilities of aircraft carriers, combined with their aircraft, made it possible that a smaller, weaker task force could win out over a superior force through better reconnaissance. The old doctrine of battleships being able to overcome an opposition force by sheer weight of bringing more guns to bear, greater accuracy in shooting those guns, or better ship handling was blown away by aircraft carriers. The aircraft carrier could release the fury of its entire air wing in a single powerful strike. If the strike could be made before the enemy launched its own aircraft it was possible to win the battle without suffering any damage whatsoever. Naval tactical experts conducted war games and studies that demonstrated that a smaller fleet could win over a superior fleet by using the intelligence gained from long-ranged reconnaissance aircraft.[3]

Patrol aircraft normally flew a course that resembled a wedge, or slice of pie. With the point of the wedge beginning at its base—either a land base or a ship—the airplane would fly out a course to its desired patrol area, then make a turn to fly along an arc at its patrol area, then fly the third leg to return to base. The size of the search area was determined by the range of the patrol aircraft and the number of aircraft available to cover the area. Naturally, the longer-ranged aircraft could extend the size of the area to be searched and a larger number of these craft allowed more intensive searches. Several patrol aircraft would usually be assigned to fly neighboring patterns to cover the desired directions from the home base. Timing was critical and patrol aircraft might be launched at varying intervals if a particular area was deserving of special attention. Another type pattern would be to fly back and forth across an area, similar to mowing a patch of lawn. Endurance was as important as range, because the maximum search area to be covered was critical.[4]

Patrolling such large areas of ocean was a task that could not be filled by Japan's Mavis (H6K) and Emily (H8K) flying boats. In the latter stages of the Pacific War, many of both types had been modified to serve as transports and were not available or suitable for patrol or bombing duties.[5] The Japanese did not have the resources to turn out thousands of patrol bombers, as the Americans had done with their Catalina (PBY) flying boats. The U.S. Navy had nearly twice as many of the Mariner (PBM) flying boats as the IJN had in all of its Mavis and Emily aircraft combined. The U.S. Navy's number of Catalina aircraft alone gave the United States roughly a ten-to-one advantage in numbers over the Japanese flying boats. Yet the Japanese had several times over the need for these extended range seaplanes. Backed into a corner, the Japanese opted to fill its needs for patrol and reconnaissance over the expanses of ocean with smaller floatplanes that were cheaper to build and operate. These floatplanes did not have the extended range capabilities of the larger flying boats, but they could be based at any island outpost or base that possessed a bay, lagoon, lake, or even a river that could serve as a runway for takeoffs and landings. The smaller floatplanes did not require the large and difficult-to-build beaching ramps and maintenance facilities required for the large flying boats. In many bases, maintenance personnel lived in tents on the beach or near the water's edge, working on their aircraft and engines in the mild Pacific climate. Hangars or shop buildings would be considered unnecessary luxuries. Operating from seaplane tenders or seaplane carriers, the floatplanes were small enough to be hoisted aboard the mother ship for operations and maintenance. The mother ships could be anchored in any protected bay, harbor, or atoll, with no need for runways.

The U.S. Navy normally operated floatplanes from its battleships and cruisers. For a while, the navy experimented with floatplanes aboard a few of its larger destroyers. These trials were conducted briefly in 1923. In 1940, the secretary of the navy ordered that six *Fletcher*-class destroyers be modified with catapults for floatplanes. The disadvantages of having to carry a tank of 1,780 gallons of volatile aviation gasoline on the deck outweighed the advantages. By late 1943, the experiment was abandoned and the destroyers were returned to their normal configuration. Later, in 1944, a system to refuel and service floatplanes by using a destroyer under way was developed. This method used an inflated rubber rearming barge towed aft of the destroyer. The purpose of this underway refueling was to service spotting aircraft from battleships and cruisers beyond their firing line, so that the larger ships did not have to withdraw from the firing line to service their spotting aircraft. After hooking onto a trailing sled, the floatplane was winched alongside the rearming barge. The aircraft could be serviced with fuel, oil, food, and water. Slight battle damage could be repaired and crews could be changed. Then, the floatplane was reeled out and with its engine restarted, the aircraft could pull ahead of the sled to take off.[6]

As the war progressed and more Japanese carriers were sunk and the Americans seized island runways, the Imperial Japanese Naval Air Force (IJNAF) was forced to make greater use of its floatplanes. In addition to floatplanes on battleships and cruisers, the water-based aircraft operated from seaplane tenders. Many more floatplanes flew from shore bases on coves and bays of Pacific islands, operating as floatplane squadrons.[7]

Having to deal with unfamiliar Japanese aircraft manufacturers' names as well as their confusing designation methods, Allied intelligence specialists and pilots had a tough time coping with these names and systems. The American intelligence specialists came up with a system that assigned female names to bombers, land-based reconnaissance aircraft, and flying boats: Betty, Dinah, and Emily; male names to fighters and reconnaissance seaplanes: Zeke and Pete; tree names to trainers: Willow and Cypress; names beginning with T (and usually female) for transports: Theresa; and bird names for gliders: Buzzard.

Jiro Horikoshi, designer of the IJNAF's Claude (A5M), was considered one of the world's foremost aircraft designers of the time. He went to work for Mitsubishi in 1927 at age twenty-three. He was sent to the United States and Europe to observe aircraft design and production. His best-known work is the famous Zero (A6M) fighter. The Zero surprised the entire aviation world as an impressive example of what the Japanese aviation manufacturers were capable of producing.

The Japanese law that required larger aircraft and engine manufacturers to be licensed by the government gave the government the control that it wanted over manufacturing techniques, equipment, and production plans. In turn, the law protected these firms with tax exemptions. The IJA and IJN, as owners of a vast pool of machine tools, loaned these tools to the builders and set up inspection and quality control procedures. Technical representatives and inspectors advised plant managers and gave the army and navy management control over the plants. Already assured of a profit, the Japanese aircraft manufacturers increased their efficiency to meet the growing demands for superior aircraft being ordered for the IJA and IJN. The Japanese aviation industry took off and increased its production fourfold between 1936 and 1940.[8]

Just as the new Claude was reaching full production and four months before it entered into combat, the IJN was already issuing specifications for its replacement. Although the Claude was an extremely agile fighting machine, it lacked the range that would be needed for the long distances in the Pacific. The performance demands specified for the new fighter would make it, unquestionably, the best fighter in the world. Those specifications called for a speed exceeding 270 knots (310.5 miles per hour) in level flight, the ability to climb to 9,843 feet within 3.5 minutes, an endurance of six to eight hours at maximum range cruising speed, and a range of 1,685 nautical miles (over 1,900 statute miles) with an auxiliary drop tank. It would be armed with two 20-mm cannon and two 7.7-mm machine guns. These specifications were so demanding that the Nakajima Company withdrew from competing for production of such an airplane, believing that the requirements were unrealistic and impossible to meet with current technologies.[9]

Designer Horikoshi noted that no minimum or maximum weight or size restrictions were placed in the specifications, but he knew that light weight would be one of the first requirements of this new super fighter. Mitsubishi, his company, proposed that its own engines be used, but the IJN wisely chose the Nakajima Sakae 12 engine because it was more reliable, produced more power, used less fuel, and weighed less than the Mitsubishi engines. The Sakae 12 engine also had a smaller frontal area, which meant that it would induce less drag than a larger engine.[10] With the Nakajima engine, the new Zero met or exceeded all of its specified requirements. When it was pitted in combat for the first time on September 13, 1940, a flight of thirteen Zeroes shot down all twenty-seven of the Chinese fighters opposing them over Chungking in less than ten minutes.[11] Brig. Gen. Claire Chennault, head of the American Volunteer Group (the Flying Tigers) in China, tried to warn American authorities of the capabilities of the new Zero. Chennault was forced to develop new fighter tactics for his less-agile fighter planes to deal with the Zero. American army and navy intelligence officers attempted to spread the word about the fantastic new Japanese fighter, but most of the American military leaders did not believe the Japanese could produce such an aircraft.[12] In addition to the magnificent new Zero fighter, the IJNAF had the best and most modern torpedo bomber of the time in the Kate (B5N). At the beginning of hostilities, the IJNAF had, in nearly all comparisons, better aircraft than those the Allies could send against them.

The IJNAF especially wanted to have a fighter seaplane that could provide air cover during the early phases of amphibious landing operations and operate from bases on the smaller islands where building runways was not practical. The famous Zero design was modified with a large central float with two small stabilizing floats under its wings. Built by Nakajima, the A6M2-N was given the code name Rufe. The float arrangement slowed the agile fighter by 60 miles per hour and only 327 of them were built.[13] Later in the war, Kawanishi, builders of the Emily, developed a floatplane fighter to replace the Rufe. The Kawanishi design was designated the N1K1 Kyofu (Mighty Wind), which had a brief combat career. The Allies assigned the code name Rex to this seldom-seen fighter. The IJNAF discovered that with its speed-reducing floats removed and equipped instead with wheeled retractable landing gear, it was a superior fighter. Its advanced design features, armament, and power made it one of the IJN's most successful land-based fighters in its late war inventory— the N1K1-J and N1K2 Shiden (Violet Lightning), code-named George by the Allies. The IJN was so impressed with the George that it gave the new fighter a much higher production priority over the Emily flying boats. This was one reason why the company's Emily was not produced in larger numbers.[14]

The U.S. Army Air Force (USAAF) was using radar-equipped Liberator (B-24) bombers in its Anti-Submarine Command. Because of the Liberator's extended range capabilities, the U.S. Navy ordered these same aircraft as the Privateer (PB4Y). The USAAF disbanded its antisubmarine units, turning these airplanes and their mission over to the navy. The USAAF then exchanged the airplanes with the navy for bomber-configured Liberators from navy orders. With their long-range capabilities, the large four-engined Privateers proved to be successful patrol bombers. At first called the Sea Liberator, its name was quickly changed to the more nautical Privateer. The Privateer had a range of almost thirty-five hundred statute miles or, on shorter missions, it could carry a bomb load of 12,800 pounds. It could protect itself with at least eight .50-

caliber machine guns. The navy began to take deliveries of a navalized version, without superchargers, designed specifically for low-altitude patrol duties.[15] The later Privateer (PB4Y-2), bristling with up to ten .50-caliber machine guns, proved to be one of the navy's most effective fighters. Navy statistical data compiled after the war's end show that the Privateers, normally flying unescorted long-range sector searches, was "one of the Navy's best fighter planes," claiming 125 Japanese bombers and 181 Japanese fighters shot down. Only the navy's dedicated fighters, the Hellcat (F6F) and the Corsair (F4U) were more successful in downing larger numbers of enemy aircraft.[16]

The U.S. Navy, on the other hand, became interested in a floatplane fighter only after encountering the Rufe in the Aleutian and Guadalcanal campaigns. The navy experimented with floats fitted to some of its more important airplanes, but without much success. A Wildcat was fitted with dual pontoon floats, which certainly did not enhance its performance. The encumbered fighter, given an unofficial designation as the F4F-3S, quickly earned a nickname as the Wild Catfish. The navy actually placed an order for one hundred of these aircraft, but its performance was so poor that the order was soon cancelled.[17] In 1938, the navy fitted floats to a Vindicator (SB2U) dive-bomber, but this proved to be a less-than-satisfactory coupling. Another later example, the Helldiver (SB2C) dive-bomber, also on large dual pontoon floats was equally unsuccessful.[18] The USAAF even experimented with its twin-engined transport, the Douglas C-47, on two huge Edo floats. The Douglas XC-47C-DL had retractable wheels built into the floats, making it an amphibian that could be operated from land runways or water. The airplane handled satisfactorily in the air and on smooth water, but suffered from a high rate of tire failures, sensitivity in crosswind landings (on land), and a critical reduction in payload. Edo was contracted to build 150 sets of floats and the float-equipped C-47s reportedly saw limited service in Alaska and New Guinea.[19]

The U.S. Navy operated only four types of single-engined floatplanes during World War II. All these aircraft were originally intended to be primarily artillery spotters for their mother ships (battleships and cruisers), with reconnaissance or scouting as secondary roles. The carriers did not use floatplanes, but usually carried a squadron of wheeled scout bombers—the ubiquitous Dauntless or later in the war, the Helldiver. Both airplanes could be land-based. The former airplane was given the label SBD—slow but deadly—and the unpopular Helldiver, designated the SB2C in official Navy parlance, was called by its crews and maintenance men, the Son-of-a-Bitch, Second Class, or the Big-Tailed Beast. The U.S. Navy's floatplanes could all be fitted with wheeled landing gear to operate from land bases, when their mother ships were in port, but most of them looked and handled awkwardly on wheels and were normally operated on floats.

The Jake (E13A) Type O Reconnaissance Seaplane was numerically the most important floatplane used by the Japanese. In 1940, Aichi won a competition that called for a three-seat reconnaissance floatplane with good speed and long range. It was powered by the reliable Mitsubishi radial engine that developed 1,050 horsepower, giving the Jake a range of over fifteen hundred miles. At reduced power, it could stay aloft for fifteen hours. The Jake could be operated from battleships, cruisers, seaplane carriers, and seaplane tenders. It made its combat debut in late 1941 in attacks on the Canton-Hankow railroad. Acting as far-reaching, searching eyes for the battleships and cruisers, the Jake also fulfilled the role of shell spotter and fleet liaison aircraft. The Jake was provided a flexible rear-firing 7.7-mm Type 92 machine gun for defense. Late production models were modified in the field with a flexible downward-firing 20-mm Type 99 cannon for use against American PT boats. The airplane could carry one 550-pound bomb or four 132-pound bombs or depth charges.

Another important floatplane in the IJN's inventory was the Pete (F1M). Its "F" designation meant that the airplane was intended to be a spotter for naval gunfire, but the Pete would prove to be capable of defending its mother ship in the fighter role. It was such a versatile machine that it was used as a dive-bomber, antishipping bomber, convoy escort, coastal patrol airplane, and even as an interceptor fighter. It was particularly active in all these duties during the Guadalcanal campaign. Even though it was lightly armed, it did score a few victories as a defense fighter.[20]

One Pete, flown by PO1c Kiyomi Katsuke of the seaplane tender *Chitose*, rammed and destroyed a Flying Fortress (B-17) bomber as it was about to attack the seaplane carrier *Nisshin* on October 4, 1942. In a dogfight near Guadalcanal, marine ace Capt. Joseph J. Foss of VMF-121 claimed "two float biplanes" (Petes), but his aircraft was so shot up by one of the Pete's rear gunners that Foss had to ditch his Wildcat (F4F) in the sea and almost drowned before he was rescued.[21] In numerous other encounters, the Pete biplane was victorious over other dive-bombers and flying boats.[22] As a biplane first flown in 1938, it looked completely outmoded, but its configuration made it extremely maneuverable. The Pete was light and had the standard armament for an observation seaplane: two fixed 7.7-mm machine guns installed in its nose, with a machine gun in its rear cockpit.[23]

In the early days of the war, some Japanese cruisers and battleships carried the two-seat Dave (E8N) biplane as their light reconnaissance floatplane. Like the Pete that replaced it, the Dave was extremely maneuverable and successfully shot down Chinese fighters on several occasions. The Dave was on board several Japanese ships as an artillery spotter during the Battle of Midway, but was relegated to training duties after that. The Dave closely resembled the handsome Corsair (O2U) biplanes that operated in the prewar U.S. Navy. The Pete and Jake aircraft had replaced the Dave types by early 1942.[24]

Later in the war, the Japanese added still more floatplanes to their inventory. Although the Jake was carrying most of the shorter ranging task load assigned to the floatplanes, the IJN produced an improved type reconnaissance floatplane in the Paul (E16A). This two-seat airplane was intended to replace the Jake, and although it was more powerful and faster, it had poor handling characteristics. It was equipped with radar and two 20-mm wing cannon and could carry a single 551-pound bomb. Unfortunately, the IJN attempted to use the Paul as a bomber. In this role, American fighters shot them down in large numbers.[25]

Kawanishi offered the IJN what it considered to be the ultimate reconnaissance floatplane with its Norm (E15K). This two-seat machine was equipped with a jettisonable main single float and inflatable stabilizing outboard floats. This float system was complicated and rarely operated as it was intended to function. The airplane's massive Mitsubishi 14-cylinder engine developed 1,850 horsepower turning contrarotating propellers that were plagued with pitch control problems. In development for over three years, the Norm was supposed to be able to reach a speed of 350 miles per hour, but could barely make 290 miles per hour, making it vulnerable to U.S. fighters. It could carry only one small 265-pound bomb. Sent to Palau Island for operational testing, twelve of the fifteen produced were quickly shot down by U.S. fighters and production was ended.[26]

The IJN learned that their practice of using torpedo bombers as reconnaissance scouts was not satisfactory, so they issued specifications for a dedicated long-range fast carrier-based reconnaissance airplane. The Saiun (C6N) was the result. Code-named Myrt by the Allies, this three-seat airplane was almost as fast as the Hellcats that pursued it in combat. With a drop tank, it had a range of over three thousand miles, and a top speed of 329 miles per hour. A total of 460 Myrt aircraft were manufactured. With the loss of most Japanese aircraft carriers near the end of the war, many of the Myrts were fitted with oblique upward-firing cannon, and used as land-based fighter-interceptors against the Superfortresses.[27]

The Seiran, or Mountain Haze, floatplane aircraft carried by the I-400 class submarines were almost as unusual as their carriers. In 1942, the Aichi firm in Japan was instructed to design a navy experimental special attack bomber especially for use with the I-400 class submarines. The original design specifications were for a fast, catapult-launched aircraft without undercarriage. The original plans were to have the aircraft return to the mother ship after their attacks and ditch in the water near the submarine. After the crew was retrieved, the aircraft would be abandoned. This scheme was revised to provide for twin detachable floats so that the airplanes could be used on more than one mission. It was designed, not as a minimal airplane like the tiny Glen (E14Y), but as a fast, robust full-fledged attack bomber.

The first prototype Seiran was completed in November 1943 and was powered by a fourteen hundred–horsepower Aichi twelve-cylinder liquid-cooled engine. This engine was patterned after the German Daimler-Benz DB603 that powered many of Germany's best fighters and bombers. The Seiran was a sleek monoplane with a complex wing, float, and tail folding system that allowed it to be stowed in the submarine hangar. Despite the complicated folding configuration, the Seiran could be prepared for flight in less than seven minutes by four trained maintenance technicians. After completing training, the skilled I-400 sailors claimed that they could surface, break out, assemble, fuel, arm, and catapult three Seiran bombers in forty-five minutes. Night assembly was facilitated by the application of phosphorescent paint to certain critical parts.

The Seiran was never assigned an Allied code name because the Allies did not know of the type's existence until the war was over. Its gross weight was ninety-eight hundred pounds loaded with crew, fuel, and either two 550-pound bombs or one 1,764-pound bomb or torpedo. The Seiran had a wingspan of over forty feet and was thirty-eight feet long. It was capable of a top speed of 295 miles per hour, and could cruise at 185 miles per hour for a range of 740 miles.[28]

At the beginning of the war, the two most prevalent types of floatplane were the Seagull (SOC) and the Kingfisher (OS2U). Both aircraft were operated primarily from the catapults of battleships and cruisers. The Seagull was an anachronistic biplane that first flew in 1934. It was powered by a six hundred–horsepower Pratt & Whitney engine, giving it a top speed of only 165 miles per hour. Armed with a fixed, forward-firing .30-caliber machine gun in its fuselage and a flexible .30-caliber gun in the rear cockpit, it could also carry two 325-pound bombs or depth charges. Production of this slow, but well-liked airplane ended in 1938, but it served to the end of the war, outlasting many of its intended replacements.[29]

The most prevalent floatplane in the U.S. Navy during World War II was the Kingfisher. Their original duties were gunnery spotting and scout observation. They were assigned to the catapults of battleships, cruisers, and seaplane tenders. Oddly enough, the Kingfishers were powered by a 450-horsepower engine and, with a top speed of 164 miles per hour and cruising at 119 miles per hour, it was not quite as fast as the old Seagull biplane. It had exactly the same armament as the Seagull—two .30-caliber machine guns. The Kingfisher found additional jobs as seaplane trainers, convoy escorts, air-sea rescue, and antisubmarine patrol aircraft. The sturdy seaplanes rescued hundreds of downed pilots and seamen. Capt. Eddie Rickenbacker, the famous World War I ace, was aboard a bomber that ditched in the Pacific. After floating for twenty-two days in a rubber raft, Rickenbacker and two crewmembers were spotted by a Kingfisher involved in the search for them. The trio was lashed to the wings and the pilot of the rugged, but overloaded, little Kingfisher, unable to take off in the rough seas, taxied for over sixty miles to complete the rescue.[30]

Two more floatplane types were to be supplied to the U.S. Navy by Curtiss to replace the Seagull and Kingfisher. Powered by a six hundred–horsepower Ranger in-line engine, the Seamew (SO3C) was meant to be a high-speed scout. The navy accepted delivery of 795, turning 250 of them over to the Royal Navy, but troublesome engines, excessive weight, and aerodynamic problems plagued the unfortunate Seamews. Their operational record was so unsatisfactory that the old Seagull biplanes, the airplanes that they were supposed to replace, were returned to duty to replace many of the Seamews. A considerable number of new Seamew airplanes were converted to be used as radio-controlled gunnery targets.[31]

Another Curtiss design, the last of a long line of Curtiss-built floatplane scouts used by the U.S. Navy, was the Seahawk (SC). It was designed to be as simple as possible for speedy production. All were delivered from the factory with fixed wheeled landing gear and the navy installed the separately purchased Edo floats as needed. This airplane had considerably more power than previous American shipboard floatplanes, being equipped with a Wright R-1820-62 engine turning out 1,350 horsepower. Its top speed was over 300 miles per hour, but it could cruise or loiter at only 125 miles per hour. A unique feature was the inclusion of two bomb cells in its central float. This fast, single-seat scout had provisions for a bunk in the fuselage that could accommodate one man in the air-sea rescue role. The Seahawk did not see action until June 1945 and production ended with the end of the war three months later.[32]

The U.S. Navy's love affair with flying boats went so far as to attempt to develop a jet fighter capable of takeoff and landing on the sea (or at least seawater in a calmed bay). This was the Sea Dart (XF2Y). The Sea Dart had twin jet engines, a water-tight hull with delta wings, and retractable skis on which it took off and landed. The test example was capable of supersonic speeds, but blew up in flight, killing the test pilot. The project was cancelled with only five examples built. They ended up in storage with one on display at the San Diego Aeronautical Museum in Balboa Park.[33]

For combat in the vast mid-Pacific, the navy wanted a surveillance airplane with a twenty-four hour endurance capability. This meant that a takeoff at midnight could place the airplane to begin its search at dawn halfway along a thousand-mile radial line. After eight to twelve hours of daylight patrol at maximum range, the airplane would still have enough fuel to return to base.[34]

In 1933, Consolidated Aircraft unveiled its new Catalina (PBY). This was an aerodynamically clean twin-engined flying boat that had evolved from a commercial design. It would prove so successful that it would become the most-produced flying boat of all time. It achieved, finally, the desired thousand-mile range capability that brought credibility to mid-ocean campaigns. Citing the flexibility and concentration in operations that it could furnish, Adm. William H. Standley, chief of naval operations, asked for large quantities of the new flying boat to be built for the navy. Many high ranking naval officers, including

Standley, Rear Adm. Edward C. Kalbus, and Rear Adm. Joseph C. Reeves, wanted masses of the Catalinas, but they wanted the airplane to be used only for surveillance and information gathering.[35]

Admiral Moffett was killed in the crash of the dirigible USS *Akron* in 1933 and was replaced as chief of the bureau of aeronautics by Rear Adm. Ernest J. King. Both officers had been involved in the development of the XP3Y-1, the airplane that would become the Consolidated Catalina. The new designation was to be PB, standing for Patrol Bomber to acknowledge the airplane's additional function as a bomber as well as a patrol airplane. King passionately believed that the new Catalina was "distinctly a naval weapon for use over the sea against naval objectives." In other words, the Catalina could bomb ships and naval bases. Rear Adm. William S. Pye of the War Plans Division agreed that massed formations of patrol bombers could probably act as "effective bombing forces."[36]

The assistant secretary of the navy for air, David S. Ingalls, and the navy's air admirals, Moffet and then King, believing that size did not count, decided for the navy to buy the smaller, twin-engined Catalina as its standard patrol bomber because it was much less expensive to purchase and to operate than the four-engined airplanes. For example, the Coronado (PB2Y) had a unit cost of $300,000—triple the cost of the smaller twin-engined Catalina. The admirals recorded their reasoning, stating that "a large plane over a given area of sea is not, necessarily, any more effective as an observation post than is a small plane . . . the small plane . . . may be at an advantage in that the facilities which made it and maintain it can make and maintain more units."[37]

The new airplane began setting records, flying nonstop from Norfolk, Virginia, to the Panama Canal, continuing on to San Francisco, setting a new distance record for seaplanes by covering 3,280 statute miles. Knowing that the new airplane could carry bombs and torpedoes, the navy gave it the production designation PBY-1. The navy placed its order for sixty of them. After a few slight improvements, fifty of the new PBY-2 were ordered, and then sixty-six PBY-3s were added. To complete the order of the early variants, thirty-three PBY-4s were delivered. One of the PBY-4s went to England in 1939 for evaluation by the British.[38] It was the first trans-Atlantic delivery of a military aircraft. At first, the patrol bomber did not impress the British. They believed that the airplane was not capable of defending itself in a combat environment. When

the Royal Air Force (RAF) found that its own Saro Lerwick twin-engined flying boat was not viable, the PBY-5 was given slightly better defensive armament, the design became more attractive, and the British gave it the name
Catalina.[39] It was an RAF Coastal Command Catalina operating from its base
in Ireland (flown by Ens. Leonard B. Smith of the U.S. Navy, one of nine
Americans secretly assigned to the RAF as special observers) that discovered
the German battleship *Bismarck* on May 26, 1941.[40] The Catalina crew
reported the *Bismarck*'s position to the British carrier *Ark Royal,* whose
Swordfish torpedo bombers hit the German battleship, crippling it. The British
battleships *King George V* and *Rodney* finished destruction of the *Bismarck* on
May 27.[41]

The Catalina proved to be a versatile aircraft and some later versions were
equipped with retractable wheel landing gear to allow landings on land or
water. The design was successful, and the United States built more than three
thousand of the amphibians. For whatever reasons, the Japanese developed
no amphibians. They either were not interested in amphibian operations or
were unwilling to use the technology to add wheels to a flying boat hull.

Admiral King at the time commanded at least a dozen squadrons of land-
and sea-based patrol planes. As a fervent advocate of naval air power, he concentrated on three priorities: to train his aviators to fly under wartime conditions; to formulate a viable doctrine for his PBY patrol bombers, and to explore
the Pacific to find bases for his patrol bombers. For two years, King and his seaplanes flew in all kinds of extreme conditions. His pilots learned to take off in
fog and high seas, at night in heavy weather and traveling extreme distances
with scant fuel reserve, as they would in war conditions. He participated in
the harrowing flights, claiming that he was "getting rid of the weaklings."
Admiral King was involved in only one serious aircraft accident in his entire
career, when his personal plane crashed on takeoff at Acapulco en route to
the Canal Zone. On this particular flight, King was a passenger, not the pilot.
All the crew and passengers were promptly rescued. The incident received some
adverse publicity, but King ignored it. His pilots continued to fly what they considered, in some cases, their terrifying training flights.[42]

Admiral King maintained that the sea offered an unlimited number of runways and his bases needed only shelter from the wind and a suitable anchorage
(in shallow water) for his seaplane tenders. He and his planes, with the seaplane

tenders following dutifully at ten knots, roamed the Pacific from the Aleutians to Panama to the central Pacific, while exploring the area for suitable seaplane bases. One of the atolls that he favored was French Frigate Shoals, the only atoll in the Hawaiian chain that possessed a large lagoon surrounded by small, low islands. In one incident, he ordered a squadron of Catalinas to take off from French Frigate Shoals in high winds and waves beyond the limits allowed by navy technical orders. The rugged Catalinas made the takeoff but because of high headwinds, their crews received King's permission by radio to divert to another destination. Postflight inspections showed that eleven of the airplanes' battered and strained hulls required repairs. King never commented on the bent hulls, but kept his faith in his rugged Catalinas.[43]

In the early months of the war in the Southwest Pacific, the attempts to use the Catalina as a bomber were disappointing. Patrol Wing Ten, initially based in the Philippines, flew dozens of bombing missions with dismal results. The defensive armament on the Catalina was inadequate for the bomber to defend itself in a combat environment against fighters. The prewar beliefs that the Catalina could be a viable bombing airplane were wrong, but the Catalina was a superb patrol and surveillance aircraft, and it did a sterling job in rescuing downed crewmembers.[44]

The IJN admired the capabilities of the Catalinas that were being produced for the U.S. Navy, but they wanted their first-line flying boats to be even more capable. The U.S. Navy had chosen the Catalina partly because it was cheaper to build and maintain than the larger four-engined flying boats. These were the qualities that prompted the IJN to request that Yokosuka Naval Arsenal design and build such a machine for them. The result was the Cherry (H5Y1). The Cherry was powered by two Mitsubishi twelve hundred–horsepower Shinten engines and had a wingspan of 103.5 feet, which was six inches shorter than that of the Catalina's with exactly the same horsepower engines. After exhaustive flight-testing, the design was found to be unfit for practical use. It failed to live up to its expected performance and production was cancelled after only six were built by 1934. The IJN never used the Cherry in combat in the Pacific War. The six examples built were used only as crew trainers.[45]

As a hedge against wartime production limitations, in 1940 the U.S. Navy began accepting delivery of a second type twin-engined flying boat—the Mariner (PBM). The Mariner was purchased in fewer numbers than the Catalina, but they were popular with their crews. The Mariner, powered by two Wright Cyclone engines developing sixteen hundred horsepower, was larger and heavier than the Catalina, and was slightly faster. It was equipped with eight .50-caliber machine guns in nose, tail, and midship power gun turrets. It could carry up to 4,000 pounds of bombs in bomb bays that were extensions of the engine nacelles.[46]

For unexplained reasons, the U.S. Navy decided that, because the Mariner could fly with more payload than it could handle on takeoff, a catapult barge would be useful to launch the airplane. As the only ship of her kind, the *Catapult Lighter No. 1* (AVC-1) was built around a single giant catapult. Known unofficially as the *Silver Queen,* the catapult barge was 424 feet long, weighed fifty-eight hundred tons, and was to be powered by diesel engines. She was launched in August 1940, but her catapult was complex and unreliable. The engines were never installed. The navy lost interest and the project was cancelled. The Mariners served well, nevertheless, by making longer, more normal takeoff runs without the aid of a catapult.[47]

A large flying boat proposed for the U.S. Navy was a rather remarkable patrol bomber, the Sea Ranger (XPBB-1), ordered in 1938. It was flown for the first time in July 1942. Its outstanding feature was its size. With a wingspan of 139 feet and weighing over one hundred thousand pounds loaded, it was the largest twin-engined flying boat built in the United States. Its wing design was the same used in the Superfortress, and was only two feet shorter than that aircraft. The Sea Ranger could carry twenty 1,000-pound bombs over short ranges, but it had a fuel capacity of 9,575 gallons. For long-range patrols, it had a theoretical endurance of seventy-two hours. Two eighteen-cylinder Wright R-3350-8 Duplex Cyclone engines powered it, each developing two thousand horsepower. It was an excellent and potentially significant patrol bomber, but the navy determined that its patrol bomber needs could be met by the ubiquitous Catalina. When production was cancelled, the sole example of the XPBB-1 was dubbed The Lone Ranger.[48]

Another flying boat was the Mars (XPB2M-1), also ordered in 1938. The Mars was originally intended to be a flying battleship, heavily armed with nose and tail gun turrets and capable of hauling ten-ton bomb loads for a range of forty-five hundred miles. On a run-in test of its Wright R-3350 engines in December 1941, an unfortunate accident changed the fate of the Mars. The number two engine threw a propeller blade and the massive twenty-two hundred–horsepower engine caught fire. The fire was put out, but serious damage had been done to the wing and engine nacelle and the propeller blade had cut a jagged hole in the fuselage. During the extensive repairs, the navy decided that the Mars would be more useful as a transport. The power gun turrets were removed from the nose and tail and the airplane was reconfigured as a large transport. It was now designated as the sole example of the XPB2M-1R and became affectionately known to its crews as the Old Lady. By January 1945, the performance of the Old Lady was so impressive that the navy decided that it wanted twenty more to be designated JRM-1. By the end of the war, only six examples of the Mars had been completed, and these sported one tall vertical stabilizer and rudder instead of the Old Lady's twin tails. The new transports began setting records for range and endurance, with one flight covering forty-six hundred miles in a flight time of thirty-two hours and seventeen minutes. The massive flying boats never served as patrol bombers, but were operated by the transport squadron VR-2 from Alameda Naval Air Station, California.[49]

That same year, Henry J. Kaiser, a prominent wartime shipbuilder, offered to build five thousand of the Mars flying boats and claimed that he could be in full production of the airplanes within ten months. His proposal was proven unworkable, but in partnership with Howard Hughes, Kaiser did receive a contract for three experimental examples of Hughes's design for an eight-engined flying boat to be built of wood. It was designated the HK-1 and after Kaiser was no longer associated with it, it became the H-4. In spite of that, it would become known as the Spruce Goose, a name that Hughes despised. After many delays, the project was cancelled, but the airplane was finally flown once by Hughes well after the war was over in November 1947, and later parked to become a tourist attraction.[50]

The Mavis was the only long-range flying boat that was serving the IJN in 1941, with a total of sixty-six of this type aircraft on strength at that time. The design team led by Yoshio Hashiguchi and Shizuo Kikuhara prepared their proposal to meet the specifications for a four-engined flying boat. It was to be powered by four 840 horsepower Nakajima Hikari 2 radial engines. Kawanishi's chief test pilot, Katsuji Kondo, first flew it on July 14, 1936.[51]

Production of the Mavis began in 1937 and the airplane was highly regarded by its pilots and crews. They liked the easy controllability and

stability of the airplane in the air and its outstanding water-handling characteristics. The Mavis had excellent load-carrying capability and range, with
reasonable speed that had been achieved by sacrificing armor plating and
self-sealing fuel tanks. It had a top speed of 208 knots (239 miles per hour),
cruised at 140 knots (161 miles per hour), and landed at a sedate 58 knots
(67 miles per hour). At cruising speed, it could remain aloft for over twenty-
six hours. It was 20 percent faster than the four-engine flying boats of other
countries at the time and had, in some cases, 50 percent more range. It could
carry two torpedoes (one on each of the wing support struts), or two 1,764-
pound bombs.[52]

At least two sources claim that the Mavis was copied from the famous
Martin M-130 China Clipper flying boat used by Pan American Airways (Pan
Am). As the famous China Clipper was being prepared for its maiden flight
from San Francisco to Honolulu on November 22, 1935, two Japanese nationals were caught tampering with the Clipper's radio direction finder. If this equipment had been set improperly, the aircraft could have been led considerably off
course. In 1936, pylon obstructions were found just beneath the surface of
San Francisco Bay. These could have damaged the Clipper as it prepared for
takeoff. Again, Japanese nationals were arrested as suspects. The Federal
Bureau of Investigations, Pan Am, and even the navy conducted investigations,
but no indictments or trials resulted and the affairs faded away. The speculation offered as the reason behind the incidents of sabotage was that the Japanese
military did not want the Clippers flying over or even near the Japanese mandated islands in the Pacific. The Japanese were illegally and secretly fortifying
the mandated islands.[53]

The two incidents of sabotage focused suspicion again on Japanese involvement when, on July 29, 1938, the Hawaiian Clipper disappeared on a routine
flight from Guam to Manila. Not a trace of the aircraft or the crew was ever
found and the complete vanishing of the flight remains a mystery. Search and
rescue vessels found no survivors or even floating debris after an exhaustive
search. This raised speculation that Japanese agents had hijacked the airplane
and had flown it to Koror in the Japanese-held Palau Islands. Two reasons have
been offered to explain the hijacking. First, a shipment of several million dol-
lars was sent to the Chinese nationalists as part of the Hawaiian Clipper's cargo.
Second, the Japanese aviation industry was interested in copying some of the

Clipper's features into their own military flying boats. One source claims that "Shortly thereafter, a Japanese version of the Martin M-130 flying boat appeared, later code-named 'Mavis' by U.S. naval planners."[54] Because the Mavis was first flown in mid-1936, none of its design features could have come from an airplane hijacked in 1938. The only real similarity between the two aircraft was that they were both four-engined flying boats.

One of the most brilliant staff officers in the IJNAF was Cdr. Tatsukichi Miyo of the Plans Division. For years, he had been urging the development of long-range flying boats in order to have a far-reaching reconnaissance airplane as well as a weapon capable of making attacks over extended ranges. Commander Miyo was regarded as one of the top airmen in the Japanese Navy. He was one of the few flyers on the staff and the first Japanese pilot to make a night landing on an aircraft carrier. He had already participated in the design of a large flying boat that would ably serve the Japanese over the vast stretches of their new Pacific Empire.[55]

Having made a thorough study of American, French, British, Italian, and German flying boat designs, Commander Miyo led the team that wrote the specifications for a new flying boat in 1938. He was confident that his country's manufacturers could turn out a flying boat that would be superior to any rivals in range, speed, armament, and overall performance.

Commander Miyo knew that his country was producing fighter and bomber aircraft that were equal to or better than most of the foreign designs the Japanese would meet in combat. This gave him confidence that Japan's aeronautical engineering talents could produce a long-range flying boat that would be superior to any such machine produced by Japan's enemies or allies. The specifications that Commander Miyo wrote would ultimately result in the production of the Emily, an airplane that would later be called "the most outstanding water-based combat aircraft of the Second World War."[56] This new airplane would augment the Mavis that was being placed in front-line service at that time (1938) by the IJNAF. The long development time that had been required for the Mavis made the IJNAF planners realize that the development of a larger, faster flying boat with longer range would take two or three years. Therefore, a development contract was awarded to Kawanishi in 1938 to begin research on an advanced design for the next generation flying boat.

The year before, the IJN had expressed a need for developing a long-range reconnaissance flying boat capable of flying nonstop from Japan to Hawaii. Because the sensitive project was top secret, the navy assigned its own Lt. Cdr. Jun Okamura to be the chief designer, with all work to be within navy facilities at Kusho. The only design requirement at that time was for an aircraft with a range of five thousand miles, which was beyond the capabilities of any airplane at that time, except one. The Germans had a flying boat, the Pencil (Do-26) that had a maximum range of 4,410 nautical miles (slightly over 5,000 statute miles). The Japanese established their specifications to match the German design.[57]

The Pencil was powered by four diesel engines, but the Japanese design would be powered by only two Junkers Jumo 205 diesel engines to be imported from Germany. The diesel engines were desired because of their low fuel consumption. The Japanese design would weigh eighteen tons when loaded and have a crew of four. The design would feature long, thin gull-like wings mounted high on a slim fuselage; it bore a strong resemblance to the Pencil. One prototype was completed in 1939 but the test flights were disappointing. The light structure lacked rigidity and there was a problem with vibration and oscillation throughout the airplane. Power was inadequate for the load to be carried and directional stability suffered. The IJN tried to correct these problems, but finally abandoned the project. Because the project was so secret, all drawings and photographs of this aircraft were destroyed. In spite of the secrecy, American intelligence specialists did learn of the airplane's existence after the war began, and even assigned a code name of Tillie to the machine, but it was never flown in operations.[58]

Although the Mavis was recognized as a good machine, the IJN was determined to have a flying boat that would be superior to any similar aircraft being flown by any other nation, either enemy or ally. The specifications written by Commander Miyo and his section called for a 30 percent increase in speed and 50 percent greater range than that of the Mavis, as well as improved maneuverability and better armament. A high degree of maneuverability comparable to smaller seaplanes was desired so that the flying boat could be used for torpedo attacks. Commander Miyo's stipulations were for the new flying boat to have better performance than the RAF's Sunderland four-engined flying boat and the U.S. Navy's experimental Sikorsky (XPBS-1). The IJNAF requirements were for a range of over 4,500 nautical miles (5,185 statute miles) at a cruising speed of 180 knots (207 miles per hour) and a top speed of 240 knots (276 miles per hour).

At the Kawanishi Kokuki Kaisha (Kawanishi Aircraft Company, Ltd.) an engineering team led by Dr. Shizuo Kikuhara began initial design work for the experimental aircraft in the summer of 1938. There were exhaustive wind tunnel and water tank tests with models. The design took shape as an aerodynamically clean, shoulder-winged monoplane flying boat of advanced concept.[59]

The demands for extreme range were met when the design team elected to use eight relatively small self-sealing fuel tanks in the wings (two tanks per engine), augmenting these with six large tanks in the hull. The wing tanks were covered with a leak-proof material composed of alternate layers of gum rubber and then rubber sheeting to a thickness of one and a half inches molded around the tanks. This was the thickest protection given to any Japanese aircraft fuel system. The hull tanks would incorporate an excellent carbon dioxide purging and fire extinguisher system and the tanks themselves would have partial self-sealing capability. The arrangement was such that if a tank were punctured, fuel would drain into a bilge collection tank and then could be pumped back into undamaged tanks by a remotely controlled pump. Representing about 29 percent of the aircraft's maximum allowable gross weight, the total fuel system held 4,502 gallons.

A manual published by the Allied Technical Air Intelligence Center (TAIC) based at the Anacostia Naval Air Station in Washington, D.C., was issued to Allied forces to provide performance and characteristics data on Japanese aircraft. The TAIC manual stated that the Emily had one-quarter inch armor plate installed behind the pilot's and copilot's seats, with the same thickness armor protection aft of the top cannon turret, extending to each side of the turret and inside the turret beside the gun.[60]

The Emily prototype was equipped with the heaviest protective armament of any flying boat. It had a flexible 20-mm Type 99, Model 1 cannon in each of the nose, dorsal, and tail turrets, with 7.7-mm (.303-caliber) Type 92 machine guns in each of two side hatches, plus a ventral position near the tail. On some Emily aircraft, even the flight deck cockpit crew compartment was provided with two 7.7-mm machine guns, protruding from the side windows. This was probably a field modification. Radio operators or mechanics manned these cockpit guns in battle.[61] All the offensive ordnance was to be suspended on external racks between the inboard and outboard engine nacelles. Optional loads could be a pair of 1,102-pound torpedoes, or 1,764-pound bombs, four 551-pound bombs, or sixteen 132-pound bombs.[62]

As with all flying boats, the Emily design shared the common shortcoming of the sometimes-fatal inability to protect itself from attack by fighters beneath it. The hull design did not permit the placement of a ball turret (as used on American bombers) or even the bathtub or dustbin gun emplacements on the belly of some German bombers to ward off fighters climbing to fire at the bomber's underside. The Emily's ventral sliding hatch near the tail with a light downward-firing machine gun was not an effective defense.[63] The universal flying boat tactic of flying close to the water's surface was not always successful. There were cases where the forced high-speed dive to the surface overstressed a fleeing flying boat to cause more structural damage than the impending gunfire that it was attempting to escape. Once near the surface, the attacking fighters could easily correct their aim by observing the water-splash patterns of their bullets. Nevertheless, the Japanese believed that their Emily, with its speed, armor, and heavy armament could take care of itself better than any other flying boat. They were correct in that belief.

The finishing touches were completed on the first prototype of the Emily on December 29, 1940, at Kawanishi's Kohnan plant at Nishinomiya, near Osaka. As an indication of the urgency that was being placed on the development program for the Emily, the maiden flight trials began the following morning with Lt. Cdr. Hiromitsu Ito at the controls. After the first flight, Ito considered the airborne performance of the airplane acceptable, but he was dissatisfied with certain other characteristics. The Emily's in-flight handling was comparatively lethargic, and there was some overbalance in the rudder.

The greatest problems encountered on the first flight were while the Emily was still on the water. When taxiing at high speed and at near takeoff speed, heavy spray was thrown into the propellers, into the cockpit, and over the wings. When the aircraft accelerated and the nose was lifted for the takeoff attitude, the massive machine became extremely unstable and difficult to control. At unstick speed (liftoff from the water), the airplane would begin to porpoise alarmingly. It would assume an exaggerated nose-high attitude, and plunge nose down into the water, with each of these oscillations becoming more severe. In several of the early taxi tests, the airplane actually capsized. The instability in the water was partially caused by the new airplane's heavy fuselage. It was four tons heavier than its original planned weight. Another instability factor was its beam width, which had been trimmed to 9.8 feet to reduce weight and resistance in the air and on the water. This was a full foot narrower than the lighter fuselage of the more stable Mavis flying boat. Emily was not a lady when it was on the surface, and its water-handling characteristics were totally unacceptable.

During takeoff trials in Kobe harbor on January 11, 1941, the aircraft's propellers were being struck by heavy spray even before reaching a speed of twenty-five knots (twenty-nine miles per hour). At higher speeds the amount of water striking the engines caused reduced power, and some propeller tips were bent.[64]

The prototype was returned to the factory for several modifications. The hull depth was increased, and the nose was lengthened for better balance. The vertical fin area was increased and the balance of the rudder was improved. The front part of the planing bottom was modified and longitudinal spray suppression chines—nicknamed *katsuobushi* (dried bonito fish)—were added to divert some of the spray. A fin was added aft of the step in the bottom of the hull along the keel to increase stability in the water. A new type of double-slotted wing flaps had been under development by the Kawanishi company since 1935, and this feature was incorporated into the design. The flaps allowed the flying boat to be airborne within thirty seconds, even when overloaded. These changes did not correct all the problems, but they made the aerodynamic and hydrodynamic characteristics of the new bomber much more acceptable. The Emily was docile on its landing touchdown at a low seventy knots (eighty miles per hour), thanks to the new flaps.[65]

The original design incorporated retractable wing-tip stabilizing floats similar to those of the Catalina, but this design feature was exchanged for strut-mounted floats to save development time and weight. When the aircraft was returned to the flight test crews, they reported that the water-handling characteristics were greatly improved. The test pilots discovered that if the proper takeoff angle was achieved and maintained during the takeoff run, a smooth, stable lift off was possible. A reference mark—called a *kanzashi* (a type of ornamental hairpin) by the test pilots—was painted onto the pitot (airspeed measurement) tube that stood vertically on the nose of the aircraft just in front of the pilot's windshield. By raising the nose so that the *kanzashi* was aligned with the horizon, the proper takeoff angle of five degrees nose-up approaching lift-off speed was assured and a smooth takeoff would result, as long as the pilot stayed within the tolerance of one degree either way.[66]

Because the new flying boat was capable of such extended range and long endurance flights, a few features for crew comfort were included in the design. Behind the cockpit area was a galley for the preparation of hot meals. Directly below the pilots' cockpit on a lower floor was an off-duty area with seats and bunks where crewmembers could relax as they ate or napped. Another advanced feature was a water-flushing toilet. Such an amenity would not appear on any other aircraft until the Boeing 707 jet airliner was introduced in the late 1950s.[67]

The single Emily prototype aircraft was officially turned over to the IJNAF on March 26, 1941, for continuing testing by navy crews. This airplane was soon joined in the testing program by three preproduction prototypes. Two of these would later be used in the second attempted bombing of Pearl Harbor. These new machines incorporated the deeper fuselage, longer nose, and modified hull that helped to partially cure the water-handling problems of the early prototype. The engines installed on the new models were four 1,530-horsepower Mitsubishi MK4A Kasei 12 fourteen-cylinder radials (the most powerful engines available in Japan at the time), driving Kawanishi-designed Sumitomo-manufactured four-bladed propellers. These propellers measured nearly thirteen feet from tip to tip. The new engines produced the same power as the previously installed engines, but added an ejection exhaust system that provided a modest thrust increase. The carburetor intake was mounted on the top of the engine, which gave better protection from water spray on takeoff and landing. The engines were upgraded to water-injected Kasei 22 engines, capable of producing 1,850 horsepower on takeoff for a 15 percent increase in power in the later production models.

A transport version of the new Kawanishi flying boat resulted from the modification of the original prototype at the Kohnon plant in November 1943. Once again, the nose cannon was replaced, this time by a 13-mm machine gun, and the dorsal turret and side gun blisters were removed. Windows were placed along the sides of the cavernous hull and twenty-nine sofa-type passenger seats were installed on two decks. Later in the war, as more and more Japanese island bases were bypassed and cut off by American forces, the transport Emily became the aerial workhorse to supply these beleaguered outposts. The twenty-nine plush seats were ripped out later and replaced by rattan chairs and benches to accommodate sixty-four passengers. Removal of several bulkheads separating compartments and the installation of a large top hatch allowed much larger and bulkier cargo to be loaded. In one noteworthy operation as part of the withdrawal from Rabaul, several Emily transport flying boats were used to evacuate six hundred personnel in one night.[68]

The earlier Mavis flying boats had been regarded as easy prey by Allied fighter pilots, because the Mavis lacked armor plating and self-sealing fuel tanks. The Emily, on the other hand, would quickly gain a reputation for being one of the most difficult of Japanese aircraft to bring down. Not only did the Emily boats have plenty of speed, armor, and a uniquely protected fuel system, the production models bristled with no fewer than five flexible 20-mm cannons in the nose, dorsal, two waist blisters, and tail turrets. In addition, there were three flexible 7.7-mm machine guns to fire through hatches in the cockpit and fuselage.[69] Several American fighter pilots reported expending their entire load of ammunition while attempting to shoot down Emily bombers and being frustrated in watching the flying boat escape. U.S. Navy fighter pilots, with grudging respect for its toughness and heavy defensive armament, soon gave the Emily another nickname—The Flying Porcupine.[70]

The suicide Ohka (MXY7) was the only aircraft designed specifically as a suicide weapon to reach operational status. Although each Ohka weighed over two tons with its warhead, its wingspan was less than seventeen feet, and it was less than twenty feet long. Powered by a rocket engine, the tiny Ohka was designed to be dropped from a twin-engined bomber to dive at a phenomenal speed of 580 miles per hour, piloted by a minimally trained kamikaze pilot. Although the Ohka rocket planes (dubbed Baka [Idiot] by the Allies) created a great deal of havoc during the American invasion of Okinawa, they were never launched from submarines because of their short range of about twenty nautical miles.[71]

The Aichi aircraft manufacturing firm did begin design work on a larger version of the Ohka, the Model 43 that was intended for operations from the Sen Toku (I-400-class) submarines. It was to have a wingspan of 26 feet, a length of 26.5 feet, and have an empty weight of 5,544 pounds. Instead of a rocket engine, it would be powered by a Ne-20 turbojet engine rated at 1,047 pounds of thrust. It was estimated to be able to attain a speed of over 398 miles per hour (considerably slower than the rocket-powered Ohka), but would have a range of about 150 miles (considerably more than the rocket-powered version). Its nose would contain 1,764 pounds of high explosives. With folding wings, several could be easily stored in the canister-hangar of the *I-400*-class submarines and launched from the deck catapult of the large sub. This combination would provide launch opportunities outside the patrol zones of U.S fighters. The Ohka Model 43A reached only the mock-up stage because there were no submarines available to carry it. The Ohka Model 43B was similar. It would have been based in coastal caves in the home islands, rolled out on rails and launched against the invading American fleet. It never left the drawing board.[72]

Except for a few experimental prototypes, neither the Japanese nor the Germans had four-engined bombers capable of large-scale extended-range attacks. Both nations had four-engined airplanes, but these were not ocean-spanning machines. Even though the Luftwaffe was an autonomous "separate Air Force" similar to Britain's Royal Air Force (RAF), the German leaders believed that the Luftwaffe's primary responsibility was to provide the close air support for the army's ground operations. Strategic and long-range bombing was not deemed necessary at the beginning of the war, so the Pedro (He-111), the Dreifinger (Ju-88), and the Pencil (Do-17) twin-engined bombers fulfilled all the roles required by the Germans.

The Imperial Japanese Army (IJA) used its Sally (Ki-21) bombers effectively in China because the distance to targets was short. The Sally was obsolescent by the beginning of the Pacific War. The Imperial Japanese Navy (IJN) believed that its long-legged flying boats could satisfy both patrol and bombing chores, even in the long distances between bases and targets in the Pacific.

The idea of merging the scouting abilities of an airplane with the stealth of a submarine was conceived in the earliest part of World War I, adding a new ingredient to the extended-range formula. The obvious advantage was the submarine's stealthy ability to approach a target area unseen, then surface to launch a bombing or reconnaissance mission. The obvious problem was creating a method of storing and securing the aircraft aboard the submarine.

Apparently the Germans thought of it first when they experimented with the combination by lashing a Friedrichshafen (FF29) floatplane onto the deck of the surface-running submarine (*U-12*). On January 6, 1915, this vulnerable coupling sailed from the occupied Belgian port of Zeebrugge. Thirty miles out to sea, the submarine flooded its tanks to submerge and depart. The float-plane floated free to take off and fly undetected along the coast of Kent, then returned directly to Zeebrugge. Several bombing raids were carried out using this aircraft-submarine combination, even to the outskirts of London. Fouled ignitions, fuel system problems, and the limited range of the German airplanes created more problems for the fliers than did the British opposition. The German high command terminated the experiments by noting in their report that "U-boats operate in the sea, aircraft in the air—there is no connection between the two."[73]

Japan, allied with Great Britain and France opposing the Germans in World War I, was quick to see the usefulness of extending the range of airplanes by launching them from ships. In September and October 1914, the *Wakamiya,* a seaplane carrier converted from a cargo ship, launched its four seaplanes to conduct reconnaissance sorties and to sink a German minelayer and damage shore installations at Tsingtao, a German concession in China. This was the first aerial bombing raid of World War I.[74] The IJN, delighted with the success of its new accomplishment, became the world's leading advocate of sea-planes.

A British raid on Christmas Day of 1915 launched seven aircraft from three modified surface vessels against the German Zeppelin sheds in the first air-craft carrier attack. The partial success of the raid led the Royal Navy to believe that they should explore additional methods of launching aircraft from ships. Under tight security, a young British naval officer, Lt. Charles D. Burney, designed a hydro-aeroplane to be built by the British and Colonial Aeroplane Company. It was a collapsible machine intended to operate from a Royal Navy submarine. Tests showed that many problems needed to be solved to combine airplanes with submarines. In 1916, two Sopwith Schneider seaplanes were used in experiments aboard the British submarine *E.22.* The tiny Sopwiths proved too fragile for open sea operations.

The Italian Navy also conducted trials of its submarines carrying different experimental seaplanes without much success.[75] The Polish Navy also toyed with the idea of placing a small, light amphibian flying boat on one of its large ocean-going submarines, the *Orzel.* Polish experimentation with this combina-tion ended with the beginning of World War II.[76]

The French Navy's pride was its large submarine, the *Surcouf,* which was launched in 1929 as the second largest submarine in the world (2,880 tons, second to Britain's HMS *X-1* at 3,050 tons). The French already possessed an aircraft that would be suitable for submarine duty. It was the angular Passepartout (MB-35), which had appeared at the 1926 Paris Air Show. The Mureaux Brothers aircraft firm built an improved version called the Petrel (MB-411) for the *Surcouf* and delivered the airplanes in 1935. The Petrel could be assembled in five minutes, but could only be launched by lowering the floatplane into the water. The *Surcouf* was not equipped with a launching catapult. Two of the Petrel airplanes operated with the submarine in the early days of World War II. The *Surcouf* sank in 1942, after being rammed by an American freighter.[77]

When they realized that several other nations were experimenting with aircraft-submarine combinations, and not wishing to be outdone, the masters of U-boat operations, the German *Reichsmarine,* rekindled their interest in this field. The German aircraft industry came up with a cranked-wing monoplane, the Arado (Ar-231), constructed so that it could be dismantled and stowed—completely with its twin floats—in a tube slightly larger than six feet in diameter. A contract was signed for six of the U-bootsaugen. This aircraft was not to be launched by catapult, but was supposed to be lowered by a crane into the sea for takeoff, then retrieved by the same method after its flight. The trials fell short of expectations. The primary objection was that the submarine needed to remain surfaced in daylight for at least ten minutes while the aircraft was hooked aboard and disassembled. This surface exposure did not appeal to submarine commanders.[78]

In 1943, the *Reichsmarine* began operating its long-range Type 1XD2 *Monsun* submarines with several of them being sent to the Indian Ocean to join forces with IJN submarines. The massive 1,760-ton German boats were furnished with a manned helicopter-kite, the Focke-Achgelis Fa-330 Bachsteltze. The Fa-330 weighed 180 pounds assembled with its three-blade twenty-four–foot diameter rotor. The helicopter-kite was stowed in its two watertight containers behind the periscopes on deck and assembled quickly (by four men in three minutes in a calm sea) after surfacing. A crewman seated himself in the helicopter-kite while the submarine accelerated into the wind to reach the required twenty knots (twenty-three miles per hour) airspeed to become airborne. A telephone line for kite-to-sub communication was included in the one thousand foot towline that allowed the kite to reach a height of 330 feet. In the event of sighting enemy aircraft, the sub had to dive quickly, so the pilot was supposed to jettison his rotor blades and unfasten his seat belt to allow the helicopter-kite to drop into the water. The pilot then descended by parachute where, in the laconic words of a Royal Navy report, "He probably drowned in the normal way." Needless to say, these machines were not popular with the crews and were rarely used.[79]

The United States Navy purchased two tiny floatplanes designed by Germany's Dr. Ernst Heinkel. The Heinkel-Caspar U-1 was an all-plywood biplane that could be dismantled to fit into a small cylinder six feet in diameter. The U-1 was remarkable in that no tools were required to assemble or disassemble the entire aircraft. Another plus was that the engine could be crankstarted from inside the cockpit, eliminating the dangerous practice of having a man straddle the floats to swing the propeller. Coincidentally, the IJN also purchased two U-1s. Deliveries to both nations were completed in 1922 in great secrecy, because armistice provisions prohibited the Germans from building military aircraft. The Americans never operated their U-1s from submarines, but the little biplanes provided design data for later types.

During 1923–24, the U. S. Navy tried operations with several aircraft especially built for the purpose: the Martin-Klemin MS-1, the Cox-Klemin XS-1, and the Loening SL-1 floatplanes.[80] The tiny Martin machine was a single-seat biplane built in 1923. It was less than eighteen feet long and its small wings spanned just eighteen feet, as well. Fully loaded, it weighed just over one thousand pounds. A sixty-horsepower Lawrence L-4 engine powered it; twelve of these little airplanes were built. Tests were conducted with the submarine USS S-1, but initially the assembly time for the airplane was almost four hours after removing it from the pressure-resistant cylinder-hangar aft of the submarine's conning tower. This was not the little airplane's only problem: It would barely fit into its cylinder-hangar and could carry only enough fuel for fifteen minutes of flight.[81]

With lessons learned from the Martin-Klemin machine, the Cox-Klemin machine was extensively modified to make its erection much simpler. It was redesignated the XS-2, and the launching crew became much more proficient in launching the little seaplane, having it airborne twelve minutes after surfacing the submarine. Only one minute longer was needed to recover, dismantle, and stow the XS-2. The U.S. Navy was interested, but not completely satisfied with its airplane-submarine combinations. Navy pilots were said to be unhappy with duty aboard the cramped old submarines that they considered dangerous.[82] In 1931, the navy experimented with the Loening XSL-2 (modified with an engine change and removal of wheels from the XSL-1) on board the old *S-1* submarine. Pilots remained unhappy with submarine duty. Prior to World War II, the United States used only the *S-1* for its experiments with the submarine-aircraft combination, but eventually tried fifteen different types of aircraft in these operations. After many trials with unfavorable results, the U.S. Navy's interest waned in operating airplanes from submarines. In September 1927, the navy's report on the "-Airplane-Submarine Experimental Type" stated that the "disadvantages of carrying an airplane . . . so far outweigh possible advantages . . . [it is] not desirable to continue expenditure . . . at this time."[83]

In 1927, the British Royal Navy converted one of its large *Monitor* submarines, the HMS *M-2*, into the first true undersea aircraft carrier by removing its 12-inch gun and waterproof turret to replace it with a watertight aircraft hangar. A compressed air catapult and retrieval derrick was added to launch and recover a specially designed two-seat floatplane, the Parnall Peto.

The Peto's small 135-horsepower engine gave it a speed of only 113 miles per hour and a low rate of climb. These shortcomings became evident in one incident when the *M-2* launched its Peto near a famous British seaside resort. On board the Peto was one of the heaviest crewmembers in the Fleet Air Arm (an observer, Lieutenant Couper, at a weight of 252 pounds). After struggling to get airborne, the pilot realized that he was unable to gain more altitude. With full power on the small engine, the airplane was headed for a row of bathhouses on the beach. The panicked pilot managed to miss all but the last bathhouse roof, hitting it with the Peto's float. The impact immediately reduced both the bathhouse and the little floatplane to piles of rubble. Standing in the shambles of the bathhouse, unhurt but nude except for a small pink towel, was the prominent Dr. Lampblough, one of the area's leading citizens. The unhurt pilot and observer were attempting to extricate themselves from the wreckage of their tiny floatplane and the shattered remains of the bathhouse. Dr. Lampblough, as he vented his rage at the crewmembers, became aware of his unclothed state and of the amusement of the gathering crowd of spectators on the beach. The

Royal Navy received a sharp complaint about its airplane-submarine operations from the good doctor. The pilot, his large observer, and the commander
of the submarine were transferred to other duties. In spite of this, experiments
continued with the submarine *M-2* and its little airplanes.

The Royal Navy saw the role of the *M-2* as a stealthy scout that could cruise
at a long distance ahead of the fleet. Its range extended by the submarine, the
aircraft could fly even farther ahead to search out enemy fleets and provide
scouting information far in advance of surface encounters.[84] The crew of the
M-2 became skillful in assembling and launching the little Peto biplanes within
five minutes. However, the *M-2* sank in 1932, and was believed to have gone
down in an accident caused by the incorrect operation of its watertight hangar
doors. Eight Peto aircraft had been built to function with the submarine and
after its loss, one of the small planes was sold to the IJN.[85]

The IJN turned out to be the only service that used submarine-borne aircraft with any success in World War II. As mentioned above, the IJN had purchased two of the Heinkel-Caspar U-1 aircraft at the same time as the U.S.
Navy. The Japanese used the U-1 to perfect its own design, the Yokosuka Naval
Arsenal–built Yokosho-1. In 1927, this airplane was operated with the submarine *I-21* that had been fitted with a hangar similar to the American *S-1* submarine. Like the *S-1*, the launching technique was to trim down the stern of the
submarine, allowing the aircraft to float free of the deck. It became apparent
that the U-1 was too slow and small for this operation. In 1930, the IJN fitted
the larger fourteen hundred–ton *I-51* with a compressed air catapult and hangar
space for the components of a new airplane, the Glen (E6Y1) Type 91 Small
Reconnaissance Seaplane, a copy of the Peto. Testing with the combination of
the Type 91 airplane and the *I-51* continued for three years. The Glen was a
low-wing two-place monoplane powered by a 340-horsepower Hitachi radial
engine. The rear-seat observer was provided a 7.7-mm machine gun for defense.
The little floatplane's top speed was only 153 miles per hour, and it could cruise
at 104 miles per hour for a range of 570 miles. This performance was only
slightly better than the Slim (E9W) biplane that later replaced it. This unique
aircraft, designed in great secrecy, was constructed so that it could be disassembled and stored in a submarine's cylindrical hangar. To reduce surface exposure time, it was common practice to supply the engine with pre-
warmed oil to reduce run-up time while the submarine was surfaced. This

procedure apparently did not cause a problem because the wings, fins, and floats were attached, the tail surfaces were unfolded, and the entire assembly was mounted on a compressed-air catapult for launching. An experienced crew could prepare the aircraft for flight within seven minutes after its mother submarine surfaced. The same crew normally needed only six minutes for recovery, disassembly, and stowage after a flight. None of the planes survived the war, even to repose in a museum.[86]

Subsequently, large fleet submarines began coming off the assembly lines in 1937 with catapults and hangars to be equipped with the first successful submarine-aircraft, the Slim two-place biplane, also known as the Type 96 Small Reconnaissance Seaplane. Thirty-six of these machines were built and used against Chinese blockade-runners as the war with China began.[87] Ten of the Slim biplanes were still aboard submarines when the Pacific War began and some of them served until July 14, 1942. With a three hundred–horsepower engine, the elderly twin-float Slim was capable of only 144 miles per hour, and cruised at 92 miles per hour for an endurance of less than five hours.[88]

At the beginning of the war, Japan had about a dozen submarines that were capable of carrying floatplanes. According to available records, during World War II the IJN had built a total of 42 aircraft-carrying submarines, but they were never all available at any one time. To operate from these submarines, the Japanese built a total of 203 floatplane aircraft.[89]

Generalleutnant Walther Wever, the first chief of the Luftwaffe general staff, was a strong advocate of the long-range bomber. He was a brilliant and dynamic leader who insisted on the development of what the Reich's air ministry called the Ural-bomber. Unfortunately for the Luftwaffe, he was not an experienced pilot and was killed when he crashed his personal He-70 aircraft in 1936.[90] Wever's successors bowed to Reichmarschall Hermann Goering's order to halt work on a long-ranged bomber. Goering, a former fighter pilot who was the top commander of the Luftwaffe, had listened to his underlings who demanded that all German bombers have dive-bombing capability—even the twenty-ton Griffon (He-177). As a result, although they turned out a few prototypes, Germany never successfully developed a strategic bomber for full production during World War II.[91]

Protected by oceans, the United States believed itself to be securely isolated from attacks by heavy bombers. So far as the Americans knew, even after the United States entered the war, the Germans and the Japanese had not even begun to develop extended-range bombers capable of crossing the Atlantic or Pacific for even one-way bombing attacks. The U.S. Army Air Force (USAAF) believed that its capable Flying Fortress (B-17), having demonstrated that it could intercept ships far at sea, could protect America's coastlines from any foreign threat.

The German high command had given a great deal of consideration that America would, sooner or later, become involved in the war. Hitler pointed out that terror bombing raids on the American cities of New York and Washington would have tremendous terror, propaganda, and morale value exceeding any physical damage done to the target cities. Hitler may have realized that when the United States did enter the war, his Luftwaffe leaders had erred in not developing a true long-ranged strategic bomber.

After America entered the war, Luftwaffe planners even discussed one-way missions, with crews ditching their aircraft to be picked up by prepositioned submarines after attacks on American cities. This plan was quickly discarded as impractical. In mid-1943, the *Reichsluftfahrt-ministerium* (state ministry of aviation) invited proposals from the German aircraft industry for a bomber capable of making the round-trip trans-Atlantic mission without refueling. It was emphasized, at that time, that the proposed bombers were to be low-priority, long-term projects. Focke-Wulf, Blohm & Voss, Messerschmitt, and Junkers submitted proposals for the extended-range bombers. Although his company had been directed to devote its efforts to the development and production of fighters, Dr. Willy Messerschmitt had already begun designing a long-range four-engined bomber in 1940.[92]

The Messerschmitt design was not developed from a previous design, as were the Blohm & Voss and Junkers airplanes. The Messerschmitt Me-264 was remarkably similar to Boeing's Superfortress (B-29) in size and configuration. The massive Messerschmitt had four engines, a smooth rounded glass-nosed cockpit, and tricycle landing gear, as did the Superfortress. The Me-264's wingspan was 141 feet, 1 inch; the Superfortress's span was 141 feet, 3 inches. The Me-264 would have a gross weight of 123,500 pounds. The Superfortress weighed 125,000 pounds when fully loaded. The most obvious difference was the twin tail configuration of the Me-264, whereas the Superfortress had a single fin and rudder. Another startling difference was that the range of the Me-264 was proposed as 9,320 statute miles. The Superfortress was capable of about half that range.

The prototype Messerschmitt Me-264V1 bomber flew for the first time in December 1942. Boeing had flown the XB-29 for the first time in September 1942. Because the United States had entered the war a year earlier, the Me-264 was openly declared the "Amerika Bomber." Design requirements for the follow-on prototypes were for increased protective armament and an increased bomb load of forty-four hundred pounds, necessitating a six-engined airplane. These design changes were to be incorporated in the Me-264V-3, given the unofficial designation of Me-364. The larger Me-364 was under consideration to be powered by various powerful new engines: one version would be driven by six piston engines and additional jets, another with four BMW 109-18 turbojets, and still a third would have BMW 109-028 turboprops. Work was begun on the upgraded design, but all work on the third prototype ground to a halt as bombing raids destroyed the first two prototypes.[93] Germany ran out of the critical materials needed in the construction of an advanced bomber. The world had learned of the existence of the four-engined Me-264 when a radio broadcast in July 1944 broke the news of the revolt of the generals following the attempted assassination of Führer Adolf Hitler. The broadcast stated that the Me-264V1 prototype airplane had been made ready at Lechfeld airfield to fly Hitler to Japan if the generals had been successful in overthrowing the Führer.[94]

For its entry into the Amerika Bomber competition, the Focke-Wulf firm offered its handsome Ta-400 six-engined reconnaissance bomber design. At a proposed speed of 447 miles per hour, it would carry a 22,000-pound bomb load and be powered by six 1.750 horsepower BMW 9-801D piston engines. Each outboard engine would be supplemented by a Junkers Jumo 109-004 turbojet engine that would develop twenty-three hundred pounds of static thrust. The design never made it past the drawing board and wind-tunnel models stage. As with the Me-264, time and materials ran out.[95]

Blohm & Voss, primarily a shipbuilding firm, had turned out a series of excellent seaplanes and flying boats for the Luftwaffe. It offered a land-plane version of its monster six-engined BV-238 flying boat, the largest airplane ever built in Germany. The Blohm & Voss design engineers replaced the boat-type planing bottom of the seaplane design with a large bomb bay and a wheeled undercarriage on the otherwise identical BV-238 to make the BV-250. The BV-250 was designed to carry a bomb load of eighty-eight hundred pounds for a distance of sixty-two hundred miles. Its range in an armed-reconnaissance role would have allowed it to cover a substantial portion of the eastern United States. Work began on four BV-250 prototypes, but in late summer 1944 the program was abandoned as material resources ran out. The BV-238 flying boat, after making only one test flight, had been destroyed by strafing American P-51 fighters.[96]

The Junkers firm completed only two prototypes of its Ju-390 reconnaissance bomber, a development of its four-engined Ju-290 transport. Three examples of the earlier Ju-290 had been modified in the spring of 1944 to carry over eighty-seven hundred gallons of fuel to allow them to fly from occupied Poland to Japanese-occupied Manchuria. These flights were intended to deliver aircraft engines and other special cargoes to the Japanese, but it is doubtful that the flights were ever made. Nevertheless, the Imperial Japanese Army Air Force (IJAAF) was so impressed with the Ju-290's range capabilities that they obtained a license agreement to build the even-longer ranged Ju-390. Major General Otani, the IJA's representative in Germany, was to receive detailed manufacturing drawings of the Ju-390 in February 1945, but this exchange was never recorded. The first Ju-390 had flown in August 1943 as a six-engined giant that carried enough fuel for an endurance of thirty-two hours. The Germans claimed that in 1944 the Ju-390 flew from Mont de Marson, south of Bordeaux, France to a point "some 20 kilometers from the U.S. coast, north of New York City, returning successfully to base." This story has persisted, but there is little or no reliable evidence that the flight really took place.[97]

Another Ju-390 prototype was supposed to be the version to be built by the Japanese as their own Amerika Bomber, but it was never completed. Nearly every German aircraft manufacturer had futuristic designs for long-ranged bombers and reconnaissance on their drawing boards, wind tunnel models, mock-ups, and a few prototypes when the war in Europe ended. The fortunes of war caused Germany to run out of materials and time to complete any of their extended-range airplanes.[98]

Even before the war, the Italians demonstrated a flair for extended-range flight in August 1939 when Angelo Tondi, Roberto Dagasso, and Ferruccio

Vignoli flew a modified Savoia-Marchetti SM.82 tri-motored transport on a nonstop closed-circuit course of 8,037.9 statute miles. In late 1942, a Savoia-Marchetti SM-75 with additional fuel tanks installed made a flight of 8,023 miles between Rome and Fussa Army airfield north of Tokyo (now Yokota AB) via a base in Japanese-held northern China. After the airplane was repainted a dull black there and adorned with Japanese *hinomaru* (rising sun) insignia, it proceeded to Japan to deliver a Campini power plant that Japan had purchased for research. The flight was remarkable in that the only navigation aid available was the airplane's compass and the first leg of the trip was flown at twenty-five hundred feet, where the airplane was exposed to antiaircraft fire over unfriendly territory.[99]

The IJA and the IJNAF had become increasingly aware that they needed large, long-range airplanes to conduct a war over the vast areas of ocean in which they operated. Their war in China had not required such aircraft, but as a confrontation with the United States and Great Britain appeared likely, the Japanese began to realize the importance of extended-range operations. Their Mavis (H6K) and Emily (H8K) flying boats were capable machines, but they were the only large aircraft possessed by the Japanese and could not measure up to all long-range missions.

The Japanese had done some experimenting with extended-range flight before the war. A round-the-world flight in late 1939 of a civilianized version of the Mitsubishi G3M Nell sponsored by the *Mainichi Shimbun* (Mainichi Press newspaper) sparked a competition. *Asahi Shimbun,* a rival newspaper, wanted to compete for reader interest by sponsoring a nonstop flight from Tokyo to New York. In 1940, the *Asahi Shimbun* requested that the Aeronautical Research Institute of the University of Tokyo design an airplane capable of such a flight. A range of 15,000 kilometers (9,321 statute miles) at a speed of no less than 300 kilometers per hour (186 miles per hour) was specified. The airplane would fly in the substratosphere and serve as a test laboratory for future stratospheric aircraft. The IJA showed its interest in the design, which was given the designation of A-26 to reflect the sponsorship of *Asahi Shimbun* and the current Japanese year, 2600 (1940). The airplane was given a beautifully streamlined fuselage and long, tapering wings. It was powered by two closely cowled Nakajima Ha-105 engines of one thousand horsepower each. The wing tanks held over twenty-five hundred gallons of fuel and gave the airplane a range of over eleven thousand miles. Engine cooling problems delayed the development of the airplane until the summer of 1942, when the two prototypes were taken over by the army as the Tachikawa Ki-77. The army wanted to use the airplanes for nonstop liaison flights to Berlin and Rome. One such flight was attempted from Singapore to Berlin in July 1943, but the Ki-77 was believed shot down somewhere over the Indian Ocean by high-flying British Spitfires. The sole remaining Ki-77 was shipped to the United States for evaluation after the war.[100]

In 1938, when Japan was in a desperate program to modernize its air forces, a large, technologically advanced airliner being developed in the United States captured their attention. This was the Douglas DC-4E with four powerful radial engines and tricycle landing gear. It had power-boosted controls, cabin air conditioning (AC), and an auxiliary power system for an AC electrical system. The Douglas Company was trying to convince the major airlines in the United States that this radical new airplane would fulfill their need for additional passenger seats. The airlines showed only mild interest, being put off by the airplane's complexity, but the Japanese showed great interest. The one DC-4E prototype was purchased by the Mitsui Trading Company ostensibly for Dai Nippon Koku (Greater Japan Air Lines) to be built under license in Japan. The airplane had been assembled in Japan by Douglas technicians, and flown on a few test flights. After a brief flurry of publicity about Japan's new transport airplane, it mysteriously disappeared from the limelight. The Douglas Company or the Japanese did not dispel rumors that it had crashed in Tokyo Bay.

In reality, the airplane was secretly dismantled for the IJN by the Nakajima Company, who carefully examined each component. The IJNAF assigned the designation LXD to the airplane. Nakajima used much of the new technology from the DC-4E in altering and improving the design of its long-ranged bomber, the Shinzan (G5N1; Mountain Recess), later code-named Liz by Allied intelligence. The Liz design used the wing, engine nacelles, and landing gear of the DC-4E, but Nakajima engineers gave the bomber twin fins and rudders (instead of three), a bomb bay, a glazed nose, and gun turrets. The Liz was powered by four 1,870-horsepower Nakajima fourteen-cylinder radial engines. The IJA was not to be outdone by the navy, so it had Nakajima draw up a similar design in 1939—the Nakajima Ki-68—for the army. It reached only the mock-up stage before it was cancelled when the army gave more priority to much-needed Nakajima fighter aircraft.[101]

The army's later Nakajima Ki-85 bomber suffered the same fate. The Japanese were, however, determined to have a bomber to outdo the Superfortress. Kawasaki's Ki-91 was a squarish bomber powered by four twenty-five hundred–horsepower Mitsubishi Ha-214 Ru engines. It was slightly larger than the Superfortress, with a wingspan of 157.5 feet, a length of 108 feet, and a gross weight of 128,000 pounds. The design speed was to be 356 miles per hour and it would be built with a pressurized cabin for operation at 32,800 feet. It would be heavily armed, bristling with twelve 20-mm cannons in five nose, tail, and fuselage turrets. It was designed for a maximum range of 6,200 statute miles, but was capable of carrying a four-ton bomb load for 2,800 statute miles. In February 1945, a Superfortress raid destroyed the tooling at the Gifu plant for the Ki-91 before the prototype was built. Production of the Ki-91 had to be cancelled.[102]

The Nakajima engineers had based their navy bomber on a flawed transport design and the Liz proved to be a lemon. It was a complex design made worse by unreliable engines. It was overweight, underpowered, and had poor performance. Four prototypes were built and they served out their careers as freight transports.[103]

Nakajima, the largest aircraft and aircraft engine manufacturer in Japan, would try again with a second four-engined bomber design. This airplane was intended to fill the need for an extended-range land-based bomber to support the fleet and be able to fly long-range bombing missions against enemy bases. This newer bomber would be designated the Nakajima G8N. The specification issued by the IJNAF in September 1943 called for a maximum speed of 368 miles per hour and a range of twenty-three hundred statute miles with a bomb load of eighty-eight hundred pounds, or a maximum range of forty-six hundred statute miles with good protective and defensive armament in all directions. This airplane, like its predecessor, the Liz, was not intended to be the Japanese version of an Amerika Bomber, but the Nakajima firm was adding to its experience as a builder of large, long-ranged bombers. Four prototypes were built, but the critical shortage of light alloys cancelled production. Code-named Rita by the Allies, one remaining example was tested in the United States after the war.[104]

The Nakajima Company was founded in 1917 by Lt. Chikuhei Nakajima, who had just retired from the navy at age thirty-three. The son of a wealthy farmer, he graduated from the Navy Engineering Academy in 1907, then went on to study engineering at the Naval Staff College. He was chosen as one of two Japanese officers to train at the Glenn Curtiss Flying School at Hammondsport, New York. He was to study manufacturing techniques and aircraft maintenance. He was not supposed to take flight training, but took up flight training on his own initiative. On return to Japan, he was reprimanded for his unauthorized flight training, but he convinced his superiors that aircraft designers should have experience in and knowledge of flying. In 1917, he resigned his commission in the navy to found his own aviation manufacturing company.[105] He entered a partnership with Seibei Kawanishi as the Nihon Hikoki Seisakusho K. K. (Japan Aeroplane Manufacturing Work Company, Ltd.). After two years of failed aeronautical efforts and frequent differences of opinion, the two partners dissolved their partnership. Nakajima secured financial backing of the strong Mitsui Trading Company, Ltd. to start his Nakajima Aeroplane Company, Ltd. Nakajima won a 9,500-yen prize in a mail-plane contest with his Nakajima Type 4. With twelve central factories encompassing fifty-five divisions, the Nakajima firm grew to become the first and largest aircraft and engine producer in Japan, capable of producing the metals and almost all parts (except propellers) needed to produce airplanes. During World War II, Nakajima produced 47 percent of all Japanese combat aircraft and 32 percent of all engines.[106]

Nakajima became an important man in wartime Japan. As one of the country's leading industrialists, he was elected as a *kokai-gin,* a member of the Diet, the Japanese parliament. He served as the emperor's minister of commerce and industry. Early in the war, Japan was optimistic with its early successes in its conquests, but Nakajima was painfully aware of the wide gap between the industrial power and natural resources of the United States and Japan. After the Japanese were defeated at Guadalcanal, he became concerned about how his country could regain an offensive capability in the war. He had learned of the new Superfortress and its long-range potential. He deduced that the Superfortresss might be ready to use against Japan by the fall of 1944 and that it would be the greatest threat of the war to Japan. Nakajima had also heard rumors of the long-ranged six-engined Peacemaker (B-36) bomber being developed by the United States. He decided that Japan needed a large extended-range bomber capable of bombing the United States directly from bases in Japan. Representatives of the IJA and IJN at first scoffed at his idea, so Nakajima decided that his company would use its own resources to develop the bomber that he named Project Z as a private venture. He believed that his company, with experience in building large airplanes, was the only firm in Japan that would be able to produce such a bomber. Other companies were then invited by the Japanese armed forces to submit their designs for an extended-range bomber. Kawanishi, the builder of the Mavis and Emily flying boats, proposed a graceful, elliptical-winged bomber with six engines as the Kawanishi Navy 19-*shi* bomber that would be designated the TB (Tranoceanic Bomber). Project Z would actually encompass several parallel designs to determine the aircraft most capable of performing the mission to carry the war to America. On January 29, 1943, Nakajima gathered his engineers to order them to begin work on a new bomber design. They would begin plans and feasibility studies that would require several months to complete.

In August 1943, Nakajima prepared a ninety-eight–page thesis, distributing fifty copies of his "Strategy for Ultimate Victory" to politicians, bureaucrats, the army and navy high commands, and Prime Minister Tojo. In six chapters, Nakajima outlined a strategy of defense and his strategy for exterminating the United States. He pointed out that all airplanes share one weakness: that they need an airport from which to operate. If their airports are destroyed, the bombers cannot take off and land. Using engineering logic, he did the math to show that sixteen hundred 1-ton bombs would be required to destroy an average airport. (At that time, most Japanese bombers could carry bomb loads of no more than 2 tons.) He maintained that such large formations of bombers would be impractical, if not impossible. He proposed a bomber large enough to carry twenty-two 1,000-pound bombs in formations of eighty airplanes to wipe out the enemy airport. He went on to point out that American construction capabilities allowed them to completely repair a destroyed airport in two weeks. Somewhat naïvely, he suggested that each airport should be bombed every other week, to deprive the Americans of their bases from which to bomb Japan.[107] The following is a verbatim translation from part of Nakajima's "Strategy for Ultimate Victory:"

Chapter Three. The New Plan of the Sure-to-Win Military Strategy.

Until now, Japan was winning the war and we felt safe that there is no chance to lose. But, now the war situation has changed. The roots of this problem are various, but the main problem is that, although Japan has created new weapons, the strategies regarding their usage remained old.

The "sure-to-win" strategy must change. It is important to change it in the correct direction and for this new strategy we must build new weapons. Let's join our efforts in order to create these new weapons. And by creating these new weapons, we will be able to quickly put together this new strategy.

The result of my research is the following plan:

1. Defense—war strategy
2. Destroy America—war strategy
3. Germany victorious—war strategy

Defense—war strategy

The most serious threats facing the Japanese mainland are the enemy "Superfortresses." There is no way to put up a perfect defense against these air raids. German General Goering has stated that his German fighters are of higher quality than the English or American airplanes, so no enemy plane will ever bomb Berlin. Yet, General Goering had to ask his people to evacuate to the bomb shelters. With the (Japanese) fighter types available at the moment, even if these types become stronger and more numerous, there is apparently no way to stop the raids of the Superfortresses. But, I say that there is a way.

In every airplane, there are faults and limitations and the most serious one is the airfield required. Without airfields, planes don't fly. Therefore, if the airfields of the enemy, from which the air raids originate, are bombed, the enemy will not be able to continue the raids. The small size of the bombers that are currently available in Japan limit them to be able to carry only one ton of bombs as their maximum load. They usually don't do any harm to the airfields of the enemy. And if they do, the damage is so small that it can be repaired easily.

It cannot be said that we can't bomb perfectly the airfields of the enemy. Large size bombers, carrying a large bomb load, are able to do this. Therefore, we have to build bombers that are larger and with a longer range than the enemy's Superfortress airplanes. If we build many of these planes and bomb the enemy's airfield, we will be able to stop the air raids.

Destroy America—war strategy.

Until now, the main war strategy to defeat an enemy was based on the destruction of his production. But, the difference between the production between [America and Japan] is vast. There is one defect in the organization of the production. That is, if a weak point is attacked, the whole production comes to a standstill. This weak point is the steel industry. And of course, the aluminum, oil and various smaller industries are weak points also.

The American steel works, aluminum factories, oil factories, etc. are scattered, so their bombardment is possible only with a small number of bombers flying a long distance. With a large number of super large sized bombers able to fly to the American mainland, Japan's limited power will be able to stop America's larger power. In the beginning, bombing the steel and aluminum industries would bring America's production to a standstill. Then, by bombing the oil industries, the enemy's planes, tanks and ships will not be able to move.

Germany Victorious—war strategy

Since this summer, Germany stopped attacking and turned to defense. The German strategy is to bring the enemy closer and cause more and more casualties both in materiel and in personnel, exhausting the enemy. But since it is very difficult to tell the difference between the casualties of personnel and materiel, it is difficult to draw conclusions whether this plan works or not.

In order to destroy the Soviet war potential, the Soviet iron, aluminum and oil industries can be bombed by large numbers of bombers in a short time. So, in order to help Germany win, large bombers able to attack the Russian mainland are needed. In the middle of 1945, America will be able to produce six-engined bombers, threatening Germany seriously. So, the Soviet war capability should be destroyed before this time. (Nakajima seemed to be hinting that his company could build and provide six-engined bombers to the Luftwaffe for this purpose.) And with Germany victorious in the East, we will hold the key to win this war.[108]

Nakajima spelled out the details of his proposal for his superbomber. He stated that, first of all, an attack radius greater than the enemy's six-engine bomber was essential. He specified a minimum operational combat radius of 8,500 kilometers (5,280 statute miles). The Japanese superbomber would carry a load of twenty-two 1,000-pound bombs. It should be at least as fast as the enemy's fighters and carry heavy defensive armament, because interception was anticipated. The airplane should be capable of flying at an altitude of more than 10,000 meters (32,800 feet). Nakajima added that the "materials necessary for the construction of the plane should be made easily accessible" for quick production, but admitted that "neither the proper high quality materials nor the proper facilities are available at the moment."[109]

The Project Z bomber's design called for six engines, each developing five thousand horsepower. (None of the warring nations were able to develop a production engine this powerful during the war.) Nakajima engineers originally proposed to develop and use the Nakajima Ha-505 (one source designates the engine as the Ha-54[110]) thirty-six cylinder radial engines. This engine was also known as the BH engine. Each of these powerful engines would be the result of joining two existing Ha-44 eighteen cylinder radial engines (each developing twenty-five hundred horsepower) in line, one behind the other, with four rows of nine cylinders. The Ha-44 engine was the most powerful available to Japan at the time. The Nakajima engine designers realized that the rear two rows of cylinders would prove VERY difficult to cool properly. A special air ducting system was designed inside the engine cowlings, but the cooling problems persisted.[111]

The Project Z bomber would be larger, far heavier, and faster than the American Superfortress, but it bore a resemblance to the Superfortress in its basic design layout. It was a graceful, sleek design with a long fuselage mounted on slender, tapered wings. The initial Project Z bomber would weigh 350,000 pounds at gross weight (loaded with bombs, crew, and gasoline); the Superfortress would have a gross weight of 125,000 pounds. The Project Z bomber would have a wingspan of 237 feet and be 144 feet long; the Superfortress's wings would measure 141 feet and it would be 99 feet long. The Project Z bomber was designed for a top speed of 422 miles per hour. The Superfortress could make 365 miles per hour at 25,000 feet. The Project Z bomber proposal listed its range at 10,000 statute miles with a bomb load of 22 tons. The monstrous Project Z bomber should be compared more equally with the postwar Consolidated Peacemaker bomber in size, weight, and performance, rather than the wartime Superfortress.[112]

The specifications for the Project Z bombers were extremely optimistic and Nakajima admitted that the envisioned aircraft was beyond the state of the technology available in wartime Japan at the time of his proposal. Nevertheless, he believed that his engineers could design such an airplane and his company would develop the technology required to produce the Project Z bomber.

Indeed, the technology needed would be impressive. The bomber's six engines were geared to drive large contrarotating propellers 15.7 feet in diameter. It would be well protected by gun turrets or flexible guns mounted in the nose, upper and lower front fuselage, two waist gun positions, upper and lower aft fuselage, and tail guns. The bomber's armament would consist of seven 13-mm machine guns and two 20-mm cannons. The crew would normally require a crew commander, pilot, copilot, two navigators, two flight engineers, two radiomen, and four gunners.

Nakajima added that the wing area would be 350 square meters (3,767 square feet), and pointed out that this was less than the Douglas B-19 experimental bomber that had a wing area of 400 square meters (4,305 square feet), "so it's by no means a monster." He went on to state that a four-engined airplane with two thousand square meters had been produced in Japan before the war.[113] (This was the Mitsubishi Ki-20 Army Type 92, based on the Junkers G-38 transport.)[114] Nakajima was attempting to demonstrate that Japan (and his company) had the technical skills to produce such an airplane, but suffered from a lack of materials only.

Nakajima was a visionary, but he was not a realist. His thesis went on to describe how such aircraft, which would become known as the Fugaku (Mt. Fuji) bombers, could be produced in several versions, all of which would result in certain victory for Japan. He proposed not only a superbomber version, but by different configurations of the same airplane a transport version, a torpedo-bomber version (to carry twenty torpedoes), and two versions of an attack bomber. One version of the attack bomber would be used for strafing attacking formations of American bombers; the other version would strafe fleets to kill shipboard personnel.[115]

To describe Nakajima's far-reaching proposal for countering enemy bombers, it is best to quote directly from his thesis:

Chapter 5. Regarding the Realization of the Plans for the Z Airplane. Defense Against Attacking Bombers

The enemy's six-engine bombers will be able to make raids on the Japanese homeland from a long distance. The Z plane as a bomber will be capable of bombing the enemy's bases from where the enemy's planes take off, there-fore eliminating the danger of the raids.

Nevertheless, there is the possibility of hidden installations in the enemy bases (secret airfields) from where the enemy's bombers could orig-inate surprise attacks against us. To counter this threat, a modified Z air-plane with ninety-six—I repeat, ninety-six—20-mm cannons installed, turned into a strafing plane—is the answer.

The maximum speed of the enemy's bombers is 550 km/hour (340 mph) while in formation. The Z plane's maximum speed is 680 km/hour (422 mph), 130 km/hour (80 mph) faster.

So, using this higher speed, the Z plane is able to approach an enemy formation from behind, get above it and shoot.

The rate of fire of the 20-mm cannon is 700 bullets per minute. If only one cannon is installed, with the speed of the Z plane, there would be 4 meter (13 feet) intervals between each bullet, which is insufficient.

So, by installing in the front and the back of the Z plane, within four meters, twelve X 20-mm cannons placed at 330-mm (13-inch) intervals and furthermore by installing more cannons at the sides of the airplane in 330-mm intervals, in eight rows, that would make 96 cannons.

So, considering the speed of the Z plane and the point where all can-nons would be fired simultaneously, there would be an area of 2.5 meters (8.2 ft) width, three km (1.86 miles) length with 330-mm (13-inch) inter-vals. Under this rain of bullets, no airplane stands a chance.

The destruction area of the 20-mm cannon shell is 350-mm (14-inches.) Keeping this in mind, success (of destruction) is assured.

Considering the length of the enemy's planes as being 30 meters (99 feet), within this 3 km, a formation of 100 enemy planes can be caught. Even in a very loose formation, at least 50 planes can be shot down with just one Z plane. Ten Z planes would be able to deal with 100 enemy bombers.

By installing radio locators (radar) at advance bases, this would give advance warning, and give us enough time for the Z planes to intercept about midway from the enemy's bases and our homeland. Even after the first intercept, Z planes, with their superior speed, would be able to catch up to any survivors on their way back to their bases. In this way, the dan-ger of enemy bombers attacking the homeland is eliminated.[116]

The Japanese conducted tests with multiple gun mounts like those described by Nakajima. The belly of a Frances (P1Y1) was fitted with sixteen 20-mm cannons all aimed forward and downward. When all the guns were fired in salvo, it was reported that the fuselage structure was bent in flight from the tremendous recoil of the guns fired in unison. The pilot complained that his head was banged sharply against the cockpit canopy when the guns were fired.

Warming to his task of describing the awesome power of the Project Z plane (and probably warmed by the heat generated by his overworked slide rule), Nakajima continued to describe another version of the Project Z plane.

Defense Against the Enemy Fleets

By remodeling Z planes to be able to carry 400 (I repeat, 400) 7.7-mm machine guns, in the same configuration as described earlier, or twenty X one-ton bombs or 20 X one-ton torpedoes, the airplanes would be able to deal with the threat of enemy fleets.

I remind you that the maximum speed of the Z plane is 680 km/hr. (422 mph). By installing forty X 7.7-mm machine guns in the front and back of the plane within ten meters (33 feet), in 250-mm (10-inch) and in ten rows with 250-mm intervals on the sides, the Z planes will be able to throw a rain of bullets on the enemy's ships. This 250-mm interval is less than the size of a man's body, either standing or lying down. So, at least one bullet would be able to hit each man on the decks of enemy carriers or even on the enemy's anti-aircraft guns. With a formation of fifteen Z planes, an area of 45 meters (148 feet) width, ten kilometers (6.2 miles) length would be showered with bullets, catching a maximum of 40 or a minimum of 20 enemy ships.

Having strafed the enemy ships, killing all exposed enemy personnel and eliminating the anti-aircraft defenses, then the Project Z bomber would follow. The Project Z bombers can carry twenty X one-ton bombs and throw them with 50-meter (164-feet) intervals. A nine Z plane formation with twenty-five meters (82-feet) distance between each plane would be able to cover an area of 200 meters (656-feet) width, one km (.62 mile) in length. In this way, two large size carriers or battleships can be dealt with for sure with a 90 Z plane formation.[117]

One account claimed that Nakajima had originally called for the building of nine thousand Fugaku—four thousand bombers (and torpedo bombers), two thousand of the superstrafer version, and five thousand transport types. Reality overtook him and Nakajima then proposed the building of a fleet of at least six hundred Fugaku airplanes in at least three configurations: one hundred bombers, one hundred of the superstrafers, and four hundred transport versions. The transports would each be capable of carrying three hundred fully-equipped troops. With his imagination still in full afterburner, Nakajima proposed a commando-style raid with the one hundred and twenty thousand airborne troops in the four hundred transports. The troops would land, either by parachute or at the commandeered Seattle-Tacoma airport, to attack the Boeing plant at Renton, Washington, destroy the Boeing plant, and then depart in their four hundred transports to return to Japan. Nakajima assumed that this would be another way of eliminating the Superfortress threat. Apparently, he was unaware that most of the Superfortresses were being built in Kansas, Nebraska, or Georgia.[118]

The IJA and the IJN both wanted a long-ranged bomber to carry the war to the mainland of the United States. The superbomber had become a rare joint army-navy project. Even though it was given a navy designation, the Nakajima G10N1, it was still called the Project Z bomber or Fugaku by all who were involved in its development. As mentioned earlier, the IJA and IJN could never agree on anything and the Fugaku was no exception. Even though it was initially conceived as a navy requirement and assigned a navy designation, the Japanese government had assigned army Captain Ando as the project manager. Ando was an expert on aircraft engines and the heart of the Fugaku would be those proposed five thousand–horsepower engines. Naturally, Ando wanted to satisfy his services' requirements and preferences for the Fugaku airplane.[119] The army specified that the bomber would operate at an altitude of 10,000 meters (32,800 feet) and be heavily armed to defend itself at that altitude. The navy wanted the airplane to fly at 15,000 meters (49,200 feet) so that it would not require as much heavy defensive armament. The navy also specified that the bomber would be able to carry at least five tons of bombs, take off from a Japanese base, bomb any place in the United States, and land at a base in Germany or occupied France.[120]

The Nakajima design team, with guidance from the army and navy, began its work on the Fugaku in earnest on February 18, 1944, working long days and nights to arrive at a solution to the many problems involved in such a large airplane with such massive engines. In August 1944, they realized that the technology was beyond their reach and gave up on the engines and the aircraft as originally conceived. Captain Ando quoted a Japanese proverb to his Navy counterparts: "We are in bed together, but we have different dreams."[121]

The huge five thousand–horsepower engines presented insurmountable cooling problems and it became evident that such engines would not be available for reliable use for many months, if at any time during the near future. The superbomber design was scaled down. The smaller design was to be powered by six Nakajima NK11A radial engines that could produce only twenty-five hundred horsepower—half the power of the proposed Ha-50s. This was the most powerful engine in production and available in Japan at the time.

The scaled-down Fugaku would now have a wingspan of 207 feet and a length of 131 feet. It could still haul 22 tons of bombs, but for only shorter distances. For its missions against mainland America, it could manage a flight of twelve thousand miles, but with only a 5.5-ton bomb load. It was designed to defend itself with two 20-mm cannons, one each in the nose and tail, plus 13-mm machine guns at various gunners' positions in the fuselage.[122]

At least one airfield to launch the giant bombers against American targets was constructed. Lt. Col. James H. Doolittle, in his autobiography *I Could Never Be So Lucky Again,* confirms that two months after the war ended, Superfortresses took off from a base (now Misawa AB) in the northern island of Hokkaido, Japan for a nonstop flight from Japan to Washington, D.C. The base had been built for the "specific purpose of sending bombers . . . from Japan to bomb America." Doolittle claimed that the bombing raids were not kamikaze-type missions, but that the giant Japanese bombers would land on convenient airfields. The Japanese crews were to have destroyed their airplanes to become prisoners-of-war. Perhaps this was another of Nakajima's ideas for the Fugaku.[123]

Although giant buildings were being constructed for the assembly of the Fugaku and some components were made, the Superfortress raids made it evident to the Japanese that their superbomber would never make it to production. For whatever reasons, the Japanese did not want any details of their superbomber to become known, even with the end of the war. All completed components, documents pertaining to the bomber, manufacturing plans, and drawings for the bomber were destroyed on August 15, 1945, when Japan surrendered. The exact configuration of the Project Z bomber as it was originally proposed or the scaled down G10N1 Fugaku is impossible to define, because no drawings remain. Only the memories of the designers describe the bomber's appearance. Artists' conceptions are basically in agreement on the overall appearance of the airplane with different versions of the airplane showing variations in cockpit configuration, gun turrets, and so on.[124]

The idea for an aircraft carrier—a ship capable of launching and landing airplanes—was formed as early as 1909. The U.S. Navy showed an interest in the 1908 flight demonstrations conducted by Orville Wright for the army. The following year, Glenn Curtiss, an American aviation pioneer, dropped simulated bombs on a floating outline of a battleship in a lake near Hammondsport, New York. This fired the first round of the controversy of airplanes versus battleships before the navy had an airplane, and it perked up the navy's interest in airplanes.

Eugene Ely, who worked for Curtiss, flew a biplane off a wooden platform built over the turrets of the light cruiser *Birmingham* in 1910 to demonstrate that an airplane could be launched from a ship. The navy accepted Curtiss's offer to teach a navy officer to fly and Lt. Theodore G. Ellyson reported for flight training at the Curtiss camp near San Diego in 1910 to become the navy's first aviator. Later that same year, Ely landed his biplane on a deck built on the fantail of the battleship *Pennsylvania*. The ship's commanding officer, Capt. C. F. Pond, proclaimed the feat "the most important landing of a bird since the dove flew back to the Ark." Captain Pond added that he was "positively assured of the importance of the aeroplane in future naval warfare, certainly for scouting purposes." He hedged by saying that, "For offensive operations, such as bomb throwing, there has as yet, to my knowledge, been no demonstration of value, nor do I think there is likely to be."[125]

The role of the aircraft carrier remained subordinate to the battleship until World War II. The large guns and heavy armor of the battleship made it the dominant weapon in battle, with the aircraft carrier (lightly armored and armed with smaller-caliber guns) relegated to the secondary role of scouting ahead of the fleet. The carriers' job was to provide the intelligence information about the location and strength of the enemy, then furnish the gunnery officers of the battleships and cruisers with shell spotting information on the fall of their salvoes, correcting their aim by radio.

With the acquisition of the new supercarriers—the *Saratoga* and *Lexington*—the U.S. Navy could concentrate its aircraft in mass air strikes. The new ships could carry up to eighty aircraft. They had size and speed, giving them unparalleled flexibility. These capabilities freed the carriers to be independent units not tied to the fleet, but to act as the centerpieces of task forces designed to meet specific projections of force. New tactics evolved for the anticarrier role. An example was the development of dive-bombing techniques, which proved to be much more accurate than high-level bombing when the targets were fast-moving ships, twisting and turning away from attack.

The IJN's carrier doctrines were similar to those of the U.S. Navy's, but the Japanese placed greater emphasis on torpedo bombers and level bombing (versus dive bombing). The Japanese possessed capable dive-bombers and used them well, but depended more on level bombers than did the U.S. Navy. A sizeable fighter escort usually protected Japanese bombers. The most amazing characteristic of the Zero (A6M) fighter, aside from its maneuverability, was its long range. When carrying a drop tank, the Zero had a range of over nineteen hundred miles (three thousand kilometers) and could stay aloft for six to eight hours at maximum range cruising speed.[126] The vast areas of the Pacific required the extended-range capabilities provided by the combination of ships and aircraft.[127]

The British Royal Navy, having observed the launching of aircraft from ships, decided that this was an interesting way to extend the range of aircraft (and ships) for fleet reconnaissance. The cruiser HMS *Hermes* was rigged to carry a short Folder hydro-aeroplane aft and a Caudron G.III amphibian forward on a railed launching platform. The *Hermes* was to participate in the fleet maneuvers of 1913, but bad weather prevented the exercise. Even so, the Royal Navy was satisfied that the experimental arrangement was a successful marriage and later converted the *Hermes* to be used as a carrier during World War I.[128]

The first flush-decked aircraft carrier, providing for takeoffs and landings on the same deck, was the Royal Navy's HMS *Argus*, converted from a merchant ship in 1917 to enter operations in the years just after the First World War. The hull was converted from a liner that had the range and speed needed for wheeled aircraft operations. Wheeled aircraft had proven themselves superior to seaplanes, especially as fighters. The first aircraft carrier designed for the purpose was the Royal Navy's HMS *Hermes,* launched in 1919 but not completed until 1924. The IJN was to have the first such ship, the *Hosho*, completed in late 1922.[129] The U.S. Navy did not possess an aircraft carrier until the U.S. Congress authorized the conversion of the fleet collier USS *Jupiter* to become *Langley*, finally commissioned in 1922. With the decision to bring the U.S. Navy up to strength, the conversion of two battle cruisers into the carriers *Lexington* and *Saratoga* put these ships in service in late 1927.[130]

The attack capability of the dive-bombers and torpedo planes was not ignored, but it was not until the 1930s that the carrier versus carrier role came to dominate in the U.S. Navy's thinking. The shell-spotting duties were turned over to floatplanes carried on the catapults of battleships and cruisers. These airplanes shared fleet reconnaissance duties with the scout bombers on carriers. The carrier's striking potential carried out the doctrine of extended range— using the carrier's mobility and flexibility in taking the airplanes to the battle area, then using the airplane's speed to strike the first blows in battle. The aircraft carriers, shifting their targets from the enemy's battleships, would attack the enemy's carriers instead in future conflicts. The ships of either side would rarely, if ever, see the ships of the opposing force. Only the ships' aircraft would make contact with the enemy. If their strikes were successful, they would prevent the enemy aircraft from finding and attacking their home carrier task force.

Production of the large *I*-class (pronounced "eee-class") Japanese submarines began in 1939, and twenty of them were built. In the initial specifications, these monster submarines would be the largest undersea boats ever built at that time, with a cruising radius of 41,575 nautical miles (nearly 48,000 statute miles, twice around the earth at the equator). These gargantuan submarines were larger in size and displacement than any destroyers and outweighed some light cruisers of World War II. They were to be true submarine aircraft carriers, equipped with a large watertight hangar capable of holding two attack aircraft and a catapult rail for launching those aircraft. Production plans were revised and, at first, delayed to accommodate the urgent need for more conventional submarines.

The *I-15*-class subs were superior to the most modern submarines of the U.S. Navy in 1941 in size, firepower, and range. With slight variations in their production, most of these Japanese craft were 356 feet long, with a beam of 30 feet, displacing 2,584 tons surfaced, 3,654 tons submerged. Propelled by twin forty-seven hundred–horsepower diesel engines, the *I-15* boats had a cruising radius of over fifteen thousand miles. Capable of 23.5 knots on the surface, these submarines were slow to dive and difficult to maneuver because of their size. Their submerged speed was only 8 knots. The *I-15* hulls were designed to dive to a depth of three hundred feet. They were armed with six 21-inch torpedo tubes, a 5.5-inch deck gun, and 25-mm antiaircraft guns. A trained deck gun crew could fire the deck gun's 82-pound shells at the rate of twelve rounds per minute. The normal crew complement was ninety-four to one hundred men. The sub's normal endurance was ninety days. Some could carry as many as twenty of the IJN's excellent Mark 95 Long Lance torpedoes. The Mark 95 torpedo was oxygen-and-kerosene fueled, left no wake, and ran at the incredible speed of 48 knots (55 miles per hour) for distances of nearly five miles.

The most unusual feature of the *I-15* class submarines was a large watertight canister-hangar on deck that could house a small, foldable reconnaissance floatplane. This airplane could be launched from a catapult on deck after being assembled, fly over its reconnaissance targets with a two-man crew, and return to land alongside the submarine to be recovered by a small onboard derrick. Like the A-1 types, the B-1 had a hangar and catapult forward of the conning tower with the main deck gun mounted aft. (These positions were reversed on the *I-17*. The *I-17* had to back up at full speed to launch its floatplane.) More of the *I-15* class were built than any of the other *I*-boats, with the first laid down in January 1938.[131]

The *I-400* Class was given the designation *Sen-Toku Sto* (Submarine, Special) and had a horizontal, rather than vertical, figure-eight pressure hull form. Construction of the *I-400* was begun at Kure on January 18, 1943. Although eighteen subs of this class were scheduled to be built, only five keels were ever laid. Both the *I-400* and *I-404* were constructed at Kure. The *I-401* and *I-402* were built at Sasebo and the *I-405* at Kawasaki, Kobe. Of these, only the *I-400, I-401,* and *I-402* were completed. The *I-405* never reached the launching stage and carrier aircraft at Kure sank the *I-404* on July 28, 1945, when it was 95 percent complete.

The twin side-by-side pressure hulls did not run for the full length of the ship. The aft crew compartment was a single pressure hull, but the twin torpedo rooms forward were stacked vertically. The wider beam provided the necessary stability for flight operations and the double hull configuration required a draft of twenty-three feet. Years later, the Russians, in their huge *Typhoon*, class missile submarines, would use a similar hull configuration. When actual construction was begun, the IJN decided that the revised *I-400* class would be even larger than originally planned. These subs would have a displacement of 5,223 tons surfaced and 6,560 tons submerged. The test depth of the pressure hull was 328 feet (82 percent of its 400-foot length). The enlarged hangar was 115 feet long and 12 feet in diameter, able to house three specially designed floatplanes. There was enough space along the walls of the hangar to store parts for a complete fourth aircraft. The hangar was capped with a large domed door that swung open to the starboard side for removing and stowing the aircraft. The bridge and conning tower were offset 7 feet to portside so that more space on the starboard side could be used for the hangar. This design feature caused some problems: The helmsman had to use a seven-degree starboard rudder to steer a straight course at two knots submerged. In a torpedo attack, the captain would have to take into account the larger turning circle to starboard than to port.

Another unique design feature was the long vertical trunk tube leading down from the conning tower outside the hangar to the control room. Full diving time was fifty-six seconds, so the bridge watch lookouts had to jump down the conning tower hatch, then slide through this long tube to man their diving stations in the control room twenty-five feet below. To cushion the landing shock of this thrilling ride, a three-foot thick canvas hassock was positioned in the control room at the foot of the conning tower tube.

The launch catapult, laid out along the foredeck, was eighty-five feet long. The recovery of the seaplanes was accomplished by having them land in the water alongside the submarine, and then they would be lifted back aboard with a heavy crane that folded flush into the foredeck when not in use. There was enough storage capacity for provisions on board for patrols of over ninety days. Below the hangar, the starboard hull contained a special compartment equipped to overhaul and test aircraft engines. In the port hull magazine, four aircraft torpedoes, fifteen bombs, and gun ammunition was stored. The entire ship was coated with "antisound" paint to make sonar detection more difficult.

Power for these gargantuan craft was supplied by four diesel engines using two sets of hydraulic couplings for two propeller screws. These engines produced seventy-seven hundred horsepower on the surface and twenty-four hundred horsepower submerged, with a snorkel-type intake system. This power produced a surface speed of 18.7 knots (21.5 miles per hour) and a submerged speed of 6.5 knots (7.5 miles per hour). The operating radius was now 37,500 miles on the surface at 14 knots—30,000 miles at 16 knots. This phenomenal range meant that the *I-400*-class submarines were capable of launching bombing missions on San Francisco, Los Angeles, the Panama Canal, Washington, or New York. These missions all received serious consideration by IJN strategists. The fuel tanks could hold five hundred and eight thousand gallons of diesel oil—enough to fill fifteen railway tank cars. Submerged radius was, because of the immense size of these monsters, reduced to 60 miles at 3 knots.

Armament for the *I*-class submarines was impressive, with a 140-mm (5.5-inch .50-caliber) cannon located aft of the conning tower, three 25-mm antiaircraft machine guns in one mount, and two twin 25-mm antiaircraft machine gun mounts. A search radar antenna, radar detectors, radio direction finder antenna, and massive pressure-proof binoculars were mounted topside. Torpedo armament consisted of eight 21-inch torpedo tubes, with twenty torpedoes normally carried. The crew complement was normally 144 officers and men, but when the *I-400* was surrendered to the U.S. Navy, there were 213 men on board.[132]

The IJN's strategic plan for the use of submarines went back to the early concept that they were to be used as a battle fleet source. The Japanese insisted on using submarines primarily for scouting and for sinking enemy warships. The Allied and German navies realized that submarines were more valuable as commerce raiders. Japanese submarine commanders tended to seek only men-of-war as their targets. They attacked tankers, cargo ships, and merchantmen and passenger ships as targets of opportunity only when warships were not to be found. Used properly, the Japanese submarine force could have delayed the rebuilding of the forces at Pearl Harbor and might have been able to significantly reduce the traffic to Australia.[133]

NOTES

Chapter 1

1. Jack Greene, *The Midway Campaign,* rev. ed. (Conshohocken, Pa.: Combined Books, Inc., 1995), 55–58.

2. Samuel Eliot Morrison, *History of United States Naval Operation in World War II,* vol. 3, *The Rising Sun in the Pacific* (Boston: Little, Brown and Co., 1984), 92–93.

3. Gordon W. Prange, with Donald M. Goldstein, and Katherine V. Dillon, *God's Samurai* (Washington, D.C.: Brassey's[US], 1990, 34–37); Capt. Mitsuo Fuchida, "I Led the Air Attack on Pearl Harbor," *Naval Institute Proceedings,* ed. Roger Pineau (September 1952), 950–52.

4. Mitsuo Fuchida and Masatake Okumiya, *Midway: The Battle That Doomed Japan* (Annapolis, Md.: Naval Institute Press, 1955), 30–32.

5. A. J. Barker, *Pearl Harbor* (New York: Ballantine Books, 1969), 120.

6. Morrison, *Rising Sun in the Pacific,* 125.

7. Gordon W. Prange, Donald M. Goldstein, and Katherine V. Dillon, *December 7, 1941* (New York: McGraw-Hill Publishing, 1988), 327–28; Gordon W. Prange, *At Dawn We Slept* (New York: Penguin Books, 1983), 542–44; and Prange and others, *Samurai,* 38–41.

8. H. P. Willmott, *Pearl Harbor* (London: Cassell & Co., 2001), 142–57.

9. Ibid., 144–54.

10. Robert J. Cressman and J. Michael Wenger, *Steady Nerves and Stout Hearts* (Missoula, Mont.: Pictorial Histories Publishing Co., 1989), 1; Cdr. Walter

Karig and Lt. Welbourn Kelly, *Battle Report: Pearl Harbor to Coral Sea* (New York: Farrar & Rinehart, Inc., 1944), 9.

11. Fuchida and Okumiya, *Midway*, 32.

12. Walter Lord, *Day of Infamy* (New York: Holt, Rinehart and Winston, 1957), 178–81; Prange and others, *Samurai*, 38–39.

13. Donald M. Goldstein and Katherine V. Dillon, eds., *The Pearl Harbor Papers* (McLean, Va.: Brassey's[US], 1993), 101.

14. Prange, *At Dawn We Slept*, 543.

15. Fuchida and Okumiya, *Midway*, 32.

16. James H. Belote and William M. Belote, *Titans of the Seas* (New York: Harper & Row, Publishers, 1975), 11; Barker, *Pearl Harbor*, 130.

17. John Prados, *Combined Fleet Decoded* (New York: Random House, 1995), 193.

18. Lord, *Day of Infamy*, 181.

19. Prange and others, *Samurai*, 41.

20. Cdr. Minoru Genda, *Shinjuwan sakusen kaikoroku* [Recollections of the Pearl Harbor Operation] (Tokyo: Yomiuri Shimbunsha, 1967; repr., Tokyo, Bungei Shunjusha, 1998), 300–301.

21. Prange, *At Dawn We Slept*, 543–44.

22. Ibid., 546–47.

23. Barker, *Pearl Harbor*, 150.

24. Ibid., 146.

25. Carl Smith, *Pearl Harbor 1941* (Oxford: Osprey Publishing, Ltd., 1999), 77; Prange, *At Dawn We Slept*, 539.

26. Prange, *At Dawn We Slept*, 547.

27. Vice Adm. Matome Ugaki, *Fading Victory: The Diary of Admiral Matome Ugaki, 1941–1945*, trans. Masataka Chihaya (Pittsburgh: University of Pittsburgh Press, 1991), 47.

28. Sidney C. Moody and photographers of the Associated Press, *War Against Japan* (Novato, Calif.: Presidio Press, n.d.), 36.

29. Prange, *At Dawn We Slept*, 435–536; Robert J. Cressman and others, *A Glorious Page in Our History* (Missoula, Mont.: Pictorial Histories Publishing Co., 1990), 21.

30. Prados, *Combined Fleet*, 231.

31. Walter J. Boyne, *Clash of Wings* (New York: Touchstone Books, 1994), 106.

32. William H. Ewing, *Nimitz: Reflections on Pearl Harbor* (Fredericksburg, Texas:

The Admiral Nimitz Foundation, 1985), 11.

33. H. P. Willmott, *Pearl Harbor* (New York: Galahad Books, 1981), 56.

34. Ewing, *Reflections on Pearl Harbor,* 10.

35. Ibid.

36. Prange and others, *December 7, 1941,* 317.

37. Ibid., 319–20.

38. Ibid., 333.

39. Ibid., 347.

40. Ewing, *Reflections on Pearl Harbor,* 10.

41. Cdr. Charles Lamb, *To War in a Stringbag,* rev. ed. (Garden City, N.Y.: Nelson Doubleday, Inc., 1980), 114–26.

42. Smith, *Pearl Harbor 1941,* 31; Boyne, *Clash of Wings,* 102–3.

43. Prange, *At Dawn We Slept,* 270.

44. Ibid.

45. Ibid.

46. Ibid., 339.

47. John Toland, *The Rising Sun: The Decline and Fall of the Japanese Empire, 1936–1945* (New York: Bantam Books, 1970), 193.

48. Ibid., 193–94; Barker, *Pearl Harbor,* 12.

49. Saburo Ienaga, *The Pacific War, 1931–1945,* trans. Frank Baldwin (New York: Pantheon Books, 1978), 133–36; John Keegan, *The Second World War* (New York: Penguin Books, 1990), 245–50.

50. Edwin P. Hoyt, *Japan's War: The Great Pacific Conflict* (New York: McGraw-Hill Book Co., 1986), 232.

51. Ibid., 152.

52. Ibid., 232–33.

Chapter 2

1. Thomas E. Griess, ed., *The Second World War: Asia and the Pacific,* The West Point Military History Series, Department of History, U.S. Military Academy (Wayne, N.J.: Avery Publishing Group, 1984), 4–5.

2. Robert H. Ferrell, *Woodrow Wilson and World War I* (New York: Harper & Row Publishers, 1985), 149–50.

3. Peter Calvocoressi, Guy Wint, and John Pritchard, *Total War,* 2nd ed. (New York: Pantheon Books, 1989), 637.

4. Paul S. Dull, *The Imperial Japanese Navy, 1941–1945* (Annapolis, Md.: Naval Institute Press, 1978), 3–4.

5. John W. Dower, *War Without Mercy* (New York: Pantheon Books, 1986), 204–5.

6. Herbert P. Bix, *Hirohito and the Making of Modern Japan* (New York: Harper Collins Publishers, 2000), 6.

7. W. G. Beasley, *The Rise of Modern Japan* (New York: St. Martin's Press, 2000), 276.

8. Edwin O. Reichauer, *The United States and Japan*, 3rd ed. (Cambridge, Mass.: Harvard University Press, 1965), 23.

9. Dull, *Imperial Japanese Navy*, 3–4.

10. H. P. Willmott, *Empires in the Balance* (Annapolis, Md.: Naval Institute Press, 1982), 48–51.

11. Ibid., 50–55.

12. Dan van der Vat, *The Pacific Campaign: The U.S.–Japanese Naval War 1941–1945* (New York, Touchstone Books, 1991), 45–82 passim.

13. John Toland, *The Rising Sun: The Decline and Fall of the Japanese Empire, 1936–1945* (New York: Bantam Books, 1970), 67.

14. Willmott, *Empires in the Balance*, 55.

15. *Samurai and the Swastika* (The History Channel, July 2, 2000).

16. H. P. Willmott, *Pearl Harbor* (London: Cassell & Co., 2001), 48–49.

17. *Samurai and the Swastika*.

18. Willmott, *Empires in the Balance*, 437–38.

19. Willmott, *Pearl Harbor*, 45.

20. van der Vat, *Pacific Campaign*, 72–73.

21. Richard B. Frank, *Downfall: The End of the Japanese Empire* (New York: Random House, 1999), 78.

22. Toland, *Rising Sun*, 106–7.

23. Edwin Hoyt, *Japan's War: The Great Pacific Conflict* (New York: McGraw-Hill Book Co., 1986), 260–61.

24. *Merriam-Webster's Geographical Dictionary*, 3rd ed. (Springfield, Mass.: Merriam-Webster, Inc., 1998), 712.

25. Dr. James A. Mowbray, "Appendix," *Seven League Boots: The Seventh Army Force at War in the South, Central and Western Pacific Ocean Areas*. n.p.; Correspondence with Dr. Mowbray, October 5, 2000.

26. Ibid.

27. Mowbray, "Appendix"; Charles Zatarain, "Helldiver Strike on Wotje," *Aviation History* (July 2000), 43–46.

28. *Building Japan's Secret Bases,* trans. Rev. Akihiko Shigemi (Tokyo: Asagumo Newspaper Co., October 10, 1970), 62.

29. Ibid., 62–63.

30. Vincent V. Loomis and Jeffrey L. Ethell, *Amelia Earhart: The Final Story* (New York: Random House, 1985), 75–82, 134.

31. John Prados, *Combined Fleet Decoded* (New York: Random House, 1995), 131–32.

32. Burke Davis, *Get Yamamoto* (New York: Bantam Books, 1971), 14–17.

33. Various authors, *Taiheiyo Senso Riku-Kaigun Kokutai* [Army and Navy Air Forces of the Pacific War], trans. Katsuhiro Uchida (Tokyo, Seibido Shuppan Co., n.d.).

34. Henry Sakaida, *Imperial Japanese Navy Aces 1937–1945* (London: Osprey Publishing, Ltd., 1998), 101; various authors, *Taiheiyo Senso Riku-Kaigun Kokutai.*

35. Davis, *Get Yamamoto,* 18.

36. Ibid., 18–19.

37. Griess, *Second World War,* 13.

38. Thomas M. Coffey, *Imperial Tragedy* (New York: World Publishing Co., 1970), 45–46.

39. Hoyt, *Japan's War,* 228.

40. William Weir, *Fatal Victories* (Hamden, Conn.: Archon Books, 1969), 12.

41. Prados, *Combined Fleet,* 131–32.

42. Edward S. Miller, *War Plan Orange: The U.S. Strategy to Defeat Japan, 1897–1945* (Annapolis, Md.: Naval Institute Press, 1991), 1–2.

43. Ibid., 1, 6–8.

44. Samuel E. Morrison, *History of United States Naval Operations in World War II,* vol. 3, *The Rising Sun in the Pacific* (Boston: Little, Brown & Co., 1984), 51.

45. Capt. Wyman H. Packard, *A Century of U.S. Naval Intelligence* (Washington, D.C.: Department of the Navy, 1996), 399.

46. H. P. Willmott, *The Barrier and the Javelin* (Annapolis, Md.: Naval Institute Press, 1983), 13–14.

47. Office of the Chief of Military History, *Japanese Monograph No. 97: Pearl Harbor Operations: General Outline of Orders and Plans* (Washington, D.C.: Naval Historical Center, n.d.), 14.

48. John J. Stephan, *Hawaii Under the Rising Sun* (Honolulu: University of Hawaii Press, 1984), 90.

49. William H. Ewing, *Nimitz: Reflections on Pearl Harbor* (Fredericksburg, Texas: The Admiral Nimitz Foundation, 1985), 11–12.

50. Walter J. Boyne, *Clash of Wings* (New York: Touchstone Books, 1994), 112.

51. van der Vat, *Pacific Campaign,* 24.

52. Norman Polmar, *Aircraft Carriers: A Graphic History of Carrier Aviation and Its Influence on World Events* (Garden City, N.Y.: Doubleday & Co., 1969), 172.

53. Naval Analysis Division, *Interrogation No. 387, File No. A-131* (San Francisco: U.S. Strategic Bombing Survey, 1945), 2–3.

54. Polmar, *Aircraft Carriers,* 28.

55. Prados, *Combined Fleet,* 228–32.

56. John Keegan, *The Second World War* (New York: Penguin Books, 1990), 256.

57. Gordon W. Prange, Donald M. Goldstein, and Katherine V. Dillon, *God's Samurai* (Washington, D.C.: Brassey's[US], 1990), 42.

58. van der Vat, *Pacific Campaign,* 29–30.

59. James H. Belote and William M. Belote, *Titans of the Seas* (New York: Harper & Row, Publishers, 1975), 32–33.

60. Polmar, *Aircraft Carriers,* 173.

61. Ibid.

62. Justice Lowe, "Japanese Air Raids at Darwin, NT on 19 February 1942," *Findings of Commission of Inquiry,* Document 224 (Darwin, Australia: Supreme Court of Victoria, March 27, 1942), 1–4.

63. Griess, *Second World War,* 99–100.

64. Ibid., 100.

65. A. J. Barker, *Midway: The Turning Point* (New York: Ballantine Books, 1971), 9–10.

66. Willmott, *Empires in the Balance,* 436–37.

67. Ibid., 1–2.

68. Prados, *Combined Fleet,* 278–80.

69. Ibid., 280–81.

70. Hoyt, *Japan's War,* 261–62.

71. Willmott, *Barrier and the Javelin,* 15.

72. Ibid., 264–65.

73. Katsuhiro Uchida, Letter to author regarding Japanese wartime flight training, December 22, 2001.

74. Rear Adm. Tsuneo Hitsuji, *Reflections of the Great Skies,* trans. David and Harumi Ziegler (Tokyo: Japan Defense Agency War History Publications, 1986), 3–4.

75. Ibid., 4–5.

76. Rear Adm. Tsuneo Hitsuji, letter to author, trans. by William Lise, July 22, 1996, 1–3.

77. Ibid., 4.

78. Hitsuji, *Great Skies,* 4.

Chapter 3

1. James F. Dunnigan and Albert A. Nofi, *Dirty Little Secrets of World War II* (New York: William Morrow and Co., 1994), 79.

2. Captain Edwin T. Layton, "Rendezvous in Reverse," *Naval Institute Proceedings* (May 1953), 478.

3. Ibid.

4. Capt. W. J. Holmes, "Discussions, Comments, Notes on 'Rendezvous in Reverse,'" *Naval Institute Proceedings* (August 1953), 897.

5. Ibid.

6. Ibid., 897–98.

7. Clarke Van Fleet and William J. Armstrong, *United States Naval Aviation, 1910–1980,* NAVAIR 00-80P-1 (Washington, D.C.: Government Printing Office, 1981), 92; James C. Fahey, *Ships and Aircraft of the U.S. Fleet,* 4 vols. (Falls Church, Va.: Ships and Aircraft, 1939; repr., Annapolis, Md.: Naval Institute Press, 1976), 19, 27.

8. Van Fleet and Armstrong, *United States Naval Aviation,* 105; Fahey, *Ships and Aircraft,* 19.

9. Rear Adm. Tsuneo Hitsuji, letter to author, "The Complete Story of Operation K," trans. Mikio Aida (November 1982), 1.

10. Dorr Carpenter and Norman Polmar, *Submarines of the Imperial Japanese Navy* (Annapolis, Md.: Naval Institute Press, 1986), 111; David R. Winans,

"Submarine Aircraft," *American Aviation Historical Society Journal*, vol. 12, no. 1 (Spring 1967), 46.

11. M. C. Richards, "Kawanishi 4-Motor Flying Boats (H6K 'Mavis' and H8K 'Emily')," *Aircraft in Profile*, vol. 11 (Garden City, N.Y.: Doubleday & Co., 1972), 241–50 passim.

12. John Prados, *Combined Fleet Decoded* (New York: Random House, 1995), 282.

13. Captain Edwin T. Layton, "Rendezvous in Reverse," *Naval Institute Proceedings* (May 1953), 479.

14. Samuel E. Morrison, *History of Naval Operation in World War II*, vol. 4, *Coral Sea, Midway and Submarine Actions* (Boston: Little, Brown & Co., 1962), 70.

15. Operational Navigation Chart ONC J-18 (St. Louis AFS, Mo.: Defense Mapping Agency Aerospace Center, 1975); Thomas B. Buell, *Master of Sea Power: A Biography of Fleet Admiral Ernest J. King* (Boston: Little, Brown & Co., 1980), 105–6.

16. Richards, "Kawanishi," 250.

17. "Submarine Operations, Dec 41–Apr 42," General Headquarters Far East Command, Japanese Research Division (*Japanese Monograph, No. 102*), Washington, D.C.

18. Dr. James A. Mowbray, "Appendix," *Seven League Boots: The Seventh Army Force at War in the South, Central and Western Pacific Ocean Areas*, n.p.

19. Prados, *Combined Fleet*, 282.

20. Layton, "Rendezvous in Reverse," 480.

21. Ibid.

22. Ibid., 480–81.

23. Ibid., 481.

24. Ibid., 480.

25. Richards, "Kawanishi," 250.

26. Ikuhiko Hata and Yashuho Izawa, *Japanese Naval Aces and Fighter Units in World War II*, trans. Don Cyril Gorham (Annapolis, Md.: Naval Institute Press, 1989), 417; letter from Katsuhiro Uchida to author with more details of Japanese wartime flight training, January 10, 2002.

27. Layton, "Rendezvous in Reverse," 481; Rear Adm. Tsuneo Hitsuji, letter to author, "Additional Details of Attack," September 25, 1995, 2.

28. Layton, "Rendezvous in Reverse," 482–83.

29. Zenji Orita and Joseph D. Harrington, *I-Boat Captain* (Canoga Park, Calif.: Major Books, 1970), 56.

30. Layton, "Rendezvous in Reverse," 483.

31. Hitsuji, "Details of Attack," 2.

32. Rear Adm. Tsuneo Hitsuji, *Reflections of the Great Skies,* trans. David and Harumi Ziegler (Tokyo: Japan Defense Agency War History Publications, 1986), 2.

33. Richards, "Kawanishi," 250.

34. Hitsuji, "Complete Story," 4.

35. Ibid.

36. Layton, "Rendezvous in Reverse," 483.

37. Ibid.

38. Hitsuji, *Great Skies,* 4.

39. Hitsuji, "Complete Story," 3.

40. Ibid.

41. M. F. Draemel, Chief of Staff, Pacific Fleet, "War Diary Entry," May 1, 1942 (Washington, D.C.: Naval Historical Center), 2.

42. John W. Lambert, *The Pineapple Air Force: Pearl Harbor to Tokyo* (St. Paul, Minn.: Phalanx Publishing Co., 1990), 7.

43. Draemel, "War Diary Entry," 2.

44. Lambert, *Pineapple Air Force,* 11.

45. Layton, "Rendezvous in Reverse," 484.

46. Lambert, *Pineapple Air Force,* 42.

47. Hitsuji, "Complete Story," 3.

48. Layton, "Rendezvous in Reverse," 484.

49. Lambert, *Pineapple Air Force,* 32.

50. Layton, "Rendezvous in Reverse," 484.

51. Peter M. Bowers, *Curtiss Aircraft, 1907–1947* (London: Putnam & Co., 1979), 496; Page Shamburger and Joe Cristy, *The Curtiss Hawks* (Kalamazoo, Mich.: Wolverine Press, 1972), 226.

52. A. J. Pelletier, *Bell Aircraft Since 1935* (Annapolis, Md.: Naval Institute Press, 1992), 28–29.

53. Bowers, *Curtiss Aircraft,* 483–84.

54. Pelletier, *Bell Aircraft,* 29.

55. Brig. Gen. H. C. Davidson to Commanding General, 7th Air Force, 24 March 1942. (Declassified 4 October 1944) (Maxwell AFB, Ala.: USAF Historical Research Center).

56. Lambert, *Pineapple Air Force,* 41–42.

57. Capt. Wesley Craig, interview by author, February 3, 1998.

58. Andrew Gennett, interview by author, November 12, 1990.

59. Ibid.

60. 7th Air Force G-3 Journal (Radar Log) from Operations of 7th Air Force, 7 December 1941–13 November 1943. (Declassified 4 October 1944) (Maxwell AFB, Ala.: USAF Historical Research Center).

61. John G. Eberhard, interview by author, February 12, 1998.

62. Richard F. Ferguson, interview by author, January 26, 1999.

63. Roy M. Foster, interview by author, October 9, 1997.

64. Hitsuji, *Great Skies,* 5.

65. Layton, "Rendezvous in Reverse," 485; Hitsuji, "Complete Story," 4; *Reflections,* 6.

66. Layton, "Rendezvous in Reverse," 485.

67. Ibid.

68. Hitsuji, "Complete Story," 4.

69. Layton, "Rendezvous in Reverse," 485.

Chapter 4

1. Herbert P. Bix, *Hirohito and the Making of Modern Japan* (New York: Harper Collins Publishers, 2000), 451–52.

2. Captain Edwin T. Layton, "Rendezvous in Reverse," *Naval Institute Proceedings* (May 1953), 485.

3. John C. Cash, letter to author, 26 October 1997.

4. "Japanese May Have Subs That Carry Planes," *Honolulu Star-Bulletin* (March 4, 1942), 1.

5. Herbert G. Hunt, Jr., letter to author, July 21, 1998.

6. Donald R. Kennedy, letter to author, December 4, 1998.

7. "Enemy Warplane Bombs Honolulu," *Honolulu Star-Bulletin* (March 4, 1942), 1.

8. "Night Alarm Wakens City," *Honolulu Advertiser* (March 4, 1942), 1.

9. "Army Hints At Raid by Single Plane," *San Francisco Chronicle* (5 March 1942), 1.

10. "New Honolulu Raid Could Be From Wake Base," *San Francisco Examiner* (March 5, 1942), 1.

11. Ken C. Rust, *Seventh Air Force Story* (Temple City, Calif.: Historical Aviation Album, 1979), 5.

12. Leonard Bridgman, ed., *Jane's All the World's Aircraft, 1945–46* (London: Sampson Low Marston, 1946; repr., New York: Arco Publishing Co., 1970), 213c, 223c.

13. "Mystery Plane Drops Four Bombs On City," *Honolulu Advertiser* (5 March, 1942), 1–2.

14. Ibid., 2.

15. Malcolm D. Aitken, letter to author, 30 August 1998.

16. Lee Kennett, *For the Duration . . .* (New York: Charles Scribner's Sons, 1985), 142.

17. Ibid., 148.

18. Rear Adm. Edwin T. Layton, *"And I Was There"* (New York: Quill William Morrow, 1985), 374.

19. Col. Frank M. Rezeli, interview by author, September 20, 1997.

20. John W. Lambert, *The Pineapple Air Force: Pearl Harbor to Tokyo* (St. Paul, Minn.: Phalanx Publishing Co., 1990), 30.

21. Peter M. Bowers, *Boeing Aircraft Since 1916* (Fallbrook, Calif.: Aero Publishers, 1966), 193–96.

22. René J. Francillon, *Lockheed Aircraft Since 1913* (London: Putnam, 1982), 169; Garry R. Pape and Warren E. Thompson, "Nocturnal Lightnings," *Air International* (August 1978), 80.

23. Owen Thetford, *Aircraft of the Royal Air Force Since 1918* (New York: Funk & Wagnalls, 1968), 202–3.

24. David Kahn, *The Codebreakers* (New York: MacMillan Co., 1967), 17.

25. Elisabeth-Anne Wheal, Stephen Pope, and James Taylor, *A Dictionary of the Second World War* (New York: Peter Bedrick Books, 1999), 286–87.

26. Stephen Budiansky, "Too Late for Pearl Harbor," *Naval Institute Proceedings* (December 1999), 47–51.

27. Kahn, *Codebreakers*, 7.

28. Capt. Joseph J. Rochefort, interview by Commander Etta-Belle Kitchen, *The Reminiscences of Captain Joseph J. Rochefort, U.S. Navy (Ret)* (Annapolis, Md., History Division: U.S. Naval Institute, 1983), 114–17.

29. Ibid., 111–13.

30. Ibid., 203–5.

31. Ibid., 205–7.

32. Walter Lord, *Incredible Victory* (New York: Harper & Row, Publishers, 1967), 17–18.

33. Kahn, *Codebreakers*, 8.

34. Ronald Lewin, *The American Magic* (New York: Farrar Straus Giroux, 1982), 97.

35. Layton, *"And I Was There,"* 372–73.

36. John Prados, *Combined Fleet Decoded* (New York: Random House, 1995), 282–83.

37. Layton, *"And I Was There,"* 373.

38. Intelligence Section, *Summary of the Situation,* Washington, D.C.: Naval Historical Center (March 6, 1942), 2.

39. M. F. Draemel, Memorandum for Flag Secretary, Washington, D.C.: Naval Historical Center (March 8, 1942).

40. 1st Lt. Thomas B. Summers, "Air Raid Alarm on Morning of 7 March 1942," *Report to S-3, Seventh Interceptor Command* (Maxwell AFB, Ala.: USAF Historical Research Center).

41. "Air Alert Sounds Over Busy City at 11:28," *Honolulu Star-Bulletin* (March 7, 1942), 1.

42. M. F. Draemel, Chief of Staff, Pacific Fleet, Intelligence Log, Washington, D.C.: Naval Historical Center (March 16, 1942), 1.

43. Rear Adm. Tsuneo Hitsuji, letter to author, "The Complete Story of Operation K," trans. Mikio Aida (November 1982), 5.

44. Layton, "Rendezvous in Reverse," 484.

45. Hitsuji, "Complete Story," 5.

46. Layton, "Rendezvous in Reverse," 485.

Chapter 5

1. Rear Adm. Tsuneo Hitsuji, letter to author, "The Complete Story of Operation K," trans. Mikio Aida (November 1982), 1.

2. Gordon Prange, Donald M. Goldstein, and Katherine V. Dillon, *Miracle at Midway* (New York: Penquin Books, 1982), 14.

3. Ibid.

4. Dr. James A. Mowbray, "Appendix," *Seven League Boots: The Seventh Army Force at War in the South, Central and Western Pacific Ocean Areas.* n.p., 6.

5. Mowbray, "Appendix," 6; Robert Sherrod, *History of Marine Corps Aviation in World War II* (Washington, D.C.: Combat Forces Press, 1952), 51–52.

6. Sherrod, *Marine Corps Aviation,* 51.

7. Hal Andrews, "Some Brewster F2A Recollections," *Skyways,* No. 55 (July 2000), 11.

8. "Brewster's Benighted Buffalo," *Air Enthusiast Quarterly,* No. 1 (1974), 83.

9. Robert J. Cressman and others, *A Glorious Page in Our History* (Missoula, Mont.: Pictorial Histories Publishing Co., 1990), 26.

10. Sherrod, *Marine Corps Aviation,* 52–53.

11. Mowbray, "Appendix," 11; John Pike, *Johnston Atoll, Kalama Atoll,* U.S. Nuclear Forces guide (FAS, Johnston Atoll, 2000), 1–2.

12. "Palmyra Atoll," *World Fact Book* (Washington, D.C.: CIA, 2000), n.p.; Mowbray, "Appendix," 16.

13. Rear Adm. Tsuneo Hitsuji, *Reflections of the Great Skies,* trans. David and Harumi Ziegler (Tokyo: Japan Defense Agency War History Publications, 1986), 9.

14. Hitsuji, *Great Skies,* 9; Hitsuji, "Complete Story," 4–5.

15. Robert C. Mikesh, *Japanese Aircraft Interiors, 1940–1945* (Sturbridge, Mass.: Monogram Aviation Publications, 2000), 313.

16. Hitsuji, "Complete Story," 4–5; "Hashizume History," TLS to Steve Horn, July 22, 1986, 4.

17. Adm. Claude C. Bloch, to Commander in Chief, Pacific Fleet, "Report of Combat Contact with Enemy Aircraft," TLS, April 1, 1942 (Washington, D.C.: Naval Historical Center), photocopy.

18. W. J. Wallace, "Report of Combat Contact with Enemy Aircraft," to CO, Fourteenth Naval District, March 10, 1942 (Washington, D.C.: Naval Historical Center).

19. Joe Mizrahi, "Farewell to the Fleet's Forgotten Fighter: Brewster F2A," *Airpower* (March 1972), 26–36; Sherrod, *Marine Corps Aviation,* 57.

20. C. J. Chapell, Radar Contact Report, to CO, MAG 22, DS March 10, 1942 (Washington, D.C.: Naval Historical Center).

21. 2nd Lt. F. McCarthy, "Pilot's Combat Report," March 10, 1942 (Washington, D.C.: Naval Historical Center).

22. 1st Lt. C. W. Somers, Jr., "Pilot's Combat Report," March 10, 1942 (Washington, D.C.: Naval Historical Center).

23. Marine Gunner Robert L. Dickey, "Pilot's Combat Report," DS by R. L. Dickey, March 10, 1942 (Washington, D.C.: Naval Historical Center).

24. Captain James L. Neefus, "Pilot's Combat Report," March 10, 1942 (Washington, D.C.: Naval Historical Center).

25. Chapell, Radar Contact Report.

26. Hitsuji, "Complete Story," 5.

27. Sherrod, *Marine Corps Aviation,* 53.

28. L. J. Wiltse, "Endorsement to Report of Combat Contact with Enemy Aircraft," from Commander in Chief, Pacific Fleet to Commander in Chief U.S. Fleet, April 1, 1942 (Washington, D.C.: Naval Historical Center).

29. Pfeiffer to Murphy, "Memo regarding Rochefort's medal award" (Washington, D.C.: Naval Historical Center, n.d).

30. Capt. Joseph J. Rochefort, interview by Commander Etta-Belle Kitchen, *The Reminiscences of Captain Joseph J. Rochefort, U.S. Navy (Ret)* (Annapolis, Md., History Division: U.S. Naval Institute, 1983), 176.

31. Hitsuji, "Complete Story," 5.

32. M. F. Draemel, Chief of Staff, Pacific Fleet, Intelligence Log, March 11, 1942 (Washington, D.C.: Naval Historical Center), 1.

33. W. J. Holmes, *Undersea Victory* (Garden City, N.Y.: Doubleday, 1966), 131.

34. Hitsuji, "Complete Story," 6; Hitsuji, "Hashizume History," 4.

35. Hitsuji, "Hashizume History," 4.

Chapter 6

1. Vice Adm. Matome Ugaki, *Fading Victory: The Diary of Admiral Matome Ugaki, 1941–1945,* trans. Masataka Chihaya (Pittsburgh: University of Pittsburgh Press, 1991), 65.

2. Mark Healy, *Midway, 1942* (London: Osprey Publishers, 1996), 9.

3. Naval Analysis Division, *The Campaigns of the Pacific War* (Washington, D.C.: United States Strategic Bombing Survey, Pacific, 1946), 3; John Keegan, *The Second World War* (New York: Penguin Books, 1990), 252.

4. Herbert P. Bix, *Hirohito and the Making of Modern Japan* (New York: Harper Collins Publishers, 2000), 439–53; Frank Gibney, *Emperor Hirohito* (*Time* Magazine, August 23–30, 1999), 29–33.

5. Hans-Joachim Krug, Yoichi Hirama, Berthold J. Sander-Nagashima, and Axel Niestlé, *Reluctant Allies: German-Japanese Naval Relations in World War II* (Annapolis, Md.: Naval Institute Press, 2001), 21–22, 44.

6. Ibid., 69.

7. Healy, *Midway,* 12–14.

8. Mitsuo Fuchida and Masatake Okumiya, *Midway: The Battle That Doomed Japan* (Annapolis, Md.: Naval Institute Press, 1955), 105.

9. Ibid, 106.

10. Carroll V. Glines, *The Doolittle Raid* (New York: Orion Books, 1988), 11–20.

11. Ibid., 20–21.

12. Ibid., 22–25.

13. Ibid., 41.

14. Ibid., 61–63.

15. Lowell Thomas and Edward Jablonski, *Doolittle: A Biography* (Garden City, N.Y.: Doubleday & Co., 1976), 178–80.

16. Glines, *Doolittle Raid*, 68–69; W. J. Holmes, *Double-Edged Secrets* (Annapolis, Md.: Naval Institute Press, Bluejacket Books, 1998), 68.

17. Stan Cohen, *Destination: Tokyo* (Missoula, Mont.: Pictorial Histories Publishing Co., 1983), 40.

18. Ibid., 48.

19. Ibid., 83–84.

20. Glines, *Doolittle Raid*, 201.

21. Col. Trevor Nevitt Dupuy, *The Air War in the Pacific: Air Power Leads the Way, Military History of World War II*, vol. 13 (New York: Franklin Watts, 1964), 39–40.

22. Bert Webber, *Retaliation: Japanese Attacks on the Pacific Coast* (Corvallis, Ore.: Oregon State University Press, 1975), 12.

23. Michael Slackman, *Target: Pearl Harbor* (Honolulu, Hawaii: University of Hawaii Press, 1990), 258.

24. Orita, Zenji, with Joseph D. Harrington, *I-Boat Captain* (Canoga Park, Calif.: Major Books, 1970), 39.

25. Slackman, *Target*, 259.

26. Prados, *Combined Fleet*, 195.

27. Orita, *I-Boat Captain*, 39.

28. Prados, *Combined Fleet*, 195.

29. Donald J. Young, "West Coast War Zone," *World War II*, 27.

30. Orita, *I-Boat Captain*, 41; Bob Hackett and Sander Kingsepp, *Sensuikan! HIJMS Submarine I-7: Tabular Record of Movement*, www.combinedfleet.com, 2001, 1–2.

31. Gordon Prange, Donald M. Goldstein, and Katherine V. Dillon, *Miracle at Midway* (New York: Penquin Books, 1982), 14–16.

32. Dan van der Vat, *The Pacific Campaign: The U.S.–Japanese Naval War 1941–1945* (New York: Touchstone Books, 1991), 172.

33. Holmes, *Double-Edged Secrets*, 71.

34. Capt. Joseph J. Rochefort, interview by Commander Etta-Belle Kitchen, *The Reminiscences of Captain Joseph J. Rochefort, U.S. Navy (Ret)* (Annapolis, Md., History Division: U.S. Naval Institute, 1983), 237.

35. Nathan Miller, *War at Sea* (New York: Oxford University Press, 1995), 240; Naval Analysis Division, *Campaigns*, 12.

36. Keegan, *Second World War*, 271–72.

37. Miller, *War at Sea*, 240.

38. Ibid., 241–42.

39. van der Vat, *Pacific Campaign*, 175; Naval Analysis Division, *Campaigns*, 53.

40. van der Vat, *Pacific Campaign*, 176; Vice Adm. Aubrey W. Fitch, "The Battle of the Coral Sea," *Battle Stations!* (New York: Wm. H. Wise & Co., 1946), 106.

41. Naval Analysis Division, *Campaigns*, 55; Edwin P. Hoyt, *Blue Skies and Blood: The Battle of the Coral Sea* (New York: Ballantine Books, 1975), 232.

42. Fuchida and Okumiya, *Midway*, 105.

43. Ibid., 106.

44. John B. Lundstrom, *The First Team* (Annapolis, Md.: Naval Institute Press, 1984), 574.

45. *The Official World War II Guide to the Army Air Forces* (New York: Bonanza Books, 1988), 52.

46. Saburo Sakai with Martin Caidin and Fred Saito, *Samurai!* (New York: Ballantine Books, 1957), 20; Healy, *Midway*, 37–38.

47. Gerald R. Weinberg, *A World at Arms* (New York: Cambridge University Press, 1994), 847–48.

48. van der Vat, *Pacific Campaign*, 176–77; Fuchida and Okumiya, *Midway*, 106.

49. Healy, *Midway*, 14–15; Fuchida and Okumiya, *Midway*, 95–96.

Chapter 7

1. Walter Lord, *Incredible Victory* (New York: Harper & Row, Publishers, 1967), 19.

2. Naval Analysis Division, *The Campaigns of the Pacific War*, U.S. Strategic Bombing Survey (Pacific) (Washington, D.C.: Government Printing Office, 1946), 79.

3. Gordon W. Prange, Donald Goldstein, and Katherine V. Dillon, *Miracle at Midway* (New York: Penguin Books, 1982), 432–34; Jack Greene, *The Midway Campaign* (Conshohocken, Pa.: Combined Books, 1995), 250–53; Mark Healy, *Midway, 1942* (London: Osprey Publishers, 1996), 24–25.

4.   Roger Chesneau, *Aircraft Carriers of the World* (Annapolis, Md.: Naval Institute Press, 1984), 163.

5. Prange and others, *Miracle at Midway*, 432–34; Greene, *Midway Campaign*, 250–53; Healy, *Midway*, 24–25; Naval Analysis Division, *Campaigns*, 74–75, 99.

6. Greene, *Midway Campaign*, 250.

7. Prange and others, *Miracle at Midway*, 432–35; Greene, *Midway Campaign*, 251; Healy, *Midway*; Naval Analysis Division, *Campaigns*, 74–75.

8. William Green, ed., "The Unrivalled Emily . . . Best of the Wartime Big Boats," *Air International*, vol. 24, No. 4 (April 1983), 186; Interrogation of Captain Ito, Navy No. 33. U.S. Strategic Bombing Survey No. 100, Tokyo (October 1946).

9. Lt. Cdr. Thomas E. Powers, "Incredible Midway," *Naval Institute Proceedings* (June 1967), 65–66.

10. Ibid., 13–15.

11. Ronald Lewin, *The American Magic* (New York: Farrar Straus Giroux, 1982), 98.

12. Capt. Duane L. Whitlock, "The Silent War Against the Japanese Navy," *Naval War College Review*, vol. 48, no. 4, (Autumn 1995), 47; Sidney C. Moody, Jr., and photographers of the Associated Press, *War Against Japan* (Novato, Calif.: Presidio Press, 1994), 55.

13. Duane L. Whitlock, *And So Was I (A Gratuitous Supplement to "I Was There" by Rear Adm. Edwin T. Layton)* (Washington, D.C.: Naval Historical Office, 1986), 78.

14. Ibid., 95.

15. "Eavesdropping on the Enemy," *World War II* (Alexandria, Va.: Time-Life Books, 1981), 60–62.

16. Rear Adm. Edwin T. Layton, *"And I Was There"* (New York: Quill William Morrow, 1985), 410.

17. Dan van der Vat, *The Pacific Campaign: The U.S.–Japanese Naval War 1941–1945* (New York: Touchstone Books, 1991), 178–79.

18. Whitlock, "Silent War," 49.

19. Lord, *Incredible Victory*, 23; van der Vat, *Pacific Campaign*, 180; Prange and others, *Miracle at Midway*, 45–46.

20. Len Walsh, *Read Japanese Today* (Tokyo: Charles E. Tuttle Co., 1969), 19–20, 155.

21. "Eavesdropping on the Enemy," 63.

22. Ibid.

23. Mitsuo Fuchida and Masatake Okumiya, *Midway: The Battle That Doomed Japan* (Annapolis, Md.: Naval Institute Press, 1955), 107.

24. Powers, "Incredible Midway," 66.

25. Rear Adm. Tsuneo Hitsuji, letter to author, "The Complete Story of Operation K," trans. Mikio Aida (November 1982), 6.

26. Fuchida and Okumiya, *Midway*, 120.

27. Lord, *Incredible Victory*, 40; Fuchida and Okumiya, *Midway*, 121.

28. David D. Lowman, "Rendezvous in Reverse II," *Naval Institute Proceedings* (December 1983), 133.

29. Ibid., 122–23.

30. Fuchida and Okumiya, *Midway*, 42.

31. Ibid., 144.

32. Samuel E. Morrison, *History of Naval Operation in World War II*, vol. 4, *Coral Sea, Midway and Submarine Actions* (Boston: Little, Brown & Co., 1962), 70; Prange and others, *Miracle at Midway*, 396; Fuchida and Okumiya, *Midway*, 249–50.

33. Layton, *"And I Was There,"* 438.

34. "Eavesdropping on the Enemy," 63.

35. Paul S. Dull, *The Imperial Japanese Navy, 1941–1945* (Annapolis, Md.: Naval Institute Press, 1978), 354.

36. Fuchida and Okumiya, *Midway*, 126–27.

37. Ibid., 133.

38. Theodore F. Cook, Jr., "Our Midway Disaster: Japan Springs a Trap, June 4, 1942," *What If?*((American Historical Publications) (New York: Berkley Books, 2000), 318–19.

39. Morrison, *Coral Sea*, 90–93; Prange and others, *Miracle at Midway*, 396; Fuchida and Okumiya, *Midway*, 249–50.

40. Fuchida and Okumiya, *Midway,* 232–39; Lord, *Incredible Victory,* 285.

41. Herbert P. Bix, *Hirohito and the Making of Modern Japan* (New York: Harper Collins Publishers, 2000), 449.

42. Ibid., 450.

43. Prange and others, *Miracle at Midway,* 362.

44. Lord, *Incredible Victory,* 286; Prange and others, *Miracle at Midway,* 362–63.

45. Prange and others, *Miracle at Midway,* 396.

Chapter 8

1. Rear Adm. Tsuneo Hitsuji, letter to the author, December 11, 1986.

2. William Green, ed. "The Unrivalled Emily . . . Best of the Wartime Big Boats," *Air International,* vol. 24, no. 4 (April 1983), 185–86.

3. Ibid., 180, 186; correspondence with Larry de Zeng IV, August 25, 2001.

4. Interrogation of Captain Ito, Navy No. 33. U.S. Strategic Bombing Survey No. 100, Tokyo (October 1946), 106–7.

5. CINCPAC Confidential Report 13 December 1945, Serial 034372 from Secret Report: *Solomon Island Campaign—Makin Island Diversion* (20 Oct 1942); Samuel E. Morrison, *History of Naval Operation in World War II,* vol. 4, *Coral Sea, Midway and Submarine Actions* (Boston: Little, Brown & Co., 1962), 235–41.

6. Fourth Marine Division History, "Penetrating the Outer Ring," USMC Historical Paper, 5; Samuel Eliot Morrison, *History of Naval Operations in World War II,* vol. 7, *Aleutians, Gilberts and Marshalls* (Boston: Little, Brown & Co., 1951), 186; Minoru Akimoto, "Directory: WWII Japanese Aircraft (11), Kawanishi Type 2 Flying Boat," *Koku-Fan* (January 1983), 153.

7. Map of *Islands of the Pacific* (Washington, D.C.: National Geographic Society, 1974).

8. Fourth Marine Division History, 5; Morrison, *Aleutians, Gilberts and Marshalls,* 186.

9. Rear Adm. Tsuneo Hitsuji, Letter to author, April 21, 1986, "More Details of Attack and Personal History," 1–2; M. C. Richards, "Kawanishi 4-Motor Flying Boats (H6K 'Mavis' and H8K 'Emily')," *Aircraft in Profile,* vol. 11 (Garden City, N.Y.: Doubleday & Co., 1972), 258–59; Capt. Rikihei Inoguchi and Cdr. Tadashi Nakajima with Roger Pineau, *The Divine Wind* (Annapolis, Md.: Naval Institute Press, 1958), 132–33.

10. M. C. Richards and Major Robert C. Mikesh, "Emily—Grand Old Lady of Japan," *Air Pictorial* (August 1969), 283.

11. Bert and Margie Webber, *Fujita: Flying Samurai* (Medford, Ore.: Webb Research Group Publishers, 2000), 82.

12. Bert Webber, *Silent Siege—III: Japanese Attacks on North American World War II* (Medford, Ore.: Webb Research Group, 1997), 136–37.

13. Webber, *Fujita: Flying Samurai,* 82.

14. Ibid., 82–87.

15. Carl Boyd and Akihiko Yoshida, *The Japanese Submarine Force and World War II* (Annapolis, Md.: Naval Institute Press, 1995), 110.

16. Webber, *Silent Siege III,* 138.

17. Webber, *Retaliation,* 11–12, 66–68; Webber, *Silent Siege,* 124–29; Nobuo Fujita and Joseph D. Harrington, "I Bombed the USA," *Naval Institute Proceedings* (June 1961), 64–69.

18. Boyd and Yoshida, *Japanese Submarine Force,* 110–11.

19. William Scheck, "Perspectives," *World War II* (July 1998), 16.

20. Donald DeNevi, *The West Coast Goes to War* (Missoula, Mont.: Pictorial Histories Publishing Co., Inc., 1998), 103.

21. Webber, *Retaliation,* 160.

22. *Los Angeles Times,* February 25, 1942, 1.

23. Wesley Frank Craven and James Lea Cate, *The Army Air Forces in World War II,* vol. 1, *Plans and Early Operations* (Chicago: University of Chicago Press, 1948), 283.

24. Robert N. Roberts, interview by the author, June 1957, notes, private collection; Lee Kennett, *For the Duration . . .* (New York: Charles Scribner's Sons, 1985), 146.

25. Webber, *Silent Siege,* 146.

26. Ibid, 93, 112–22.

27. Norman Polmar, *Aircraft Carriers: A Graphic History of Carrier Aviation and Its Influence on World Events* (Garden City, N.Y.: Doubleday & Co., 1969), 318.

28. W. J. Holmes, *Undersea Victory* (Garden City, N.Y.: Doubleday, 1966), 254; Fujita and Harrington, 68.

29. Thomas Paine, "The Transpacific Voyage of HIJMS I-400" (Los Angeles and Santa Barbara, Calif.: Tom Paine's Journal, rev. 1991), 6; James F. Dunnigan and Albert A. Nofi, *Dirty Little Secrets of World War II* (New York: William Morrow and Co., 1994), 242.

30. Richard O'Neill, *Suicide Squads* (New York: Ballantine Books, 1981), 174.

31. Background information from the Doyusha instruction sheet for a Japanese model of the *I-400* submarine.

32. Holmes, *Undersea Victory,* 472.

33. O'Neill, *Suicide Squads,* 175.

34. Paine, "Transpacific Voyage," 10–11; Holmes, *Undersea Victory,* 473.

35. Capt. E. John Long, "Japan's Undersea Carriers," *Naval Institute Proceedings* (June 1950), 609.

36. Robert C. Mikesh, *Japan's World War II Balloon Bomb Attacks on North America* (Washington, D.C.: Smithsonian Institute Press, 1973), 8, 13–15, 58.

37. Tanaka Tetsuko, *Making Balloon Bombs;* Haruko and Theodore Cook, eds., *Japan at War* (New York: The New Press, 1992), 188–92.

38. Mikesh, *Balloon Bomb Attacks,* 3–6.

39. Dale Andradé, "Trial by Fire," *The Retired Officer Magazine* (February 2002), 58–59; Don Thompson, "First Black Paratroopers Saw Little Combat," *Greenville News* (S.C.) (June 18, 2000), F1-4.

40. Mikesh, *Balloon Bomb Attacks,* 67.

Epilogue

1. Edward Davidson and Dale Manning, *Timeline of World War II* (London: Cassell & Co., 1999), 198, 202.

2. Ibid., 219, 224.

3. John Ray Skates, *The Invasion of Japan: Alternative to the Bomb* (Columbia, S.C.: University of South Carolina Press, 1994), 101.

4. Ibid., 102–9.

5. U.S. Strategic Bombing Survey, *Japanese Air Power* (Washington, D.C.: Government Printing Office, July 1946), n.p.; Robert C. Mikesh, *Broken Wings of the Samurai* (Annapolis, Md.: Naval Institute Press, 1993), 28; Dennis Warner and Peggy Warner with Cdr. Sadao Seno, *The Sacred Warriors* (New York: Van Nostrand Reinhold Co., 1982), 292.

6. Hitsuji, correspondence with the author, 22 July 1986.

7. Gordon W. Prange, Donald M. Goldstein, and Katherine V. Dillon, *God's Samurai* (Washington, D.C.: Brassey's[US], 1990), passim.

8. Burke Davis, *Get Yamamoto* (New York: Bantam Books, 1971), 69–72; Hiroyuki Agawa, *The Reluctant Admiral,* trans. John Bester (Tokyo: Kodansha International Ltd., 1979), 344–46.

9. David Kahn, *The Codebreakers* (New York: MacMillan Co., 1967), 598; Carroll V. Glines, *Attack on Yamamoto* (Atglen, Pa.: Schiffer Military History, 1993), 1–3.

10. Glines, *Attack on Yamamoto*, 31–37.

11. Ibid., 61.

12. Ibid., 108.

13. Ibid., 109; Davis, *Get Yamamoto*, 142–43.

14. Pete Azzole, *Cryptology* (Corvallis, Ore.: The U.S. Naval Cryptologic Veterans Association, 1995), n.p.

15. Bert and Margie Webber, *Fujita: Flying Samurai* (Medford, Ore.: Webb Research Group Publishers, 2000), 93, 108–9, 113, 128.

16. Major Robert C. Mikesh, "Japanese Giant of WW-2," *Air Progress* (January 1967), 48–47.

17. Ibid., 47.

18. Ibid., 60.

19. Ibid., 60–61.

20. Ibid., 62; Flight Test Division, "Final Report of Evaluation of 'Emily' Flying Boat," U.S. Naval Air Test Center, Patuxent River, June 10, 1947, 4.

21. Flight Test Division, "Final Report," 4–7.

22. Dorr Carpenter and Norman Polmar, *Submarines of the Imperial Japanese Navy* (Annapolis, Md.: Naval Institute Press, 1986), 111; Erminio Bagnasco, *Submarines of World War Two* (London: Cassell & Co., 1977), 194–95.

23. Carpenter and Polmar, 110; Bagnasco, *Submarines*, 189.

24. Frank Gibney, *Emperor Hirohito* (*Time* Magazine, August 23–30, 1999), n.p.

25. Ibid.

26. Edward Behr, *Hirohito: Behind the Myth* (New York: Villard Books, 1989), chap. 11, 12, 13, passim; Herbert P. Bix, *Hirohito and the Making of Modern Japan* (New York: Harper Collins Publishers, 2000), 439–46.

27. Gibney, "Hirohito," n.p.

28. Leonard Mosely, *Hirohito: Emperor of Japan* (Englewood Cliffs, N.J.: Prentice-Hall, Inc., 1966), 329–30.

29. Warner and Warner, *Sacred Warriors*, 308; Thomas M. Coffey, *Imperial Tragedy* (New York: World Publishing Co., 1970), 491–92.

30. Richard O'Neill, *Suicide Squads* (New York: Ballantine Books, 1981), 278.

31. Behr, *Hirohito,* xvi.

32. Ibid., xvii.

33. Bix, *Hirohito,* 676.

34. Ibid., 680.

35. Ibid., 684–85.

36. Toshikazu Kase, *Journey to the* Missouri (New Haven, Conn.: Yale University Press, 1950), 271–72.

Appendix

1. Thomas E. Griess, ed., *West Point Atlas for the Second World War, Asia and the Pacific* (Wayne, N.J.: Avery Publishing Group, 1985), 4, 14; Freeman Westell, "Japan's Forlorn Floatplane Flotilla," *Airpower* (July 2000), 46.

2. James F. Dunnigan and Albert A. Nofi, *Victory at Sea* (New York: Quill, William Morrow & Co., 1995), 197.

3. Edward S. Miller, *War Plan Orange: The U.S. Strategy to Defeat Japan, 1897–1945* (Annapolis, Md.: Naval Institute Press, 1991), 175.

4. Dunnigan and Nofi, *Victory at Sea,* 199.

5. René J. Francillon, *Japanese Aircraft of the Pacific War* (New York: Funk & Wagnalls, 1970), 307, 313.

6. William T. Larkins, *Battleship and Cruiser Aircraft of the U.S. Navy, 1910–1949* (Atglen, Pa.: Schiffer Military/Aviation History, 1996), 224–26.

7. Dunnigan and Nofi, *Victory at Sea,* 200.

8. Francillon, *Japanese Aircraft,* 3–4.

9. Robert C. Mikesh, *Zero* (Osceoa, Wis.: Motorbooks International, 1944), 16.

10. Staff of *Aireview Magazine, General View of Japanese Military Aircraft of the Pacific War* (Tokyo: Kanto Sha Co., Ltd, English text, 3rd ed., 1958), 16.

11. Ibid, 38–39.

12. William M. Leary, "The Zero Fighter," *Aerospace Historian* (Winter 1987), 19–20.

13. Francillon, *Japanese Aircraft,* 426–28.

14. Ibid., 317–21.

15. John Wegg, *General Dynamics Aircraft and their Predecessors* (Annapolis, Md.: Naval Institute Press, 1990), 89–90, 99–100; Gordon Swanborough and Peter

M. Bowers, *United States Navy Aircraft Since 1911* (Annapolis, Md.: Naval Institute Press, 1968), 103–6.

16. Air Branch, Office of Naval Intelligence, *Naval Aviation Combat Statistics, World War II,* OPNAV—P23V No. A129 (Washington, D.C: Office Of Chief of Naval Operations, June 17, 1946), 58–59.

17. Mitch Mayborn, and others, *Grumman Guidebook,* American Aircraft Series, Book 4 (Dallas: Flying Enterprise Publications, 1976), 30.

18. Peter M. Bowers, *Curtiss Aircraft, 1907–1947* (London: Putnam & Co., 1979), 426.

19. René J. Francillon, *McDonnell Douglas Aircraft Since 1920,* vol. 1 (Annapolis, Md.: Naval Institute Press, 1988), 230.

20. Henry Sakaida, *Imperial Japanese Navy Aces 1937–1945* (London: Osprey Publishing, Ltd., 1998), 109.

21. John Guttman, "Japan's Feisty Floatplane," *Aviation History* (January 2001), 36.

22. Ibid., 32.

23. Guttman, "Feisty Floatplane," 30; Francillon, *Japanese Aircraft,* 358–62.

24. William Green, *Warplanes of the Second World War,* vol. 6, *Floatplanes* (Garden City, N.Y.: Doubleday & Co., 1962), 132–33.

25. Westell, "Floatplane Flotilla," 48, 51.

26. Green, *Floatplanes,* 126–28; Westell, "Floatplane Flotilla," July 2000, 52; *General View of Japanese Military Aircraft in the Pacific War* (Tokyo: Kanto-Sha Co., Ltd., 1958), 60.

27. J. R. Smith and Antony Kay, *German Aircraft of the Second World War* (London: Putnam & Co. Ltd., 1972), 312–13; Herwig and Rode, *Luftwaffe Secret Projects,* 80.

28. Francillon, *Japanese Aircraft,* 291–94; Green, *Floatplanes,* 118–20.

29. Green, *Floatplanes,* 157–60; Swanborough and Bowers, *United States Navy Aircraft Since 1911,* 159–61.

30. Gerard P. Moran, *Aeroplanes Vought, 1917–1977* (Temple City, Calif.: Historic Aviation Album, 1979), 72–74; Swanborough and Bowers, *United States Navy Aircraft Since 1911,* 447–48.

31. Peter M. Bowers, *Curtiss Aircraft, 1907–1947* (London: Putnam & Co., 1979), 419–21; Swanborough and Bowers, *Navy Aircraft,* 164–65.

32. Green, *Floatplanes,* 166–68; Bowers, *Curtiss Aircraft,* 169–70; Swanborough and Bowers, *Navy Aircraft,* 169–70.

33. Capt. Richard C. Knott, *The American Flying Boat* (Annapolis, Md.: Naval Institute Press, 1979), 236–37.

34. Miller, *War Plan Orange,* 176.

35. Ibid, 178.

36. Fleet and Armstrong, *United States Naval Aviation,* 84; Miller, *War Plan Orange,* 179.

37. Ray Wagner, *America's Combat Planes,* 3rd ed. (Garden City, N.Y.: Doubleday & Co., 1982), 314.

38. Bert Kinzey, *PBY Catalina* (Carrollton, Texas: Squadron/Signal Publications, 2000), 4–5.

39. John Wegg, *General Dynamics Aircraft and their Predecessors* (Annapolis, Md.: Naval Institute Press, 1990), 70–71.

40. Nathan Miller, *War at Sea* (New York: Oxford University Press, 1995), 162.

41. Winston Churchill, *The Grand Alliance: The Second World War,* vol. 3 (New York: Bantam Books, 1962), 267, 270.

42. Thomas B. Buell, *Master of Sea Power: The Biography of Fleet Admiral Ernest J. King* (Boston: Little, Brown & Co., 1980), 102–3.

43. Ibid., 105.

44. Dwight R. Messimer, *In the Hands of Fate: The Story of Patrol Wing Ten, 8 December 1941–11 May 1942* (Annapolis, Md.: Bluejacket Books, 2002), 308.

45. Staff of *Aireview Magazine, General View of Japanese Military Aircraft of the Pacific War* (Tokyo: Kanto Sha Co., Ltd, English text, 3rd ed., 1958), 63.

46. Wagner, *America's Combat Planes,* 316; Knott, *Flying Boat,* 149.

47. Andrew Toppan, "Aviation Oddities, Part III: Barges, Landing Ships, and Other Platforms," *Haze Gray,* hazegray.com, 1.

48. Kenneth Munson and Gordon Swanborough, *Boeing: An Aircraft Album,* No. 4 (New York: Arco Publishing Co., 1971), 86; Peter M. Bowers, *Boeing Aircraft Since 1916* (Fallbrook, Calif.: Aero Publishers, 1966), 216–17.

49. Gordon Swanborough and Peter M. Bowers, *United States Navy Aircraft Since 1911* (Annapolis, Md.: Naval Institute Press, 1968), 512; Knott, *The American Flying Boat,* 182–83.

50. Leonard Bridgman, ed., *Jane's All the World's Aircraft, 1943–1944* (New York: Macmillan Co., 1943), 202c; Knott, *The American Flying Boat,* 193–99.

51. M. C. Richards, "Kawanishi 4-Motor Flying Boats (H6K 'Mavis' and H8K 'Emily')," *Aircraft in Profile,* vol. 11 (Garden City, N.Y.: Doubleday & Co., 1972), 242.

52. Ibid., 261.

53. Justin Libby, "Pan Am Gets a Pacific Partner." *Naval History* (October 1999), 28.

54. Stan Cohen, *Wings to the Orient* (Missoula, Mont.: Pictorial Histories Publishing Co., 1985), 42; Libby, "Pan Am Gets a Pacific Partner," 28.

55. John Prados, *Combined Fleet Decoded* (New York: Random House, 1995), 282.

56. Francillon, *Japanese Aircraft,* 307.

57. William Green, *Warplanes of the Third Reich* (Garden City, N.Y.: Doubleday & Co., 1970), 139.

58. Robert C. Mikesh and Shorzoe Abe, *Japanese Aircraft, 1910–1941* (Annapolis, Md.: Naval Institute Press, 1990), 281–82.

59. Richards, "Kawanishi," 243; William Green, ed. "The Unrivalled Emily . . . Best of the Wartime Big Boats," *Air International,* vol. 24, no. 4 (April 1983), 182–83.

60. OPNAV-16-VT #301, *Japanese Aircraft: TAIC Manual No. 1.* (Washington, D.C: Technical Air Intelligence Center, 1944), n. p.

61. Hitsuji, Rear Adm. Tsuneo, correspondence with the author, February 7, 1986.

62. Francillon, *Japanese Aircraft,* 304–8.

63. Hitsuji, correspondence with the author, February 7, 1986.

64. Green, "The Unrivalled Emily," 184.

65. Ibid., 184–85.

66. Richards, "Kawanishi," 243–45.

67. Ibid., 246.

68. Green, "The Unrivalled Emily," 186.

69. Hitsuji, correspondence with the author, February 7, 1986.

70. Francillon, *Japanese Aircraft,* 186.

71. Richard O'Neill, *Suicide Squads* (New York: Ballantine Books, 1981), 175–77.

72. Tadeusz Janusqewski, *Japanese Submarine Aircraft* (Redbourn, U.K.: Mushroom Model Publications, 2002), 84–85.

73. Terry C. Treadwell, *Strike From Beneath the Sea* (Charleston, S.C.: Tempus Publishing Inc., 1999), 13–14.

74. René J. Francillon, *Japanese Aircraft of the Pacific War* (New York: Funk & Wagnalls, 1970), 37; Roger Chesneau, *Aircraft Carriers of the World* (Annapolis, Md.: Naval Institute Press, 1984), 157.

75. Jonathan Thompson, *Italian Civil and Military Aircraft, 1930–1945* (Fallbrook, Calif.: Aero Publishers, Inc., 1963), 176, 219.

76. Treadwell, *Beneath the Sea,* 80.

77. William Green, *Warplanes of the Second World War,* vol. 6, *Floatplanes* (Garden City, N.Y.: Doubleday & Co., 1963), 8; David R. Winans, "Submarine Aircraft," *American Aviation Historical Society Journal,* vol. 12, no. 1 (Spring 1967), 44–45.

78. Green, *Floatplanes,* vol. 6, 138–40.

79. Winans, "Submarine Aircraft," 44–45.

80. Kenneth E. Wixey, *Parnall Aircraft Since 1914* (Annapolis, Md.: Naval Institute Press, 1990), 147.

81. William T. Larkins, *Battleship and Cruiser Aircraft of the United States Navy, 1910–1949* (Atglen, Pa.: Schiffer Military/Aviation History, 1996), 224, 231, 225.

82. Winans, "Submarine Aircraft," 41–42; William T. Larkins, *U.S. Navy Aircraft 1921–1941 and U.S. Marine Corps Aircraft 1914–1959* (New York: Orion Books, 1988), 26, 30, 54, 60.

83. Bert Webber, *Silent Siege—III: Japanese Attacks on North America in World War II* (Corvallis, Ore.: Webber Research Group, 1997), 277.

84. Treadwell, *Beneath the Sea,* 42–45.

85. Ibid., 43; Maurice Allward, *An Illustrated History of Seaplanes and Flying Boats* (New York: Barnes & Nobles Books, 1981), 64–65.

86. Ibid., 138–40.

87. Webber, *Retaliation,* 11–12.

88. Green, *Floatplanes,* 137–38.

89. Webber, *Retaliation,* 11.

90. Harold Faber, ed., *Luftwaffe: A History* (New York: Times Books, 1977), 7; John Killen, *A History of the Luftwaffe* (New York: Berkley Medallion Books, 1969), 74–75.

91. Faber, *Luftwaffe,* 168–71.

92. William Green, *Warplanes of the Third Reich* (Garden City, N.Y.: Doubleday & Co., 1970), 640–41.

93. Dieter Herwig and Heinz Rode, *Luftwaffe Secret Projects: Strategic Bombers, 1935–1945* (Leicester, U.K.: Midland Publishing, 2000), 41.

94. Kenneth Munson and Gordon Swanborough, *Boeing, An Aircraft Album No. 4* (New York: Arco Publishing Co., 1972), 87–91; Green, *Third Reich*, 641.

95. J. R. Smith and Antony Kay, *German Aircraft of the Second World War* (London: Putnam & Co. Ltd., 1972), 312–13; Herwig and Rode, *Luftwaffe Secret Projects*, 80.

96. Green, *Third Reich*, 98–99; Ray Wagner and Heinz Nowarra, *German Combat Planes* (Garden City, N.Y.: Doubleday & Co., 1971), 360–63; Staff of *Aireview* Magazine, *German Military Aircraft in the Second World War* (Tokyo: Kanto-Sha Co., Ltd., 1960), 59, 93–94.

97. Green, *Third Reich*, 519; Smith and Kay, *German Aircraft*, 456; Wagner and Nowarra, *German Combat Planes*, 313–14.

98. Smith and Kay, *German Aircraft*, 455–56; Green, *Third Reich*, 519–20.

99. Jonathan Thompson, *Italian Civil and Military Aircraft: 1930–1945* (Fallbrook, Calif.: Aero Publishers, Inc., 1963), 276; Robert C. Mikesh, *Japanese Aircraft Code Names & Designations* (Atglen, Pa.: Schiffer Military/ Aviation Publications, 1993), 161.

100. Francillon, *Japanese Aircraft*, 262–64.

101. Robert C. Mikesh, *The Japanese Giants*, Part 1, *Wings* (June 1981), 10–14.

102. Francillon, *Japanese Aircraft*, 484; Staff of *Aireview*, *General View*, 78–79 and 129.

103. Francillon, *Japanese Aircraft*, 423–25.

104. Ibid., 440–42.

105. David C. Evans and Mark R. Peattie, *Kaigun: Strategy, Tactics and Technology in the Imperial Japanese Navy 1887–1941* (Annapolis, Md.: Naval Institute Press, 1997), 529; Robert C. Mikesh and Shorzoe Abe, *Japanese Aircraft, 1910–1941* (Annapolis, Md.: Naval Institute Press, 1990), 198.

106. Francillon, *Japanese Aircraft*, 24–26.

107. *Japanese Military Aircraft Illustrated*, vol. 2, *Bombers*, trans. George and Kiri Elephtheriou, and by Akihiko Shegemi (Tokyo: Bunrin-do, n.d.), 252–53.

108. Ibid., 254–56.

109. Ibid., 257; and Shigeru Nohara, *The X-Planes of the Imperial Japanese Army and Navy, l924–1945*, trans. George and Kiri Elephtheriou (Tokyo: Green Arrow Publishing, 2000), n. p.

110. Nohara, *The X-Planes of the Imperial Japanese Army and Navy*, 260.

111. Ibid., 260–61.

112. *Japanese Military Aircraft Illustrated*, 257–61; Peter M. Bowers, *Boeing Aircraft Since 1916* (Fallbrook, Calif.: Aero Publishers, 1966), 282.

113. Yoshiro Ikari, *SABARA KUJUSENKAN FUGAKU: Maboroshi no America hondo daikusu FUGAKU* [Good-bye, Battleship in the Air—The Dream of Bombing the American Mainland], trans. George and Kiri Elephtheriou and Akihiko Shegimi (Tokyo: Kougin-sha, 2002), n.p.

114. Mikesh and Abe, *Japanese Aircraft 1910–1941*, 182.

115. Ikari, *FUGAKU*, n.p.

116. Ibid.

117. Ibid.

118. Ibid.; Bowers, *Boeing Aircraft Since 1916*, 278.

119. Kiyoshi Tanaka, *Nainenkikan (Internal Combustion Engines)*, trans. Akihiko Shegimi (Tokyo: n.p., 1972).

120. Robert C. Mikesh, *The Japanese Giants*, Part 2, *Airpower* (July 1981), 34.

121. Ikari, *FUGAKU*, n.p.

122. Ibid., n.p.

123. Gen. James H. "Jimmy" Doolittle, *I Could Never Be So Lucky Again* (New York: Bantam Books, 1992), 426.

124. *Japanese Military Aircraft Illustrated*, vol. 2, 252–61; Francillon, *Japanese Aircraft*, 493; Staff of *Aireview*, *General View*, 125.

125. Norman Polmar, *Aircraft Carriers: A Graphic History of Carrier Aviation and Its Influence on World Events* (Garden City, N.Y.: Doubleday & Co., 1969), 1–7.

126. Robert C. Mikesh, *Zero* (Oceola, Wisc.: Motorbooks International Publishers, 1994), 16.

127. Ibid., 35.

128. Chesneau, *Aircraft Carriers*, 79.

129. Len Deighton, *Blood, Tears and Folly* (New York: Harper Collins, 1994), 631–32; Chesneau, *Aircraft Carriers*, 157.

130. Chesneau, *Aircraft Carriers*, 198, 201.

131. *Jane's Fighting Ships of World War II* (London: Jane's Publishing Co., 1946–47: repr. New York: Crescent Books, 1992), 198; John Ellis, *World War II: The Encyclopedia of Facts and Figures* (New York: The Military Book

Club, 1993), 301; Dorr Carpenter and Norman Polmar, *Submarines of the Imperial Japanese Navy* (Annapolis, Md.: Naval Institute Press, 1986), 101–2; Erminio Bagnasco, *Submarines of World War Two* (London: Cassell & Co., 1977), 190–91; Donald J. Young, "West Coast War Zone," *World War II* (July 1998), 27.

132. Hajime Fukaya, ed. by Martin E. Holbrook, "Three Japanese Submarine Developments," *Naval Institute Proceedings* (August 1952), 866–67; Capt. E. John Long, "Japan's Undersea Carriers," *Naval Institute Proceedings* (June 1950), 612; Thomas Paine, "The Transpacific Voyage of HIJMS I-400" (Los Angeles and Santa Barbara, Calif.: Tom Paine's Journal, rev. 1991), 2–3.

133. Edwin P. Hoyt, "The Downfall of the *I*-Boats," *The American Legion Magazine* (December 1980), 18.

GLOSSARY OF AIRCRAFT

Allies' Code Name	Designator	Builder	Notes
Airacobra	P-39	Bell	A single-engined fighter aircraft.
Avenger	TBF	Grumman	A single-engined torpedo bomber. It was used operationally for the first time in the Battle of Midway. Four of six Avengers used at Midway were shot down in its battle debut.
Betty	G3M	Mitsubishi	A twin-engined land-based bomber.
Black Widow	P-61	Northrop	A large twin-engined night fighter. It was the first U.S. fighter designed specifically for night fighter duties.
Bolo	B-18	Douglas	A long-range bomber.
Boston	A-20	Douglas	A twin-engined light bomber. It was very fast at low altitude.

Allies' Code Name	Designator	Builder	Notes
Boston/Havoc	A-20/P-70	Douglas	A twin-engined bomber. Some Bostons were equipped with radar equipment and additional nose guns and redesignated as P-70, codenamed Havoc. They were used as night fighters until replaced in 1944 by the Black Widow.
Buffalo	F2A-3	Brewster	Single-engined navy fighter. It was the U.S. Navy's first monoplane fighter, but was obsolescent by the beginning of the war in the Pacific.
Catalina	PBY	Consolidated	A large twin-engined flying boat. The U.S. Navy used it throughout World War II for patrol and attack duties. It was a slow, but a versatile aircraft that was used also for bombing, as a torpedo bomber, and for search and rescue. Later models were modified with retractable wheels so that it could function as an amphibian.
Claude	A5M1	Mitsubishi	A fighter.
Clipper	M-130	Martin	A civilian flying boat operated by Pan American Airways.

Allies' Code Name	Designator	Builder	Notes
Coronado	PB2Y	Consolidated	A large four-engined flying boat. It was expensive and the U. S Navy puchased fewer of these in favor of the smaller Catalina. It was used primarily as a transport and rarely for patrol duties.
Corsair	O2U/F4U	Vought	Single-engined prewar biplane observation floatplane. It used for artillery spotting for battleships and cruisers, and was copied by most prewar navies.
Dauntless	SBD	Douglas	Single-engined dive-bomber. It served extremely well, especially during the Battle of Midway.
Dragon	B-23	Douglas	A twin-engined bomber developed as a successor to the Bolo.
Dreifinger	Ju-88	Junkers	A twin-engined nightfighter bomber.
Emily	H8K	Kawanishi	Four-engined flying boat.
Flying Fortress	B-17	Boeing	A four-engined heavy bomber.
Frances	P1Y1	Nakajima	A twin-engined bomber. Frances was fast and maneuverable.
Fugaku	G10N1	Nakajima	A six-engined land-based bomber. No Allied nickname; it was called Fugaku (Mount Fuji) by the Japanese.

Allies' Code Name	Designator	Builder	Notes
Glen	E14Y	Yokosuka	A submarine-based reconnaissance floatplane.
Hellcat	F6F	Grumman	A carrier-based fighter.
Helldiver	SB2C	Curtiss	A single-engined dive-bomber.
Hudson	A-29	Lockheed	A twin-engined light bomber. It was adapted as a bomber for the RAF from a light transport.
Jake	E13A	Aichi	A reconnaissance float plane.
Jean	B4Y	Yokosuka	A biplane torpedo bomber.
Judy	D4Y	Yokosuka	A dive-bomber.
Kate	B5N2	Nakajima	A carrier-borne attack bomber.
Kingfisher	OS2U	Aichi	A single-engined observation-scout float-plane. It was used through-out the war, launched by catapult from battleships and cruisers.
Kittyhawk	P-40	Curtiss	A single-engined fighter aircraft. It gained its primary fame as the aircraft used by the Flying Tigers in China. The Kittyhawk was the USAAF's primary fighter in the early days of the war in the Pacific.
Liberator	B-24	Consolidated	A four-engined heavy bomber. Slightly faster and with a longer range than the Flying Fortress, it was used in every theater of World War II. See also PB4Y.

Allies' Code Name	Designator	Builder	Notes
Lightning	P-38	Lockheed	A twin-engined fighter aircraft. It was easily recognizable by its twin-boom tail configuration.
Lily	Ki-48	Kawasaki	A twin-engined light bomber.
Liz	G5N1	Nakajima	
Marauder	B-26	Martin	A twin-engined medium bomber. Similar to the Mitchell in size and performance, the Marauder was modified to carry torpedoes in the Battle of Midway.
Mariner	PBM	Martin	A twin-engined flying boat.
Mars/Old Lady	XPB2M	Martin	A flying boat.
Mavis	H6K	Kawanishi	A four-engined flying boat.
Mitchell	B-25	North American	A twin-engined medium bomber. It was fast, rugged, and could carry a bomb load of three thousand pounds. The Mitchell was used by the Doolittle Raiders.
Mustang	P-51	North American	A single-engined fighter aircraft.
Myrt	C6N	Nakajima	A single-engined carrier-based reconnaissance aircraft.
Norm	E15K	Kawanishi	

Allies' Code Name	Designator	Builder	Notes
Ohka/Baka	MXY-7		A purpose-built kamikaze (suicide) aircraft used by Japan toward the end of World War II. The Japanese name was Ohka (Cherry Blossom), but U.S. servicemen gave the aircraft the name Baka (Japanese for "fool").
Passepartout	MB-35	Marcel-Besson	
Paul	E16A1	Aichi	
Peacemaker	B-36	Consolidated	A six-engined very heavy bomber. Its design was begun in 1941 to give the U.S. Army Air Force the extended range capability to be able to bomb Europe or Japan from U. S. bases.
Peashooter	P-26	Boeing	
Pedro	He-111	Heinkel	A twin-engined bomber.
Pencil	Do-17	Dornier	A twin-engined bomber.
Pete	F1M	Mitsubishi	A biplane.
Privateer	PB4Y		A large four-engined land-based heavy bomber, adapted by the navy from the army's Liberator. The navy used it for land-based long-range bombing, ASW, and reconnaissance missions.
Rex	N1K1	Kawanishi	
Rita	G8N	Nakajima	
Sally	Ki-21	Mibsubishi	A bomber.

Allies' Code Name	Designator	Builder	Notes
Sea Dart	XF2Y	Convair	An experimental twin-engined fighter/ flying boat.
Seagull	SOC	Curtiss	Single-engined biplane observation aircraft. It served throughout the war, outlasting its intended replacements on the catapults of battleships and cruisers.
Seahawk	SC	Curtiss	Single-engined scout floatplane. It came into service just at the end of the war.
Seamew	SO3C	Curtiss	
Seiran	M6A	Aichi	A single-engined submarine-borne attack bomber with twin detachable floats. No Allied nickname; it was called the Seiran (Mountain Haze) by the Japanese.
Slim	E9W	Watanabe	Reconnaissance aircraft for submarines; a small biplane.
Spruce Goose	HK-1/H4	Kaiser	An experimental flying boat.
Superfortress	B-29	Boeing	A long-range heavy bomber.
Swordfish		Fairey	A frame-and-fabric biplane torpedo bomber.
Val	D3A/D4Y	Aichi	A carrier-based dive-bomber.
Vindicator	SB2U	Vought	Single-engined navy and marine dive-bomber. It was obsolescent before the war began.

Allies' Code Name	Designator	Builder	Notes
Wildcat	F4F	Grumman	Single-engined navy fighter. It was the navy's first-line World War II fighter until 1943, replacing the Buffalo.
Wirraway	CA-1	Commonwealth	A bomber with a three-bladed propeller, two fixed .303-inch machine guns and a third in the rear cockpit, and bomb rack for up to 500 pounds of ordnance.
Zero	A6M	Mitsubishi	A carrier-borne fighter aircraft. One of the best all-around carrier-based fighters of the early 1940s.

BIBLIOGRAPHY

Primary Sources

7th Air Force G-3 Journal (Radar Log) from Operations of 7th Air Force, 7 December 1941–13 November 1943. (Declassified October 4, 1944), Maxwell AFB, Ala.: USAF Historical Research Center.

"Air Alert Sounds Over Busy City; Off at 11:28." *Honolulu Star-Bulletin,* March 7, 1942, 1.

Aitken, Malcom D. Letter to author, August 30, 1998.

"Army Hints at Raid by Single Plane." *San Francisco Chronicle,* March 5, 1942.

Bloch, Claude C., to Commander in Chief, Pacific Fleet. "Report of Combat Contact with Enemy Aircraft." TLS, April 1, 1942, Washington, D.C.: Naval Historical Center.

Cash, John C. Letter and war diary excerpt to author, October 26, 1997.

Chapell, C. J. "Radar Contact Report." March 10, 1942, Washington, D.C.: Naval Historical Center.

"CINCPAC Confidential Report." December 13, 1945, Serial 034372 from Secret Report: *Solomon Islands Campaign—Makin Island Diversion.* October 20, 1942, Declassified.

Craig, Wesley P. Interview and letter to author, February 3, 1998.

Davidson, H. C., to Commanding General, 7th Air Force, 24 March 1942. (Declassified October 4, 1944), Maxwell AFB, Ala.: USAF Historical Research Center.

de Zeng, Larry, IV. Letters to author regarding organization and deployment of Japanese flying boat units, August 20, 21, and 25, 2001.

Dickey, Robert L. "Pilot's Combat Report." March 10, 1942, Washington, D.C.: Naval Historical Center.

Draemel, M. F. "Intelligence Log." March 11, 1942, Washington, D.C.: Naval Historical Center.

———. "Intelligence Log." March 16, 1942, Washington, D.C.: Naval Historical Center.

———. "Memorandum for Flag Secretary." March 8, 1942, Washington, D.C.: Naval Historical Center.

———. "War Diary Entry." May 1, 1942, Washington, D.C.: Naval Historical Center.

Eberhard, John G. Letter to author, February 12, 1998.

"Enemy Warplane Bombs Honolulu." *Honolulu Star-Bulletin,* March 4, 1942, 1.

Ferguson, Richard F. Letter to author, January 26, 1999.

Flight Test Division. "Final Report of Evaluation of Japanese 'Emily' Flying Boat." Patuxent River: U. S. Naval Air Test Center, Md., June 10, 1947.

Foster, Roy M. Letter to author, October 9, 1997.

Fujita, Nobuo, and Joseph D. Harrigan. "I Bombed the USA." *Naval Institute Proceedings,* (June 1961).

General View of Japanese Military Aircraft in the Pacific War, 4th ed, Two volumes (Vol. 2 is English trans). Tokyo: Kanto-sha Co, Ltd., 1958.

Gennett, Andrew. Interview by author, November 12, 1990.

Hajime Fukaya. "Three Japanese Submarine Developments." Edited by Martin E. Holbrook. *Naval Institute Proceedings,* (August 1952).

"Hashizume History," TLS to Steve Horn, July 22, 1986.

Hitsuji, Rear Adm. Tsuneo. Letter to author, February 7, 1986, "Details of 'Emily' aircraft."

———. Letter to author, April 21, 1986, "More Details of Attack and Personal History."

———. Letter to author, July 22, 1998. "Hashizume and Crew."

———. Letter to author, December 11, 1986, "Seaplane Operations II."

———. Letter to author, September 25, 1995, "Additional Details of Attack."

———. Letter to author, July 22, 1996. Lise, William, translator.

Hunt, Herbert G., Jr. Letter to author, July 21, 1998.

Ikari, Yoshiro. *SABARA KUJUSENKAN FUGAKU: Maboroshi no America Hondo daikusu FUGAKU* [Goodbye, Battleship of the Air—The Dream of Bombing the American Mainland]. Translated by George and Kiri Elephtheriou and by Akihiko Shegimi. Tokyo: Kougin-sha, 2002.

Instruction sheet for Doyusha (Japan) scale model of *I-400* submarine.

Intelligence Section, Pacific Fleet. "Situation Summary," March 6, 1942, Washington, D.C.: Naval Historical Center.

"Japanese May Have Subs That Carry Planes." *Honolulu Star-Bulletin,* March 4, 1942, 1.

Kennedy, Donald R. Letter to author, December 4, 1998.

Lowe, Justice. "Japanese Air Raids at Darwin, NT on 19 February 1942." *Findings of Commission of Inquiry,* Document 224. Darwin, Australia: Supreme Court of Victory, 27 March 1942.

Map of Islands of the Pacific. Washington, D.C.: National Geographic Society, 1974.

McCarthy, F. P. "Pilot's Combat Report." March 10, 1942, Washington, D.C.: Naval Historical Center.

Mowbray, James A. "Appendix," *Seven League Boots: The Seventh Army Force at War in the South, Central and Western Pacific Ocean Areas.* (Unpublished.)

———. Correspondence with author regarding Pacific bases and airfields, October 5, 2000.

"Mystery Plane Drops Four Bombs on City." *Honolulu Advertiser,* March 5, 1942, 1.

Neefus, J. L. "Pilot's Combat Report." March 10, 1942, Washington, D.C.: Naval Historical Center.

"New Honolulu Raid Could Be From Wake Base." *San Francisco Examiner,* March 5, 1942, 1.

"Night Alarm Wakens City." *Honolulu Advertiser,* March 4, 1942, 1.

Nohara, Shigeru, *The X-Planes of the Imperial Japanese Army and Navy.* Translated by George and Kiri Elephtheriou and by Akihiko Shegimi. Tokyo: Green Arrow Publishing, 2000.

"Operational Navigation Chart ONC J-18." St. Louis AFS, Mo.: Defense Mapping Agency Aerospace Center, 1975.

"Pfeiffer to Murphy. Memo regarding Rochefort's medal award." n.d, Washington, D.C.: Naval Historical Center.

Rezeli, Frank M. Interview by author, September 20, 1997.

Roberts, Robert N. Interview by author, June 1957.

Somers, Charles W, Jr. "Pilot's Combat Report." March 10, 1942. Washington, D.C.: Naval Historical Center.

Tanaka, Kiyoshi. *Nainenkikan (Internal Combustion Engines)*. Translated by Akihiko Shegimi. Tokyo: n.p. 1972.

Uchida, Katsuhiro. Letter to author regarding Japanese wartime flight training, December 22, 2001.

————. Letter to author with more details of Japanese wartime flight training, January 10, 2002.

Wiltse, L. J. Endorsement to Report of Combat Contact with Enemy Aircraft, from Commander in Chief, Pacific Fleet to Commander in Chief U.S. Fleet. April 1, 1942, Washington, D.C.: Naval Historical Center.

Secondary Sources

Agawa, Hiroyuki. *The Reluctant Admiral*. Translated by John Bester. New York: Kodansha International/USA, 1979.

Akimoto, Minoru. "Directory: WWII Japanese Aircraft (11), Kawanishi Type 2 Flying Boat, *Koku-Fan*." Tokyo: Bunrindo Co., 1983.

Allward, Maurice. *An Illustrated History of Seaplanes and Flying Boats*. New York: Barnes & Nobles Books, 1981.

Andradé, Dale. "Trial by Fire." *The Retired Officer Magazine* (February 2002).

Andrews, Hal. "Some Brewster F2A Recollections." *Skyways* no. 55 (July 2000).

Azzole, Pete. *Cryptolog*. Corvallis, Ore.: The U. S. Naval Cryptologic Veterans Association, 1995.

Bagnasco, Erminio. *Submarines of World War Two*. London: Cassell & Co, 1977.

Barker, A. J. *Midway: The Turning Point*. New York: Ballantine Books, 1971.

————. *Pearl Harbor*. New York: Ballantine Books, 1969.

Beasley, W. G. *The Rise of Modern Japan*. New York: St. Martin's Press, 2000.

Behr, Edward. *Hirohito: Behind the Myth*. New York: Villard Books, 1989.

Belote, James H., and William M. Belote. *Titans of the Seas*. New York: Harper & Row, 1975.

Bix, Herbert P. *Hirohito and the Making of Modern Japan*. New York: Harper Collins Publishers, 2000.

Bowers, Peter M. *Boeing Aircraft Since 1916*. Fallbrook, Calif.: Aero Publishers, 1966.

———. *Curtiss Aircraft, 1907–1947*. London: Putnam & Co., 1979.

Boyd, Carl, and Akihiko Yoshida. *The Japanese Submarine Force and World War II*. Annapolis, Md.: Naval Institute Press, 1995.

Boyne, Walter J. *Clash of Wings*. New York: Touchstone Books, 1994.

"Brewster's Benighted Buffalo." *Air Enthusiast Quarterly*, no. 1 (1974).

Bridgman, Leonard, ed. *Jane's All the World's Aircraft, 1943–1944*. New York: MacMillan Co., 1943.

———. *Jane's All the World's Aircraft, 1945–1946*. London: Sampson Low Marston, 1946; reprinted New York: Arco Publishing Co., 1970.

Budiansky, Stephen. "Too Late for Pearl Harbor." *Naval Institute Proceedings* (December 1999).

Buell, Thomas B. *Master of Sea Power: A Biography of Fleet Admiral Ernest J. King*. Boston: Little, Brown & Co., 1980.

"Building Japan's Secret Bases." Translated by Rev. Akihiko Shigemi. *Asagumo Newspaper Co*, October 10, 1970.

Calvocoressi, Peter, Guy Wint, and John Pritchard. *Total War*, 2nd Edition. New York: Pantheon Books, 1989.

Carpenter, Dorr, and Norman Polmar. *Submarines of the Imperial Japanese Navy*. Annapolis, Md.: Naval Institute Press, 1986.

Chesneau, Roger. *Aircraft Carriers of the World, 1914 to the Present*. Annapolis, Md.: Naval Institute Press, 1984.

Churchill, Winston. *The Grand Alliance: The Second World War*, Vol. 3. New York: Bantam Books, 1962.

Coffey, Thomas M. *Imperial Tragedy*. New York: World Publishing Co, 1970.

Cohen, Stan. *Destination: Tokyo*. Missoula, Mont.: Pictorial Histories Publishing Co., 1984.

———. *Wings to the Orient*. Missoula, Mont.: Pictorial Histories Publishing Co., 1985.

Cook, Theodore F., Jr. *Our Midway Disaster: Japan Springs a Trap, June 4, 1942. What If?* American Historical Publications. New York: Berkley Books, 2000.

Craven, Wesley Frank, and James Lea Cate, eds. *The Army Air Forces in World War II*, Vol. 1: *Plans and Early Operations*. Chicago: University of Chicago Press, 1948.

Cressman, Robert J., Steve Ewing, Barrett Tillman, Mark Horan, Clark Reynolds, and Stan Cohen. *A Glorious Page in Our History*. Missoula, Mont.: Pictorial Histories Publishing Co., 1990.

Cressman, Robert J., and J. Michael Wenger. *Steady Nerves and Stout Hearts*. Missoula, Mont.: Pictorial Histories Publishing Co., 1989.

Davidson, Edward, and Dale Manning. *Timeline of World War II*. London, Cassell & Co., 1999.

Davis, Burke. *Get Yamamoto*. New York: Bantam Books, 1971.

Deighton, Len. *Blood, Tears and Folly*. New York: Harper Collins, 1994.

DeNevi, Donald. *The West Coast Goes to War*. Missoula, Mont.: Pictorial Histories Publishing Co., 1998.

Doolittle, James H. *I Could Never Be So Lucky Again*. New York: Bantam Books, 1992.

Dower, John. *War Without Mercy*. New York: Pantheon Book, 1986.

Dull, Paul S. *The Imperial Japanese Navy, 1941–1945*. Annapolis, Md.: Naval Institute Press, 1978.

Dunnigan, James F., and Albert A. Nofi. *Dirty Little Secrets of World War II*. New York: William Morrow and Co., 1994.

———. *Victory at Sea*. New York: Quill, William Morrow and Co., Inc., 1995.

Dupuy, Trevor Nevitt. *The Air War in the Pacific: Air Power Leads the Way. The Military History of World War II*, Vol. 13. New York: Franklin Watts, Inc., 1964.

"Eavesdropping on the Enemy." *World War II*. Alexandria, Va.: Time-Life Books, 1981.

Ellis, John. *World War II: The Encyclopedia of Facts and Figures*. New York: The Military Book Club, 1993.

Evans, David C., and Mark R. Peattie. *Kaigun: Strategy, Tactics and Technology in the Imperial Japanese Navy, 1887–1941*. Annapolis, Md.: Naval Institute Press, 1997.

Ewing, William H. *Nimitz: Reflections on Pearl Harbor*. Fredericksburg, Texas: The Admiral Nimitz Foundation, 1985.

Faber, Harold. *Luftwaffe: A History*. New York: Times Books, 1977.

Fahey, James C. *The Ships and Aircraft of the United States Fleet*, 4 vols. Falls Church, Va.: *Ships and Aircraft*, 1939; reprint, Annapolis, Md.: Naval Institute Press, 1977.

Ferrell, Robert H. *Woodrow Wilson and World War I*. New York: Harper & Row, Publishers, 1985.

Fitch, Aubrey W. The Battle of the Coral Sea. *Battle Stations!* New York: Wm. H. Wise & Co., 1946.

Fourth Marine Division History. "Penetrating the Outer Ring." Washington, D.C.: USMC Historical Center.

Francillon, René J. *McDonnell Douglas Aircraft Since 1920,* Vol. 1. Annapolis, Md.: Naval Institute Press, 1990.

———. *Japanese Aircraft of the Pacific War.* New York: Funk & Wagnalls, 1970.

———. *Lockheed Aircraft Since 1913.* London: Putnam, 1982.

Frank, Richard B. *Downfall: The End of the Japanese Empire.* New York: Random House, 1999.

Fuchida, Mitsuo. "I Led the Air Attack on Pearl Harbor." Edited by Roger Pineau. *Naval Institute Proceedings* (September 1952).

Fuchida, Mitsuo, and Masatake Okumiya. *Midway: The Battle That Doomed Japan.* Annapolis. Md.: Naval Institute Press, 1955.

Fukaya, Hajime. "Three Japanese Submarine Developments." Edited by Martin E. Holbrook. *Naval Institute Proceedings,* (August 1952).

Genda, Minoru. *Shinjuwan sakusen kaikoroku* [Recollections of the Pearl Harbor Operation]. Tokyo: Yomiuri Shimunsha, 1967; reprinted, Tokyo: Bungei Shunjusha, 1998.

Glines, Carroll V. *The Doolittle Raid.* New York: Orion Books, 1988.

Green, William, ed. "Unrivalled Emily . . . Best of the Wartime Big Boats." *Air International* 24 no. 4 (April 1983).

Griess, Thomas E., ed. *West Point Atlas for the Second World War, Asia and the Pacific.* Wayne, N.J.: Avery Publishing Group, 1985.

Hata, Ikuhiko, and Yashuho Izawa. *Japanese Naval Aces and Fighter Units in World War II.* Translated by Don Cyril Gorham. Annapolis, Md.: Naval Institute Press, 1989.

Healy, Mark. *Midway 1942.* London: Osprey Publishers, 1993.

Herwig, Dieter, and Heinz Rode. *Luftwaffe Secret Projects: Strategic Bombers, 1935–1945.* Leicester, U.K.: Midland Publishing, 2000.

Hitsuji, Tsuneo. "The Complete Story of Operation K." Translated by Mikio Aida. November 1982.

———. *Reflections of the Great Skies.* Translated by David and Harumi Ziegler. Tokyo: Japan Defense Agency War History Publications, 1986.

Holmes, W. J. "Discussions, Comments, Notes on 'Rendezvous in Reverse.'" *Naval Institute Proceedings* (August 1953).

———. *Double-Edged Secrets.* Annapolis, Md.: Naval Institute Press, 1998.

———. *Undersea Victory.* Garden City, N.Y.: Doubleday & Co., 1966.

Hoyt, Edwin P. *Blue Skies and Blood: The Battle of the Coral Sea.* New York: Pinnacle Books, 1975.

———. "Downfall of the *I*-Boats." *The American Legion Magazine* (December 1980).

———. *Japan's War: The Great Pacific Conflict.* New York: McGraw-Hill Publishing, 1986.

Hudson, Alec [W. J. Holmes]. "Rendezvous." *The Saturday Evening Post* (August 2 and 9, 1941).

Ienaga, Saburo. *The Pacific War, 1931–1945.* Translated by Frank Baldwin. New York: Pantheon Books, 1978.

Inoguchi, Rikihei, and Tadashi Nakajima, with Roger Pineau. *The Divine Wind.* Annapolis, Md.: Naval Institute Press, 1958.

Interrogation of Captain Ito, Navy No. 33. U. S. Strategic Bombing Survey No. 100. Tokyo, October 1946.

Jane's Fighting Ships of World War II. London: Jane's Publishing Co., 1947; reprint, New York: Crescent Publishing Co., 1992.

Janusqewski, Tadeusz. *Japanese Submarine Aircraft.* Redbourn, U.K.: Mushroom Model Publications, 2002.

Japanese Military Aircraft Illustrated, Vol. 3, *Reconnaissance, Flying Boat/ Trainer/Transport.* (Kolu-fan Illustrated Special). Translated by George and Kiri Elephtheriou, and by Akihiko Shegemi. Tokyo: Bunrin-do Co., Ltd., n.d.

Kahn, David. *The Code Breakers.* New York: The MacMillan Co., 1967.

Karig, Walter, and Welbourn Kelly. *Battle Report: Pearl Harbor to Coral Sea.* New York: Farrar & Rinehart, Inc., 1944.

Kase, Toshikazu. *Journey to the* Missouri. New Haven, Conn.: Yale University Press, 1950.

Keegan, John. *The Second World War.* New York: Penquin Books, 1990.

Kennett, Lee. *For the Duration. . . .* New York: Charles Scribner's Sons, 1985.

Killen, John. *A History of the Luftwaffe.* New York: Berkley Medallion Books, 1969.

Kinzey, Bert. *PBY Catalina: Detail and Scale.* Carrollton, Texas: Squadron/ Signal Publications, 2000.

Knott, Richard C. *The American Flying Boat*. Annapolis, Md.: Naval Institute Press, 1979.

Krug, Hans-Joachim, Yoichi Hirama, Berthold J. Sander-Nagashima, and Axel Niestlé. *Reluctant Allies: German-Japanese Naval Relations in World War II*. Annapolis, Md.: Naval Institute Press, 2001.

Lamb, Charles. *To War in a Stringbag*. Revised edition. Garden City, N.Y.: Nelson Doubleday, Inc., 1980.

Lambert, John W. *The Pineapple Air Force: Pearl Harbor to Tokyo*. St. Paul, Minn.: Phalanx Publishing Co., 1990.

Larkins, William T. *Battleship and Cruiser Aircraft of the United States Navy, 1910–1949*. Atglen, Pa.: Schiffer Military/Aviation History, 1996.

———. *U. S. Navy Aircraft, 1921–1941*, one vol. 1961; *U. S. Marine Corps. Aircraft, 1914–1959*, one vol. 1959. Reprint (two vols. in one), New York: Orion Books, 1988.

Layton, Edwin T. *And I Was There*. New York: Quill William Morrow, 1985.

———. "Rendezvous in Reverse." *Naval Institute Proceedings* (May 1953).

Leary, William M. "The Zero Fighter." *Aerospace Historian* (Winter 1987).

Lewin, Ronald. *The American Magic*. New York: Farrar Straus Giroux, 1982.

Libby, Justin. "Pan Am Gets a Pacific Partner." *Naval History* (October 1999).

Long, E. John. "Japan's Undersea Carriers." *Naval Institute Proceedings* (June 1950).

Loomis, Vincent V., and Jeffrey L. Ethell. *Amelia Earhart: The Final Story*. New York: Random House, 1985.

Lord, Walter. *Day of Infamy*. New York: Holt, Rinehart and Winston, 1957.

———. *Incredible Victory*. New York: Harper & Row, 1967.

Lowman, David D. "Rendezvous in Reverse II." *Naval Institute Proceedings* (December 1983).

Lundstrom, John B. *The First Team*. Annapolis, Md.: Naval Institute Press, 1984.

Mayborn, Mitch, et al. *Grumman Guidebook*, American Aircraft Series, Book 4. Dallas: Flying Enterprise Publications, 1976.

Merriam-Webster's Geographical Dictionary, 3rd Edition. Springfield, Mass.: Merriam-Webster, Inc., 1997.

Messimer, Dwight R. *In the Hands of Fate: The Story of Patrol Wing Ten, 8 December 1941–11 May 1942*. Annapolis, Md.: Bluejacket Books, 2002.

Mikesh, Robert C. *Broken Wings of the Samurai.* Annapolis, Md.: Naval Institute Press, 1993.

———. *Japanese Aircraft Code Names and Designations.* Atglen, Pa.: Schiffer Military/Aviation Books, 1993.

———. *Japanese Aircraft Interiors, 1940–1945.* Sturbridge, Mass.: Monogram Aviation Publications, 2000.

———. "Japanese Giant of WW-2." *Air Progress* (January 1967).

———. "The Japanese Giants, Part 1." *Wings* (June 1981).

———. "The Japanese Giants, Part 2." *Airpower* (July 1981).

———. *Japan's World War II Balloon Bomb Attacks on North America.* Washington, D.C.: Smithsonian Institute, 1973.

———. *Zero.* Osceola, Wisc.: Motorbooks International, 1994.

Mikesh, Robert C., and Shorzoe Abe. *Japanese Aircraft, 1910–1941.* Annapolis, Md.: Naval Institute Press, 1990.

Miller, Edward S. *War Plan Orange: The U. S. Strategy to Defeat Japan, 1897–1945.* Annapolis, Md.: Naval Institute Press, 1991.

Miller, Nathan. *War at Sea.* New York: Oxford University Press, 1995.

Mizrahi, Joe. "Farewell to the Fleet's Forgotten Fighter: Brewster F2A." *Airpower* (March 1972).

Moody, Sidney C., Jr., and photographers of the Associated Press. *War Against Japan.* Novato, Calif.: Presidio Press, 1994.

Moran, Gerald P. *Aeroplanes Vought, 1917–1947.* Temple City, Calif.: Historic Aviation Album, 1979.

Morrison, Samuel E. *Aleutians, Gilberts and Marshalls,* Vol. 7, *History of United States Naval Operations in World War II.* Boston: Little, Brown & Co., 1951.

———. *Coral Sea, Midway and Submarine Actions,* Vol. 4, *History of United States Naval Operations in World War II.* Boston: Little, Brown & Co., 1962.

———. *The Rising Sun in the Pacific, History of United States Naval Operations in World War II,* Vol. 3. Boston: Little, Brown & Co., 1984.

Mosely, Leonard. *Hirohito: Emperor of Japan.* Englewood Cliffs, N.J.: Prentice-Hall, Inc., 1966.

Munson, Kenneth, and Gordon Swanborough. *Boeing: An Aircraft Album,* No. 4. New York: Arco Publishing Co., 1971.

Naval Analysis Division. U.S. Strategic Bombing Survey, Interrogation No. 387, File No. A-131. San Francisco: n.p., 1945.

Naval Analysis Division. U.S. Strategic Bombing Survey (Pacific). *The Campaigns of the Pacific War.* Washington, D.C.: Government Printing Office, 1946.

Office of the Chief of Military History. *Japanese Monograph No. 97: Pearl Harbor Operations: General Outline of Orders and Plans.* Washington, D.C.: Naval Historical Center, n.d.

———. *Japanese Monograph, No. 102: Submarine Operations, Dec 41–Apr 42.* General Headquarters Far East Command, Japanese Research Division. Washington, D.C.

The Official World War II Guide to the Army Air Forces. New York: Bonanza Books, reprint 1988.

O'Neill, Richard. *Suicide Squads.* New York: Ballantine Books, 1981.

OPNAV-16-Vt. #301. *Japanese Aircraft: TAIC Manual No. 1.* Anacostia, Md.: Technical Air Intelligence Center, 1944.

Orita, Zenji, with Joseph D. Harrington. *I-Boat Captain.* Canoga Park, Calif.: Major Books, 1970.

Packard, Wyman H. *A Century of U. S. Naval Intelligence.* Washington, D.C.: Department of the Navy, 1996.

Paine, Thomas. *The Transpacific Voyage of H.I.J.M.S. I-400.* Los Angeles and Santa Barbara: Tom Paine's Journal, 1991.

Palmyra Atoll. *World Fact Book.* Washington, D.C.: CIA, 2000.

Pape, Garry R., and Warren E. Thompson. "Nocturnal Lightnings." *Air International* (August 1978).

Pelletier, A. J. *Bell Aircraft Since 1935.* Annapolis, Md.: Naval Institute Press, 1992.

Pike, John. *Johnston Atoll, Kalama Atoll.* U. S. Nuclear Forces Guide. FAS, Johnston Atoll, 2000.

Polmar, Norman. *Aircraft Carriers: A Graphic History of Carrier Aviation and Its Influence on World Events.* Garden City, N.Y.: Doubleday & Co., 1969.

Powers, Thomas E. "Incredible Midway." *Naval Institute Proceedings* (June 1967).

Prados, John. *Combined Fleet Decoded.* New York: Random House, 1995.

Prange, Gordon W., with Donald M. Goldstein and Katherine V. Dillon. *At Dawn We Slept.* New York: Penquin Books, 1982.

———. *December 7, 1941.* New York: McGraw-Hill Book Co., 1988.

———. *God's Samurai.* Washington, D.C.: Brassey's (US), Inc., 1990.

———. *Miracle at Midway.* New York: Penguin Books, 1982.

Reichauer, Edwin O., *The United States and Japan*, 3rd Edition. Cambridge, Mass.: Harvard University Press, 1965.

Richards, M. C. "Kawanishi 4-Motor Flying Boats (H6K 'Mavis' and H8K 'Emily')." *Aircraft in Profile*, Vol. 11. Garden City, N.Y.: Doubleday & Co., 1972.

Richards, M. C., and Robert C. Mikesh. "'Emily'—Grand Old Lady of Japan." *Air Pictorial* (August 1969).

Rochefort, Joseph J. Interview by Commander Etta-Belle Kitchen. *The Reminiscences of Captain Joseph J. Rochefort, U. S. Navy (Ret.)*. Annapolis, Md.: History Division, U. S. Naval Institute, 1983.

Rust, Ken C. *Seventh Air Force Story*. Temple City, Calif.: Historical Aviation Album, 1979.

Sakai, Saburo, with Martin Caiden and Fred Saito. *Samurai!* New York: Ballantine Books, 1957.

Sakaida, Henry. *Imperial Japanese Navy Aces, 1937–1945*. London: Osprey Publishing, 1988.

Samurai and the Swastika. The History Channel. July 2, 2000.

Scheck, William. "Perspectives." *World War II*. (July 1998).

Shamburger, Page, and Joe Cristy. *The Curtiss Hawks*. Kalamazoo, Mich.: Wolverine Press, 1972.

Sherrod, Robert. *History of Marine Corps Aviation in World War II*. Washington, D.C.: Combat Press, 1952.

Skates, John Ray. *The Invasion of Japan: Alternative to the Bomb*. Columbia, S.C.: University of South Carolina Press, 1994.

Slackman, Michael. *Target: Pearl Harbor*. Honolulu: University of Hawaii Press, 1990.

Smith, Carl. *Pearl Harbor 1941*. Oxford: Osprey Publishing, Ltd., 1999.

Smith, J. R., and Antony Kay. *German Aircraft of the Second World War*. London: Putnam & Co., Ltd., 1972.

Staff of *Aireview* Magazine. *General View of Japanese Military Aircraft of the Pacific War*. Tokyo: Kanto Sha Co., Ltd. English text, 3rd Edition, 1958.

———. *German Military Aircraft in the Second World War*. Tokyo: Kanto-Sha Co., Ltd., English text, 2nd Edition, 1960.

Stephan, John J. *Hawaii Under the Rising Sun*. Honolulu: University of Hawaii Press, 1984.

Swanborough, Gordon, and Peter M. Bowers. *United States Navy Aircraft Since 1911*. Revised edition. Annapolis, Md.: Naval Institute Press, 1990.

Taiheiyo Senso Riku-Kokutai [Army and Navy Air Forces of the Pacific War]. Translated by Katsuhiro Uchida. Tokyo: Seibido Shuppan Co, n.d.

Tanaka, Tetsuko. "Making Balloon Bombs." In *Japan at War,* edited by Haruko and Theodore Cook. New York: The New Press, 1992.

Thetford, Owen. *Aircraft of the Royal Air Force Since 1918.* New York: Funk & Wagnalls, 1968.

Thomas, Lowell, and Edward Jablonski. *Doolittle: A Biography.* Garden City, N.Y.: Doubleday & Co., 1976.

Thompson, Don. "First Black Paratroopers Saw Little Combat." *Greenville (S.C). News* (June 18, 2000).

Thompson, Jonathan. *Italian Civil and Military Aircraft, 1930–1945.* Fallbrook, Calif.: Aero Publishers, 1963.

Toland, John. *The Rising Sun: The Decline and Fall of the Japanese Empire, 1936–1945.* New York: Bantam Books, 1970.

Toppan, Andrew. "Aviation Oddities, Part III: Barges, Landing Ships and Other Platforms." *Haze Gray* at www.Hazegray.org.

Treadwell, Terry C. *Strike From Beneath the Sea.* Charleston, S.C.: Tempus Publishing, Inc., 1999.

Ugaki, Matome. *Fading Victory: The Diary of Admiral Matome Ugaki, 1941–1945.* Translated by Masataka Chihaya. Pittsburgh, Pa.: University of Pittsburgh Press, 1991.

van der Vat, Dan. *The Pacific Campaign: The U. S.–Japanese Naval War 1941—1945.* New York: Touchstone Books, 1991.

Van Fleet, Clarke, and William J. Armstrong. *United States Naval Aviation, 1910–1980,* NAVAIR OO-80-P-1. Washington, D.C.: Government Printing Office, 1981.

Wagner, Ray. *American Combat Planes,* 3rd Edition. Garden City, N.Y.: Doubleday & Co., 1982.

Wagner, Ray, and Heinz Nowarra. *German Combat Planes.* Garden City, N.Y.: Doubleday & Co., 1971.

Walsh, Len. *Read Japanese Today.* Tokyo: Charles E. Tuttle Co., 1969.

Warner, Dennis, and Peggy Warner, with Sadao Seno. *The Sacred Warriors.* New York: Van Nostrand Reinhold Co., 1982.

Webber, Bert. *Retaliation: Japanese Attacks on the Pacific Coast.* Corvallis, Ore.: Oregon State University Press, 1975.

———. *Silent Seige-III: Japanese Attacks on North America in World War II.* Medford, Ore.: Webber Research Group, 1997.

Webber, Bert, and Margie Webber. *Fujita: Flying Samurai.* Medford, Ore.: Webb Research Group Publishers, 2000.

Wegg, John. *General Dynamics Aircraft and their Predecessors.* Annapolis, Md.: Naval Institute Press, 1990.

Weinberg, Gerald R. *A World at Arms.* New York: Cambridge University Press, 1994.

Weir, William. *Fatal Victories.* Hamden, Conn.: Archon Books, 1969.

Westell, Freeman. "Japan's Forlorn Floatplane Flotilla." *Airpower* (July 2000)

Wheal, Elizabeth-Anne, Stephen Pope, and James Taylor. *A Dictionary of the Second World War.* New York: Peter Bedrick Books, 1999.

Whitlock, Duane L. *And So Was I (A Gratuitous Supplement to "I Was There" by Rear Adm. Edwin T. Layton).* Washington, D.C.: Naval Historical Office, 1986.

———. "The Silent War Against the Japanese Navy." *Naval War College Review* 48 no. 4 (Autumn 1995).

Willmott, H. P. *The Barrier and the Javelin.* Annapolis, Md.: Naval Institute Press, 1983.

———. *Empires in the Balance.* Annapolis, Md.: Naval Institute Press, 1982.

———. *Pearl Harbor.* New York: Galahad Books, 1981.

———. *Pearl Harbor.* London: Cassell & Co., 2001.

Winans, David R. "Submarine Aircraft." *American Aviation Historical Society Journa,* 12 (Spring 1967).

Wixey, Kenneth. *Parnall Aircraft Since 1914.* Annapolis, Md.: Naval Institute Press, 1990.

Young, Donald J. West Coast War Zone. *World War II.* July, 1998

Zatarain, Charles. "Helldiver Strike on Wotje." *Aviation History* (July 2000).

Suggested Further Reading

Primary Sources

7th Air Force Intelligence Section. Extracts from Operations of 7th Air Force, 7 December 1941–13 November 1943. (Declassified 4 October 1944) Maxwell AFB, Ala.: USAF Historical Research Center.

Aeronautical Vest-Pocket Handbook. United Technologies, Pratt & Whitney Aircraft of Canada, Ltd., 1981.

Air Branch, Office of Naval Intelligence. *Naval Aviation Combat Statistics, World War II,* OPNAV-P23V No A129. Washington, D.C.: Office of Chief of Naval Operations, 17 June 1946.

Allen, Riley H. "This is War." *Honolulu Star-Bulletin,* March 4, 1942. Editorial. Photocopied.

Allison, Thomas M. "Clear Sky." *The Navigator,* March 3, 1988.

Borg, Jim. "Tantalus Bombing May Have Altered World War II." *Honolulu Star Bulletin,* March 3, 1984.

Chief of Staff, Combined Fleet to Chief of Staff, 4th Fleet. Orders for Operation K, January 16, 1942, translated by Mikio Aida.

Creswell, H. T., J. Hiraoka, and R. Namba. *A Dictionary of Japanese Military Terms: Japanese-English; English-Japanese.* Chicago: The University of Chicago Press, 1946.

Director, Naval Intelligence. "Daily Information Briefing Report." March 5, 1942: Washington, D.C.: Naval Historical Center.

Director, Naval Intelligence. "Daily Information Briefing Report." March 7, 1942: Washington, D.C.: Naval Historical Center.

Director, Transportation Museum. Letter to author, Tokyo, 12 February 1997.

Draemel, M. F. Memorandum for Flag Secretary. March 5, 1942: Washington, D.C.: Naval Historical Center.

————. Report of Attack, March 4, 1942. March 8, 1942: Washington, D.C.: Naval Historical Center.

"Enemy Means Business Here." *Honolulu Advertiser,* March 5, 1942. Editorial, 4.

"Enemy Plane Traced by Army." *Honolulu Star-Bulletin,* March 5, 1942, 1.

Intelligence Section, Pacific Fleet. "Situation Summary." March 5, 1942: Washington, D.C.: Naval Historical Center.

————. "Situation Summary." March 9, 1942, Washington, D.C.: Naval Historical Center.

————. "Situation Summary." March 11, 1942, Washington, D.C.: Naval Historical Center.

Ishibashi, Kenji. Letter to author, March 11, 1983.

McGoran, John H. Letter to author, Corte Madera, Calif, November 9, 1998.

Nazzaro, Mathew, Robert McLean, and Mike Cross, Aircraft Restoration Museum Specialists. Interview by the author, tape recording, Paul Garber Facility of the National Air and Space Museum, Silver Hill, Md. August 10, 2000.

Nee, Roland W. Letter to author, February 10, 1998.

Summers, Thomas B. "Air Raid Alarm on Morning of 7 March 1942." *Report to S-3, Seventh Interceptor Command.* Maxwell AFB, Ala.: USAF Historical Research Center.

Taiheiyo Senso Tiku-Kaigun Kokutai [Army and Navy Air Forces of the Pacific War]. Translated by Katsuhiro Uchida. Tokyo: Seibido Shuppan Co., n.d.

Vlach, Vincent. Letter to author, Riverside, Calif., June 2, 1998.

Wallace, W. J. CO, MAG-22. Report of Combat Contact with Enemy Aircraft. to CO., 14th Naval District. March 10, 1942, Washington, D.C.: Naval Historical Center.

Secondary Sources

A-20 Havoc, A Douglas 'Great,' *Air Enthusiast,* No. 36.

Alexander, Joseph H. "Trial by Fire at Coral Sea." *Military History Quarterly* 13 no. 1 (Autumn 2000).

Anderson, Fred. *Northrop: An Aeronautical History.* Los Angeles: The Northrop Corporation, 1976.

Andrews, C. F. *Vickers Aircraft Since 1908.* London: Putnam, 1969.

Arakaki, Leatrice, and John Kuborn. *7 December 1941.* Hickam AFB, Hawaii: PACAF History Office, 1991.

Barnes, C. H. *Shorts Aircraft Since 1900.* Annapolis, Md.: Naval Institute Press, 1967, revised by Derek James, 1989.

Beck, Alfred M., ed. *With Courage: The U. S. Army Air Forces in World War II,* Washington, D.C.: Government Printing Office, 1994.

Bird, Roy. "Seabee in the South Pacific." *Military History* (October, 2000).

Birdsall, Steve. *Log of the Liberators.* Garden City, N.Y.: Doubleday & Co., 1973.

Botting, Douglas, et al. *The Giant Airships.* The Epic of Flight. Alexandria, Va.: Time-Life Books, 1980.

Bowers, Everett P. "Aerial Attack on Oregon." *Military History* (June 2000).

Boyd, Carl. *American Command of the Sea Through Carriers, Codes and the Silent Service: World War II and Beyond.* Newport News, Va.: The Mariners' Museum, 1995.

Boyne, Walter J. *Clash of Titans.* New York: Simon & Schuster, 1995.

Breuer, William B. *Secret Weapons of World War II.* New York: Wiley and Sons, Inc., 2000.

Campbell, Christy. *Air War Pacific.* New York: Crescent Books, 1990.

Cohen, Elliot A. "The Might-Have-Beens of Pearl Harbor." *Military History Quarterly* 4, no. 1 (Autumn 1991).

Cohen, Stan. *East Wind Rain*. Missoula, Mont.: Pictorial Histories Publishing Co., 1981.

Conn, Stetson, Rose C. Engleman, and Byron Fairchild. *Guarding the United States and Its Outposts*. volume unknown. *United States Army in World War II*, Washington, D.C.: Office of the Chief of Military History, 1964.

Costello, John. *Days of Infamy*. New York: Pocket Books, 1994.

————. *The Pacific War*. New York: Rawson-Wade Publishers, 1981.

Daniel, J.-M. "Emily a Retrouve son Soleil." *L'Aviation*. Translated by Frances M. Horn (April 1983).

Davies, R. E. G. *Pan Am: An Airline and Its Aircraft*. New York: Orion Books, 1987.

Donald, David, ed. *The Complete Encyclopedia of World Aircraft*. New York: Barnes & Nobles Books, 1997.

Dorr, Robert F. *B-24 Liberator Units of the Pacific War*. Osprey Combat Aircraft No. 11. Oxford, Great Britain: Osprey Publishing Ltd., 1999.

Finnegan, John Patrick. *Military Intelligence*. Washington, D.C.: Center of Military History, U.S. Army, 1998.

Fukudome, Shigeru. "Hawaii Operation." *Naval Institute Proceedings* (December 1955).

Hart, B. H. Liddell. *History of the Second World War*. New York: G. P. Putnam's Sons, 1970.

Hill, Douglas. "Countdown to Disaster." *Military History Quarterly* 4 no. 1 (Autumn 1991).

Hinz, Earl. *Pacific Island Battlegrounds of WWII*. Honolulu: Bess Press, 1995.

Infield, Glenn B. *Unarmed and Unafraid*. New York: Macmillan Co., 1970.

Jablonski, Edward. *Sea Wings: The Romance of the Flying Boats.*, Garden City, N.Y.: Doubleday & Co., Inc., 1972.

Jackson, Paul, ed. *Jane's All the World's Aircraft, 1999–2000*. Coulson, U.K.: Jane's Information Group, 2000.

Jane's Fighting Aircraft of World War II. New York: Military Press, 1989.

"Japanese Air Force." *Aviation* (September 1941).

Japanese Imperial Army and Navy Aircraft Color and Markings. Koku-Fan Illustrated No. 42. Tokyo: Bunrindo Co., 1988.

Japanese Imperial Navy Aircraft. Koku-Fan Illustrated No. 38. Tokyo: Bunrindo Co., 1987.

Japanese Military Aircraft Illustrated. Vol. 2, *Bombers.* Koku-fan Illustrated Special. Tokyo: Bunrindo Co., Ltd., n.d.

Japanese Military Aircraft Illustrated. Vol. 1, *Fighters.* Tokyo: Bunrindo Co., n.d.

Kinzey, Bert. *B-25 Mitchell: Detail and Scale.* Carrollton, Texas: Squadron/ Signal Publications, 1999.

Larson, George, George Hall, and Baron Wolman. *The Blimp Book.* Mill Valley, Calif.: Squarebooks, 1977.

Lindley, John M. *Carrier Victory: The Air War in the Pacific.* New York: E. P. Dutton, 1978.

Maurer, Maurer. *Air Force Combat Units of World War II.* Washington, D.C.: U. S. Government Printing Office, 1961.

McDowell, Ernest R. *B-25 Mitchell in Action.* Carrollton, Texas: Squadron/ Signal Publications, 1978.

Mueller, A. J. "Games the Black Cats Played." *Aviation* (May 1994).

Musciano, Walter A. *Warbirds of the Sea: A History of Aircraft Carriers and Carrier-Based Aircraft.* Atglen, Pa.: Schiffer Military/Aviation History, 1994.

"Nocturnal Nighthawk." *Air Enthusiast,* no. 27 (1985).

O'Conner, Raymond. Introduction and commentary to *The Japanese Navy in World War II.* Annapolis, Md.: Naval Institute Press, 1969.

Office of the Chief of Military History. *Monograph No. 108: Second Demobilization Unit. Submarine Operations.* Washington, D.C.: Naval Historical Center, n.d.

Okumiya, Masatake, and Jiro Horikoshi, with Martin Caidin. *Zero!* New York: Ballantine Books, 1956.

Ostrowski, David W. "Anacostia Flight Tests: Brewster XF2A-1, F2A-1, XF2A-2 Fighters; Details: Brewster F2A Fighter." *Skyways* (July 2000).

Polmar, Norman, et al. "Historic Aircraft: The Last Flying Boat." *Naval History* 13, no. 4 (1999).

Prange, Gordon W., with Donald M. Goldstein and Katherine V. Dillon. *Pearl Harbor: The Verdict of History.* New York: Penguin Books, 2001.

Sakaida, Henry. *Pacific Air Combat.* St. Paul, Minn.: Phalanx Publishing Co., 1993.

Sekigawa, Eiichiro, ed. *Aireview's German Military Aircraft in the Second World War,* 2nd edition. Two volumes (Vol. 2 is English text). Tokyo: Kanto-Sha Co., Ltd., 1960.

Smurthwaite, David. *The Pacific War Atlas: 1941–1945*. New York: Facts on File, 1995.

Spennemann, Dirk H. R. *Japanese Sea Plane Operations in the Marshall Islands*. Albury, NSW, Australia: Charles Stuart University, 1995.

Spurr, Russell. *A Glorious Way to Die*. New York: Newmarket Press, 1981.

Stinnet, Robert B. *George Bush: His World War II Years*. Washington, D.C.: Brassey's (U.S.), Inc., 1992.

Thorpe, Don. *Japanese Naval Air Force Camoflage*. Fallbrook, Calif.: Aero Publishers, 1977.

Thorpe, Don, and Ed Maloney. *Tora! Tora! Pearl Harbor*. Corona Del Mar, Calif.: Planes of Fame, 1991.

Toland, John. *Infamy: Pearl Harbor and Its Aftermath*. Garden City, N.Y.: Doubleday & Co., 1982.

Type 2 Flying Boat. Famous Airplanes of the World, No. 49. Tokyo: Bunrindo Co., 1994.

Wagner, Ray. *Prelude to Pearl Harbor*. San Diego, Calif.: San Diego Aerospace Museum, 1991.

Westell, Freeman. "Floatplane Follies." *Airpower* (March 2000).

Young, Donald J. *First 24 Hours of War in the Pacific*. Shippensburg, Pa.: Burd Street Press, 1998.

INDEX

ABOUT THE AUTHOR

Lt. Col. Alton "Steve" Horn (Ret.) was born in Forest City, North Carolina, in 1927. He enlisted in the Navy at the age of seventeen and served for a period of sixteen months. He later served as a pilot in the Air Force and was a member of the Strategic Air Command. He retired from the Air Force after twenty-five years of service and then worked for Lear Aircraft.

He attended Mars Hill College, University of North Carolina, and University of Nebraska, where he received his B.A. degree. In 2000, he received his M.A. degree in Humanities at the University of North Carolina in Asheville, North Carolina.

His primary interests and hobbies all revolve around airplanes.

He and his wife, Frances, reside in Greenville, South Carolina.